Rational Emotive Behaviour Therapy

A Reader

edited by
WINDY DRYDEN

SAGE Publications
London • Thousand Oaks • New Delhi

First published 1995

SAGE Publications Ltd
6 Bonhill Street
London EC2A 4PU

SAGE Publications Inc
2455 Teller Road
Thousand Oaks, California 91320

SAGE Publications India Pvt Ltd
32, M-Block Market
Greater Kailash - I
New Delhi 110 048

British Library Cataloguing in Publication data

A catalogue record for this book is available from the British Library.

ISBN 0 8039 7858 8
ISBN 0 8039 7859 6 (pbk)

Library of Congress catalog card number 94–74902

Typeset by Type Study, Scarborough
Printed in Great Britain by The Cromwell Press Ltd,
Broughton Gifford, Melksham, Wiltshire

Contents

Preface

The purpose of this Reader is to present a collection of articles that address important issues in the practice of Rational Emotive Behaviour Therapy (REBT). The Reader begins with an overview of the theory and practice of REBT (Chapter 1) written by Albert Ellis, its founder, for those who are unfamiliar with REBT or who want an updated account of this approach to psychotherapy.

The following six chapters are concerned with three issues that need to be considered before change-directed interventions are used. In Chapter 2, I outline the importance of building a therapeutic alliance with clients, while in Chapters 3 and 4 Norman Macaskill and Russ Grieger address the importance of educating clients about REBT. Finally Raymond DiGiuseppe (Chapters 5 and 7) and I (Chapter 6) consider different aspects of assessing clients' problems.

The bulk of the Reader, however, is devoted to therapeutic intervention. Since disputing irrational beliefs is a core technique in REBT, I have included two chapters on it (Chapters 8 and 9). As Albert Ellis shows in the opening chapter, REBT is an active-directive approach to psychotherapy and two chapters address different aspects of activity and directiveness. Chapter 10 explores the use of force and energy in the practice of REBT, while what I have called vivid techniques are discussed in Chapter 11.

Albert Ellis has often said, semi-humorously, that he was born with a gene for efficiency and therefore it is not surprising that he views REBT as an efficient therapy. Chapter 12 considers several important dimensions of therapeutic efficiency as exemplified by this approach. One way that an approach can demonstrate its efficiency is how it tackles resistance which is a ubiquitous phenomenon in psychotherapy. In Chapter 13, Albert Ellis identifies the major sources of resistance and outlines techniques to deal with them.

In the following two chapters, Joseph Yankura and I outline two important aspects of the practice of the REBT. In Chapter 14, we discuss the REBT counselling sequence which outlines the steps needed to be followed when dealing with a single client problem, while in Chapter 15 we take an overall look at the process of REBT from beginning to end. Then, in Chapters 16 and 17, I consider two ways in which REBT therapists have to demonstrate flexibility. First, in Chapter 16, I outline the compromises that REBT therapists sometimes have to make when they cannot help their clients to effect a philosophic change, while in Chapter 17, I show that REBT is an eclectic form of therapy where a broad range of interventions can be used by its practitioners informed as they are by a decided theoretical perspective.

The Reader ends with an exploration of why many therapists are critical of REBT. Steve Weinrach argues that one reason may be due to the fact that REBT is a tough-minded approach existing in a tender-minded profession. If it continues to exist it will be because articles such as those in this Reader will have shown the power of this therapeutic approach.

A word on terminology. In 1993, Albert Ellis decided to change the name of the therapy from Rational-Emotive Therapy to Rational Emotive Behaviour Therapy to emphasize that the approach does have a definite behavioural emphasis as well as an emotional and a rational (cognitive) focus. Since most of the articles that appear in this Reader were published before 1993, the old term, Rational-Emotive Therapy or RET is used as it does in their original published form. However, the actual approach has not changed, just its name.

Windy Dryden
London

Acknowledgements

Chapter 1 by Albert Ellis is a revised and expanded version of a chapter first published in Windy Dryden and Larry K. Hill (eds), *Innovations in Rational-Emotive Therapy* (Sage, Newbury Park, 1993), pp. 1–32.

Chapter 2 by Windy Dryden was first published in *Current Issues in Rational-Emotive Therapy* (Croom Helm, Beckenham, 1987).

Chapter 3 by Norman D. Macaskill and Chapter 4 by Russell M. Grieger were first published in Windy Dryden and Peter Trower (eds), *Cognitive Psychotherapy: Stasis and Change* (Cassell, London, 1989), pp. 87–98 and pp. 99–120.

Chapter 5 by Raymond DiGiuseppe was first published in Michael E. Bernard (ed.), *Using Rational-Emotive Therapy Effectively: A Practitioner's Guide* (Plenum Press, New York, 1991), pp. 151–72.

Chapter 6 by Windy Dryden was first published in the *Journal of Rational-Emotive and Cognitive Behavior Therapy*, 7(2) (1989), pp. 59–66.

Chapter 7 by Raymond DiGiuseppe was first published in Windy Dryden and Peter Trower (eds), *Developments in Rational-Emotive Therapy* (Open University Press, Milton Keynes, 1988).

Chapter 8 by Raymond DiGiuseppe was first published in Michael E. Bernard (ed.), *Using Rational-Emotive Therapy Effectively: A Practitioner's Guide* (Plenum Press, New York, 1991), pp. 173–95.

Chapter 9 by Thomas H. Harrell, Irving Beiman and Karen LaPointe was first published in *Rational Living*, 15(1) (1980), pp. 3–8.

Chapter 10 by Albert Ellis was first published in the *Journal of Contemporary Psychotherapy*, 10(2) (1979), pp. 83–97.

Chapter 11 by Windy Dryden was first published in Albert Ellis and Russell M. Grieger with contributors, *Handbook of Rational-Emotive Therapy*, Vol. 2 (Springer, New York, 1986), pp. 221–45. (It combines articles originally published in *Rational Living*, 18 (1983), pp. 7–12 and *Journal of Rational-Emotive Therapy*, 1 (1983), pp. 9–14 and 2 (1984), pp. 27–31.)

Chapter 12 by Albert Ellis was first published in *Psychotherapy: Theory, Research and Practice*, 17(4) (1980), pp. 414–19.

Chapter 13 by Albert Ellis was first published in Albert Ellis and Russell M. Grieger with contributors, *Handbook of Rational-Emotive Therapy*, Vol. 2 (Springer, New York, 1986), pp. 221–45. (It combines articles originally published in *British Journal of Cognitive Psychotherapy* 1(1) (1983), pp. 28–38 and 1(2) (1983), pp. 1–16.)

Chapters 14 and 15 were first published in Windy Dryden and Joseph Yankura, *Counselling Individuals: A Rational-Emotive Handbook*, 2nd edn (Whurr Publishers, London, 1993), pp. 149–88 and 189–221.

Chapter 16 was first published in Windy Dryden, *Current Issues in Rational-Emotive Therapy* (Croom Helm, Beckenham, 1987).

Chapter 17 by Windy Dryden was first published in *The Counsellor*, 3(5) (1982), pp. 15–22.

Chapter 18 by Stephen G. Weinrach is being publisned simultaneously in the *Journal of Counseling and Development*, Jan/Feb 1995.

The editor and publishers wish to thank the following for permission to reprint copyright material: the American Counseling Association for Chapter 18, copyright © 1995 American Counseling Association; Cassell PLC for Chapters 3 and 4; Windy Dryden for Chapters 2, 6, 7, 11, 16, 17; Windy Dryden and Joseph Yankura for Chapters 14 and 15; Albert Ellis for Chapters 12 and 13; Plenum Publishing Corporation for Chapters 5, 8, 9 and 10; Sage Publications Inc. for Chapter 1, copyright © 1993.

Every effort has been made to trace all the copyright holders, but if any interested parties have been inadvertently overlooked, we shall be pleased to include an acknowledgement at the earliest opportunity.

OVERVIEW

1

Fundamentals of Rational Emotive Behavior Therapy for the 1990s

Albert Ellis

In some ways, rational emotive behavior therapy (REBT) is remarkably similar in the 1990s to the fundamentals that I first began to delineate in 1955; but in other ways it is distinctly different. In this chapter, I shall describe its distinctive features today and shall try to concentrate on the most important aspects of its present day theory and practice.

The Basic Theory of REBT

'Causes' of Emotional Disturbance

Emotional disturbance – and especially what is often called neurosis – has several important cognitive, emotive and behavioral sources and does not only arise from but is heavily influenced by cognition or thinking. Humans are born easily disturbable, but they live in a social and physical environment, so that their 'healthy' and 'unhealthy' behaviors are 'caused' by the interactions among their innate predispositions and their external milieu, particularly their social milieu. As I noted in my early writings (Ellis, 1958) people rarely, if ever, have 'pure' thoughts, feelings or behaviors. Instead:

> Thinking . . . is, and to some extent has to be, sensory, motor, and emotional behavior. . . . Emotion, like thinking and the sensory-motor processes, we may define as an exceptionally complex state of human reaction which is integrally related to all the other perception and response processes. It is not one thing, but the combination and holistic integration of several seemingly diverse, yet actually closely related, phenomena. . . . Thinking and emoting are so closely interrelated that they usually accompany each other, act in a circular cause and effect relationship, and in certain (though hardly all) respects are essentially the same thing, so that one's thinking becomes one's emotion and emotion becomes one's thought. (Ellis, 1958: 35–6)

Following the views of several early philosophers, especially Buddha, Confucius, Epicurus, Seneca, Epictetus and Marcus Aurelius, REBT holds that people are largely responsible for their 'emotional' disturbances and that they overtly and tacitly, consciously and unconsciously 'choose' to disturb themselves. Consequently, they can consciously and actively, for the most part, choose to 'undisturb' and to fulfill themselves (Ellis, 1957b, 1962, 1991e; Ellis and Dryden, 1987, 1990, 1991). They mainly (not only) do this by taking their strong preferences for achievement, approval, comfort and health and making them (yes, destructively changing them) into dogmatic, absolutist musts, shoulds, oughts and demands.

The REBT view of neurotic disturbance, following ancient and modern phenomenalism, posits an ABC model. People start with goals (Gs), usually to remain alive and be reasonably happy, and then often encounter activating events or adversities (As) that block or thwart their desires for success, love and comfort. They then tend to create or construct cognitive, emotive and behavioral consequences (Cs) about these As – particularly, unhealthy or self-defeating feelings of anxiety, depression and rage, as well as such dysfunctional behaviors as withdrawal, procrastination and compulsions.

They construct these self-sabotaging Cs largely by their beliefs (Bs). These consist of, first *rational beliefs* (rBs), which are preferences and wishes and of, second, *irrational beliefs* (iBs), which are dogmatic musts and imperative demands. Thus, when *adversities* like failure and rejection occur (or people imagine or make occur) at point A, they choose rational beliefs (rBs) at point B – such as 'I don't *like* failing and being rejected, but it's not the end of the world and I can still find some degree of happiness' – and they then feel healthily (self-helpingly) sorry and disappointed, and try to change what is happening at point A. And they also choose irrational beliefs (iBs) at point B – such as, '*I absolutely must not* fail or be rejected. How *awful*. What an *incompetent and unlovable person* I am!' – and they then unhealthily (self-defeatingly) feel anxious, depressed and self-hating.

People, then, largely (not completely) choose both rBs and iBs about the adverse As they experience; and REBT theory says that if they *only* choose the former and never the latter, they would often create very strong *healthy* feelings of sorrow, regret, frustration, and discomfort but would rarely create *un*healthy feelings and neurotic behaviors. Moreover, REBT theory states, when people do construct their own destructive feelings and acts, they frequently create *secondary* consequences (Cs) about their primary consequences. Thus, when they feel panicked, they create iBs like, 'I *must* not be panicked! I'm no good for being panicked!' and thereby bring on panic *about* their panic. And when they behave neurotically – say, foolishly procrastinate – they tell themselves iBs like, 'I *absolutely should not* procrastinate. I'm a no-good procrastinator!' and they thereby hate themselves *for* procrastinating (Ellis, 1979a, 1980a, 1986a; Ellis and Dryden, 1991).

The ABCs of rational emotive behavior therapy seem to be very simple and can easily be explained to disturbed people who want to help themselves, but they are exceptionally interactional and therefore in many ways complex (Ellis, 1985c, 1991d). This is because *activating events* (As) are perceived and thought about, and therefore have some beliefs (Bs) included in them and are also affected by past consequences (behaviors and feelings), and therefore have some Cs included in them. Similarly, beliefs (Bs) are affected by activating events (past and present) as well as by consequences (Cs), especially by feelings. Finally, consequences (Cs) are importantly influenced by activating events (As) and especially by one's belief system (B). As noted above, people's cognitions, emotions, and behaviors importantly affect and include each other and are never really 'pure,' but the same goes for their ABCs, which again are interactional and far from pure (Ellis, 1991e).

To make things more complicated, when two or more people relate to each other, their As, Bs and Cs often significantly affect each other's As, Bs and Cs. For example, if Joe is married to Joann and he criticizes her, he creates an unpleasant activating event (A) for her. She may then tell herself – at B, her belief system – 'He must not unfairly criticize me like that, that worm!' and at C, her consequence, largely makes herself furious at Joe. He then can experience her C, rage and tell himself, 'It looks like I criticized her too much, as I absolutely *should* not have done! How *awful* of me to act so badly!' and he may thereby make himself feel, at C, guilty and depressed. Then Joann may note his depression, think that she has gone too far with her rage, tell herself at B, 'I was wrong in showing him so much rage. I *must not* be that wrong!' and she, while still feeling very angry at Joe, may cause herself to be quite guilty and depressed.

So Joe's rational beliefs (rBs) ('Joann acted badly and I wish she wouldn't!') may lead to his healthy feelings of sorrow and disappointment and to his mildly criticizing her supposedly 'poor' behavior; and his irrational beliefs (iBs) ('She *must* not act badly! I *can't stand* her acting this way!') may lead to his anger and his severe criticism of her. Joe's cognitions about Joann's consequence (C), rage, may lead him to have rational beliefs (rBs) ('I don't like Joann's rage, but I can live with it and still be happy'), and his cognitions about her rage may lead him to construct irrational beliefs (iBs) ('I criticized her too much, as I absolutely *should not* have done! How *awful* of me to act so badly!') and to thereby make himself depressed.

Similarly, Joann is affected or 'pushed' by Joe's beliefs and emotional consequences to create both rational and irrational Bs and to bring about her own healthy (self-helping) and unhealthy (self-defeating) consequences. When Joe and Joann have children, in-laws, friends and business associates, you can see that the ABCs and the cognitions, emotions and behaviors of all these individuals may importantly affect each other and may encourage each other to have (though not *absolutely make* each other have) self-helping and self-sabotaging (not to mention socially helpful and socially sabotaging) consequences.

REBT, then, agrees with many systems-oriented thinkers that humans invariably live in some kind of (material and social) system; that the system importantly affects the people in it; that all the individuals in it affect each other and affect the system; and that to understand how people usually and abnormally behave, we had better understand (a) how people affect themselves (the ABCs of their thoughts, feelings, and behaviors); (b) how they affect each other; (c) how they affect the system; and (d) how the system affects them (Bateson, 1979; DiSalvo, 1989; Ellis, 1989a, 1991d; Huber and Baruth, 1989).

The difference between REBT and most of the other personality and psychotherapy theories is that REBT clearly distinguishes people's standards, goals and values from their musts about these rules. REBT agrees that, because they are innately teachable or gullible, most people most of the time significantly accept or learn the values and standards of their family, peers, teachers, and religious and political groups. Not always, of course, but often! They also partly, but only partly, learn or adopt musts or commands *about* these standards. Thus, when their parents say, 'You must not be lazy!' they first learn that it is 'wrong' or 'undesirable' to be lazy – that in their social group they will probably be penalized for laziness and rewarded for effort.

Their learning the rules of their culture is generally good, because otherwise they would be severely penalized. They also invent their own personal rules – such as, 'I will only try to succeed at tennis but not at golf.' Or, 'I only will try tennis for three months, and if I don't get pretty good at it, I will quit and try golf.' Both their socially and personally acquired rules are okay as long as they are *preferences* and not *absolutist demands*.

People also take musts from their parents, teachers, peers and cultures, but wrongly think that they are unconditional rather than conditional musts. Thus, your parents tell you, 'You *must* do your homework,' but really mean, 'You *preferentially should* do your homework, or else you will fail at school and get bad results.' If they literally meant, '*Under all conditions*, at *all times*, you must do your homework,' they would see you as a *thoroughly horrible person* when you didn't, and perhaps boycott you or give you away. Actually, they scold you for a short while and then go back to being nice to you – proving that they deplore your *behavior* but still accept and love *you* in spite of it.

You, however, frequently take their *preferential should* too seriously and turn it into an absolute, ever-to-be-obeyed *command*. You then tell yourself, 'If I don't do my homework, as I *must*, I am acting badly and *I* am a *bad person* for acting that way.' Your parents (and others) rarely damn *you* for your poor behavior. But you easily damn *yourself*.

Similarly, you construct or invent absolutist musts *on your own*. You take your parents', your society's, and your personal preferences, even when they are expressed only and clearly as desires, and you change them into rigid musts. Thus, you take the view, 'It is desirable to make a lot of money,' and change it to, '*I have to* become a millionaire or see myself as a *total failure*!' You, like almost all people, are a born 'musturbator' and will almost inevitably take parental, societal and personal rules and foolishly make them into imperatives. So most – not all – of your profound musturbation is self-constructed, self-repeated, self-learned.

You often – not always – construct your dogmatic musts during your early childhood, when you tend to think badly, rigidly and crookedly. Then you may carry them on, in spite of evidence that they are not valid and don't work, forever. But you also may easily construct many of them during adolescence and adulthood and, conversely, can also change or surrender them as you get older and wiser. The main thing REBT emphasizes is that virtually all humans seem to be *active* acceptors of preferences and musts, *active* creators of demands *about* their desires, and *active* ongoing re-creators of self-disturbing and antisocial commands on themselves, on others, and on the world (Ellis, 1990f, 1991a, 1991e; Ellis and Dryden, 1987, 1991; Ellis, Young and Lockwood, 1987).

The Primacy of Absolutist Shoulds and Musts

When I first posited the ABCs of REBT, I listed 10 major irrational beliefs (iBs) that people largely use to upset themselves, and that I empirically derived from asking my clients what they thought or told themselves when they were 'emotionally' upset (Ellis, 1957a, 1957b, 1958, 1962). These have been put into 30 or more tests of irrational or dysfunctional beliefs and literally hundreds of studies have shown that disturbed people do acknowledge holding many of these beliefs (Baisden, 1980; Beck, 1991; DiGiuseppe et al., 1979; Ellis, 1979c; Smith, 1989).

When people change their irrational to more rational or functional beliefs, they significantly improve (Beck, 1991; DiGiuseppe et al., 1979; Ellis, 1957b, 1979c; Engels and Diekstra, 1986; Haaga and Davison, 1989; Jorm, 1987; Lyons and Woods, 1991; McGovern and Silverman, 1984). After using REBT for a few years, I was surprised to find that the original 10 iBs and my later additions to them (Ellis and Whiteley, 1979) could be put under three – yes, only three – main headings; and that each of these core iBs included an absolutist, rigid should or must. Thus: (1) '*I* (ego) absolutely *must* perform well and win significant others' approval or else *I* am an *inadequate, worthless person*.' (2) '*You* (other people) *must* under all conditions and at all times be nice and fair to me or else *you* are a *rotten, horrible person*!' (3) '*Conditions* under which I live absolutely *must* be comfortable, safe and advantageous or else the world is a rotten *place, I can't stand it*, and life is hardly worth living.'

Other cognitive-behavior therapies – such as those of Beck (1976), Maultsby (1984) and Meichenbaum (1977) – also accept these shoulds and musts as irrational and disturbance-producing, but they do not, as REBT does, see them as primary and do not see that the misleading inferences, attributions, and overgeneralizations that also are irrational largely stem from, or are tacitly derived from, disturbed people's musts, and would much less often exist without them. Thus, emotionally dysfunctional people, as REBT has pointed out since the 1950s, catastrophize, awfulize, overgeneralize, personalize, jump to invalid conclusions, use emotional-reasoning, dichotomize, damn themselves and others, and make other major unrealistic, anti-empirical, often false inferences and attributions (Ellis, 1958, 1962, 1987c, 1987d).

If, for example, I reject your invitation to go to a movie, you may quickly infer: (a) You were wrong to ask me to go; (b) You selected a stupid movie; (c) I dislike you; (d) I hate movies; (e) You are a fool for inviting me, and so on. All these inferences are probably false, but you still create and believe them, and thereby may make yourself feel anxious, depressed and self-hating.

Why does an intelligent person like you quickly manufacture such dubious, often ridiculous, attributions? The REBT theory says, first, because you are naturally, innately, and by experiential training a slippery thinker who *easily* makes questionable or false inferences from observable (or imaginable) data. So you often, harmlessly or harmfully, see rightly and conclude wrongly. Many experimental and social psychologists agree with REBT about this (Ellis, 1987c, 1987d; Epstein, 1990; Kahneman et al., 1982; Korzybski, 1933; Taylor, 1990).

REBT adds another theory: that when you are 'emotionally' disturbed by your erroneous inferences and attributions, these are usually (not always) derived from and secondary to your dogmatic, imperative musts. Thus, in the illustration given two paragraphs back, you *bring* to your inviting me to a movie the underlying, implicit, tacit and preconscious powerful must: 'Whenever I invite anyone I really like, such as Albert Ellis, to a movie, *he absolutely* must accept my invitation and clearly show he truly likes me or else.' Because you devoutly, rigidly believe, and keep holding on to this *demand*, you *easily, semi-automatically, and rigidly* jump to the questionable conclusions, when I refuse your invitation (as I *must* not!), that you were wrong to ask me, selected a stupid movie, made me dislike you, discovered that I disliked movies, are a fool for inviting me, and so on.

REBT assumes, in other words, that you are often a profound musturbator and that once you strongly construct absolutist *musts* and *must nots* you will very easily and often, when you, others, and the world contradict them, slide yourself into 'logical' but misleading inferences that 'confirm' and add to your disturbed reactions. Unlike cognitive-behavior therapy (CBT), therefore, REBT's cardinal rule when people are thinking, feeling and acting neurotically is 'Cherchez le should! Cherchez le must! Look for the should! Look for the must!' REBT assumes that people with disturbances overtly and/or tacitly have one, two or three underlying musts, that these can usually be quickly found, and then actively and forcefully Disputed and changed back to preferences. However, to dislodge people's dysfunctional shoulds and musts thoroughly, REBT also looks for and actively shows them how to Dispute their misleading inferences – especially their catastrophizing, awfulizing, I-can't-stand-it-itis, self- and other-damning, and overgeneralizing (Ellis, 1962, 1971, 1987d, 1991e; Ellis and Dryden, 1987; Ellis and Grieger, 1977, 1986; Ellis, Young and Lockwood, 1987).

Disturbance about Disturbance

Soon after I started using the ABCs of REBT, I realized that, once they disturb themselves (or accept the irrational beliefs of others), people largely construct secondary disturbances – or disturbances about their disturbances. Thus, they make themselves anxious about their anxiety, depressed about their depression, or self-hating about their anger at others (Dryden, 1990a, 1990b; Ellis, 1962, 1971, 1973b, 1985c, 1988a, 1991a, 1991e; Ellis and Dryden, 1987, 1990, 1991). They also, as shown in the next section, often create ego disturbance about their low frustration tolerance or discomfort disturbance; and they create discomfort disturbance about their ego disturbance. REBT, therefore, assumes that clients have primary and secondary emotional-behavioral problems, looks for both, and, if they exist, helps clients uproot both these important kinds of disturbances (Ellis, 1979a, 1980a).

REBT and Discomfort Disturbance

When I first originated and practiced REBT, I rightly emphasized ego disturbance – that is, people's damning themselves for not achieving success and winning others' approval. I soon saw, however, that although almost all my clients (and relatives and friends!) often tended to dysfunctionally denigrate their *self* or *being*, and not merely their poor *performances*, they also had *discomfort disturbance* or *low frustration tolerance* (LFT) in the course of which they destructively *demanded* that other people and external conditions *absolutely must* act and be exactly the way they preferred them to act and be. I therefore added to ego disturbance the central REBT theory of discomfort disturbance or low frustration tolerance (Bard, 1980; Dryden, 1990b; Ellis, 1963a, 1979c, 1980a, 1985c, 1988a; Ellis and Knaus, 1977; Grieger and Boyd, 1980; Walen et al., 1992; Warren and Zgourides, 1991; Wessler and Wessler, 1980).

As I have noted in my writings and in many therapy sessions, ego and discomfort disturbance often coexist and significantly interact to cause severe neurotic problems. Thus, phobias may start with a client strongly convincing herself 'It's *too* uncomfortable and dangerous driving across a bridge! I *can't* stand it!' and thereby creating LFT about bridges. Then she may put herself down (ego disturbance) by telling herself, 'I *must not* be afraid of bridges! What a *weak person* I am for avoiding them!' and may thereby create a secondary disturbance. But she may also irrationally believe, 'My life is *unbearable* when I avoid bridges and when I hate myself for having this phobia! How horrible for me to be this incapacitated!' and she may then have discomfort depression or LFT *about* her phobia and *about* her self-downing. Her interactions among her discomfort disturbance and her ego disturbance may make her doubly or triply upset; and because of her LFT – 'It's *too hard* for me to work on my emotional-behavioral problems! I *shouldn't* have to take so much time and energy to ameliorate them!' – she may refuse to give up her interactional disturbances. REBT practitioners, therefore, assume that most clients have *both* LFT and self-damnation and try to help their clients discover and undo both kinds of disturbance.

REBT and the Scientific Method

REBT has always tried to be scientific in its theory and in checking its practice, but it first wrongly followed logical positivism (Ellis, 1962). Since 1976, it is close to Popper's (1962, 1985) critical realism (Ellis, 1985c, 1988a; Mahoney, 1991; Rorer, 1989), which focuses on critically assessing theories and trying to learn by falsifying them rather than on striving for their 'truth' or 'validity.' As science recently has become more open-minded and probabilistic, REBT in some respects tends to be synonymous with the scientific method.

How so? Well, modern science – and not, of course, dogmatic scientism – has three main facets. (1) It checks its theories with realism and empiricism to see whether they are falsifiable and anti-empirical. (2) It uses logic to see if theories are consistent with their own tenets and if they are contradicted by opposing, and presumably better, theories. (3) It is never dogmatic, doesn't claim that any theory is perfectly true under all conditions and at all times, and happily seeks for better, more workable, alternative theories (Bartley, 1962; DiGiuseppe, 1986; Popper, 1962, 1985).

I realized, after I had used REBT for several years, that if people rigorously – not rigidly! – followed this kind of scientific outlook in their personal lives they would have a difficult time making themselves needlessly self-defeating or neurotic. They would presumably create few or no absolutist, dogmatic shoulds, oughts, and musts (because doing so is to be antiscientific) and if they did so, they would fairly easily and quickly challenge and dispute them empirically and logically – just as they are shown to do in REBT!

REBT, in other words, theorizes that much (not all) 'emotional' disturbance is closely related to, and often essentially the same thing as, antiscientific, inflexible, absolutist thinking and that the main elements of 'mental health' are flexibility, open mindedness, and alternative-thinking. So REBT's theory of neurotic disturbance dovetails with contemporary scientific methods in several important ways.

The REBT Theory of Force

I first thought, along with several ancient and modern philosophers, that people who had more irrational beliefs (iBs) were more 'emotionally' disturbed than those with fewer such beliefs, and I still think that this concept has some evidential support. But then I changed REBT so that it focuses mainly (not exclusively!) on the kinds of iBs that people hold – particularly on their absolutist shoulds, oughts and musts.

A great deal of clinical evidence, however, led me to conclude, as Abelson (1963) had posited, that cognitions can be 'cool' and 'hot.' I added to this theory that they could also be 'warm.' Thus, the cognition, 'This is a deadly gun' is a 'cool' cognition that merely describes an object. The cognition, 'I dislike this deadly gun' is a 'warm' cognition that evaluates the same object.

The cognition, 'I hate this deadly gun and I think that it has to be immediately destroyed, along with all other guns like it!' is a 'hot' cognition that powerfully, forcefully evaluates this object, and constitutes a command, rather than a desire, about it.

REBT now holds that when people have self-disturbing thoughts, these thoughts are often, perhaps usually, 'hot' cognitions that they could hold mildly or lightly, on the one hand, or forcefully and heavily, on the other hand. People may easily, at one and the same time, have a 'warm' or preferential cognition – 'I like success but I can accept failure, learn from it, and still lead a happy life' – and also have a contradictory 'hot,' musturbatory cognition – 'I really *must* succeed, *must* not fail, and can only be quite miserable if I do!' REBT theory says that if they hold the latter irrational belief (iB) more frequently and/or more strongly than the former rational belief (rB) they will tend to disturb themselves needlessly, while if they hold the rB more frequently and/or more strongly than the iB they will tend to make themselves less frequently and less strongly disturbed (Ellis, 1985c, 1988a).

Because REBT asserts that people hold rBs and iBs weakly and strongly, it also theorizes that if people lightly and namby-pambily dispute their iBs and lightly or parrotingly change them into rBs, they often will still powerfully and tacitly hold onto their underlying iBs and, therefore, will only temporarily and weakly surrender their emotional-behavioral disturbances. Consequently, REBT has invented and adapted a number of strong, dramatic-evocative, emotive therapy techniques, some of which are described below (Ellis, 1985c, 1988a; Ellis and Dryden, 1987, 1991). Preferential REBT, unlike general REBT and CBT, almost invariably employs vigor, force and emotive, as well as cognitive and behavioral, methods of therapy (Ellis and Whiteley, 1979).

REBT and the Concept of Efficiency

I started to do REBT in 1955 largely because, as I jokingly and yet seriously often say in my talks and workshops, I have a gene for efficiency while poor Sigmund Freud – not to mention Carl Jung, Melanie Klein and Wilhelm Reich – had a gene for inefficiency. Almost all methods of therapy work to some extent with some people – especially when they include the therapist giving the client unconditional positive regard and encouraging some kind of in vivo desensitization. But psychoanalytic and many other therapies take much too long in many instances – while, alas, the clients are painfully and needlessly suffering.

REBT, therefore, has always espoused efficiency-oriented methods to supplement relationship, support, desensitization and other conventional, widely used (and often effective) techniques. For the most part, it also minimizes or avoids, except in unusual cases, long-winded, inefficient methods like free association, dream analysis, detailed 'explanations' of past history, and other methods that lead nowhere in the short, and often in the long, run. As noted below, on theoretical grounds it favors active-directive, questioning and challenging, distinctly didactic, homework-assigning, and other designed-to-be-efficient techniques (Ellis, 1962, 1971, 1973b, 1988a, 1990b; Grieger and Boyd, 1980).

By *efficiency*, REBT means a therapeutic theory and practice that is designed to get at clients' fundamental problems rapidly and show them, within a few sessions, how to start working to ameliorate these problems. It also means a system that shows clients, as rapidly as feasible, how to achieve what REBT calls an 'elegant' or profound philosophical change, which is described below.

REBT and the Self System

REBT has been somewhat pioneering in being a 'self' psychology, even more so than the psychoanalytic 'self systems,' such as those of Klein (Klein and Riviere, 1964), Hartman (1964), Guntrip (1971), Kohut (1977) and Kernberg (1975). This is because it gives more importance to people's self-constructions, even during their early childhood, than any of the psychoanalytic theories. As noted above, it sees humans as individuals who live in a social group (as also do the Adlerians and the object relations theorists). But it sees them as largely adopting social standards and values and then constructing or making them into rigid, absolutist musts and commands.

It is each person's unique 'self' or 'ego' that does most of this constructing and that is embedded in a social context, and even takes much of its 'personality' from its sociality – as Adler (1964) and Sampson (1989) and others have shown. But one's 'self' is both a taker and a creative constructor; and it largely runs human existence. REBT objects strongly to *rating* or *measuring* one's 'self' (as noted below), but it particularly favors self-development and self-actualization, as long as they are not taken to harmful extremes (Ellis, 1963c, 1973b, 1991a).

As for 'object relations,' REBT agrees with the neo-Freudian analysts, especially Bowlby (1969, 1973), that people have a tendency to make their relationships with others of paramount importance and to believe strongly that they not only *preferably should have* but *absolutely need* the approval and love of their parents and early caretakers. They also believe that if they do not get 'validated' by significant others they then have little *personal worth* and are *bad people*. Unlike psychoanalytic and many other therapies, however, REBT holds that lack of early love and succoring does not *necessarily* seriously disturb all children, nor does it *give them* 'personality disorders.' Instead, most of the people with such disorders (as well as the psychotics) seem to have other, largely biological, deficits that contribute to their extreme neediness and severe disturbance. Because of the severity of their problems, they usually require more prolonged and intensive therapy than most 'neurotics' (Ellis, 1989b).

REBT especially tries to help personality disordered and psychotic individuals to fully accept themselves *with* their severe disturbances. It specializes in treating their neurosis *about* their psychosis and while it hardly cures the latter state, it appreciably helps many of them to achieve happier lives.

Humanistic and Existential Aspects of REBT

REBT has always been one of the humanistic-existential psychotherapies (Ellis, 1962, 1972b, 1983a, 1983b, 1985a, 1987b, 1987e, 1988a, 1990d, 1990f, 1991a). Although it has sometimes been accused of being sensationalistic and overly 'rationalist' (Mahoney, 1991), REBT is actually one of the most 'constructivist' therapies. It holds that people do not merely *get*, or are 'conditioned' to be, disturbed but that they largely create or construct their own grandiose musts and demands and that they actively, though often tacitly or 'unconsciously,' keep reconstructing them for the rest of their lives (Ellis, 1972b, 1985c, 1990f, 1991a, 1991e, 1991f).

As I noted in Dryden and DiGiuseppe (1990: 79–93):

> Unlike some of the other cognitive-behavior therapies, REBT takes a definite humanistic-existential approach. It is not purely objective, scientific, or technique-centred in that it adheres to the following principles:
>
> 1 It deals with disturbed *human* evaluations, emotions, and behaviors. It sees humans as the basic creators or inventors of their own emotional problems and therefore as *humanly* capable of minimizing these problems.
> 2 It is highly rational and scientific but uses rationality and science in the service of humans in an attempt to enable them to live and be happy. It is hedonistic but espouses long-range instead of short-range hedonism so that people may achieve the pleasure of the moment and the future and arrive at maximum freedom and discipline.
> 3 It hypothesizes that nothing superhuman probably exists and that devout belief in superhuman agencies tends to foster dependency and increase emotional disturbance (Ellis, 1983a; Ellis and Tisdale, 1990; Ellis and Yeager, 1989).
> 4 It assumes that no humans, whatever their antisocial or obnoxious behavior, are damnable or subhuman. It respects and accepts all people just because they are alive and human.
> 5 It attempts to help people maximize their individuality, freedom, self-interest, and self-control rather than to submit to the control and direction of others (including their therapists). At the same time, it tries to help people live in an involved, committed, and selectively loving manner with other humans and to foster social as well as individual interest.
> 6 It particularly emphasizes the importance of will and choice in human affairs, even though it accepts the likelihood that some human behavior is partially determined by biological, social, and other forces.

Biological Bases of Human Irrationality and Disturbance

REBT, more than most other psychotherapies, accepts the familial and societal influences on human irrationality and disturbance, but it *also* emphasizes their biological origins (Ellis, 1976a; Franklin, 1987). It does this for several reasons:

1 Practically all humans have a number of neurotic self-defeating tendencies, no matter where or in what culture or what ethnic group they were reared (Ellis, 1987c; Frazer, 1959; Freud, 1965; Hoffer, 1951; Levi-Strauss, 1962).
2 Although people tend to be more frequently and more severely disturbed when they are reared by dysfunctional, abusive, incest-ridden families, they can also be highly neurotic when reared by highly functional, nonabusive, and nonincestuous families.
3 When people's disturbance is family-related, they often inherit a strong genetic factor from their close relatives. Several of the more serious mental-emotional disturbances – such as manic-depressive, severe depressive, schizophrenic and obsessive-compulsive disorders – appear to have a distinct genetic component.
4 Even when seriously disturbed individuals – such as borderline personalities – significantly improve as a result of intensive therapy, they frequently fall back to disturbed ways of functioning.
5 Most therapists and their children display many unrealistic and self-defeating ideas and behaviors.
6 People commonly not only disturb themselves but needlessly depress and panic themselves about their disturbances. The 'solutions' they choose for their problems often become part of or embrace the problem (Ellis, 1979a, 1980a, 1985a, 1985c, 1986a, 1987c, 1988a; Watzlawick et al., 1974).
7 When people acknowledge their disturbances and their disadvantages, they still commonly resist working to change them (Ellis, 1985c; Wachtel, 1982). When they temporarily change themselves, they frequently fall back to self-defeating ways (Ellis, McInerney, DiGiuseppe and Yeager, 1988).
8 Not only absolutist musts but erroneous attributions, inferences and overgeneralizations seem to be ubiquitous among all humans (Beck, 1976; Burns, 1980; Ellis, 1957a, 1962, 1985c, 1987d; Korzybski, 1933; Russell, 1965).

Because REBT practitioners accept the biological as well as the social and interpersonal 'causes' of human disturbance, they realize how difficult it is for people to make real and lasting changes, often show their clients that this is so, and encourage them to keep working and practicing to improve and to maintain their improvements (Ellis, 1985c, 1988a, 1991e).

Distinctive Practices of REBT

REBT was the original cognitive-behavior therapy (CBT) when I started using it in the beginning of 1955 and has always, in its general form, been synonymous with CBT (Ellis, 1969a, 1980b; Ellis and Whiteley, 1979; Lazarus, 1990). Like CBT, it uses a large number of cognitive, emotive and behavioral methods, and it has many important integrative aspects, as it selectively adapts and employs a number of methods that are also used in existential, humanistic, eclectic and other therapies. In its preferential form, however, it uniquely stresses a number of practices that most other modes of CBT and other therapies rarely espouse, such as the following techniques.

Active-Directive REBT

REBT practitioners assume that many, though hardly all, clients can actively and directively be taught the ABCs of REBT from the first session onward and can soon learn to use them effectively. I personally am highly active and directive with the great majority of my clients and find that at least a third of them can start improving within a few weeks. If they prove to be, as I experiment with rapid-fire REBT, borderline or resistant, I usually slow down, repeat the main REBT procedures and, avoiding my own possible low frustration tolerance, still keep pushing them to change for longer periods of time (and in a few cases for a number of years). I assume, however, that many neurotic, hardworking clients can benefit by an encouraging, active-directive approach, and that REBT is one of the few intrinsically brief (or at least brief*er*) therapies for a good many less resistant clients (Ellis, 1992a). I originated REBT mainly because psychoanalysis and other therapies that I used up to 1955 were too inefficient and too prolonged. So I designed REBT so that it can, but doesn't have to be, done in a relatively brief, highly directive manner (Bernard, 1991; Dryden, 1990a, 1990b; Ellis, 1962, 1973b, 1988a; Ellis and Abrahms, 1978; Ellis and Becker, 1982; Ellis and Dryden, 1987, 1991; Walen et al., 1992; Wessler and Wessler, 1980).

During the first few sessions, I outline the main principles of REBT to my clients, especially show them how they largely disturb themselves; help them look for and dispute their musts and their other irrational beliefs; work out with them suitable cognitive, emotive and behavioral homework assignments; and encourage them to unconditionally accept themselves and to improve their low frustration tolerance. Usually, one or two main symptoms – such as social anxiety, depression, and addiction – are repetitively tackled. But as my clients continue to improve, a more elegant, profound philosophic change is investigated and sought for (as is explained in the next section).

REBT and the Concept of Elegant Change

Unlike some psychotherapies, such as pure behavior therapy and hypnosis, REBT not only tries to help clients 'cure' themselves of their presenting symptoms but also tries to help them achieve an 'elegant' or profound philosophic change (Ellis, 1980b, 1985c, 1988a, 1994; Ellis and Whiteley, 1979; Ellis, Young and Lockwood, 1987). This includes several possibilities:

1 Clients become less disturbed or even free of their presenting symptoms (e.g., of panic, depression, rage or self-hatred).
2 They minimize their related and other disturbances (e.g., if they come to therapy about their sexual anxiety, they also make themselves less anxious about work problems and overcome their neurotic procrastination).
3 They recognize and minimize their disturbances about their disturbance (e.g., their anxiety about their anxiety, depression about their depression, or self-downing about their rage).
4 They maintain their improvement for a long period of time, preferably permanently.
5 They rarely seriously disturb themselves about almost anything in the future.
6 When they feel disturbed again, they quickly use REBT to reduce or eliminate the new disturbances.
7 By practicing REBT over the years, they become less disturbable and prophylactically keep warding off potential needless upsets.
8 When even the worst things happen to them or their loved ones, they tend to disturb themselves minimally and mainly to feel *healthily* sad, sorry, regretful, frustrated and annoyed.
9 While steadily working at minimally disturbing themselves, they optimistically and energetically strive for greater happiness and self-fulfillment (Ellis and Dryden, 1991).

It is assumed in REBT that people can make inelegant, though important, symptomatic changes through a number of different methods, including many of those used in REBT. But when they make the kind of elegant change outlined above, they usually make a *profound philosophic change*. This can be achieved in several ways, especially by working hard and persistently to have strong preferences instead of grandiose demands. REBT favors critical realistic acceptance, including:

Acceptance of self-change through hard work and practice.
Unwhining acceptance of what one cannot change.
Acceptance of human fallibility and imperfection.
Unconditional acceptance and nondamnation of oneself and others.
Acceptance of long-range rather than short-range hedonism.
Acceptance of probability and uncertainty.
Acceptance of the importance of one's self and one's social group.
Acceptance of one's own and others' mortality.
Acceptance of one's talents for greater happiness and self-actualization as one keeps working to minimize one's disturbance.

Clients are shown that though they can often make important personality and behavioral changes within a few months, their making an elegant change requires something of a lifelong dedication to acquiring, reconstructing and steadily implementing an enthusiastic self-helping attitude. Therapy sessions are important but working in between sessions and after therapy has ended to be self-reliant and unconditionally self-accepting is even more crucial. REBT sessions may be brief and infrequent, but self-determination and action to become consistently preferential and anti-musturbatory is endless (Ellis and Dryden, 1987, 1990, 1991; Ellis and Velten, 1992).

Therapeutic Relationship and Self-help Materials

Theoretically, REBT can be taught to people through books, pamphlets, audio-visual materials, lectures, courses, workshops and intensives, with no personal relationship between a therapist and his or her clients. So can person-centered therapy, though Carl Rogers (1961) has denied this. Some of the most helped REBTers I have known had little or no individual or group therapy; and a few mainly figured out its principles for themselves.

At the Institute for Rational-Emotive Therapy in New York, we use many self-help materials, especially some of my books and cassettes (Ellis, 1957a, 1972a, 1972d, 1973a, 1973c, 1974, 1975, 1976c, 1977a, 1977b, 1977d, 1978a, 1979b, 1980c, 1987f, 1988a, 1988b, 1990b; Ellis and Becker, 1982; Ellis and Harper, 1975; Ellis and Knaus, 1977) and those of Beck (1988), Burns (1980), Dryden and Gordon (1991), Hauck (1973, 1974, 1977), Knaus (1983), and Young (1974). We find that clients who use these materials tend to improve faster and more intensively than those who neglect them (Ellis, 1978b, 1990c, 1991c).

Like the writings and cassettes of Abraham Low (1952), REBT is also well designed for self-help groups. In 1987, Jack Trimpey (1989) started Rational Recovery, which already has hundreds of self-help groups in the United States and several other countries that include alcohol, food, and other addicts who specifically use REBT to help themselves with their emotional and behavioral problems (Ellis, 1991c; Trimpey and Trimpey, 1990). Many regular psychotherapy groups throughout the world – including eight weekly groups at the Institute for Rational-Emotive Therapy in New York – also use REBT and CBT (Ellis, 1987a, 1990g; Ellis and Dryden, 1987; Ellis and Harper, 1961).

Ideally, however, people receive individual sessions of REBT together with the use of REBT self-help materials. Seriously neurotic and personality disordered individuals particularly benefit from this combination (Ellis, 1989b). Realizing that perhaps the majority of therapy clients have a dire need for approval and love, including that of their therapist, REBT practitioners usually avoid relating too closely to their clients and avoid having them maintain or increase their dependency tendencies. At the same time, they tend to be highly collaborative, encouraging, supportive and mentoring (Ellis, 1990c, 1990d; Ellis and Dryden, 1991).

Most of all, REBT practitioners, like person-centered therapists, unconditionally accept all their clients, *whether or not* these clients behave well in and out of therapy, and *whether or not* they are nice and lovable. Unlike Rogerians, moreover, they actively, forcefully teach their clients to *accept themselves* unconditionally. People can do this *practically*, REBT teaches, by merely *deciding* that they are 'good' or 'worthy' just because they are alive and human. Or they can achieve unconditional self-acceptance more elegantly by deciding and actively practicing to rate *only* their deeds and performances and *not* to measure or evaluate their total *self* or *being* at all (Bard, 1987; Ellis, 1962, 1963c, 1972b, 1976b, 1988a, 1991e; Ellis and Becker, 1982; Ellis and Dryden, 1987, 1990, 1991; Ellis and Harper, 1975; Hauck, 1992).

Active Disputing of Musts and Other Irrational Beliefs

Many cognitive-behavior therapies use the ABCs of REBT, then go on to D, Disputing of the clients' irrational Beliefs (iBs), and then proceed to E (Effective New Philosophy). But they often do so in a somewhat hesitant, unforceful manner. Uniquely, REBT usually Disputes iBs actively, directly and forcefully and, simultaneously, teaches clients how to do their own persistent and vigorous Disputing as cognitive homework.

REBT particularly, and almost invariably, shows neurotics their absolutistic shoulds, oughts and musts, and Disputes them (and their other iBs) in three major ways:

1 *Empirical or Realistic Disputing*: A client who, let us say, insists that she absolutely must succeed in her career may be questioned as follows:

Therapist: Why *must* you have a great career?
Client: Because I very much want to have it.
Therapist: Where is the evidence that you *must* fulfill this strong desire?
Client: I'll feel much better if I do.
Therapist: Yes, you probably will. But how does your feeling better prove that you must succeed?
Client: But that's what I really want more than anything else in the world.
Therapist: I'm sure you do. But if we take 100 people like you, all of whom want a great career, want it more than anything else in the world, and would feel much better if they achieved it, do they all *have* to succeed at it?
Client: If they are to have any joy in life, they have to do so.
Therapist: Really? Can't they have *any* pleasure if they fail to get a great career?
Client: Well, yes. I guess they can have *some* pleasure.
Therapist: And could some of them have a great deal of pleasure?
Client: Um. Probably yes?
Therapist: Probably?
Client: Well, highly probably.
Therapist: Right. So, no matter how much people greatly want success and would feel better about gaining it, they don't have to get it. Right?
Client: Well, yes.
Therapist: Reality is that way – isn't it?
Client: It seems so.
Therapist: Back to you. Does *your* great desire for a successful career mean that you *absolutely must* achieve it – that the world *has* to fulfill this desire?
Client: I see what you mean. Reality is the way it is, no matter how unpleasant I find it to be.

Therapist: Exactly. Make a note of that Effective New Philosophy you just arrived at and keep thinking that way until you thoroughly believe it!

2 *Logical Disputing*: A client who insists that because he treated his friend very nicely and fairly this friend *should* treat him the same way may be shown how illogical his demand is, as follows:

Therapist: Let's suppose that you're describing the situation with your friend accurately and that he treats you shabbily and unfairly after you consistently treat him well. How does it follow that because of your good behavior he has to respond in kind?
Client: But he's very unfair if he doesn't!
Therapist: Yes, we're agreeing on that. He *is* unfair and you are fair. Can you jump from 'Because I'm very fair to him, he *has to be* fair to me?'
Client: But he's wrong if he isn't fair when I am.
Therapist: Agreed. But because you're fair, and presumably right, and because he takes advantage of your fairness, does it *still* follow that he has to be right and to treat you fairly?
Client: It logically follows.
Therapist: Does it? It looks like a complete non sequitur to me.
Client: How so?
Therapist: Well it's logical or consistent that he preferably should treat you fairly when you treat him well. But aren't you making an illogical – or 'magical' – jump from 'Because he *preferably* should treat me fairly he *absolutely has to* do so?' What 'logical' law of the universe leads to your 'He absolutely has to do so?'
Client: No law, I guess.
Therapist: No, in logic we get necessitous conclusions, such as 'If all men are human and John is a man, John must be human.' But your 'logic' says 'People who get treated fairly often treat others fairly; I treat my friend fairly; therefore it is absolutely *necessary* that he treat me similarly.' *Is* that a logical conclusion?
Client: I guess not.
Therapist: Moreover, you seem to be claiming that because you act fairly and your friend behaves unfairly his unfair *acts* make him a *rotten person*. Is that logical thinking?
Client: Why not?
Therapist: It's illogical because you're overgeneralizing. You're jumping from one of his rotten *behaviors* – or even one of his *traits* – to categorizing *him*, his totality as 'rotten'. How does that overgeneralization follow from a few of his behaviors?
Client: I can see now that it doesn't.
Therapist: So what could you more logically conclude instead?
Client: Well, I could think that he *isn't* one of his main behaviors. He is a person who often but not always acts rottenly.
Therapist: Good! Alfred Korzybski and his followers in General Semantics would approve of your new conclusion!

3 *Pragmatic Disputing*: A client insists that if she is anxious and perfectionistic she will succeed better at school and win others' approval. She can be shown that this irrational Belief will probably produce poor results.

Client: If I am anxious about doing poorly at school because, as you say, I think that I absolutely must do well, won't my must and my anxiety motivate me to do better?
Therapist: Yes, in part. But won't they also defeat you?
Client: How so?
Therapist: If you keep making yourself very anxious with 'I must do well! I must

perform perfectly!' won't it preoccupy yourself so much that you *detract* from the time and energy you can give to studying?

Client: Maybe. But I'll still feel quite motivated.

Therapist: Mainly motivated to obsess! You'll be *driven* to study. And, while you drive yourself, you'll keep thinking, 'But suppose I fail! Wouldn't that be *awful*?' You'll worry about what your texts will be like, how you will handle them, how you will subsequently perform, etc. How will keeping the *future* so much in mind help you focus on the *present* studying?

Client: It may not help.

Therapist: No, it's much more likely to sabotage. Moreover, even if you somehow succeed in your courses do you want to be miserably anxious, and perhaps depressed, *while* you are succeeding?

Client: Frankly, no.

Therapist: And do you want to be *so* absorbed in worrying about school that you have little time for relationships, sports, music and other enjoyments?

Client: I don't think so. I passed my courses last term but was able to do little else.

Therapist: See! And what about the physical results of your constant worry and perfectionism.

Client: My physician thinks they are making my digestive tract hyperactive.

Therapist: I'm not surprised. And when you constantly worry, how do you feel about *you* for being such a worrier.

Client: Pretty shitty.

Therapist: Is *that* feeling worth it? But even if you just felt bad about your anxiety and didn't put *yourself* down for having it, you would still bring on endless frustration and disappointment by indulging in it.

Client: You may be right.

Therapist: Don't take my word for it. Look for yourself at the results you get from your perfectionist demands and figure out what you could say to yourself to replace them.

Client: Well, I could tell myself, 'It's great to do well at school but I *don't have to be perfect*. Even if my anxiety sometimes helps me to get good marks, it, too, has too many disadvantages and isn't worth it.'

Therapist: Good! That's a much better way to think!

REBT Disputing also actively challenges client's *awfulizing* and *terribilizing* and helps them to see that if something is 'awful' it is (1) *totally* bad, (2) *more than* (101 percent) bad, and (3) badder than it *absolutely should be*. But all these extreme statements are unrealistic, illogical and self-defeating.

REBT practitioners show clients that when they vigorously claim that they *absolutely can't stand* unfortunate Activating Events (As) they can Dispute this exaggeration by showing themselves that they rarely will die from *awful* happenings and that they can – if they *think* they can – have *some degree* of happiness in spite of them.

REBT particularly helps people Dispute their *self*-ratings by showing them that they are only good or bad *persons* by arbitrarily and overgeneralized *definition*. Their *self* or *being*, as already noted, cannot accurately be given any global rating because it is too complex, executes millions of good and bad *acts*, and has no *general* criterion, and certainly no absolutist one, by which it can be judged (Ellis, 1962, 1972b, 1973b, 1976b; Ellis and Harper, 1975; Ellis and Velten, 1992).

Just about all the irrational Beliefs (iBs) that I originally listed in the 1950s and early 1960s, and that Beck (1976), Burns (1980), Maultsby (1984) and other cognitive behavior therapists outlined and disputed a decade and more later, are actively and vigorously Disputed in REBT empirically, logically and pragmatically. Rational emotive behavior therapy mainly defines *rational* as being self-helping and society-abetting Beliefs and defines *irrational* as self-defeating and society-sabotaging Beliefs. It teaches hard-heading Disputing of human irrationalities.

Other Cognitive Techniques of REBT

Apart from the disputing techniques just discussed, REBT uses a number of other cognitive techniques. Some of its most popular ones are as follows:

Use of Rational Coping Statements When clients work at Disputing their irrational Beliefs (iBs) and at challenging their shoulds, oughts, musts, awfulizing and I-can't-stand-its, they come up with E, their Effective New Philosophy, which can be put into rational coping statements. They can write these down (or put them on a cassette tape), go over them many times, and think about *why* they are sensible, until they come to really believe them. Thus, they can repeat to themselves, 'I never absolutely *need* what I want. I only, only *prefer* it and can live reasonably happily even if I am deprived of it.' 'No matter how many times I fail, I am never *a failure*, nor an *inadequate person*' (Ellis and Abrahms, 1978).

Referenting the Disadvantages of Dysfunctional Behaviors REBT clients, when addicted to unhealthy habits – such as smoking or procrastination – can make a long list of the disadvantages of these behaviors, write them down on cards, and read them and think about them at least five times a day, to sink them into their heads and hearts (Ellis, 1988a; Ellis and Velten, 1992).

Modeling Clients are often encouraged to find models of good behavior – in their real life or in biographies and autobiographies – and to model themselves after the self-helping and productive thoughts, feelings and actions of these models (Ellis and Velten, 1992).

Cognitive Distractions As a technique to temporarily allay their anxiety, rage and depression, and to give themselves leeway to get around to effective REBT Disputing of their irrational Beliefs, clients are shown how to use cognitive distraction techniques. Thus, they can use biofeedback, progressive relaxation, Yoga and meditation to help them become less disturbed. REBT, however, would then encourage them to *also* do active Disputing of their iBs (Ellis, 1985a, 1990b).

Cognitive Homework REBT uses several self-help forms and encourages clients to do them as a form of cognitive homework. On these forms they write out the ABCs of REBT, indicate exactly how they can Dispute their irrational Beliefs, and come up with Effective New Philosophies (Es) that help make them more functional and happy. They can go over these self-help forms with their therapist, with their therapy group, with their friends, or with other people to see whether they are filling them out properly and getting satisfactory results (Dryden, 1990b; Ellis, 1988a, 1991f; Ellis and Velten, 1992).

Reframing REBT clients are encouraged to reframe some of the 'awful' and 'horrible' things that occur in their lives and to see that these often have 'good' sides as well. Thus, they are shown how being quickly rejected by someone can save them time and energy vainly trying to win that person's approval; and they can be shown how failing to get a job may lead them to get more education and to find better employment (Ellis, 1988a; Ellis and Abrahms, 1978). They are also shown how to reframe 'bad' events so as to stubbornly refuse to make themselves depressed and miserable about them, and instead only make themselves feel healthily sorry and disappointed. (Ellis, 1985c, 1988a).

Semantic Corrections REBT, as noted elsewhere in this chapter, follows some of the principles of Alfred Korzybski (1933), who originated the science and philosophy of General Semantics. It therefore shows clients how they often use language improperly to overgeneralize and falsely tell themselves constructions like, 'I *am* a stupid person because some of the things I *do* are stupid!' So REBT teaches people how to correct misleading self-statements, such as 'People *make me* angry by doing unfair acts,' and to change them to statements such as, 'I choose to anger myself about the bad acts that people sometimes do' (Ellis, 1988a; Ellis and Abrahms, 1978; Ellis and Harper, 1975).

Emotive Techniques of REBT

As noted above, REBT hypothesizes that people often *forcefully* and *powerfully* create and hold on to their dysfunctional thoughts, feelings, and behaviors. Therefore, it has designed and adapted and almost always employs, a number of vigorous evocative-emotive techniques. For example:

Shame Attacking These exercises encourage clients to go out in public and deliberately do some act they consider 'foolish' or 'shameful' while working cognitively and emotively to feel *only* healthily sorry and disappointed and *not* ashamed or self-downing when they receive disapproval (Ellis, 1969b, 1973a, 1988a; Ellis and Abrahms, 1978; Ellis and Becker, 1982; Ellis and Harper, 1975).

Rational-Emotive Imagery People imagine one of the worst things that could happen to them, implode their *unhealthy* feelings of horror, terror, depression and rage, and then work to make themselves feel *healthily* sorry, disappointed or frustrated (Ellis, 1988a; Ellis and Harper, 1975; Ellis and Velten, 1992; Maultsby, 1971; Maultsby and Ellis, 1974).

Forceful Coping Statements Clients are shown how to create realistic and philosophic rational self-statements and how to sink them *vigorously* into their heads and hearts until they *convincingly* believe them (Ellis, 1969b, 1988a; Ellis and Becker, 1982; Ellis and Dryden, 1987, 1991; Ellis and Harper, 1975).

Forceful Self-dialogues Clients make a tape describing their irrational beliefs (iBs), vehemently dispute them on the tape, listen to their own disputing, and have others listen to it to see if it is sufficiently powerful and convincing (Ellis, 1985c, 1988a, 1990b; Ellis and Velten, 1992).

Use of Humor REBT uses many forms of disputing a client's irrational beliefs, especially that of reducing them to absurdity. Disturbed people frequently lose their sense of humor, and it has been found that, if they interrupt their over-seriousness by laughing at some of their errors and inanities, they emotively as well as cognitively distract themselves from and tend to surrender some of their dysfunctional beliefs (Ellis, 1977c, 1987f; Fry and Salameh, 1987).

I began using a group of rational humorous songs, with my own lyrics set to popular tunes, in 1976. At the Institute for Rational-Emotive Therapy's psychological clinic in New York, we find that they are often effective when used with individual and group clients and in REBT-oriented talks, workshops and intensives (Ellis, 1977d, 1981, 1987f).

Use of Group Processes and Exercises I began to apply REBT to group processes in the late 1950s because I found that clients gained support from others who learned and used REBT with them and that, when actively disputing others' irrational beliefs, they became more adept at and interested in disputing their own iBs. Consequently, REBT uses several small and large-scale group processes, including regular group therapy, special women's and men's groups, workshops and intensives. In the course of these groups – as well as in REBT individual sessions – many experiential and emotive-evocative exercises are used (Dryden, 1990a; Ellis, 1969b, 1973b, 1975, 1977a, 1979c, 1980c, 1985b, 1985c, 1987a, 1988a, 1990b, 1990c, 1990d, 1990g, 1990h, 1991a, 1991c, 1991f; Ellis, Sichel, Leaf and Mass, 1989).

Interpersonal Relationships From the start, REBT has emphasized interpersonal and family relationships because most clients have problems in these areas and many would not come to therapy if they did not have them. REBT actively deals with how people upset *themselves* about their relations with others, but it also shows them how to relate and cooperate better with others in the course of individual and group therapy and in workshops and intensives. It is consequently one of the main interpersonal relationship therapies (Crawford and Ellis, 1982; Ellis, 1957a, 1962, 1969b, 1971, 1973b, 1975, 1976c, 1977a, 1977b, 1979b, 1980c, 1985a, 1985b, 1986b, 1988a, 1988b, 1990b, 1990d, 1992a, 1992b; Ellis and Becker, 1982; Ellis and Bernard, 1985; Ellis and Dryden, 1985, 1987; Ellis and Harper, 1961; Ellis, Sichel, Yeager, DiMattia and DiGiuseppe, 1989; Hauck, 1977).

REBT Role Playing Clients role play with a therapist, group member or friend and stop when they display anxiety, rage or depression to see what they are telling themselves to create their disturbed feelings (Ellis, 1988a; Ellis and Abrahms, 1978).

Reverse Role Playing The rational emotive behavior therapist or a friend of the client plays the client's role and rigidly holds on to his or her irrational beliefs (iBs), until the client is able to talk the role player out of these dysfunctional ideas (Ellis, 1988a; Ellis, Sichel, Yeager, DiMattia and DiGiuseppe, 1989).

Other Emotive Techniques REBT includes a number of other emotive-evocative methods, such as the therapist's using strong encouragement, forceful disputing, self-disclosure, stories, analogies, metaphors, and so on (Bernard, 1986; Bernard and Joyce, 1984; Ellis and Abrahms, 1978; Ellis and Dryden, 1987, 1991; Ellis and Yeager, 1989; Lazarus, 1990; Muran, 1991; Vernon, 1989).

Behavioral Techniques of REBT

Because I got myself over my public speaking and social phobias at the age of 19 by forcing myself to *act against* them, REBT has always heavily used a number of behavioral methods, and therefore pioneered in cognitive-behavior therapy (Ellis, 1962, 1969a, 1969b, 1971, 1972c, 1973b, 1988a, 1990e, 1991b; Ellis and Becker, 1982; Ellis and Dryden, 1987, 1990, 1991; Ellis and Harper, 1975; Warga, 1989). Some of the most frequently employed behavioral methods of REBT are discussed below.

In Vivo Desensitization Rather than rely on Wolpe's (1982) imaginal systematic desensitization, REBT favors in vivo desensitization and urges clients to do repetitively what they are afraid to do, such as speaking in public, encountering potential sex-love partners, and going for difficult job interviews (Ellis, 1962, 1971, 1988a; Ellis and Becker, 1982; Ellis and Dryden, 1987, 1990, 1991; Ellis and Harper, 1961, 1975).

Implosive Desensitization In encouraging clients to do what they are afraid to do in order to overcome their dysfunctional fears, REBT often favors implosive rather than gradual desensitization (Ellis, 1983b). Thus, people with elevator fears are encouraged to enter 20 elevators a day for about 30 days in a row while forcefully telling themselves, 'I can handle this! I won't get stuck in this elevator and if I do, it's only a damned inconvenience, not a horror!' Not all clients agree to do their fear-attacking homework implosively, but when they do, they usually get better and quicker results than when they do so gradually – for they then experientially *see* that it is only uncomfortable, not harmful or 'horrible' (Ellis, 1971, 1973a, 1985c, 1988a, 1991b).

Remaining in 'Awful' Situations REBT often encourages clients to remain temporarily in 'awful' situations – such as staying in a 'rotten' marriage or with a 'horrible' boss – until they work out their emotional problems and stop making themselves panicked, depressed or enraged. *Then* they may be helped to leave the situation (Ellis, 1985c, 1988a; Ellis and Abrahms, 1978).

Response Prevention With serious obsessive-compulsives, they are sometimes shown how to get a friend or relative to steadily monitor and restrain them, so that they are effectively prevented from indulging in their compulsive rituals (Ellis, 1985c; Ellis and Velten, 1992; Marks, 1978).

Penalization REBT not only uses a good deal of reinforcement when clients do their difficult agreed-upon homework assignments, but also recommends self-imposed penalties when they steadily refuse to do so. Thus, difficult customers (DCs) are urged to burn a hundred dollar bill or send it to an organization they violently disagree with when they fail to keep their promises to themselves to change their behavior. If necessary, they enlist a friend or relative to monitor their carrying out self-assigned penalties (Ellis, 1979c, 1985c, 1988a; Ellis and Abrahms, 1978; Ellis and Becker, 1982).

Medication REBT shows many clients how to live with little or no medication – such as large doses of Valium – but also often recommends experiments with antidepressants, lithium and other suitable medication for clients afflicted with endogenous depression, manic-depressive illness, obsessive-compulsive disorder, and other serious emotional-behavioral problems. It specializes in helping clients to work on their low frustration tolerance and thereby be able to follow medical and psychopharmacological routines that they are dysfunctionally avoiding (Ellis, 1985c; Ellis and Abrahms, 1978).

Skill Training REBT, as I have noted on several occasions, is a 'double-systems' therapy in that it usually first helps people function better in their present family, work, school or social system and then, as therapy proceeds, helps them change the system so that they can lead happier, more fulfilling lives. Consequently, it often shows clients how to change the activating events (As) they encounter, how to solve practical problems, and how to acquire pleasure-enhancing skills. It has pioneered in teaching clients assertion training (Ellis, 1963a, 1975; Wolfe, 1974; Wolfe and Fodor, 1975), and it frequently emphasizes relationship, communication, sex and social skills training (Ellis, 1957a, 1962, 1963a, 1963b, 1971, 1973a, 1973b, 1975, 1976c, 1977a, 1979b, 1980c, 1985b, 1986b, 1988a, 1992b; Ellis and Becker, 1982; Ellis and Dryden, 1987, 1991; Ellis and Grieger, 1977, 1986; Hauck, 1977).

Avoidance of Inefficient Procedures

REBT, as noted above, strives for efficient therapy and, therefore, largely (though not completely) avoids ineffective and potentially harmful therapy techniques. Thus, it is skeptical of and often avoids (a) Extensive free association; (b) Extensive dream analysis; (c) Too much therapist's warmth and enhancing of client's dependency; (d) Compulsive exploration of clients' early life and endless narration of their present complaints and experiences; (e) Compulsive talking about clients' feelings; and (f) Overemphasis on positive thinking and on positive visualization rather than on Disputing of irrational beliefs (Bernard, 1986, 1991; Ellis, 1991f; Ellis and Dryden, 1985).

Emphasis on Self-actualization

As mentioned previously, REBT has two main aspects: helping people overcome their cognitive-emotive-behavioral disturbances and helping them actively to seek and arrange for a fuller, happier, and more self-actualizing existence. More specifically, as I point out in a recent paper (Ellis, 1991a: 15) and as I have collaboratively worked out with Ted Crawford (Crawford and Ellis, 1989), REBT encourages clients to work at (a) actively choosing self-actualizing paths that they individually select; (b) preferring but not demanding that they solve self-actualizing problems; (c) unconditional acceptance of oneself and others; (d) overcoming procrastination and low frustration tolerance; (e) framing self-actualizing as a systemic problem to be designed and redesigned; (f) moving from either/ors toward and/alsos – by accepting ambiguity, paradox, inconsistency and confusion and then pushing toward an integrated wholeness.

The REBT approach to self-actualization, like its approach to treating cognitive-emotional disturbance, heavily emphasizes openness, skeptical questioning and ceaseless experimentation. Critical realism is ever its watchword.

References

Abelson, R.P. (1963) Computer simulation of 'hot' cognition. In S.S. Tompkins and S. Messick (eds), *Computer Simulation of Personality*. New York: John Wiley.

Adler, A. (1964) *Social Interest: A Challenge to Mankind*. New York: Capricorn.
Baisden, H.E. (1980) *Irrational Beliefs: A Construct Validation Study*. Unpublished doctoral dissertation, University of Minnesota, Minneapolis.
Bard, J. (1980) *Rational-Emotive Therapy in Practice*. Champaign, IL: Research Press.
Bard, J. (1987) *I Don't Like Asparagus*. Cleveland, OH: Cleveland State University, Psychology Department.
Bartley, W.W. (1962) *The Retreat to Commitment*. New York: Knopf. (Rev. edn, Knopf, New York, 1985).
Bateson, G. (1979) *Mind and Nature: A Necessary Unit*. New York: E.P. Dutton.
Beck, A.T. (1976) *Cognitive Therapy and the Emotional Disorders*. New York: International Universities Press.
Beck, A.T. (1988) *Love is Never Enough*. New York: Harper and Row.
Beck, A.T. (1991) Cognitive therapy: A 30-year retrospective, *American Psychologist*, 46, 382–9.
Bernard, M.E. (1986) *Staying Alive in an Irrational World: Albert Ellis and Rational-Emotive Therapy*. South Melbourne, Australia: Carlson/Macmillan.
Bernard, M.E. (ed.) (1991) *Using Rational-Emotive Therapy Effectively: A Practitioner's Guide*. New York: Plenum.
Bernard, M.E. and Joyce, M.R. (1984) *Rational-Emotive Therapy with Children and Adolescents*. New York: John Wiley.
Bowlby, J. (1969) *Attachment and Loss. I: Attachment*. New York: Basic Books.
Bowlby, J. (1973) *Attachment and Loss. II: Separation*. New York: Basic Books.
Burns, D.D. (1980) *Feeling Good: The New Mood Therapy*. New York: Morrow.
Crawford, T. and Ellis, A. (1982) Communication and Rational-Emotive Therapy. Workshop presented in Los Angeles in October.
Crawford, T. and Ellis, A. (1989) A dictionary of rational-emotive feelings and behaviors, *Journal of Rational-Emotive and Cognitive-Behavior Therapy*, 7(1), 3–27.
DiGiuseppe, R. (1986) The implication of the philosophy of science for rational-emotive theory and therapy, *Psychotherapy*, 23, 634–9.
DiGiuseppe, R., Miller, J.J. and Trexler, L.D. (1979) A review of rational-emotive psychotherapy outcome studies. In A. Ellis and J.M. Whiteley (eds), *Theoretical and Empirical Foundations of Rational-Emotive Therapy* (pp. 218–35). Monterey, CA: Brooks/Cole.
DiSalvo, J. (1989) *Beyond Revolution: On Becoming a Cybernetic Epistemologist*. New York: Vantage.
Dryden, W. (1990a) *Dealing with Anger Problems: Rational-Emotive Therapeutic Interventions*. Sarasota, FL: Professional Resource Exchange.
Dryden, W. (1990b) *Rational-Emotive Counseling in Action*. London: Sage.
Dryden, W. and DiGiuseppe, R. (1990) *A Primer on Rational-Emotive Therapy*. Champaign, IL: Research Press.
Dryden, W. and Gordon, J. (1991) *Think Your Way to Happiness*. London: Sheldon Press.
Ellis, A. (1957a) *How to Live with a Neurotic: At Home and at Work*. New York: Crown. (Rev. edn, Wilshire, North Hollywood, CA, 1975)
Ellis, A. (1957b) Outcome of employing three techniques of psychotherapy, *Journal of Clinical Psychology*, 13, 344–50.
Ellis, A. (1958) *Rational Psychotherapy*. New York: Institute for Rational-Emotive Therapy. (Reprinted from *Journal of General Psychology*, 1958, 59, 35–49).
Ellis, A. (1962) *Reason and Emotion in Psychotherapy*. Secaucus, NJ: Citadel.
Ellis, A. (1963a) *The Intelligent Woman's Guide to Manhunting*. New York: Lyle Stuart and Dell. (Rev. edn, *The Intelligent Woman's Guide to Dating and Mating*, Lyle Stuart, Secaucus, NJ, 1979)
Ellis, A. (1963b) *Sex and the Single Man*. Secaucus, NJ: Lyle Stuart.
Ellis, A. (1963c) Showing the patient that he is not a worthless individual, *Voices*, 1(2), 74–7. (Reprinted and revised as *Showing Clients they are not Worthless Individuals*, Institute for Rational-Emotive Therapy, New York, 1985)

Ellis, A. (1969a) A cognitive approach to behavior therapy, *International Journal of Psychiatry*, 8, 896–900.
Ellis, A. (1969b) A weekend of rational encounter, *Rational Living*, 4(2), 1–8. (Reprinted in A. Ellis and W. Dryden, *The Practice of Rational-Emotive Therapy*, Springer, New York, 1987).
Ellis, A. (1971) *Growth Through Reason*. North Hollywood, CA: Wilshire.
Ellis, A. (Speaker) (1972a) *Conquering Low Frustration Tolerance* [Cassette recording]. New York: Institute for Rational-Emotive Therapy.
Ellis, A. (1972b) *Psychotherapy and the Value of a Human Being*. New York: Institute for Rational-Emotive Therapy. (Reprinted in A. Ellis and W. Dryden, *The Essential Albert Ellis*. New York: Springer, 1990)
Ellis, A. (1972c) Psychotherapy without tears. In A. Burton (ed.), *Twelve Therapists* (pp. 103–26). San Francisco: Jossey-Bass.
Ellis, A. (Speaker) (1972d) *Solving Emotional Problems* [Cassette recording]. New York: Institute for Rational-Emotive Therapy.
Ellis, A. (Speaker) (1973a) *How to Stubbornly Refuse to be Ashamed of Anything* [Cassette recording]. New York: Institute for Rational-Emotive Therapy.
Ellis, A. (1973b) *Humanistic Psychotherapy: The Rational-Emotive Approach*. New York: McGraw-Hill.
Ellis, A. (Speaker) (1973c) *Twenty-one Ways to Stop Worrying* [Cassette recording]. New York: Institute for Rational-Emotive Therapy.
Ellis, A. (Speaker) (1974) *Rational Living in an Irrational World* [Cassette recording]. New York: Institute for Rational-Emotive Therapy.
Ellis, A. (Speaker) (1975) *RET and Assertiveness Training* [Cassette recording]. New York: Institute for Rational-Emotive Therapy.
Ellis, A. (1976a) The biological basis of human irrationality, *Journal of Individual Psychology*, 32, 145–68. (Reprinted, Institute for Rational-Emotive Therapy, New York, 1976)
Ellis, A. (1976b) RET abolishes most of the human ego. New York: Institute for Rational-Emotive Therapy. (Reprinted from *Psychotherapy*, 1976, 13, 343–8)
Ellis, A. (1976c) *Sex and the Liberated Man*. Secaucus, NJ: Lyle Stuart.
Ellis, A. (1977a) *Anger – How to Live With and Without It*. Secaucus, NJ: Citadel.
Ellis, A. (Speaker) (1977b) *Conquering the Dire Need for Love* [Cassette recording]. New York: Institute for Rational-Emotive Therapy.
Ellis, A. (1977c) Fun as psychotherapy, *Rational Living*, 12(1), 2–6. (Also available as a cassette recording [1977] from Institute for Rational-Emotive Therapy, New York)
Ellis, A. (Speaker) (1977d) *A Garland of Rational Humorous Songs* (Cassette recording and songbook). New York: Institute for Rational-Emotive Therapy.
Ellis, A. (1978a) *I'd Like to Stop but . . . Dealing with Addictions* [Cassette recording]. New York: Institute for Rational-Emotive Therapy.
Ellis, A. (1978b) Rational-emotive therapy and self-help therapy, *Rational Living*, 13(1), 2–9.
Ellis, A. (1979a) Discomfort anxiety: A new cognitive behavioral construct. Part 1, *Rational Living*, 14(2), 3–8.
Ellis, A. (1979b) *The Intelligent Woman's Guide to Dating and Mating* (rev. edn). Secaucus, NJ: Lyle Stuart. (Original work published as *The Intelligent Woman's Guide to Manhunting*, Lyle Stuart and Dell, New York, 1963)
Ellis, A. (1979c) Rational-emotive therapy: Research data that support the clinical and personality hypotheses of RET and other modes of cognitive-behavior therapy. In A. Ellis and J.M. Whiteley (eds), *Theoretical and Empirical Foundations of Rational-Emotive Therapy* (pp. 101–73). Monterey, CA: Brooks/Cole.
Ellis, A. (1980a) Discomfort anxiety: A new cognitive behavioral construct. Part 2, *Rational Living*, 15(1), 25–30.
Ellis, A. (1980b) Rational-emotive therapy and cognitive behavior therapy: Similarities and differences, *Cognitive Therapy and Research*, 4, 325–40.
Ellis, A. (Speaker) (1980c) *Twenty-two Ways to Brighten up your Life* [Cassette recording]. New York: Institute for Rational-Emotive Therapy.
Ellis, A. (1981) The use of rational humorous songs in psychotherapy, *Voices*, 16(4), 29–36.

Ellis, A. (1983a) *The Case Against Religiosity*. New York: Institute for Rational-Emotive Therapy.
Ellis, A. (1983b) The philosophic implications and dangers of some popular behavior therapy techniques. In M. Rosenbaum, C.M. Franks and Y. Jaffe (eds), *Perspectives in Behavior Therapy in the Eighties* (pp. 138–51). New York: Springer.
Ellis, A. (1985a) Intellectual fascism, *Journal of Rational-Emotive Therapy*, 3(1), 3–12.
Ellis, A. (1985b) Love and its problems. In A. Ellis and M.E. Bernard (eds), *Clinical Applications of Rational-Emotive Therapy* (pp. 32–54). New York: Plenum.
Ellis, A. (1985c) *Overcoming Resistance: Rational-Emotive Therapy with Difficult Clients*. New York: Springer.
Ellis, A. (1986a) Anxiety about anxiety: The use of hypnosis with rational-emotive therapy. In E.T. Dowd and J.M. Healy (eds), *Case Studies in Hypnotherapy* (pp. 3–11). New York: Guildford. (Reprinted in A. Ellis and W. Dryden, *The Practice of Rational-Emotive Therapy*, Springer, New York, 1987)
Ellis, A. (1986b) Rational-emotive therapy applied to relationship therapy, *Journal of Rational-Emotive Therapy*, 4, 4–21.
Ellis, A. (1987a) Critical incidents in group therapy: Rational-emotive therapy. In J. Donigan and R. Malnati (eds), *Critical Incidents in Group Therapy* (pp. 87–91, 105–9, 123–8, 141–6, 166–72, 189–92). Monterey, CA: Brooks/Cole.
Ellis, A. (Speaker) (1987b) *The Enemies of Humanism – What Makes them Tick?* (Cassette recording, no. 108). New York and Alexandria, VA: Audio Transcripts.
Ellis, A. (1987c) The impossibility of achieving consistently good mental health, *American Psychologist*, 42, 364–75.
Ellis, A. (1987d) A sadly neglected cognitive element in depression, *Cognitive Therapy and Research*, 11, 121–46.
Ellis, A. (1987e) Testament of a humanist, *Free Inquiry*, 7(2), 21.
Ellis, A. (1987f) The use of rational humorous songs in psychotherapy. In W.F. Fry, Jr. and W.A. Salameh (eds), *Handbook of Humor and Psychotherapy* (pp. 265–87). Sarasota, FL: Professional Resource Exchange.
Ellis, A. (1988a) *How to Stubbornly Refuse to Make Yourself Miserable about Anything – Yes, Anything!* Secaucus, NJ: Lyle Stuart.
Ellis, A. (Speaker) (1988b) *Unconditionally Accepting Yourself and Others* [Cassette recording]. New York: Institute for Rational-Emotive Therapy.
Ellis, A. (1989a) Foreword. In J. DiSalvo, *Beyond Revolution . . . On Becoming a Cybernetic Epistemologist* (pp. xi–xii). New York: Vantage.
Ellis, A. (1989b) *The Treatment of Psychotic and Borderline Individuals with RET*. New York: Institute for Rational-Emotive Therapy. (Original work published 1965)
Ellis, A. (1990a) The Advantages and Disadvantages of Self-help Materials. Paper presented at the 98th Annual Conference of the American Psychological Association, Boston.
Ellis, A. (Speaker) (1990b) *Albert Ellis Live at the Learning Annex* [Cassette recording]. New York: Institute for Rational-Emotive Therapy.
Ellis, A. (1990c) How can psychological treatment aim to be briefer and better? The rational-emotive approach to brief therapy. In J.K. Zeig and S.G. Gilligan (eds), *Brief Therapy: Myths, Methods and Metaphors* (pp. 291–302). San Francisco: Jossey-Bass.
Ellis, A. (1990d) Is rational-emotive therapy (RET) 'rationalist' or 'constructivist'? In A. Ellis and W. Dryden, *The Essential Albert Ellis* (pp. 114–41). New York: Springer.
Ellis, A. (1990e) My life in clinical psychology. In C.E. Walker (ed.), *History of Clinical Psychology in Autobiography* (pp. 1–37). Homewood, IL: Dorsey Press.
Ellis, A. (1990f) A Rational-Emotive Approach to Peace. Paper delivered at the 98th Annual Convention of the American Psychological Association, Boston.
Ellis, A. (1990g) Rational-emotive therapy. In I.L. Kutash and A. Wolf (eds), *The Group Psychotherapist's Handbook* (pp. 298–315). New York: Columbia University Press.
Ellis, A. (1990h) Special features of rational-emotive therapy. In W. Dryden and R. DiGiuseppe, *A Primer on Rational-Emotive Therapy* (pp. 79–93). Champaign, IL: Research Press.

Ellis, A. (1991a) Achieving self-actualization. In A. Jones and R. Crandall (eds), *Handbook of Self-actualization*. Corte Madera, CA: Select Press.
Ellis, A. (1991b) Foreword. In P. Hauck, *Hold your Head up High* (pp. 1–4). London: Sheldon.
Ellis, A. (1991c) The Future of Cognitive-Behavioral Therapies. Paper presented at the 99th Annual Convention of the American Psychological Association, San Francisco.
Ellis, A. (1991d) Rational Recovery Systems: Alternatives to AA and Other 12-step Programs. Paper presented at the 99th Annual Convention of the American Psychological Association, San Francisco.
Ellis, A. (1991e) The revised ABCs of rational-emotive therapy. In J. Zeig (ed.), *Evolution of Psychotherapy: II*. New York: Brunner/Mazel. (Expanded version in *Journal of Rational-Emotive and Cognitive-Behavior Therapy*, 1991, 9(3), 139–72)
Ellis, A. (1991f) *Using RET Effectively: Reflections and Interview*. In M.E. Bernard (ed.), *Using Rational-Emotive Therapy Effectively* (pp. 1–33). New York: Plenum.
Ellis, A. (1992a) Brief therapy: The rational-emotive method. In S. Budman, J. Hoyt and S. Friedman (eds), *First Sessions of Brief Psychotherapy*. New York: Guilford.
Ellis, A. (1992b) Rational-emotive approaches to peace, *Journal of Cognitive Psychotherapy*, 2, 79–104.
Ellis, A. (1994) *Reason and Emotion in Psychotherapy*. Revised edn. New York: Carol Publishing.
Ellis, A. and Abrahms, E. (1978) *Brief Psychotherapy in Medical and Health Practice*. New York: Springer.
Ellis, A. and Becker, I. (1982) *A Guide to Personal Happiness*. North Hollywood, CA: Wilshire.
Ellis, A. and Bernard, M.E. (eds) (1985) *Clinical Applications of Rational-Emotive Therapy*. New York: Plenum.
Ellis, A. and Dryden, W. (1985) Dilemmas in giving warmth or love to clients: An interview with Windy Dryden. In W. Dryden, *Therapists' Dilemmas* (pp. 5–16). London: Harper and Row.
Ellis, A. and Dryden, W. (1987) *The Practice of Rational-Emotive Therapy*. New York: Springer.
Ellis, A. and Dryden, W. (1990) *The Essential Albert Ellis*. New York: Springer.
Ellis, A. and Dryden, W. (1991) *A Dialogue with Albert Ellis: Against Dogma*. Stony Stratford, Milton Keynes, England: Open University Press.
Ellis, A. and Grieger, R. (eds) (1977) *Handbook of Rational-Emotive Therapy* (Vol. 1). New York: Springer.
Ellis, A. and Grieger, R. (eds) (1986) *Handbook of Rational-Emotive Therapy* (Vol. 2). New York: Springer.
Ellis, A. and Harper, R.A. (1961) *A Guide to Successful Marriage*. North Hollywood, CA: Wilshire.
Ellis, A. and Harper, R.A. (1975) *A New Guide to Rational Living*. North Hollywood, CA: Wilshire.
Ellis, A. and Knaus, W.J. (1977) *Overcoming Procrastination*. New York: New American Library.
Ellis, A., McInerney, J.F., DiGiuseppe, R. and Yeager, R.J. (1988) *Rational-Emotive Therapy with Alcoholics and Substance Abusers*. Elmsford, NY: Pergamon.
Ellis, A., Sichel, J., Leaf, R.C. and Mass, R. (1989) Countering perfectionism in research on clinical practice. I: Surveying rationality changes after a single intensive RET intervention, *Journal of Rational-Emotive and Cognitive-Behavior Therapy*, 7, 197–218.
Ellis, A., Sichel, J., Yeager, R., DiMattia, D. and DiGiuseppe, R. (1989) *Rational-Emotive Couples Therapy*. Elmsford, NY: Pergamon.
Ellis, A. and Tisdale, J.R. (1990) The Ellis-Tisdale debate, *Newsletter of the Transpersonal Psychology Interest Group of the American Psychological Association*, 9, 3–11.
Ellis, A. and Velten, E. (1992) *When AA Doesn't Work for You: Rational Steps to Quitting Alcohol*. New York: Barricade Books.

Ellis, A. and Whiteley, J.M. (1979) *Theoretical and Empirical Foundations of Rational-Emotive Therapy*. Monterey, CA: Brooks/Cole.
Ellis, A. and Yeager, R. (1989) *Why Some Therapies Don't Work: The Dangers of Transpersonal Psychology*. Buffalo, NY: Prometheus Books.
Ellis, A., Young, J. and Lockwood, G. (1987) Cognitive therapy and rational-emotive therapy: A dialogue, *Journal of Cognitive Psychotherapy*, 1(4), 137–87.
Engels, G.I. and Diekstra, R.F.W. (1986) Meta-analysis of rational-emotive therapy outcome studies. In P. Eelen and O. Fontaine (eds), *Behavior Therapy: Beyond the Conditioning Framework* (pp. 121–40). Hillsdale, NJ: Lawrence Erlbaum.
Epstein, S. (1990) Cognitive experiential theory. In L. Pervin (ed.), *Handbook of Personality Theory and Research*. New York: Guilford.
Franklin, J. (1987) *Molecules of the Mind*. New York: Delta.
Frazer, J.G. (1959) *The Golden Bough*. New York: Macmillan.
Freud, S. (1965) *Standard Edition of the Complete Psychological Works of Sigmund Freud*. New York: Basic Books.
Fry, W.F., Jr. and Salameh, W.A. (eds) (1987) *Handbook of Humor and Psychotherapy*. Sarasota, FL: Professional Research Exchange.
Grieger, R. and Boyd, J. (1980) *Rational-Emotive Therapy: A Skills-based Approach*. New York: Van Nostrand Reinhold.
Guntrip, H. (1971) *Psychoanalytic Theory, Therapy and the Self*. New York: Basic Books.
Haaga, D.A. and Davison, G.C. (1989) Outcome studies of rational-emotive therapy. In M.E. Bernard and R. DiGiuseppe (eds), *Inside Rational-Emotive Therapy* (pp. 155–97). San Diego, CA: Academic Press.
Hartman, H. (1964) *Ego Psychology and the Problem of Adaptation*. New York: International Universities Press.
Hauck, P.A. (1973) *Overcoming Depression*. Philadelphia: Westminster.
Hauck, P.A. (1974) *Overcoming Frustration and Anger*. Philadelphia: Westminster.
Hauck, P.A. (1977) *Marriage is a Loving Business*. Philadelphia: Westminster.
Hauck, P.A. (1992) *Overcoming the Rating Game*. Louisville, KY: Westminster.
Hoffer, E. (1951) *The True Believer*. New York: Harper and Row.
Huber, C.H. and Baruth, L.G. (1989) *Rational-Emotive Systems Family Therapy*. New York: Springer.
Jorm, A.P. (1987) *Modifiability of a Personal Trait Which is a Risk Factor for Neurosis*. Paper presented at World Psychiatric Association, Symposium on Epidemiology and the Prevention of Mental Disorder, Reykjavik.
Kahneman, D., Slovic, P. and Tversky, A. (eds) (1982) *Judgement under Uncertainty: Heuristics and Biases*. New York: Cambridge University Press.
Kernberg, O. (1975) *Borderline Conditions and Pathological Narcissism*. New York: Jason Aronson.
Klein, M. and Riviere, J. (1964) *Love, Hate and Reparation*. London: Hogarth.
Knaus, W.J. (1983) *How to Conquer your Frustrations*. Hillsdale, NJ: Lawrence Erlbaum.
Kohut, H. (1977) *The Restoration of the Self*. New York: International Universities Press.
Korzybski, A. (1933) *Science and Sanity*. San Francisco: International Society of General Semantics.
Lazarus, A.A. (1990) *The Practice of Multimodal Therapy*. Baltimore, MD: Johns Hopkins University Press.
Levi-Strauss, C. (1962) *The Savage Mind*. Chicago: University of Chicago Press.
Low, A.A. (1952) *Mental Health Through Will Training*. Boston: Christopher.
Lyons, L.C. and Woods, P.J. (1991) The efficacy of rational-emotive therapy: A quantitative review of the outcome research, *Clinical Psychology Review*, 11, 357–69.
Mahoney, M.J. (1991) *Human Change Processes*. New York: Basic Books.
Marks, D.F. (1978) *Living with Fear*. New York: McGraw-Hill.
Maultsby, M.C., Jr. (1971) Rational-emotive imagery, *Rational Living*, 6(1), 24–7.
Maultsby, M.C., Jr. (1984) *Rational Behavior Therapy*. Englewood Cliffs, NJ: Prentice-Hall.

Maultsby, M.C. and Ellis, A. (1974) *Technique of Using Rational-Emotive Imagery*. New York: Institute for Rational-Emotive Therapy.
McGovern, T.E. and Silverman, M.S. (1984) A review of outcome studies of rational-emotive therapy from 1977 to 1982, *Journal of Rational-Emotive Therapy*, 2(1), 7–18.
Meichenbaum, D. (1977) *Cognitive-Behavior Modification*. New York: Plenum.
Muran, J.C. (1991) A reformulation of the ABC model in cognitive psychotherapies: Implications for assessment and treatment, *Clinical Psychology Review*, 11, 399–418.
Popper, K.R. (1962) *Objective Knowledge*. London: Oxford University Press.
Popper, K.R. (1985) *Popper Selections* (David Miller, ed.). Princeton, NJ: Princeton University Press.
Rogers, C.R. (1961) *On Becoming a Person*. Boston: Houghton Mifflin.
Rorer, L.G. (1989) Rational-emotive theory: I. An integrated psychological and philosophical basis, *Cognitive Therapy and Research*, 13, 475–92.
Russell, B. (1965) *The Basic Writings of Bertrand Russell*. New York: Simon & Schuster.
Sampson, E.E. (1989) The challenge of social change in psychotherapy, *American Psychologist*, 44, 914–21.
Smith, T.W. (1989) Assessment in rational-emotive therapy. In M.E. Bernard and R. DiGiuseppe (eds), *Inside Rational-Emotive Therapy* (pp. 135–53). San Diego, CA: Academic Press.
Taylor, S.E. (1990) *Positive Illusions: Creative Self-Deception and the Healthy Mind*. New York: Basic Books.
Trimpey, J. (1989) *Rational Recovery from Alcoholism: The Small Book*. New York: Delacorte.
Trimpey, L. and Trimpey, J. (1990) *Rational Recovery from Fatness*. Lotus, CA: Lotus Press.
Vernon, A. (1989) *Thinking, Feeling, Behaving: An Emotional Education Curriculum for Children*. Champaign, IL: Research Press.
Wachtel, P. (1982) *Resistance*. New York: Plenum.
Walen, S.R., DiGiuseppe, R. and Dryden, W. (1992) *A Practitioner's Guide to Rational-Emotive Therapy* (2nd edn). New York: Oxford University Press.
Warga, C. (1989) *Profile of Psychologist Albert Ellis*. New York: Institute for Rational Emotive Therapy. (Original version published in *Psychology Today*, September, 1988)
Warren, R. and Zgourides, G.D. (1991) *Anxiety Disorders: A Rational-Emotive Perspective*. Elmsford, NY: Pergamon.
Watzlawick, P., Weakland, J. and Fisch, R. (1974) *Change*. New York: Norton.
Wessler, R.A. and Wessler, R.L. (1980) *The Principles and Practice of Rational-Emotive Therapy*. San Francisco, CA: Jossey-Bass.
Wolfe, J.L. (1974) *Rational-Emotive Therapy and Women's Assertiveness Training* [Cassette recording]. New York: Institute for Rational-Emotive Therapy.
Wolfe, J.L. and Fodor, I.G. (1975) A cognitive-behavioral approach to modifying assertive behavior in women, *Counseling Psychologist*, 5(4), 45–52.
Wolpe, J. (1982) *The Practice of Behavior Therapy* (3rd edn). Elmsford, NY: Pergamon.
Young, H.S. (1974) *A Rational Counseling Primer*. New York: Institute for Rational-Emotive Therapy.

PART 1
ALLIANCE, EDUCATION AND ASSESSMENT

2
The Therapeutic Alliance in Rational-Emotive Therapy

Windy Dryden

Bordin's Concept of the Therapeutic Alliance

As a rational-emotive therapist I have found the work of Ed Bordin (1979) on the concept of the therapeutic alliance particularly helpful in developing a basic framework for the conduct of RET. Bordin argues that the therapeutic alliance refers to the complex of attachments and shared understandings formed and activities undertaken by therapists and clients as the former attempt to help the latter with their psychological problems.

Bordin has stressed that there are three major components of the therapeutic alliance: (1) bonds – which refer to the interpersonal connectedness between therapist and client; (2) goals – which refer to the aims of both therapist and client; and (3) tasks – which are activities carried out by both therapist and client in the service of the latter's goals.

I will consider each of these components separately and show that rational-emotive therapists have important clinical decisions to make in each of the three alliance domains so as to individualise therapy for each client and thus maximise therapeutic benefit.

At the outset it should be noted that Bordin (1979) has speculated that effective therapy occurs when therapist and client (1) have an appropriately bonded working relationship; (2) mutually agree on the goals of the therapeutic enterprise; and (3) both understand their own and the other person's therapeutic tasks and agree to carry these out to implement the client's goals.

Bonds

The major concern of rational-emotive therapists in the bond domain should be to establish and maintain an appropriately bonded relationship that will encourage each individual client to implement his or her goal-directed therapeutic tasks. It should be underlined that there is no single effective bond that can be formed with clients in RET; different clients require different bonds. This observation became clear to me when, on a six months' sabbatical at the Center for Cognitive Therapy in Philadelphia in 1981, I saw two clients on the same afternoon who benefited from a different bonded relationship with me. At 4 p.m. I saw Mrs G., a 50-year-old married business woman, who was impressed with my British professional qualifications and whose responses to initial questions indicated that she anticipated and preferred a very formal relationship with her therapist. I provided such a relationship by using formal language, citing the research literature whenever appropriate, wearing a suit, shirt and tie and by referring to myself as Dr Dryden and to my client as Mrs G. On one occasion I inadvertently used her first name and was put firmly in my place concerning the protocol of professional relationships. On another occasion I disclosed a piece of personal information in order to make a therapeutic point and was told in no uncertain terms: 'Young man, I am not paying you good money to hear about your problems.' Here, a therapist is faced with the choice of respecting and meeting a client's bond anticipations and preferences or examining the reasons why, for example, this client was so adamantly against her therapist's informality. In my experience the latter strategy is rarely productive and rational-emotive therapists are recommended to fulfil their clients' preferences for therapy style as long as doing so does not reinforce the client's psychological problems.

At 5 p.m. on the same afternoon I regularly saw Mr B., a 42-year-old male nurse who indicated that he did not respond well to his previous therapist's neutrality and formality. Our therapy sessions were thus characterised by an informal bond. Before seeing him I would remove my jacket and tie that I wore for Mrs G.; in sessions we would use our first names and would both have our feet up on my desk. We also developed the habit of taking turns to bring in cans of soda and my client referred to our meetings as 'rap sessions' while I conceptualised my work as therapy within an informal context.

I maintain that Mrs G. would not have responded well to an informal therapy relationship nor would Mr B. have done as well with a highly formal mode of therapy. Thus, I argue that it is important that rational-emotive therapists pay attention to the question: 'Which bond is likely to be most effective with a particular client at a given time in the therapeutic process?' Drawing upon social-psychological principles, certain writers have argued that some clients show more progress when the therapeutic bond is based on liking and trustworthiness, while others flourish more when the bond emphasises therapist credibility and expertness (Strong and Claiborn, 1982; Beutler, 1983; Dorn, 1984). Future research in RET could fruitfully address the issue of which bond is effective with which clients. However, until we have such data, therapists could make decisions about which type of bond to foster on the basis of an early assessment of the client's anticipations and preferences in the bond domain and to try to meet such expectations, at least initially. This is one reason why I would caution novice therapists against emulating the therapy style of leading RET practitioners whose bond with clients may be based mainly on prestige and expertness. Rational-emotive therapists should thus be prepared to emphasise different aspects of themselves with different clients in the bond domain, without adopting an inauthentic façade, and to monitor transactions in this domain throughout therapy.

How can this best be done? One way would be to administer a modified portion of Lazarus's (1981) Life History Questionnaire which focuses on clients' expectations regarding therapy. The items: 'How do you think a therapist should interact with his or her clients?' and 'What personal qualities do you think the ideal therapist for you should possess?' are particularly relevant and could usefully provide impetus for further exploration of this issue at the outset of therapy. If the client has had therapy previously, the current therapist could usefully explore which aspects of the previous therapist(s') interactive style and behaviour were deemed by the client to be both helpful and unhelpful. Particular emphasis should be placed on the exploration of the instrumental nature of previous therapeutic bonds since statements such as 'He was warm and caring' are of little use unless the client evaluated these qualities positively and attributed therapeutic progress to these factors.

Furthermore, and for similar reasons, I have found it helpful to explore clients' accounts of people in their lives who have had both positive and negative therapeutic influence on their personal development. Such exploration may provide the therapist with important clues concerning which types of therapeutic bonds to promote actively with certain clients and which bonds to avoid developing with others.

Therapeutic style is another aspect of the bond domain which requires attention. Interpersonally oriented therapists (e.g., Anchin and Kiesler, 1982) have argued that practitioners need to be aware that therapeutic styles have a 'for better or worse' impact on different clients. Rational-emotive therapists tend to be active and directive in their style of conducting therapy. This therapy style may not be entirely productive with both passive clients and, as Beutler (1983) has argued, clients who are highly reactive to interpersonal influence. Clients who tend to be passive in their interpersonal style of relating may 'pull' an increasingly active style from their therapists who may in turn reinforce these clients' passivity with their increased activity. Clients whose psychological problems are intrinsically bound up with a passive style of relating are particularly vulnerable in this regard. It is important that rational-emotive therapists need to engage their clients productively at a level which constructively encourages increased activity on their part but without threatening them through the use of an overly passive style of practising RET.

Beutler (1983) has argued that all approaches to psychotherapy can be viewed as a process of persuasion and this is particularly true of RET practitioners who aim to 'persuade' clients to re-evaluate and change their irrational beliefs. As such, rational-emotive therapists need to be especially careful in working with clients for whom such persuasive attempts may be perceived as especially threatening (i.e., highly reactant clients). Here it is important that therapists execute their strategies with due regard to helping such clients to preserve their sense of autonomy, emphasising throughout that these clients are in control of their own thought processes and decisions concerning whether or not to change them. At present, the above suggestions are speculative and await full empirical ènquiry, but my clinical work has led me to question the desirability of establishing the same therapeutic bond with all clients and of practising rational-emotive therapy in an unchanging therapeutic style.

Goals

The major concern of rational-emotive therapists in the goal domain of the alliance is to ensure that there is agreement between therapist and client on the client's outcome goals for change. A prerequisite of such agreement concerns client and therapist arriving at a shared understanding of the client's most relevant problems as defined by the client (Meichenbaum and Gilmore, 1982). Difficulties may occur here when the therapist uncritically accepts the client's initial accounts of his or her problem because such accounts may well be biased by the client's internalised values, for example, the views of significant others in the client's life. In addition, although most rational-emotive therapists consider that early goal-setting with the client is important, clients' initial statements about their goals for change may well be coloured by their psychological disturbance as well as by their internalised values concerning what these goals should be. Rational-emotive therapists need to walk a fine line between uncritically accepting clients' initial goals for change and disregarding them altogether. A helpful solution here involves establishment and maintenance of a channel of communication between client and therapist which deals with metatherapy issues (i.e., issues concerning matters relating to therapy itself). I have referred to the activities that occur within this channel as involving negotiations and renegotiations about therapeutic issues (Dryden and Hunt, 1985). Rational-emotive therapists need to take the main responsibility for keeping this communication channel open in order to monitor clients' goals over time and to determine the reasons for shifts in these goals.

Pinsof and Catherall (1986) have made the important point that clients' goals occur (implicitly or explicitly) in reference to their most important relationships and their therapists need to be mindful of the impact that these systems are likely to have on both the selection of such goals and the client's degree of progress towards goal attainment. Adopting this focus may well possibly mean involving parts of the client's interpersonal system in therapy itself. It also suggests that future theorising in RET could profitably assign a more central role to interpersonal issues (compare Safran, 1984; Kwee and Lazarus, 1986).

Tasks

Rational-emotive practitioners tend to subscribe to the following therapeutic process. Initially, having agreed to offer help to the client, the therapist attempts to structure the therapeutic process for the client and begins both to assess his or her problems in rational-emotive terms and also to help the client to view his or her problems within this framework. Goals are elicited based on a rational-emotive assessment, and therapeutic strategies and techniques are implemented to effect the desired changes. Finally, obstacles to client change are analysed and, it is hoped, overcome, and therapeutic gains are stabilised and maintained.

Therapists have tasks to execute at each stage in the rational-emotive therapeutic process and these will now be outlined.

Structuring Effective RET depends in part on each participant clearly understanding their respective responsibilities in the therapeutic endeavour and upon each agreeing to discharge these responsibilities in the form of carrying out therapeutic tasks. It is the therapist's major responsibility to help the client to make sense of this process by providing an overall structure of mutual responsibilities and tasks. It is important to stress that structuring occurs throughout therapy and not just at the outset of the process. Sensitive therapists who pay attention to alliance issues will structure the process using language which the client can understand and analogies which make sense to each individual person. Thus, it is often helpful to discover clients' hobbies and interests so that apt and personally meaningful structuring statements can be made. Thus, if a client is interested in golf, ascertaining how that person learned the game may be valuable in drawing parallels between the processes of learning coping skills and learning golfing skills. Both involve practice and failures can be realistically anticipated in each activity.

Assessment and Conceptualisation of Clients' Problems During the assessment process, rational-emotive therapists traditionally attempt to gain a full understanding of the cognitive and behavioural variables that are maintaining their clients' problems. During this stage two issues become salient from an alliance theory perspective. First, it is important for therapist and client to arrive at a shared definition of the client's problems (i.e., what these problems are). Secondly, as Meichenbaum and Gilmore (1982) have noted, it is important for them to negotiate a shared conceptualisation of the client's problems (i.e., an explanation of what accounts for the existence of these problems) so that they can work productively together in the intervention stage of therapy.

When working towards shared problem conceptualisation, I argue that it is important for RET practitioners to use, wherever possible, the client's own language and concepts, particularly when providing alternative explanations of their problems. This helps therapists to work within the range of what clients will accept as plausible conceptualisations of their problems. If clients' own ideas about the origins of their problems and more particularly what maintain them are ignored, then they may well resist accepting their therapists' conceptualisations. As Golden (1985) has noted, sometimes therapists often have to accept initially, for pragmatic purposes, a client's different (i.e., to the therapist's) conceptualisation of his or her problems in order to arrive later at a shared one. In addition, rational-emotive therapists may well privately (i.e., to themselves) conceptualise a client's problems in rational-emotive terms (irrational beliefs) while publicly (to the client) using the client's conceptualisation (e.g., negative self-hypnosis). To what extent the effectiveness of RET is based on negotiation or on the unilateral persuasion attempts of the therapist is a matter for future empirical enquiry.

Change Tactics Once the therapist and client have come to a mutually agreed understanding of the client's problems, the therapist then discusses with the client a variety of techniques that the client can use to reach his or her goals. Here it is important to realise that both client and therapist have tasks to execute.

Effective RET in the task domain tends to occur when:

1 Clients understand what their tasks are.
2 Clients understand how executing their tasks will help them achieve their goals.
3 Clients are, in fact, capable of executing their tasks and believe that they have this capability.
4 Clients understand that change comes about through repeated execution of their tasks.
5 Clients understand the tasks of their therapists and can see the link between their therapists' tasks, their own tasks and their goals.
6 Therapists adequately prepare their clients to understand and execute the latter's tasks.
7 Therapists effectively execute their tasks (i.e., they are skilled in the techniques of RET) and use a wide range of techniques appropriately.
8 Therapists employ techniques which are congruent with their clients' learning styles. While some clients learn best through action, others learn best through reading bibliotherapy texts, etc.
9 Therapists employ techniques that clients have selected (from a range of possible procedures) rather than unilaterally selecting techniques without client participation.
10 Therapists pace their interventions appropriately.
11 Therapists employ techniques which are potent enough to help clients achieve their goals (e.g., using exposure methods with clients with agoraphobic problems – Emmelkamp et al., 1978).

Failures in RET

I have been practising RET now for over 15 years in a variety of settings. I have worked in (1) a university therapy service; (2) a general practice; (3) a National Health Service psychiatric clinic; (4) a local marriage guidance council; and (5) private practice. I have seen in these settings a wide range of moderately to severely disturbed individuals who were deemed to be able to benefit from weekly counselling or psychotherapy. While I do not have any hard data to substantiate the point, I have found rational-emotive therapy to be a highly effective method of individual psychotherapy with a wide range of client problems.

However, I have of course had my therapeutic failures, and I would like, in this final section, to outline some of the factors that in my opinion have accounted for these failures. I will again use Bordin's (1979) useful concept of the therapeutic working alliance as a framework in this respect.

Goals

I have generally been unsuccessful with clients who have devoutly clung to goals where changes in other people were desired. (In this regard, I have also failed to involve these others in therapy.) I have not been able to show or to persuade these clients that they make themselves emotionally disturbed and that it would be better if they were to work to change themselves before attempting to negotiate changes in their relationships with others. It is the devoutness of their beliefs which seems to me to be the problem here.

Bonds

Unlike the majority of therapists of my acquaintance, I do not regard the relationship between therapist and client to be the sine qua non of effective therapy. I strive to accept my clients as fallible human beings and am prepared to work concertedly to help them overcome their problems, but do not endeavour to form very close, warm relationships with them. In the main, my clients do not appear to want such a relationship with me (preferring to become close and intimate with their significant others). However, occasionally I get clients who do wish to become (non-sexually) intimate with me. Some of these clients (who devoutly believe they need my love) leave therapy disappointed after I have failed to get them to give up their dire need for love or refused to give them what they think they need.

Tasks

In this analysis I will assume throughout that therapists are practising RET effectively and thus the emphasis will be on client variables.

My basic thesis here is that when therapist and client agree concerning (1) the view of psychological disturbance as stated in rational-emotive theory, (2) the rational-emotive view on the acquisition and perpetuation of psychological disturbance, and (3) the rational-emotive view of therapeutic change, such agreements are likely to enhance good therapeutic outcome. Furthermore, the greater the disagreement between the two participants on such matters, the greater the threat that exists to the therapeutic alliance with all the negative implications that this has for good therapeutic outcome. I should say at the outset that this hypothesis has yet to be tested and should thus be viewed sceptically.

I will illustrate my points by using clinical examples from my experience as a therapist.

Conceptualisation of Psychological Disturbance Rational-emotive theory states that much psychological disturbance can be attributed to clients' devout, absolutistic evaluations (irrational beliefs) about themselves, other people and life events. RET practitioners assume that most clients do not enter therapy sharing this viewpoint and, thus, one of the therapist's major tasks is to persuade the client to adopt this viewpoint if effective RET is to ensue. Of course, not all clients will be so persuaded because they have their own (different) ideas about the nature of their psychological problems and what causes them and are not prepared to relinquish these. In my experience, the following clients are not good candidates for RET unless they change their ideas about the determinants of their problems: those who believe that their problems are caused by (1) external events (including events that happened in childhood), (2) physical, dietary or biochemical factors, (3) repressed basic human impulses, (4) fate or astrological factors and (5) blockages in the body.

I once had a referral from a social worker who confused RET with Reichian therapy. The client specifically wanted to work on his character armour blockages which he considered were at the source of his problems. I explained that an error had been made and that I was a rational-emotive therapist and gave him a brief outline of the rational-emotive view of his problems. He responded with incredulity, saying that he hadn't heard such intellectualised clap-trap in a long while and asked me whether I knew of anyone who could really help him. I referred him to a local bioenergetics therapist who, apparently, helped him considerably.

Acquisition and Perpetuation of Psychological Disturbance Rational-emotive theory de-emphasises the value of understanding acquisition variables in helping clients change. Rather, it stresses the importance of understanding how people perpetuate their psychological problems. This is because the theory hypothesises that while past events may well have contributed to clients' psychological disturbance, these did not make them disturbed, since people bring their tendency to make themselves disturbed to these events and experiences. Thus, clients who come to therapy in order to trace their psychological problems back to their roots tend not to benefit greatly from the present-centred and future-oriented focus of RET. Clients who are prepared to look for and challenge their currently held irrational beliefs do much better in RET than clients who are preoccupied with discovering how they came to hold such beliefs in the first place.

A 60-year-old woman with agoraphobic and panic problems was firmly convinced that the origins of her panic lay in buried childhood feelings towards her parents, who while kindly disposed to my client, had placed undue burdens on her as a child. Not only did we have different views concerning the 'cause' of her present problems, but we differed as to the most appropriate time focus for the therapy. I did discuss her childhood with her, but as a stimulus to help her re-focus on her present disturbance-perpetuating beliefs, but to no avail. She quit therapy with me and started consulting a Jungian therapist who has seen her now for two years with little impact on her panic disorder.

Views on Therapeutic Change RET can be viewed as a therapeutic system which has a 'Protestant Ethic' view of therapeutic change. Clients are urged to 'work and practise' their way to emotional health by using a variety of cognitive, emotive and behavioural methods designed to help them to change their irrational beliefs. Clients who are not prepared to put in the necessary hard work usually have less successful therapeutic outcomes than clients who challenge repeatedly their irrational beliefs in thought, feeling and deed.

It follows from the above that RET places most emphasis on the activities that clients initiate and sustain outside therapy as the major agent of change. Clients who consider that change will occur primarily from therapy sessions usually do not gain as much from RET as clients who are in accord with the rational-emotive viewpoint on this matter.

During my six-month stay at the Center for Cognitive Therapy in Philadelphia, I saw briefly a client who had heard of cognitive therapy for depression and wished to try it. I was learning this approach at the time and was keen to do it 'by the book'. The client had recently moved to Philadelphia from Los Angeles where she had consulted an experiential therapist with whom she had had a very close relationship which, in my opinion, had encouraged her to be more dependent on love and approval than she was before she consulted him. The client had come to believe that therapeutic change depended on a very warm, close therapeutic relationship in which completing homework assignments and 'Daily Record of Dysfunctional Thoughts' sheets had no place. Despite my attempts to change her views on such matters, she left cognitive therapy to seek another experiential therapist.

Ellis's Study on Failure in RET Ellis (1983) has published some interesting data which tend to corroborate my own experiences of therapeutic failure in RET. He chose 50 of his clients who were seen in individual and/or group RET and were rated by him, and where appropriate by his associate group therapist, as 'failures'. In some ways, this sample consisted of fairly ideal RET clients in that they were individuals (1) of above average or of superior intelligence (in Ellis's judgement and that of their other group therapist); (2) who seemed really to understand RET and who were often effective (especially in group therapy) in helping others to learn and use it; (3) who in some ways made therapeutic progress and felt that they benefited by having RET but who still retained one or more serious presenting symptoms, such as severe depression, acute anxiety, overwhelming hostility or extreme lack of self-discipline; and (4) who had at least one year of individual and/or group RET sessions, and sometimes considerably more.

This group was compared with clients who were selected on the same four criteria but who seemed to benefit greatly from RET. While a complete account of this study – which, of course, has its methodological flaws – can be found in Ellis (1983), the following results are most pertinent. First, in its cognitive aspects, RET emphasises the persistent use of reason, logic and the scientific method to uproot clients' irrational beliefs. Consequently, it ideally requires intelligence, concentration and high-level, consistent cognitive self-disputation and self-persuasion. These therapeutic behaviours would tend to be disrupted or blocked by extreme disturbance, by lack of organisation, by grandiosity, by organic disruption and by refusal to do RET-type disputing of irrational ideas. All these characteristics proved to be present in significantly more failures than in those clients who responded favourably to RET.

Second, RET also, to be quite successful, involves clients' forcefully and emotively changing their beliefs and actions, and their being stubbornly determined to accept responsibility for their own inappropriate feelings and vigorously work at changing these feelings (Ellis and Abrahms, 1978; Ellis and Whiteley, 1979). But the failure clients in this study were significantly more angry than those who responded well to RET; more of them were severely depressed and inactive, they were more often grandiose, and they were more frequently stubbornly resistant and rebellious. All these characteristics would presumably tend to interfere with the kind of emotive processes and changes that RET espouses.

Third, RET strongly advocates that clients, in order to improve, do in vivo activity homework assignments, deliberately force themselves to engage in many uncomfortable activities until they make themselves comfortable, and notably work and practise its multimodal techniques. But the group of clients who signally failed in this study showed abysmally low frustration tolerance, had serious behavioural addictions, led disorganised lives, refrained from doing their activity homework assignments, were more frequently psychotic and generally refused to work at therapy. All these characteristics, which were found significantly more frequently than were found in the clients who responded quite well to RET, would tend to interfere with clients using the behavioural methods of RET.

Thus it appears from the above analysis that the old adage of psychotherapy applies to RET: namely that clients who could most use therapy are precisely those individuals whose disturbance interferes with their benefiting from it.

References

Anchin, J.C. and Kiesler, D.J. (eds) (1982) *Handbook of Interpersonal Psychotherapy*. New York: Pergamon.

Beutler, L.E. (1983) *Eclectic Psychotherapy: A Systematic Approach*. New York: Pergamon.

Bordin, E.S. (1979) The generalizability of the psychoanalytic concept of the working alliance, *Psychotherapy: Theory, Research and Practice*, 16, 252–60.

Dorn, F.J. (1984) *Counseling as Applied Social Psychology: An Introduction to the Social Influence Model*. Springfield, IL: Thomas.

Dryden, W. and Hunt, P. (1985) Therapeutic alliances in marital therapy. II. Process issues. In W. Dryden (ed.), *Marital Therapy in Britain. Volume 1: Context and Therapeutic Approaches*. London: Harper and Row.

Ellis, A. (1983) Failures in rational-emotive therapy. In E.B. Foa and P.M.G. Emmelkamp (eds), *Failures in Behavior Therapy*. New York: Wiley.

Ellis, A. and Abrahms, E. (1978) *Brief Psychotherapy in Medical and Health Practice*. New York: Springer.

Ellis, A. and Whiteley, J.M. (eds) (1979) *Theoretical and Empirical Foundations of Rational-Emotive Therapy*. Monterey, CA: Brooks/Cole.

Emmelkamp, P.M.G., Kuipers, A.C.M. and Eggeraat, J.B. (1978) Cognitive modification versus prolonged exposure in vivo: A comparison with agoraphobics as subjects, *Behavior Research and Therapy*, 16, 33–41.

Golden, W.L. (1985) An integration of Ericksonian and cognitive-behavioral hypnotherapy in the treatment of anxiety disorders. In E.T. Dowd and J.M. Healy (eds), *Case Studies in Hypnotherapy*. New York: Guilford.

Kwee, M.G.T. and Lazarus, A.A. (1986) Multimodal therapy: The cognitive behavioural tradition and beyond. In W. Dryden and W.L. Golden (eds), *Cognitive-Behavioural Approaches to Psychotherapy*. London: Harper and Row.

Lazarus, A.A. (1981) *The Practice of Multimodal Therapy*. New York: McGraw-Hill.

Meichenbaum, D. and Gilmore, J.B. (1982) Resistance from a cognitive behavioral perspective. In P.L. Wachtel (ed.), *Resistance*. New York: Plenum.

Pinsof, W.M. and Catherall, D.R. (1986) The integrative psychotherapy alliance: Family, couple and individual scales, *Journal of Marital and Family Therapy*, 12, 137–51.

Safran, J.D. (1984) Assessing the cognitive-interpersonal circle, *Cognitive Therapy and Research*, 8, 333–47.

Strong, S.R. and Claiborn, C.D. (1982) *Change through Interaction*. New York: Wiley Interscience.

3

Educating Clients about Rational-Emotive Therapy

Norman D. Macaskill

Introduction

The majority of clients have significantly distorted expectations of psychotherapy and do not understand their role in the psychotherapeutic process (Garfield and Wolpin, 1963). These misunderstandings impair therapeutic progress and may lead to premature termination and/or poor therapeutic outcome (Goldstein, 1962). Preparing clients for psychotherapy by educational methods has been shown to reduce the early dropout rate and improve therapeutic outcome (Macaskill and Macaskill, 1983).

The main issues regarding which clients may have serious misconceptions are:

1 The rationale of therapy;
2 The client's role in therapy;
3 The therapist's role;
4 The therapeutic techniques;
5 The process of change.

This chapter addresses these issues in relation to educating clients about what to expect in rational-emotive therapy (RET). To date this issue has been largely neglected in the clinical literature on RET. The review by Macaskill and Macaskill (1983) found no experimental work on educating clients about RET. A few RET writers have touched on issues related to educating clients, for example, Dryden (1984) on the therapeutic alliance, Golden (1983) on resistance and Young (1984) on doing RET with difficult client groups, but apart from these papers little explicitly related to educating clients about the process of RET has been written.

Many RET therapists, of course, have supplemented their therapeutic work with regular bibliotherapy assignments, for example, *A New Guide to Rational Living*, by Ellis and Harper (1975). This undoubtedly has been a valuable adjunct for many clients, and probably for many therapists is seen as sufficient education about RET. However, bibliotherapy has several critical limitations. First, it is too distant from the individual client's experience with his or her therapist. Second, it does not adequately address issues such as the client's role, the therapist's role, or the impact of various RET techniques. Finally, it allows the therapist and client to view education about the therapeutic process as a peripheral and transient hurdle rather than a central and continuous part of the therapeutic work.

Personal experience in using RET and discussion with other therapists would suggest that educating clients about RET in a systematic manner, and viewing it as a continuous process is particularly important in RET because of certain demand characteristics of the approach.

RET is an active, directive, focused and challenging therapy with a range of diagnostic and cognitive-restructuring techniques which place considerable demands on the client's capacity to think clearly and logically. In addition RET techniques frequently and rapidly release powerful and unpleasant emotions as core irrational beliefs (iBs) are uncovered and challenged. These emotions can at times severely test the client's capacity to collaborate with the therapist in the assessment and disputing phases of RET.

Unless the therapist therefore takes these characteristics of RET into account and, as this chapter suggests, educates clients adequately then there are risks that the client's understanding, and cooperation, may periodically be impaired substantially as a result of misconception, confusion or emotional overload.

With these comments in mind the specific aspects of educating clients about the process of RET will now be discussed.

Rationale of Therapy

RET espouses the view that emotional problems and dysfunctional behaviour are largely, if not exclusively, determined by client's irrational beliefs (iBs) related to their view of the world, others and themselves. RET holds that elucidation of these irrational beliefs, and replacement by adaptive beliefs, will significantly reduce or abolish the problematic emotions and behaviours.

The therapist often is called upon to spend considerable time and energy educating clients in the ABCs of RET. Many clients have environmental, biological or developmental theories of emotional disturbance and find considerable difficulty in accepting a cognitive perspective on their problems. Even when they do acquire such a perspective, clients in therapy frequently revert to previously held views of disturbance so that the therapist needs to be alert to the necessity of repeatedly educating his or her client about the RET model when a cognitive intervention is employed.

Furthermore, having accepted the ABC model of disturbance, clients may have misconceptions about its emphasis which can cause problems. The two commonest problems are 'downgrading the A' and 'downgrading the C'. In the former, clients misinterpret the therapist as saying that the *only* problems which they have concern the way in which they evaluate reality. That is, the A is unimportant. For example, a client whose marriage is breaking up may feel that his therapist is concerned only with his iBs about the break-up of his marriage, and not at all with the stressful activating event itself. This leads to the belief that the client's reality problems are being dismissed and trivialized. In introducing an ABC analysis of such situations it is often helpful to anticipate such a reaction by using a 'two-problem model'. The therapist emphasizes that the client has significant reality problems which merit attention, but also indicates that the client's irrational evaluations, iBs, of this problem are important variables which exacerbate the reality problem. Thus, when the therapist focuses on the iBs the client will collaborate effectively having seen that the reality problem has been acknowledged and may also be a focus of therapeutic work.

Problems related to 'downgrading the C' occur when clients perceive their therapist as ignoring their dysfunctional emotions (Cs), other than for the purpose of efficiently providing pointers to linked iBs. Here the client feels that his emotions are being dismissed and trivialized, and by extension his sense of personal significance. Very marked hostile reactions towards the therapist can develop if this misconception is not modified. Such reactions can be minimized if the therapist is able, (a) to acknowledge and reflect the distress the client is experiencing when a problem is brought up for discussion; and (b) to elicit feedback regularly as to whether the therapist is being perceived by the client in such a negative manner. This may at times substantially slow the pace of a session, but is very worthwhile in the service of maintaining a therapeutic alliance, particularly in working with very disturbed clients.

In addition to the ABC model of disturbance, RET espouses a clear life philosophy. This philosophy includes enlightened hedonism, self-acceptance, stoicism, tolerance and scientific thinking (Dryden, 1984). Misconceptions about this aspect of RET abound and may seriously impede therapy. For example, clients may view RET as amoral, antisocial, antireligious, endorsing mediocrity and passive acceptance of injustice, or may fear they will be transformed into emotionless robots (Young, 1984).

Because such potent misconceptions exist, and because it is easy for clients to misinterpret therapists' views and technical interventions as endorsing these misconceptions, it is important for the therapist to look for and quickly clarify such issues. This can frequently be done when the client's goals are being discussed as it is in this area that the philosophical underpinnings of RET become concrete and open to observation.

The Client's Role

Clients frequently approach therapy with the expectation that they will be relatively passive participants in the process. If sophisticated, they may assume that they will be expected to talk, emote and then acquire transforming insights. In RET the expectation is that clients will be hard-working, active participants, who will take a major role in specifying problems and goals, and in identifying and modifying irrational beliefs.

Unless these aspects of therapy are adequately explained to clients, considerable problems may occur. Clients who anticipate a passive role and have irrational beliefs centred around dependency may initially resent their adult autonomous role in therapy. If clients are hopeless and depressed they may not participate because they only anticipate failure and humiliation.

In educating clients about their role in RET, it is often useful to provide them with an analogy with which they can identify. For example, learning a skill where the client's role is likened to that of a student or an apprentice. Equally, it is helpful if the client's role can be described in such a way as to indicate that participating in the therapeutic process has some pleasurable aspects. This is important with some clients as otherwise the stoic aspects of RET can have a negative effect on the client's motivation for therapy.

The Therapist's Role

It is important also for clients to have a clear understanding of what they may expect in terms of the therapist's behaviour and her role in the therapeutic relationship.

Clients frequently expect the therapist to provide advice and direct remedies, or alternatively to be a sympathetic listening ear who will magically remove their problems by a process of catharsis and insight. Less frequently, clients with some knowledge of RET anticipate an aggressive, confrontational style peppered with profanities. As such misconceptions can very quickly impede therapy it is generally helpful for the therapist to describe and explain her therapeutic role. Portraying the therapist as a tutor or coach can help the client to adjust to the essentially adult-to-adult, collaborative nature of the relationship. It is worthwhile then exploring the client's reactions to these analogies as for some clients these have very negative meanings. Thus clients who resent the pupil–teacher analogy will have difficulty in cooperating when therapeutic adjuncts such as a blackboard are used in sessions, or terms such as homework, are employed for between-session assignments.

Within the model of tutor or coach, RET therapists vary in style from the didactic to the evocative or Socratic. Increasingly there is a recognition of the value of therapists flexibly varying their style according to the needs of their clients (Eschenroeder, 1979). Again it is useful to anticipate that each of these styles, and changes from one to another, can cause problems which can be minimized by explaining to the client the purpose of any given style coupled with eliciting the client's reactions to it. For example, the didactic style may be experienced as dogmatic and impersonal, leading to rebellion or passive compliance. On the other hand, the evocative approach can leave clients feeling that they are floundering stupidly or are being cleverly driven into a corner by Socratic questions.

The RET therapist is also a problem-solver, and it is important to discuss this aspect of her role with the client. Most clients work well within this framework, but there are some who will initially misconstrue this approach as being mechanistic and dehumanizing.

Once the client is clear about his role in therapy, the therapist's role, and the rationale of therapy the therapeutic work subsequently focuses on applying RET principles to specific client problems. Here a variety of misconceptions may occur.

Therapeutic Techniques

Eliciting Irrational Beliefs

Eliciting clients' irrational beliefs is a major RET therapist skill. Therapists are encouraged to expose efficiently and systematically clients' iBs which are deemed to underpin their specific emotional and behavioural problems. Eliciting techniques, including sentence completion and inference chaining (Moore, 1983), get quickly to clients' core beliefs. In so doing, almost invariably, they release intense and unpleasant emotions.

Clients who are not adequately helped to understand why such techniques are used and the fact that release of intense dysphoria sometimes accompanies their use, report a variety of problems. They experience confusion and disorganization when multiple iBs are elicited in quick succession. They feel dehumanized if, in addition, the process of eliciting multiple iBs is done as if the therapist were merely gathering data rather than dealing with a personally significant emotional experience. If intense dysphoria results clients often report feeling overwhelmed and panic may result. Some clients feel persecuted when exposed to such eliciting techniques. Depressed patients may report considerable amplification of their depressive affect. When using eliciting techniques, it is therefore important for therapists to take these possibilities into account. This can frequently be best done by helping clients to anticipate potential difficulties in working with these techniques and by asking them to take charge of the process (as behaviour therapists frequently do when working with clients in an exposure programme). This serves to reduce secondary anxiety due to fear of loss of control, increases therapist–client collaboration, and establishes a more appropriate and individually paced therapeutic programme.

In addition, it is often useful to indicate to clients that techniques such as inference chaining may lead to the discovery of core iBs apparently far removed from the original presenting problem. If clients are not forewarned about this, the experience can otherwise lead to marked secondary panic in clients which are again frequently due to beliefs about loss of control. On occasion clients may judge that they are being persecuted by their therapist as they experience themselves as being totally unprotected from exploration by the latter.

Because some core iBs are probably acquired when the client was at a preverbal level of development, both therapist and client need to be aware of potential difficulties in attempting to elicit some iBs as verbal statements. Such clients are more likely to have images linked with emotional states and experience verbal descriptions of iBs as inaccurate. It is often useful, therefore, to find out early on in therapy whether clients are predominantly imagers or self-talkers. Helping clients to anticipate such difficulties can prevent loss of credibility in the therapist and/or his techniques. Beck and Emery (1979) suggest that anxious clients tend to think in images, while depressed clients have self-statement patterns of thinking. This dichotomy has also considerable implications for preparing clients for the use of disputational or cognitive-restructuring techniques.

Disputing Irrational Beliefs

Disputing clients' irrational beliefs in order to produce a philosophical change by helping them to adopt more adaptive rational beliefs is another core therapist skill. In the literature there is a strong emphasis on logical or philosophical disputing as the major method of changing iBs. However, if disputing is to be effective, preparatory interventions are necessary.

First and foremost, the client needs to be motivated to explore and change an irrational belief. For this reason emphasis should be placed on specifying the substantial disadvantages of maintaining the belief, and conversely the substantial advantages of modifying it. Until this is firmly established the client will only weakly dispute his iB.

Second, some clients fear losing their iBs as they equate them with their personal identity. Unless this misconception is clarified many clients will resist the process which they fear could leave them feeling anchorless disembodied selves.

Third, clients may not vigorously dispute their iBs when they are preoccupied with a desire to explore their personal past in order to understand the historical origins of their iBs. The RET focus on here-and-now disputation frequently needs careful and sensitive exploration as otherwise clients may view RET as superficial. With some clients it is important, in the service of maintaining the therapeutic alliance, to be flexible and allow such an exploration, however limited, to take place.

Clients should also understand that the process of disputing is often one of 'trial-and-error'. With some clients a particular verbal dispute may hit home, while other disputes may be quite ineffective. In addition, verbal disputes may be ineffective with imagers, and likewise imaginal disputes may not be helpful with self-talkers. The therapist needs, therefore, to be flexible and creative in her use of disputing methods.

The Process of Change

RET very clearly recognizes that changing beliefs is hard work and requires sustained practice. Clients frequently, however, have unrealistic expectations about the process of changing their irrational beliefs. Many expect that disputing will easily, rapidly and permanently lead to healthier feelings and constructive life philosophies. It is vital, therefore, to help clients anticipate that the process is likely to be arduous, and here using analogies such as learning and maintaining new skills, for example, playing the piano or learning a new language to the point of proficiency, are invaluable. If this is not done clients may give up disputing their irrational beliefs very quickly because it feels phoney, or later, when it fails to be totally and permanently effective. Equally, many clients need to be taught that in many instances effective disputations reduce but may not eliminate faulty thinking.

Clients may also need to be educated to anticipate the frequently observed phenomenon that disputations that are effective in the therapy sessions may for a considerable time be less effective when applied in vivo. This issue is closely allied to another problem that is encountered when clients dispute beliefs which are held across a wide variety of situations. For example, a client may express a need for approval from a variety of significant people in his or her life. When disputing this iB in relation to these significant others the client may experience what appears to be unpredictable successes and failures in modifying his dysfunctional emotions. This may lead to a sense of failure and bewilderment unless the client is educated about hierarchies of intensity of dysfunctional Cs in relation to individual iBs, similar to hierarchies of anxiety in connection to phobic stimuli. That is, a client may experience minor levels of dysphoria related to disapproval from some people, and moderate or severe levels of dysphoria in relation to disapproval from others. Initially, disputing methods are likely to be effective only when a minor level of dysphoria is attached to the iB. It is often useful to work out hierarchies of dysfunctional Cs in relation to a specific iB and encourage clients to work systematically through this hierarchy. Without such education, clients may be inadvertently 'thrown in at the deep end' and hence experience marked failure in disputing their irrational beliefs (McMullin and Giles, 1981).

One final problem commonly met with in practice in the working through process but not discussed in the RET literature needs to be mentioned. The problem is one of an unacknowledged mourning process.

As clients dispute their iBs they are frequently involved in giving up a view of themselves, the world or others that they have greatly cherished. In other words, repeated disputation provokes a mourning process, akin to that which occurs in losing a limb, spouse or symbolically significant object. In mourning, fluctuating grief, repeated attempts to regain the lost object, protest and despair occur before the loss is accepted. In RET a similar, if sometimes attenuated, process can occur. It is helpful to educate clients to anticipate this and doing so seems to ease the abandonment of the old iB. Failure to understand and acknowledge this 'mourning' process can lead to client resistance.

The Education Process

How does the therapist educate clients about RET?

Such education is a *process* that occurs throughout therapy, and is not a specific technique or package of techniques. The issues that require education are often idiosyncratic to each therapist–client dyad. Furthermore, the therapist has to provide educational input as misconceptions arise. One-off standardized educational interventions at the beginning of therapy are therefore inadequate.

The therapist fosters the educational process by a combination of anticipatory skills and specific technical interventions. Many client misconceptions about RET can be anticipated if the therapist (a) is alert to the potential significance of information derived from the initial assessment, and (b) elicits feedback from clients as to their response to therapy and the therapist, particularly when the client shows no signs of overt resistance. These anticipatory skills provide the therapist with a sensitive guide as to the specific need for, and timing of, educational interventions with individual clients.

Many of the common problems requiring client education can be anticipated. To do this the therapist's initial assessment of the client and his problems should cover the following areas: (1) personal history, (2) cognitive style, (3) personality structure, and (4) degree of symptomatic decompensation. For example, the client's personal history may reveal previous therapy failures which may have left the client with maladaptive attitudes to further therapy. A history indicating strong fundamental religious beliefs will indicate the need for careful discussion of the philosophical basis of RET. Exploration of the client's cognitive style may elicit a preference for feeling rather than thinking as a mode of experiencing, with obvious implications for the way in which the therapist presents RET therapy and philosophy. Assessment of the client's personality structure may reveal, for example, marked impulsiveness and low frustration tolerance threshold. Clients with these traits have very marked discomfort anxiety problems and tend to do poorly in RET. Early preparation involving the necessity of work, practice and facing discomfort are necessary if therapy is to have any chance of success with such clients. Equally, personality assessment may reveal marked narcissistic, borderline or schizo-typal character traits. Clients with marked traits in any of these categories require substantially greater inputs of therapist time and effort along educational lines, than is usual with typically neurotic individuals. Finally, assessing the client's degree of symptomatic decompensation revealing, for example, a high score on the Beck Depression Inventory, would indicate the need for caution in introducing and pacing RET techniques which aim to elicit the client's iBs.

Some of these issues and the methods that can be used to prepare clients for them will now be illustrated with case examples.

Case Examples

Mary's Case

Mary was a single university student in her late 20s who came to therapy with a 10-year history of depression. Her history revealed that she was an ardent feminist, active in socialist politics and had two previous experiences in psychoanalytically oriented therapy, both of which had failed to help her. She also reported that on several occasions during previous therapies her depressive symptomatology had reached suicidal proportions. These details suggested that Mary might have considerable misconceptions about, and problems during, RET. During the initial assessment sessions the therapist therefore focused extensively on clarifying the philosophical basis of RET, indicating that it was an active problem-solving therapy with an emphasis on social hedonism, personal responsibility and humanism. This discussion helped reduce Mary's fear that RET would be antagonistic to her philosophy of life and turn her into a passive insensitive person. Discussion of the ABC model with the emphasis on vigorous disputation and regular homework assignments overcame Mary's fears that RET would be a superficial therapy which would not help her cope with the deeper issues in her life. It also helped in pointing out the significant differences between RET and her previous therapies. In addition, exploration of the therapist's active directive role and the rationale for this helped her anticipate potential problems related to her fear of dominance by males. This problem was also reduced by asking her to take control of the sessions, and to indicate to her therapist when he seemed to be behaving dogmatically or insensitively.

The key remaining issue that the therapist prepared Mary for was the potential upsetting effect of eliciting irrational beliefs related to her self-worth. This was addressed in view of her apparent decompensation in previous therapy when painful issues were explored extensively. The author suggested that Mary take charge of the pace of the eliciting process and maintain it at a level where she could feel able to achieve sufficient cognitive distance to continue working on her problems.

Debbie's Case

Debbie was an anorexic teenager who, prior to entering RET, had had several years in a psychiatric hospital during which she received supportive individual therapy and psychoanalytically-oriented family therapy. Debbie showed a marked tendency to blame others for her problems and extreme fear of disapproval. Education about RET focused initially on the issue of personal responsibility and the cognitive basis of emotional disturbance. Considerable emphasis was put on this in view of Debbie's strong tendency to blame others and to perceive herself as the victim of her developmental history. The process was completed successfully after Debbie was able to accept that individuals could respond differently to extremely unpleasant events, for example, quadriplegia. Following this, Debbie was able to collaborate on eliciting irrational beliefs related to her anger at her parents, although on occasion she considered that her therapist was being insensitive. On a number of occasions she felt confused by the fluctuations in her emotions from anger to despair as she examined her beliefs. Here Debbie's confusion was lifted when the therapist introduced the idea that giving up irrational beliefs involved a process of grieving.

At a later stage in therapy Debbie began to dispute her need for approval from many people in her life. However, she made erratic progress initially. Her therapist eventually resolved this by helping Debbie construct a disapproval hierarchy and getting her to work her way systematically up this hierarchy.

Having outlined the education process and illustrated it in the above case examples, it should be clear that educational interventions fall into two main categories. The first of these concerns the provision of new information which may relate to any of the main areas of therapy.

The second main category concerns the provision of appropriate conceptual models. Examples are the presentation of the teacher–client relationship, and the grief process as a model for understanding the vicissitudes of aspects of the change process.

In practice the author utilizes the following interventions:

1 At the beginning of the first assessment session the client's ideas about the assessment interview are elicited to clarify any major misconceptions that might impede the interview.
2 In the latter part of the first assessment session the therapist utilizes a semi-structured interview, guided by assessment of the areas mentioned above to elicit the client's views of therapy, and RET in particular. An explanation of the ABC framework is given and illustrated and the process of change is also described. This interview takes 20–30 minutes on average.
3 At the end of the interview the client is given a copy of *A New Guide to Rational Living* (Ellis and Harper, 1975).
4 At the next session the author discusses and clarifies any misconceptions arising from the reading assignment and the assessment interview.
5 In subsequent sessions, guided by feedback from the client's reaction to therapy and the therapist, corrective information is provided verbally and reinforced by giving the client a tape of the session to review at several points before the next session.

Conclusion

This chapter has indicated how and where patients may benefit from education about RET. It is suggested that each of the stages of therapy assessment, socialization, disputation and working through can be sources of misunderstanding for clients.

These misunderstandings and confusions can be conceived of as arising from two main sources. First, clients may *enter* therapy with a variety of attitudes, misconceptions or prejudices about RET and specifically about therapy in general. Second, problems can *arise* in therapy due to the impact of RET techniques on the client's cognitive and emotional status and the meanings given by the client to the impact of the therapist's style and interventions on the client's sense of personal significance. In short, therapy, the therapist and the client's emotional state can be potent sources of dysfunctional ABCs. It may be extremely difficult to maintain the thrust of therapy at these points as clients are not able to distance themselves from their immediate cognitive-emotional state.

The therapist can anticipate many of the potential problems from these two sources. Much of the skill in educating clients about RET relies on sensitive anticipation, guided by a good knowledge of the client's personal history, cognitive style, personality characteristics, and degree of symptomatic decompensation. In addition to sensitive anticipation, a therapeutic style that seeks and incorporates regular feedback from clients in sessions on their reaction to the therapeutic process can help the therapist become aware of the need to do further educational work.

As outlined in this chapter, much of the educational work with clients involves the provision of appropriate information. However, it is also important that the therapist paces therapy appropriately to reduce cognitive and affective overload. This pacing and support can often be achieved through the judicious use of reflection, empathic comments and clarifications along person-centred lines.

In choosing adjunctive educational materials a wide variety of options are available to the therapist. Lectures, group exercises, audiotapes and videotapes can be utilized. The contention of this chapter, however, is that while such materials may be available, individually tailored interventions, matched to the specific misunderstandings of each client, will be the most efficient and effective method of educating clients about RET, particularly if the therapist views such education as a central potentially continuous aspect of the therapeutic work.

References

Beck, A.T. and Emery, G. (1979) *Cognitive Therapy of Anxiety and Phobic Disorders*. Philadelphia: Center for Cognitive Therapy.

Dryden, W. (1984) *Rational-Emotive Therapy: Fundamentals and Innovations*. London: Croom Helm.

Ellis, A. and Harper, R.A. (1975) *A New Guide to Rational Living*. North Hollywood, CA: Wilshire.

Eschenroeder, C. (1979) Different therapeutic styles in rational-emotive therapy, *Rational Living*, 14(2), 3–7.

Garfield, S.L. and Wolpin, M. (1963) Expectations regarding psychotherapy, *Journal of Nervous and Mental Diseases*, 137, 353–62.

Golden, W.L. (1983) Resistance in cognitive-behaviour therapy, *British Journal of Cognitive Psychotherapy*, 1(2), 33–42.

Goldstein, A.P. (1962) *Therapist–patient Expectancies in Psychotherapy*. New York: Wiley.

Macaskill, N.D. and Macaskill, A. (1983) Preparing patients for psychotherapy, *British Journal of Clinical and Social Psychiatry*, 2, 80–4.

McMullin, R.E. and Giles, T.R. (1981) *Cognitive-Behavior Therapy: A Restructuring Approach*. New York: Grune and Stratton.

Moore, R.H. (1983) Inference as 'A' in RET, *British Journal of Cognitive Psychotherapy*, 1(2), 17–23.

Young, H.S. (1984) Special issue on the work of Howard S. Young, *British Journal of Cognitive Psychotherapy*, 2(2).

4

A Client's Guide to Rational-Emotive Therapy

Russell M. Grieger

Introduction

It has long been my observation that few people who enter psychotherapy are equipped to participate effectively in their own changes and betterment. As I have said elsewhere (Grieger and Boyd, 1980), psychotherapy clients, and perhaps most people, have the worst of two worlds. First, because of biological predispositions (Ellis, 1976) and years of habituating practice (Maultsby, 1984), they are very good at being disturbed. Second, they are poor at working through their problems and changes.

There are many reasons why people often find it difficult to change, even though they have taken the significant step of entering therapy. Some simply are ignorant of what to do to change and of what their role is in therapy. Others are embarrassed about having emotional problems or seeking professional help, and they consequently deny or play down their problems. Others are fearful of giving up their familiar, though debilitating ways of thinking, acting and feeling; they then tenaciously hold onto their old self-defeating patterns. Others are too emotionally overwrought or confused to participate; they find it impossible to focus their attention anywhere but on how bad they feel or on the frustrating circumstances of their lives. Still others believe that they are hopelessly disturbed: either that they are too far gone to get better, or their problems are foisted on them by uncontrollable outside sources. And still others are such committed pleasure-seekers that they are unwilling to do the sustained, hard work necessary to change. The list could go on, and I refer the interested reader to Ellis (1985), Grieger and Boyd (1980), and Maultsby (1975, 1984) for further discussions of this.

People, therefore, have two points against them when they enter therapy; and this is why I have always agreed with Ellis (1976, 1978) who argues that therapists who are active, directive, commanding, forceful, scientific, and psychoeducational are more effective than those who are not – these stances, I have found, help people more easily cut through roadblocks to change and move purposely on the road to recovery.

Notwithstanding this, perhaps the bottom line in elegant and long-lasting psychotherapeutic change is for the client to learn to take responsibility for his or her life. In rational-emotive theory this means a good many things, but most generally and importantly it means that people acknowledge, appreciate, and act on the premise that they are mainly responsible for their actions and feelings and for the choices they make and the results they get in their lives. In RET practice this means that people actively participate in their own psychotherapy by accepting the above and committing themselves to do what is necessary to get different results in their lives. To me, it is one of the brilliant features of Ellis's ABC framework that it communicates all of this.

The guide (pp. 55–71) evolved as an attempt to assist the client to be an active, collaborative and responsible participant in the psychotherapeutic process. It is my premise that the more the client knows about human psychology and about the RET process, the more he or she can participate thoroughly in treatment, and the more difficult it will be to shirk responsibility. The guide therefore, is not a self-help book, like, for example, *A New Guide to Rational Living* (Ellis and Harper, 1975). Rather, it is the client's equivalent of a how-to-do-it book for practitioners. It outlines for the client the sequential steps in therapy, and, for each step, it gives the rationale and goals, what the therapist will do and why, and what are the client's responsibilities. All in all, the general message is what I tell most of my clients: 'I want you to know as much as I do and try as hard as I will so that we can work together, as partners, equally and actively, to solve your problems and bring about the changes you want.'

Benefits of the Guide

In summary, the guide is a procedural and explanatory aide to RET that brings the client into the role of acting as his or her own therapist-problem-solver from the outset. In so doing, some of the benefits I have observed through using the guide are as follows:

Facilitates Responsibility

If clients have this guide, it becomes harder for them to blame the therapist, outside circumstances or the past for their troubles, while encouraging them to accept responsibility for their emotional problems and for doing something about them. Alternatively, it leads them to ask the question, 'Have I done everything I can today to further my psychological or interpersonal betterment?'

Encourages Collaboration

The guide emphasizes what the client is to do at each step of the therapeutic process, including between-session homework which is typical of RET. It thus underscores the client's role as self-helper and his or her job in acting as partner to the therapist in the change process.

Facilitates Efficiency

By telling the client what will happen in therapy and why, the guide gives an organized, step-by-step procedure for change. Thus, like a workbook, all the client has to do is follow the recipe (with, of course, commitment and vision).

Promotes Hope

By breaking the process of psychotherapy down to a series of logical and understandable steps, the guide lets clients know that there is a defined procedure that can help them. This knowledge tends to undercut the notion that psychological change is an ambiguous or mysterious process that works by chance. This knowledge also, again, brings the client into the driver's seat in the change process and gives them tasks that they can do to get better.

Rationalizes Emotional Problems

It is now common knowledge that people, once emotionally disturbed, tend to make themselves more emotionally disturbed about their original disturbance (Ellis, 1987; Grieger and Boyd, 1980). In other words, once anxious, depressed, enraged, or guilty, people usually create further anger or depression about having these problems. Again, by seeing to it that people understand the mechanics of their disturbance and the six-step process of change, the guide helps them see their problems as just that – problems or low points in their lives to be handled rather than horrors to be feared.

Promotes Self-help

Rational-emotive therapy has two general goals: (1) to facilitate change in the presenting problem; (2) to teach the client the skills of RET so that he or she can take future problems without the need of a professional therapist. The guide serves both these goals. Coincidentally, it reinforces the ideal of client responsibility of a life value.

Having thus reviewed some of the guide's benefits, it is now presented in the same form as is given to clients.

THE GUIDE

Dear Client
The reason you entered psychotherapy is to resolve problems you are having in your life. I will do my best to help you in this. Together we want to work as

efficiently as we can to get you to feel better, to function more effectively in your job or at school, and to relate better with others.

So that we may make the quickest possible progress, I have prepared this booklet to guide you through your psychotherapy. While all of us are unique, and while no one's therapy is exactly like anyone else's, you will find this step-by-step guide helpful in understanding what we are doing and knowing what are your responsibilities. This book will also suggest things for you to do to make the most of your therapy. These will include the following:

1 Doing periodic reading. The readings will be particularly relevant to understanding and overcoming the problems or concerns on which you wish to work.
2 Doing written and behavioural homework. These will help you efficiently work against and overcome your problems.
3 Listening to tapes of our sessions. A great deal often happens in psychotherapy. Some of it can be remembered, while some cannot. To get the most out of our sessions, I will audiotape them and give the tape to you to listen to before the next one. Please do so and bring the tape to our next appointment. We can then discuss things from it, save it for future reference, or record over it.

Please feel free to discuss any or all of this with me. I look forward to working with you. I want you to know that I am committed to helping you achieve a quick and thorough resolution of your concerns.

Sincerely,

Step One: Committing Oneself to Change

> Commitment is what transforms a promise into reality.
> It is the words that speak boldly of your intentions. And the actions that speak louder than the words.
> It is making time when there is none. Coming through time after time, year after year.
> Commitment is the stuff character is made of; the power to change the face of things.
> It is the daily triumph of integrity over skepticism.
>
> Shearson Lehman,
> American Express Advertisement

By the time you decided to enter psychotherapy you had most likely spent a great deal of time innocently and unwittingly engraining the ways of acting and reacting that you now find painful and self-defeating. It is understandable that, with all this 'practice', you find it easy to think, feel and act as you do.

While I will certainly do my best to help you undo these self-defeating patterns, I and many others have found that people change to the extent to which they themselves work in psychotherapy – that is, when they *do* what is necessary to change. This depends on a full, personal, and responsible commitment for solving their problems and for bringing about their own growth and change.

It follows, then, that the first, crucial step in your psychotherapy is to commit yourself to doing the work necessary to bring about the changes you want. Without this commitment, your efforts may very well be sporadic and half-hearted, and your gains will be slow, accidental and incomplete. So, to facilitate your commitment, take some time (about half an hour) to read, reflect upon, and complete Assignment 1, which immediately follows. Bring it to your next session so that I can help you refine it and so that we can both be clear about and agree upon the directions you are headed.

Assignment 1: Commitment Contract (please complete)

I commit myself to and take full responsibility for doing whatever is necessary to overcome the following painful and/or self-defeating feelings and actions.

(1) ______________________________

____

(2) ______________________________

____

(3) ______________________________

____

(4) ______________________________

____

(5) ______________________________

____

I commit myself to and take full responsibility for doing whatever is necessary to develop the following pleasurable and/or self-enhancing feelings and actions.

(1) ______________________________

____

(2) ______________________________

____

(3) ______________________________

____

(4) ______________________________

____

(5) ______________________________

____

I will continue to keep my commitment for doing whatever is necessary to eliminate my self-defeating patterns and for promoting my well-being for the duration of this therapy and for the rest of my life.

Signed ______________________________

Date ______________________________

Good! Congratulations! You have now taken the first major step toward solving your problems. So that you will keep your commitment alive, I suggest you read this commitment contract at least once a day, and perhaps sellotape it in a prominent place, or copy it and carry it in your pocket, so that you can frequently look at it.

Step Two: Understanding Emotional Disturbance and its Treatment

> People are disturbed not by things but by the views they take of them.
>
> Epictetus, 1st Century AD

A world-famous clinical psychologist and psychotherapist, Albert Ellis, has said: 'I have long been convinced that people become and remain emotionally disturbed largely because they do not clearly define what their "disturbance" is and what they can do to minimize it' (1971). I wholeheartedly agree with Dr Ellis. The more you know about your emotional disturbance and how to overcome it, the more focused will be your efforts and the more efficient will be your change.

The second step in your psychotherapy, then, is to become educated about the nature of emotional problems and their treatment. Your responsibility now is to complete reading assignments that will give you this knowledge. These assignments will, in addition to being interesting, help you understand what your problems are and what we will do to overcome them. Perhaps most important, they will help you to see your role in creating and maintaining the problems that you so much want to be rid. Bring anything that you do not understand or agree with to my attention and we will discuss it fully.

Now, complete Assignment 2, which follows.

Assignment 2: Reading Assignment

I will assign some items from the list below for you to read. Read these items carefully at least twice. Underline what you find important, take notes (space is provided following the reading list), and do anything else that will help you understand the concepts and relate them to your problems. Remember! Be *vitally interested* in your own well-being, as if you are the most important person in the world to you! Take this reading *seriously*, as it can lay the foundation for effective and long-lasting change! Be *committed* to the promises you made in Assignment 1, for your commitment will make a difference!

PAMPHLETS/ARTICLES

Ellis, Albert (1971) Emotional disturbance and its treatment in a nutshell, *Canadian Counselor*, 5(3), 168–71.

Ellis, Albert (1973) The no cop-out therapy, *Psychology Today*, July.

Ellis, Albert (1975) *RET abolishes most of the human ego*. Paper delivered at the American Psychological Association National Convention, September.
Ellis, Albert (1973) Unhealthy love: its causes and treatment. In Mary Ellen Curtin (ed.), *Symposium on Love*. New York: Behavioral Publications.
Burns, David D. (1980) The perfectionist's script for self-defeat, *Psychology Today*, November, 34–5.

BOOKS

Burns, David D. (1980) *Feeling Good: The New Mood Therapy*. New York: William Morrow.
Burns, David D. (1985) *Intimate Connections*. New York: William Morrow.
Ellis, Albert and Harper, Robert A. (1975) *A New Guide to Rational Living*. North Hollywood, CA: Wilshire.
Ellis, Albert and Becker, Irving (1982) *A Guide to Personal Happiness*. North Hollywood, CA: Wilshire.
Miller, Tom (1983) *So, You Secretly Suspect You're Worthless! Well . . . .* Skaneateles, NY: Lakeside Printing.
Ellis, Albert (1975) *How to Live with a Neurotic*. North Hollywood, CA: Wilshire.
Maultsby, Maxie C., Jr (1975) *Help Yourself to Happiness*. New York: Institute for Rational Living.

Notes about the Reading Material

Step Three: Uncovering and Appreciating your Irrational Thinking

> Until an individual accepts the fact that he is responsible for what he does, there can be no treatment. It is not up to therapists to advance explanations for irresponsibility. Individual responsibility is the goal of treatment and unhappiness is the result and not the cause of irresponsibility.
>
> William Glasser, MD

I have summarized below some of the crucial insights you learned in your reading assignment. Read this summary and refer back to the readings if you need to do so. Some people find these insights bitter pills to swallow; they resist them. Nonetheless, they are true. I cannot emphasize enough how important it is to your getting better for you to understand and accept them. If you have any questions, concerns, or disagreements about any of these insights, please raise them with me now since what we will do in psychotherapy follows from them.

INSIGHT 1

How you feel and behave is largely determined *by the way you think*, not by the things that happen to you or by the actions of others. That is, your *moment-by-moment thoughts*, which usually represent deeply believed attitudes or philosophies, '*cause*' you to feel and act as you do. We represent this in terms of the ABC theory, whereby: 'A' stands for the Activating Event, or what happened; 'B' stands for your beliefs, or what you thought and believed when it happened; and 'C' stands for your emotional and behavioral reactions, or how you felt and acted *by thinking what you did* when it happened.

INSIGHT 2

Regardless of what happened to you in the past (for example, whether your parents loved you or not), you first became disturbed *when you adopted, endorsed, or bought into your irrational beliefs* (your iBs). In other words, no matter how badly you were treated, or how irrational was the thinking of significant people in your life, it was when *you* decided to *believe* what you do, or when *you agreed with* the nutty ideas that others held, that your troubles began. And, you get upset and are disturbed today because you continue to indoctrinate yourself with the same irrational beliefs that you learned in the past.

INSIGHT 3

Although you are responsible for creating and maintaining your own irrational thinking, it is important not to judge or condemn yourself. Humans find it very easy to think irrationally and self-defeatingly. First, we come into this world with a strong capacity to err and to think crookedly; second, we are bombarded in our society with irrational, neurotic ideas. Therefore, it is important to be gentle with yourself. Realize that you share with the vast majority of people the problems you have, and forgive and accept yourself even though you have created and maintained your own problems. This is insight 3. Please heed and practice it.

INSIGHT 4

Insight 4 follows from the fact that by the time you entered therapy you have so propagandized yourself to believe what you do that you probably simply accept what you believe as truth. You most likely think and believe what you do without much awareness and certainly without question. It follows, then, that *an energetic and sustained effort* first to become aware of your irrational thoughts and beliefs and second to assault them are necessary to give them up. This insight, then, says that you 'must' work long and hard to give up your current, self-defeating way of thinking if you are to get over your emotional problems.

Now with these insights firmly in place, you are ready for Step Three in your psychotherapy. Your job here is twofold; one, to find out specifically what are your irrational thoughts and beliefs; two, to appreciate how these beliefs cause your painful feelings and your self-defeating actions. Both the discovery of these beliefs and their appreciation is extremely important, for knowledge without appreciation does little good.

To help you uncover and appreciate your irrational thinking, Step Three involves both taking a brief, self-administered and self-scored test and also doing written homework.

Testing for your Irrational Thinking There are several irrational belief tests now on the market. The two that I find most useful are the Dysfunctional Attitude Scale (DAS)[1] and the Irrational Beliefs Test (IBT).[2] I will select one of these for you to take. Each one asks you to mark the degree to which you agree or disagree with a series of statements. Each also gives you scoring instructions and helps you interpret what the scores mean. Taking the test can be fun and the results should prove both interesting and helpful.

Assignment 3: Taking the Test

Please be serious about this. Bring both the test itself and your questions and insights to our next session. It may be a good idea to insert the test and the results in this book for frequent reference.

Written Homework It not only is important to know what general irrational beliefs you hold, but it also is important to become skilled at 'hearing' your irrational thoughts on a moment-by-moment basis. In learning to spot what you are thinking to upset yourself at any given moment (and recognizing the irrational beliefs behind these thoughts), you are well positioned to do the things necessary to change your self-defeating thinking. Without this skill, you will probably go on reacting to your own thinking without any power to act and feel as you want.

Assignment 4, which immediately follows, is designed to help you learn to track down and recognize your irrational thinking. With this skill, you will be ready to move to step four, the change process.

Assignment 4: The Irrational Thinking Log

Your assignment now is a daily one. Your instructions are to devote from 15 to 30 minutes each day to filling out one of the thinking logs that follow. I have provided 14 of these to last you two weeks, but I will give you more if you want to do more than one per day or if you need to continue this for more than two weeks. Remember! The purpose of this homework is to help you become very conscious of your own irrational self-defeating thinking. The more aware you become of your irrational thinking, the more you will be able to overcome it.

The irrational thinking log is very simple to follow and do, although you may initially have trouble identifying your irrational thinking. Don't worry if you find this difficult. You will become quite skilled at this in a very short time if you persistently do the homework. I will coach you so bring your sheets to each session. Instructions are as follows:

1 Each day, take a time when you become upset over something. Use getting upset as a cue to do your log. Then, either as soon after the event as possible or at some designated later time, begin by *briefly writing down what happened* – the Activating Event, or the 'A'. Do not belabor this describing it endlessly, as the real cause of your problems is your thinking (at B) about the event, not the event itself.
2 Briefly describe *how you felt* and *what you did* in relation to the event. This is the 'C' or the consequence of your thinking about the event. A mistake people often make here is to confuse what they thought with how they felt. For example, people often write, 'I felt he should not have done that.' In fact this is a thought ('I *thought* he should not have done that!'). This thought caused the emotions. Feelings refer to anger, guilt, depression, anxiety and the like, and are to be reported here.
3 As a last step in this homework assignment, write down in sentence form *what you thought*, at B, to make you feel and act at C as you did about the event. Two hints here. First, to help you discover the thoughts, ask yourself: 'What was going through my head when I first started feeling/acting as I did?' Second, listen very carefully for your *demands* (expressed with words like should, ought, must, and need), your *catastrophizing* (expressed as awful, horrible, terrible and tragic) and your *self-downing* (as in, 'I'm a failure', or 'I'm bad'). After you've written your thoughts, double check to see if one of these themes is hidden there; if so, rewrite the thought to include it.

Again, ask any questions of me to help you become skilled at uncovering your irrational thinking. Becoming good at this is important. Happy hunting!

A caution. Your goal in doing your written homework is to become quite sensitive to your irrational thinking. In doing so, you may be surprised how frequently you think these thoughts and how deeply you believe what you do. Some people are shocked at this and conclude that they are worse off than they really are and that there is too much in their heads to conquer. Do not fall into this trap. Rather than taking this attitude, remember that getting better requires awareness of your thinking. The more you become tuned into these thoughts, the better positioned you will be to bring about the changes you want.

Irrational Thinking Log

A	**B**	**C**
Activating event →	Irrational thoughts/beliefs	→ Emotional and/or behavioral consequences

1 Briefly describe the activating event.
2 Briefly record the painful emotion(s) (e.g., anxiety, guilt, depression, anger) you experienced in relation to A.
Briefly record your self-defeating behavior(s) in relation to A.
3 Write down the thoughts you had which caused your painful emotions and self-defeating behaviors. Write them in sentence form. Number them consecutively.

(1)

(2)

(3)

(4)

(5)

Step Four: Changing your Irrational Thinking

> If we do not change our direction, we are likely to end up where we are headed.
>
> Chinese Proverb

> We cannot solve life's problems except by solving them. This statement may seem idiotically tautological or self-evident, yet it is seemingly beyond the comprehension of much of the human race. This is because we must accept responsibility for a problem before we can solve it. We cannot solve a problem by hoping that someone else will solve it for us. I can solve a problem only when I say 'This is *my* problem and it's up to me to solve it.' But, many, so many, seek to avoid the pain of their problems by saying to themselves: 'This problem was caused me by other people, or by social circumstances beyond my control, and therefore it is up to other people or society to solve this problem for me. It is not really my personal problem.'
>
> M. Scott Peck, MD

So far you have committed yourself to change, learned about the nature of your emotional problems and become familiar with the specific irrational beliefs that cause your problems. You are now well-positioned to bring about the changes you want – to breaking the habit of responding to situations with your automatic irrational thoughts, *and* to giving up the deeply held, harmful ideas or beliefs that create your painful feelings and self-defeating behaviors.

A word to the wise is important here! In order to change it will be necessary for you to work hard – to devote time and energy to doing the work necessary to change. After all, you have believed these irrational ideas for years and have thought about and dealt with scores of situations with them. In effect, they have become habitual, deeply endorsed, 'second nature'. Furthermore, you may never have learned, or perhaps have gotten rusty at, the critical thinking skills important for change, and you may therefore have to bone up on these skills.

So, some hard work is now in order. But, you can do the work, and it is worth it! All you have to do is be willing to spend the time and energy. Rather than seeing this work as a burden or chore, I encourage you to think of it as an adventure. After all, you are working to change some extremely important things about yourself that will lead to all sorts of benefits, clearly a project worthy of effort and excitement.

To bring about the changes in your thinking, acting and feeling, I will give you assignments in each of three areas. I will describe each in turn, but you will be doing all three concurrently.

1 READING ASSIGNMENT

Yes, more reading! This time, your reading is designed to help you clearly understand what is illogical, false and self-defeating about the ideas or beliefs (at B) that underpin your problems. These readings will also serve to teach you new, alternative ideas that are contrary to your irrational ones and that both make more sense and pay off for you. The goal is for you to acquire a new knowledge base that you can learn, endorse, and eventually adopt, thereby bringing about better results for yourself.

Assignment 5: Reading Assignment

From the list of readings in Step 2, and possibly from other sources, I will now assign you readings. Again, please read the material carefully, digest it, and discuss it with me at the next session. A couple of blank sheets follow on which to take notes.

Notes about the Reading Material

2 BEHAVIORAL ASSIGNMENTS

It has been found that one of the most effective methods of destroying irrational beliefs is to act contrary to them. Doing this not only serves to call up our irrational thinking, which we can then combat with written homework (see (3), below) and other methods, but it also serves to help us see that our irrational beliefs are nonsense – that for example, we do not need to act perfectly, that we won't perish if we are rejected, that the world doesn't end if we are in some way frustrated.

Thus, I will assign you things to do each day to help you give up your irrational thinking. Probably these will be one or more of the following, which I will fully explain in our sessions.

Pleasurable pursuits – committing yourself to activities.
Rational-emotive imagery – vividly picturing difficult events and practicing thinking rationally about them.
Shame-attacking exercises – performing 'silly' or 'embarrassing' acts in public to show yourself that you do not need *ever* to feel ashamed.
Courting discomfort – deliberately doing things you find uncomfortable, or staying in uncomfortable situations a little longer.
Risk-taking – doing things you fear.
Behavioral rehearsal – practicing doing things at which you are unskilled or are fearful of doing.
Rewarding and penalizing – pleasuring or punishing yourself for doing or not doing something.

Sometimes people react with fear to undertaking behavioral assignments. Other people resent doing them. Still others find them boring. These are all typical reactions, yet reactions to be ignored. It is important to follow through on these behavioral assignments as they are important techniques for ridding yourself of your irrational beliefs.

Assignment 6: Behavioral Assignment

I will assign you things to do between now and our next session. These assignments are designed to help you see that your beliefs are both irrational and self-defeating and to encourage you to give them up. If you find yourself reluctant to do this assignment, either because of anxiety, resentment, or boredom, ignore these feelings and do the assignments anyway. We can talk about these feelings and what are behind them in our sessions. The long-range benefits will far outweigh the short-term or brief (and irrelevant) discomfort that you may feel. On the sheet provided, keep a log of *your behavioral assignment* and *any* thoughts you had about doing it.

Weekly Behavioral Assignment Log

Assigned activity: ______________________________

____

____

Reward: ______________________________

Punishment: ______________________________

Date	Completed: yes/no	Irrational thoughts

3 WRITTEN HOMEWORK

Written homework is designed for you to destroy your irrational thoughts and beliefs by a direct, active, energetic assault on them. In this homework you will employ the logico-empirical method of *repeated and persistent scientific questioning and disputing*. The idea is to take your long-held beliefs and, instead of automatically believing them as you have done for so long, to hold them up to scrutiny. You want to identify what is wrong with them, why they are nonsense, how they hurt you, and what evidence there is to refute them. In other words, you will want to *debate against* them, perhaps for the first time in your life, instead of automatically endorsing and acting on them as you have done for so long. This task will probably be difficult for you at first, but you will soon become quite good at it.

We are fortunate to have many different written 'disputation' forms from which to choose. Some of these come from Dr David Burns' book, *Feeling Good*; others derive from Dr Albert Ellis' work at the Institute for Rational-Emotive Therapy in New York City; and still others have been developed by psychotherapists around the world. I will choose one that best suits your particular problems.

Assignment 7: Written Disputation of your Irrational Beliefs

This assignment is absolutely crucial to your change. You are to reserve from 15 to 30 minutes per day for at least one month to do your written homework. You may do more than this, but this is an absolute minimum. During this time you are to complete at least one homework sheet. I will supply you with a month's supply to get you started.

Take this assignment very seriously. This is as important as anything else in your life right now. Remember that you have spent a lifetime practicing and rehearsing the way you presently think and believe; you have the nonsense down pat. It only follows that strong, persistent effort against this habit, and these beliefs, is necessary for change to take place. *Bring your written homework* to our sessions so that I can go over it with you. I want to coach you in getting better and better at doing it. In becoming skilled at this, you, in effect, learn to be your own psychotherapist for future problems you may have in your life.

Step Five: Combatting and Overcoming Resistance

> Any real change implies the breakup of the world as one has already known it. The loss of all that gave one an identity, the end of safety. And at such a moment, unable to see and not daring to imagine what the future will now bring forth, one clings to what one knew, or thought one knew; to what one possessed or dreamed that one possessed. Yet it is only when persons are able, without bitterness or self-pity, to surrender a dream they have long cherished or a privilege they have long possessed that they are set free – they have set themselves free – for higher dreams, for greater privileges. All people have gone through this; go through it, each according to their degrees, throughout their lives. It is one of the irreducible facts of life.
>
> Author Unknown

The fact that you are now reading this suggests that you have come a long way in your psychotherapy. Your progress has been tremendous, and your level of self-awareness is much beyond that of most people.

Nevertheless, you may to your own surprise find yourself fighting against me, against your therapy, or even against yourself. You may, for example, start denying that you have problems; you may not want to attend your sessions or to bring up important difficulties; you may be tempted to argue against some of my observations and messages; and you may at first agree but later refuse to carry out your homework assignments.

All of this is a fairly typical stage in the psychotherapy process, a stage recognized by almost all people who do psychotherapy. It is called *resistance*, and, in fact, is so typical that whole books have been written to guide people like myself in helping people work through it. The *danger* is that you will allow your resistance to interfere with your progress and even cause you to stop your psychotherapy entirely.

In order to guard against this and to continue to get better, your task now is to understand what resistance is and what you can do about it so as not to let it undermine both what you've already accomplished and what you can further accomplish. So, now your goal is to understand and overcome your resistance.

First, resistance often comes about from confusion or a lack of understanding. You may, for example, not fully understand what I am saying, or what are your tasks or how to execute your assignments, or how your tasks relate to your goals. If you find any of these true, please bring them to my attention. I can then help to clarify things for you and get you back on track.

A second, perhaps more serious form of resistance often comes about from unrealistic fears and irrational misconceptions on your part. These fears and misconceptions, while unfounded, may appear entirely reasonable to you. I assure you, however, that they are entirely untrue. Once you let go of them, or ignore them, and continue your therapeutic working through, you will find that your fears are groundless and that your life will indeed be much better without your symptoms.

Dr Albert Ellis, the founder of rational-emotive therapy, has written an excellent book titled *Overcoming Resistance*. In his book he has listed many resistances that clients can hold, all of which result from false logic, including the following:

1 Fear of discomfort – believing that the effort to change is too difficult, that you cannot tolerate the discomfort and hassle of doing your homework, that it's easier to drift along with your problems than to make the effort to change them.
2 Fears of disclosure and shame – believing that you should not feel, think or act the way you do; that you are stupid, bad, or awful for all that; and that it would be terrible if I or anyone else knew how you really felt or thought.
3 Feelings of powerlessness and hopelessness – believing that you are unable to change, that your problems are too big to overcome, that you are too weak and small to conquer your problems.
4 Fears of change – believing you must have safety and certainty and, therefore, that you have to keep your symptoms, even though they are uncomfortable, because you are used to them.
5 Fear of failure and disapproval – believing that you must always succeed, you may fear that your symptoms may lead you to risk subsequent failure and disapproval (for example, overcoming a public speaking anxiety may prompt you to talk in public, do poorly, and get disapproval).
6 Self-punishment – in believing you are a bad person, you may believe that you must continue to suffer for your 'badness'.
7 Rebelliousness – believing you have to completely control your destiny and have absolutely perfect freedom to do what you like, you may rebel against me or your psychotherapy because you see it as an impingement on your freedom or power.
8 Secondary gain – having received payoffs for your symptoms, you may not want to give up your symptoms for fear of losing these payoffs (for example, you may get attention and sympathy for acting depressed or helpless).

In addition to the resistances mentioned above, I have observed that some people also hold the following ones:

9 Discouragement – believing that, since you don't feel better immediately after identifying your irrational beliefs or after disputing them a time or two, you can never overcome your disturbance.

10 Fear of loss of identity – believing that you are your feelings, you may incorrectly conclude you won't be you anymore if you change the way you feel.
11 Fear of loss of feelings – believing that thinking rationally will lead to no emotions at all, you may resist changing your beliefs for fear you'll become cold, unemotional, mechanized or dull.
12 Self-hate – believing that you are a bad person, you may block your working through so that you will continue to suffer to punish yourself for your 'badness'.
13 Fear of mediocrity – believing that you must be perfect, you may not want to give up your perfectionistic demands for fear this will lead to less than ideal behavior and thus condemn yourself to mediocrity and worthlessness.
14 Righteousness – believing that other people should act perfectly well, particularly toward you, you may refuse to give up your anger-producing beliefs because this lets them off the hook. You may not want to admit that they, as fallible human beings, have the right to make mistakes, that they are not condemnable because of their bad behavior, and that it is not correct for you to set out to make them suffer.

Like the irrational beliefs we are working to overcome, these phony ideas 'should' be seen for what they are – as irrational and self-defeating! – and 'should' be worked against. As with your main irrational beliefs, use the A–B–C theory to organize your assault against them, as per the diagram that immediately follows.

A ⟶	B ⟶	C ⟶
The prospect of thinking, feeling, and acting differently	Irrational, resistant thoughts	Resistant feelings and behaviors

Assignment 8: Overcoming your Resistances

In overcoming your resistance I will instruct you to do many of the things you were to do for Step Four, Changing your Irrational Beliefs. This time, though, you are to use these techniques to do violence to your resistant thoughts. So, for this assignment, you are to do two things. One, you are to ignore your resistance and do the assignments previously given you for Step Four. In other words, have your resistances (your fears, your doubts) if you like, but force yourself to continue your step four work anyway.

In order to combat your resistant ideas directly, I will now also assign you both behavioral and written homework to search out and destroy these ideas. Be sure to do this work as it would be a shame to come this far and stop yourself from completing your change. Be willing to take the risk of working against your irrational beliefs. After all, if you do not like the results, you can always go back to thinking, acting and feeling the way you did before.

Step Six: Going Forward

> Life shrinks or expands in proportion to one's courage.
>
> Anaïs Nin

> Responsibility is a unique concept. It can only reside and inhere in a single individual. You may share it with others, but your portion is not diminished. You may delegate it, but it is still with you. You may disclaim it, but you cannot divest yourself of it.
>
> Admiral Hyman Rickover

> Life is either a daring adventure or nothing.
>
> Helen Keller

Congratulations! You have come a long, long way from where you started. You have, with your own efforts, made fundamental changes in yourself and in the quality of your life. You have every right to be proud of what you have done.

But a word to the wise is in order. Remember the insights you have already learned, especially (1) that it is exceptionally easy to think irrationally, and (2) that hard work against your irrational thinking is necessary to change. The bad news now is that it is easy to backslide – to get lazy and to stop working on your thinking. You will, at times, still think and act irrationally (after all, that is human nature); *and*, if you are not careful, you will stop working altogether and drift back into your old way of doing things.

The good news, though, is that you are in the driver's seat. You have the choice whether to drift or whether to continue to devote regular time, each day, to your ongoing well-being and happiness. I encourage you to think of the long-range benefits of the brief and sometimes inconvenient efforts you would be wise to make each day. I encourage you to think of doing daily psychological workouts for your mental health much as you would do daily physical workouts for your physical health.

To finish your therapy, then, I will share with you ways to maintain your gains and strategies for dealing with backsliding. Fortunately, Dr Albert Ellis has written a pamphlet titled, 'How to use rational-emotive therapy (RET) to maintain and enhance your therapy gains,' that we can use as a guideline in this. I urge you to adopt many of those strategies as part of your daily routine.

Finally, and ultimately, your life is *your* responsibility. Whether you go forward with what you have learned or whether you backslide depends on your keeping alive your commitment to your own well-being. While I will always be available to you as a resource in case you find yourself in serious difficulties or in case you simply want a tuneup, it would be wonderful if my services became irrelevant to you in the future. Therefore, your final assignment is to renew the commitments you made in the first part of your therapy, as per Assignment 9, which follows.

Assignment 9: Lifetime Commitment Contract

I commit myself to, and take full responsibility for, doing whatever is necessary to maintain and enhance the following thoughts/beliefs, feelings, and behaviors.

(1) ______________________________
____

(2) ______________________________
____

(3) ______________________________
____

(4) ______________________________
____

(5) ______________________________
____

I commit myself to, and take full responsibility for, doing the following things to maintain and enhance my therapy gains (be sure to indicate the frequency for each).

(1) ______________________________
____

(2) ______________________________
____

(3) ______________________________
____

(4) ______________________________
____

(5) ______________________________
____

Notes

1 The Dysfunctional Attitude Scale (DAS) was developed by Dr Arlene Weissman. A brief version of this scale is presented by David Burns, MD in his book, *Feeling Good: The New Mood Therapy* (see reference for this in Step Two).

2 The Irrational Beliefs Test (IBT) was developed in 1969 as part of R.G. Jones's doctoral dissertation.

References

Ellis, A. (1976) The biological basis of human irrationality, *Journal of Individual Psychology*, 32, 145–68.

Ellis, A. (1978) Family therapy: a phenomenological and active-directive approach, *Journal of Marriage and Family Counseling*, 4(2), 43–50.

Ellis, A. (1985) *Overcoming Resistance: Rational-emotive Therapy with Difficult Clients*. New York: Springer.

Ellis, A. (1987) The impossibility of achieving consistently good mental health, *American Psychologist*, 42(4), 364–75.

Ellis, A. and Harper, R. (1975) *A New Guide to Rational Living*. North Hollywood, CA: Wilshire.

Grieger, R. and Boyd, J. (1980) *Rational-Emotive Therapy: A Skills-Based Approach*. New York: Van Nostrand Reinhold.

Maultsby, M.C., Jr (1975) *Help Yourself to Happiness: Through Rational Self-counseling*. New York: Institute for Rational-Emotive Therapy.

Maultsby, M.C., Jr (1984) *Rational Behavior Therapy*. Englewood Cliffs, NJ: Prentice Hall.

5
A Rational-Emotive Model of Assessment

Raymond DiGiuseppe

Rational-emotive therapy has always been presented as an active, directive, efficient form of psychotherapy (Ellis, 1957, 1962, 1985, 1989a). It is often described as a no-nonsense, no-cop-out form of therapy because it advocates forceful, active disputing, challenging and confronting clients' irrational beliefs. An extensive RET literature has developed that explicates the theory (Bernard and DiGiuseppe, 1989; Ellis, 1962, 1973, 1985), specifies the application of RET to different populations and hypothesizes specific irrational beliefs likely to be held by various client populations (Ellis and Bernard, 1983, 1985; Ellis, McInerney, DiGiuseppe and Yeager, 1988; Ellis, Sichel, DiMattia, Yeager and DiGiuseppe, 1989), and details disputing strategies to be used with clients (Ellis, 1985; Ellis and Dryden, 1987).

The missing topic in the RET literature has been assessment. Most recent books on RET spend little time discussing assessment. The consideration of assessment in the RET literature is usually limited to one chapter focusing on discovering the client's As, Bs and Cs, and on detailed hypotheses concerning which irrational beliefs probably underlie the problem in the client group being discussed. Few, if any, systematic procedures or comprehensive rationales for assessment are outlined in the RET literature. Rational-emotive theory and therapy appear to lack a conceptual statement on the place of assessment.

This state of affairs has probably emerged because of Ellis's attitude toward traditional assessment strategies in mental health services and his commitment to efficient intervention strategies. In my 15 years of teaching workshops and lectures on RET with Dr Ellis he has repeatedly commented that most traditional psychological assessment is a waste of time and is highly inefficient.

Are all diagnostic judgments irrelevant in RET? Do RET therapists avoid treatment decisions based on the client's type or degree of psychotherapy or personality style? How does a psychotherapist using RET choose what to dispute? Many clinicians watch Ellis perform a demonstration of RET and wonder how he starts disputing so quickly. They fail to see anything that resembles assessment.

Ellis's professional history and list of publications (American Psychological Association, 1985) reveals that he is no stranger to psychological assessment. His doctoral dissertation investigated the psychometric properties of the Minnesota Multiphasic Personality Inventory (MMPI). He published several research reviews of personality inventories in the 1940s and 1950s. He was director of a statewide psychological assessment unit for many years. All of these accomplishments occurred before he initiated rational-emotive therapy.

It would be correct to say that Ellis has been dismayed by the inefficiency of traditional intake procedures in mental health settings. It would be correct to say that, as a result, Ellis's past and present clinical practice and his writings on RET eschew the traditional assessment strategies in mental health. It is correct to say that assessment has been underplayed in the RET literature. However, it would be incorrect to conclude that Ellis and other rational-emotive therapists do not have any assessment strategies. In fact, clinicians at the Institute for Rational-Emotive Therapy who work with Ellis frequently share stories concerning the amount of information he recalls about his clients, or how he uncovers important clinical information in just a session or two.

In this chapter, I propose that RET has a distinct approach to assessment and that RET's active-directive reputation is derived more from its assessment strategies than from its intervention strategies. Based on my work with Ellis for 15 years, having listened to hundreds of his therapy tapes and having discussed clinical and training issues with him, I attempt here to specify the rational-emotive approach to assessment. I compare the rational-emotive model of assessment on a number of assumptions with the traditional approach to psychological assessment.

Overview of Rational-Emotive Assessment Procedures

Clients who come for therapy at the Institute for Rational-Emotive Therapy in New York are typically told to come for their appointment about an hour early. They are asked to complete a four-page biographical information form, the Millon Clinical Multiaxial Inventory II (Millon, 1987), the short form of the Beck Depression Inventory (Beck and Beck, 1972; Beck et al., 1974), the General Psychological Well Being Scale (DuPuy, 1984), the General Health Questionnaire (Goldberg, 1972), the Satisfaction with Life Scale (Diener et al., 1985), and the Attitudes and Beliefs Scale 2 (DiGiuseppe et al., 1988). Usually, clients are not finished before the session begins, and the scales are completed after the first session. The scales are computer-scored on the premises and are usually available to the therapist by the second session. The brief version of the Beck Depression Inventory, the General Psychological Well Being Scale, the General Health Questionnaire, and the Satisfaction with Life Scale are repeated every four weeks so that therapists and clients can review their progress.

Although therapists at the Institute for Rational-Emotive Therapy do use standardized assessment instruments, diagnostic assessment is not the first task of the therapist. The first task is to develop a therapeutic alliance. Assessment is dynamic, not static. By *dynamic*, I mean that it is ongoing. The therapist is always aware that diagnostic impressions are hypotheses and subject to change on attainment of new information. Also, ongoing assessment provides information on the effectiveness of the interventions, which subsequently helps to guide the therapist's clinical decisions.

RET assessment is hypothesis-driven. Rational-emotive theory rejects logical positivism and its emphasis on induction. It acknowledges that therapists are always creating hypotheses about their clients and postulates that it is best to test such hypotheses as quickly as possible.

RET assessment does not follow the medical model. Assessment is treatment-oriented. The most important aspects of assessment are those that lead to treatment decisions. The treatment utility of all assessment strategies guides the therapist.

RET versus Traditional Models of Assessment

It is proposed here that the traditional models of assessment in psychotherapy, psychiatry and mental health are based on certain assumptions and models of psychopathology and epistemology. Typically, the medical model is contrasted with the behavioral model. Such a contrast usually compares a trait view of behavior with a behavioral or environmental view. RET appears to be a hybrid theory in this regard, in that it postulates traitlike irrational beliefs but also considers the role of the environment.

The traditional models of assessment appear to rest on the view that assessment and treatment are separate activities. Clinicians have traditionally perceived a clear demarcation between their role as diagnostician and their role as therapist (Blatt, 1975). The traditional models of psychopathology and epistemology that have guided assessment are, respectively, the medical model of mental and emotional disorder and the logical-positivist position of knowledge. In addition, the medical model of psychopathology leads to a medical model of assessment. This model, which assumes clients' willingness to self-disclose, fails to place priority on establishing a therapeutic relationship before assessment. Rational-emotive theory differs from traditional models of assessment because it takes different positions on these issues, as is discussed below.

Medical Model of Assessment

The medical model of behavioral disorders assumes that a complete diagnosis and a total assessment of the problem are necessary before any treatment begins. Mental health clinics and psychiatric hospitals are dominated by the medical profession. The result has been the adoption of the medical model of assessment as the primary paradigm in the mental health field. In medicine there is usually a specific treatment for specific disorders. One does not receive the same antibiotic regardless of the type of infection. The physician performs tests to diagnose the specific flora that have invaded one's body and then prescribes a medication designed to treat that infection. Based on the medical model, mental health treatment also requires a complete diagnostic assessment. This will include a social history, followed by a psychiatric or intake interview. Next, psychological testing may be done. Finally, the case is discussed at a clinical case conference, a diagnosis is reached, and a treatment plan is mapped out. At this time, the case is assigned to a therapist. After several weeks have gone by, the client has spoken with a number of professionals. There are three major criticisms of the traditional medical model of mental health assessment made here: (1) it interferes with developing the therapeutic alliance; (2) differential diagnosis does not lead to differential treatment; and (3) the inductive procedure fails to help clinicians disconfirm their hypotheses.

In private practice, where multidisciplinary teams are rarely used, therapists often perform the necessary tasks themselves, spending a considerable amount of time obtaining a psychosocial history, assessing clients' functioning in all areas of his or her life, and acquiring a full history of the symptoms. Does the client understand the purpose of the assessment? Does the process of delving into so much information, which may be viewed as irrelevant by the client, really enhance the therapeutic relationship? I would say not. And I would go so far as to suggest that, in addition to being inefficient and costly, the medical model of assessment often alienates clients. The problem with placing a priority on diagnostic assessment before therapy is the brief number of sessions most clients remain in therapy. Depending on the study and the population sampled, from 25 percent to 90 percent of clients terminate therapy by the fifth session. Up to 80 percent may leave by the eighth session (see review by Garfield, 1986). I would hypothesize that the high dropout rate in psychotherapy (Garfield, 1986) is partly due to the traditional intake process. Therapists may not have sufficient time to perform a diagnostic assessment before the client leaves.

A recent internal study at the Institute for Rational-Emotive Therapy of 731 clients who had terminated therapy revealed that RET is most often a brief therapy. The mean number of sessions was 16.5, the median was 11 sessions; 30 percent of the clients had had 5 sessions or fewer, 42 percent had had 8 sessions or fewer, and only 25 percent had had 23 sessions or more. Actually, RET ends up having somewhat longer session lengths because fewer people drop out in the first five or so sessions.

Clients come to us in psychological pain. They want help. They may perceive their being shuffled around to different professionals as being abandonment. They may perceive therapists' questions concerning their past, family, and other areas of their lives as voyeuristic and irrelevant. They may perceive the lack of an intervention as a sign of incompetency.

The medical model assumes that a diagnosis is necessary before any treatment can begin because specific disorders respond to different treatments. However, this practice is usually not the case in psychotherapy. Ask any therapist you know if she or he uses different treatments for different diagnoses. In fact, ask yourself if you would be more likely to use Gestalt approaches with one client, behavioral approaches with another, and psychoanalytic approaches with yet a different client. The answer clearly is no.

Psychologists have questioned the utility of diagnostic assessment before therapy. Several authors have concluded that therapists do not find the information revealed in a diagnostic assessment useful for treatment planning or for enhancing therapeutic effectiveness (Adams, 1972; Daily, 1953; Meehl, 1960; Moore et al., 1968). Clearly, the present diagnostic taxonomy and our present knowledge in psychotherapy do not yet lead to prescriptive psychotherapy (Beutler, 1989). The single best predictor of the type of treatment a client receives is the theoretical orientation of the therapist. All theoretical orientations in psychotherapy claim that their orientation is appropriate for all disorders. Decision rules in psychotherapy treatment manuals concerning which clients are unlikely to benefit from psychodynamic (Luborsky, 1984; Strupp and Binder, 1984), interpersonal (Klerman et al., 1984), cognitive (Beck et al., 1979), and experiential therapy (Daldrup et al., 1988) are based on patients' motivation and acceptance of therapeutic philosophy and psychological-mindedness rather than on diagnostic judgments from the third edition of the *Diagnostic and Statistical Manual* (DSM-III; American Psychiatric Association, 1980). Reviews of comparative outcome studies with homogeneous samples have failed to indicate the different successes of specific therapies (Beutler, 1989; Beutler and Crago, 1987).

The best way to start therapy may be to ask the client what problem brought him or her to therapy. Cummings (1986) argued that it is best to ask what motivated clients to come when they did. This problem focus communicates to the client the therapist's willingness to help alleviate his or her pain. From the RET perspective, the assessment of the activating events, the emotional consequences, and the irrational beliefs (Dryden and DiGiuseppe, 1990) may be the most efficient use of the client's and the therapist's time. This kind of assessment helps the therapist apply his or her theoretical orientation to the problem that the client is most willing to present. This kind of assessment also helps the client evaluate the trustworthiness and competence of the therapist and gives the client a chance to evaluate the therapist's orientation. Applying the ABC problem-solving model to the first problem that the client raises also helps the client learn the model on a less difficult problem. As a result, it may be easier to apply RET to the most important issues when the client chooses to discuss them.

Although Ellis and his associates have eschewed assessment for diagnosis, the RET literature has focused on client behaviors and personality characteristics that may influence the course of therapy (Ellis, 1973, 1985; Ellis and Dryden, 1987; Walen et al., 1980). As proposed by Hayes et al. (1987), RET advocates that assessment focus on issues that are relevant to treatment. In addition to the activating events, emotions and irrational beliefs, RET recommends that therapists assess clients' introspection, cognitive flexibility, social-problem-solving skills, the presence of secondary emotional reactions, and secondary gain.

There are a few diagnostic categories that may lead to different treatment. These are psychotic syndromes, organic brain impairment and biologically based depression. All of these disorders may best be treated with medication. However, two points are worth noting. Although these disorders often do respond to medication, the patients often require or benefit from psychotherapy as well. Second, there is no reason why one has to perform the entire ritual of assessment to uncover these problems. Perhaps a more focused style of assessment would uncover these disorders efficiently. The process of identifying and challenging irrational beliefs provides the RET therapist with much information about the way the client thinks. Such cognitive processing information is more likely than a social history to suggest or corroborate the diagnosis of organicity or psychosis.

Therapists can pursue a hypothesis-driven assessment once they suspect one of these disorders. For example, certain things that the client says may suggest to the therapist the presence of a major depression or another diagnostic category that will respond to medication. Once a therapist develops such a hypothesis, she or he would construct questions to corroborate or disconfirm it immediately. This process is discussed in more detail in the next section.

Static versus Dynamic Assessment

The medical model of assessment and the medical model of psychopathology present assessment as static. Emotional and behavioral disorders are mental symptoms of intrapsychic diseases that are categorically diagnosed. They are present or absent at intake, as are irrational beliefs. The therapist performs an assessment first to formulate a diagnosis and then begins treatment.

The RET model assumes that assessment is an ongoing process, although we are still searching for stable traits. All diagnostic impressions are tentative. Therapists had better be prepared to shift their conceptualization of the client as new information is revealed throughout the progression of therapy. An attitude of ongoing assessment means that assessment is an integral part of all therapy sessions, as similarly stressed in behavior therapy (Wolpe, 1969). RET advocates the scientist-practitioner model (Barlow et al., 1984) of ongoing assessment to monitor the effectiveness of the therapy. If an intervention is not working, the case can be reformulated and a new strategy tried. Ongoing assessment means that the successful outcomes are assessed for the systemic effect that they may bring about (Freeman, 1986). For example, a depressed client may overcome his or her depression and behave in newly assertive and independent ways. These behaviors may be a threat to other family members, who will try to subvert them. The client may not have the skills to cope with the sabotage. The therapist who assesses for the potential of these possible outcomes can work either with the primary client on new goals or with the family members to help them adjust to the client's new behavior.

Therapeutic Relationships and Self-disclosure

Ellis (1962, 1985, 1989a) has attempted to help clients identify the irrational beliefs causing their emotional difficulties as quickly as possible. He frequently engages in the disputation of an irrational belief in the first session, possibly 20–30 minutes into the session. RET assumes that clients may be reluctant to reveal their problems at the initial session. Ellis attempts to actively teach clients a process of resolving emotional problems to increase the clients' confidence in the efficacy of treatment.

The traditional model of psychological assessment gathers information to achieve a diagnosis before treatment begins. This strategy assumes that clients will reveal their deepest, darkest secrets, symptoms, thoughts, and emotions in the first couple of contacts with mental health professionals *before* a therapeutic *alliance* is established. I would argue that clients are likely to withhold shameful, important information about themselves or about their reason for seeking therapy until after they have established a therapeutic alliance. Such a therapeutic alliance involves trusting that the therapist will accept them regardless of their problems. A therapeutic alliance also requires confidence that the therapist is sufficiently skilled to handle a problem if the client does risk revealing himself or herself. Traditional mental health assessment is poorly designed to build a therapeutic relationship. Interviews designed to obtain all the information necessary for a psychosocial history and diagnosis require a significant amount of immediate disclosure, and to a professional whom the client does not know and may not see again. Also, the information requested in such an interview may not seem *relevant to the client*. If clients believe in a historical insight model of therapy, this information may seem relevant. However, many clients (as well as many therapists) do not perceive the relevance of the psychosocial history. The possible perception of irrelevance further detracts from the therapeutic alliance. Finally, clients usually seek therapy when they are in psychological pain. Rational-emotive theory postulates that a therapeutic alliance is best developed by offering the client some interventions as quickly as possible to demonstrate the therapist's willingness and ability to perceive and respond to the client's pain.

Recall, Recognition and Private Thoughts

Traditional assessment strategies in psychology assume that clients are able to report their inner thoughts and feelings. It has long been established that the clients who are good candidates for psychotherapy have good verbal skills. The clients who benefit from therapy the most are termed *YAVIS clients*. This acronym stands for 'young, attractive, verbal, intelligent and successful'. People who have poor verbal skills, or who are not psychologically minded or introspective, are considered poor candidates for the 'talking cure'. Even therapists who are not cognitively oriented seem to believe that clients are capable of verbally expressing their feelings. I would like to suggest that the reason that verbal skills have been considered such a prerequisite for psychotherapy is that therapy involves a translation process.

Bernard (1981) pointed out that irrational beliefs and other such private thoughts may not be readily accessible for verbal report. Research in cognitive psychology suggests that people are capable of expressing all of their cognitive processes (Nisbett and Wilson, 1977). Bernard suggested that cognitive approaches to clinical phenomena consider the relationship between thought and language suggested by Vygotsky (1962; also see Fodor, 1973). According to Vygotsky, thought and language are not synonymous. Children think before they develop linguistic abilities; therefore, people's thoughts are not encoded in the words of their spoken language. Once language is developed, thoughts can still be generated without language. Thoughts appear to be encoded in shorthand. A great many associations can be connected to a particular thought, and those associations can be experienced almost instantaneously. To communicate a thought to another, the person has to formulate the equivalent ideas in his or her native language. As an example, think of your mother – only for a second. How many different associations and ideas come to your mind? Now, try to imagine translating all of those associations into spoken English. Do all the thoughts and feelings have direct equivalents in our language? How much longer would it take to verbalize all the associations than it took to think them? Because it would take much longer to say them, you may struggle with which associations are most important. Because thought and language are not the same, Bernard suggested that clients may not always be able to express their irrational beliefs and, I would add, any other thoughts or feelings.

The relationship between programming and processing languages in computers may demonstrate the relation between thought and language. Information in a computer is encoded in a series of electronic impulses. The code used to derive meaning from these series of impulses is called *binary*. For the computer to communicate with the user, the binary code is translated into the programming language: Pascal, Basic, Fortran, or some other. There are limits on the information that can be communicated because of the limitations of any program language. There are limits on the speed with which the information can be retrieved depending on the hardware of the computer. Although I recognize that the computer is a poor model of human thought, this aspect of the computer demonstrates the importance of the translation process.

Thoughts are encoded in some physiological neural engram that science does not yet understand. In order for a person to share his or her thoughts with others, the thoughts have to be translated into the person's native language. Some languages are better suited to the expression of certain points than others, and some human hardware is better suited to the translation task than others.

Bernard suggested that another reason why private thoughts may be hard to recall is the distinction between linguistic and episodic memory. Memory of linguistic information and memory of information concerning events or episodes are organized separately (Tulving, 1972). Historic events and early experiences that may be associated with a disturbed emotion or evaluation of a class of stimuli would most likely be stored in episodic memory and easily accessible to linguistic recall.

Self-disclosure in therapy requires that clients go through two processes: (1) uncovering ideas that are organized in episodic memory and encoded in the neuronal coding system, which is dense with connections and (2) extracting the central idea and translating it into their native language. This could be a difficult task, as it involves the recall of information and expressive language. Most forms of psychotherapy rely on these expressive and recall processes. Clients have to recall their feelings and thoughts and then express the translation. Clients with proficient verbal skills are good at this task. However, the recall of information is always more difficult than recognition, and receptive language is always more difficult than expressive language. Clients who have not learned to be psychologically minded, or who have limited emotional vocabularies, or who have limited intellectual and verbal abilities, do less well. But we let them suffer through this process anyway.

Clients who have difficulty with the translation process may benefit from a recognition or receptive language task in therapy. This is precisely what occurs when the therapist offers interpretations or hypotheses. If the hypothesis formulated by the therapist is similar to an idea or feeling experienced by the client, the client recognizes it and affirms the hypothesis. If the hypothesis is off the mark, and the client does not recognize it as reflecting her or his own experience, the client disconfirms the hypothesis, and the therapist starts over again. I would argue that such hypothesis-driven assessment, as practiced in RET, is more effective – and is perceived as more friendly and less threatening by clients with poor insight and limited verbal skills. I would also hypothesize that clients with poorer verbal skills benefit more from therapy with hypothesis-driven assessment than those who are more verbal and who can benefit from self-discovery.

Epistemology

Another major difference between RET and traditional models of psychological assessment concerns the directiveness of the interviewer. Traditionally, assessment is thorough and comprehensive. Interviewers refrain from offering hypotheses about the client's behavior. After all the information is collected, the professional team sifts through the data looking for conclusions about the client. The assessment process in the mental health professions appears to follow the same epistemological model that psychology advocates for the process of science: logical positivism (Ayer, 1936; Cook and Campbell, 1979). Logical positivism in psychology has always placed a premium on inductive logic and reasoning. According to this model, scientists (or clinicians) collect as much data as possible and do so 'objectively' and dispassionately. They then search for patterns of results present in the data. Following this model, the therapist asks questions in all areas of clients' lives and functioning, including the social, family, medical, academic, and vocational arenas. A complete history is taken in each of the above-mentioned areas. A good interviewer avoids any premature conclusions until all the data are collected. If the therapist has any hypotheses, she or he does not share them with the client.

Rational-emotive theory has rejected the logical-positivist approach to epistemology (Ellis, 1989a; Woolfolk and Sass, 1989) and instead posits a constructivistic, hypotheticodeductive view of epistemology based on the philosophy of science (Hempel, 1966; Lakatos, 1970) and Bartley's (1984) comprehensive critical rationalism (DiGiuseppe, 1986a; Ellis, 1989a, 1989b; Ellis, Sichel, DiMattia, Yeager and DiGiuseppe, 1989). Rational-emotive theory holds that humans can not help but make up theories. One tests one's theories by logically deducing hypotheses from the theory and empirically testing them. Although this model of epistemology has been applied to clients' irrational beliefs and has lead to identifying disputing strategies, its implications for therapist behavior have not been fully explored.

The primary reason why the philosophy of logical positivism is inappropriate as a model for clinical assessment is that therapists cannot collect data in the manner suggested by this philosophy. Therapists (and people) cannot dispassionately collect data and wait for an inductive, logically accurate conclusion (Polanyi, 1958). I propose that all therapists formulate hypotheses concerning clients' diagnoses within minutes of the interview. Ask yourself how long it takes you to have a working hypothesis the next time you see a new client. A novice therapist may take longer, but before the session is over, they will still have some hypothesis.

So why does human hypothesis formation pose a problem to the inductive model of reasoning? The answer follows from the way human memory works. Humans (and therefore clinicians) tend to remember confirmatory information more than disconfirmatory information (Achenbach, 1985). Let us suppose two clinicians are interviewing a client together. During the interview, they develop different hypotheses concerning the client's diagnosis. They stick to the structured, inductive way of asking questions concerning all of the areas mentioned above. They share their different impressions after the interview. Because of human nature, each clinician will claim that he or she is correct and will recall information from the interview to support his or her hypothesis. The two could discuss their differences and reach a consensus. Based on this model, in most clinical instances there would have to be another interviewer present to remember information that supports a rival hypothesis.

Another problem involves the possible distorting of the process of induction through the interviewer's influence on the data gathering. Once a clinician has formulated a hypothesis concerning the diagnosis (or other aspects of the client's personality), she or he is more interested in hearing confirmatory than in hearing disconfirmatory information. The interviewer may be inclined to show more interest when the client speaks about topics that confirm her or his hypothesis. This differential interest on the part of the therapist may be expressed in his or her facial expression, tone of voice, or body posture. The therapist's actions may reinforce the client to talk more about some topics than about others. The fact that such nonverbal, innocuous reinforcers can affect the responses of the interviewee has been well documented in behavioral psychology and is referred to as the *Greenspoon effect* (Greenspoon, 1965).

Achenbach (1985) argued that there are a number of such cognitive distortions in clinicians' judgments. His solution to the problem is the use of objective, standardized, normed questionnaires to collect data. Although I concur with Achenbach, there is an alternative solution. The solution to the problems of clinician errors in judgment is to change the model of science on which the assessment strategies are based. Rather than rely on an inductively driven model based on logical positivism, clinicians can base their interviewing strategies on a constructivist, modern, hypotheticodeductive philosophy of science.

Historians of science (Kuhn, 1970) have argued that science has not progressed by induction. In fact, scientists are not dispassionate, objective data gatherers (Polanyi, 1958). Scientists formulate hypotheses or theories and then develop deductions from their theories that are testable empirically (Hempel, 1966; Lakatos, 1970). Philosophers of science such as Popper (1962) have argued the importance of deduction from theories of testable hypotheses that can be falsified. Popper's method is important precisely because humans are apt not to give up their constructed hypotheses and theories.

The resulting interviewing strategy includes the following elements: (1) assessment is viewed as an ongoing process, not as an activity for the initiation of treatment; (2) it is acknowledged that clinicians formulate hypotheses quickly in any interview; (3) questions are developed in the interview with the intent of testing the theory about the client that the clinician has formulated; (4) attempts to disconfirm hypotheses are given as much importance as or more importance than attempts to confirm them; and (5) after a hypothesis is rejected, the information gathered to disconfirm the hypothesis is used to formulate new hypotheses.

Hypothesis-driven Assessment

RET advocates training clinicians to develop hypotheses concerning their clients and to test them as quickly as possible. One must be careful not to confuse the two uses of the term *induction* and must discriminate between logical induction and psychological induction. The term *logical induction* refers to a form of testing the truth of a statement and involves drawing a conclusion of a general rule from observing all particular elements (Bachhuber, 1957). Psychological induction is a process of construing theories or hypotheses concerning things based on observations (Holland et al., 1989). The psychological induction used by a therapist (or a scientist) to develop a theory concerning a client does not imply that the theory or hypothesis generated by the therapist has been proved by the logical rules of induction. The therapist (or scientist) must develop ways to test the theory. I would argue that, because therapists develop theories about clients all the time, and because the traditional data-gathering strategies can foster the logical errors mentioned above, it is best for therapists to actively test their theories immediately. This can be done in several ways. First, they can deduce other facts that they would expect to be true if their theory is correct. Second, they can construct questions to ascertain if this hypothesis is correct. Third, the therapist can ask the client if the hypothesis is true. The client can provide a large amount of confirmatory or disconfirmatory evidence.

Consider this example. After listening to the client discuss the reasons for coming to therapy, a therapist learns that the client is fatigued, sleepless, and unmotivated and does not enjoy life. The therapist develops the theory that this client is depressed. The therapist can let the client go on reporting and search her reports for more evidence of depressive symptoms, or she can develop a set of questions that will help to rule in favor of or to disconfirm depression. The therapist thinks about what other symptoms accompany depression. She decides to ask the client if he has the cognitive triad associated with depression (Beck et al., 1979). The client responds affirmatively. The therapist may ask for more data: 'Do you feel extremely sad, or do you lack energy to complete activities?' The client responds yes. Now that the hypothesis is confirmed, the therapist's mind is still active. Based on the body posture and the way the client enters the room, the therapist wonders if the client's depression is biologically based. What would one expect if this were true? She recalls her knowledge of the difference between exogenous and endogenous depression. She then asks the client if there are any vegetative symptoms. He answers no. She is unsure yet what to conclude. If his depression is endogenous, it is less likely to be reactive to a particular event. So she asks, 'Was there anything that happened to you that preceded your depression?' The client responds affirmatively and reports that the depression started when his wife left him and that he had never been depressed before. The therapist surrenders her notion of endogenous depression and hypothesizes that the client's main irrational belief leading to the depression is a demand for love and approval.

In this brief example, the therapist quickly creates a theory about this client, refers to a knowledge base from which to deduce a series of questions that will help corroborate or disconfirm the theory, and develops questions based on this knowledge. The therapist also develops new ideas after each confirmation or disconfirmation of her hypothesis. This is an active-directive hypothesis-driven model of assessment. Therapists are constantly using their experience and knowledge to test and disconfirm hypotheses and, finally, to develop new hypotheses. Therapists avoid the errors of memory and leading the client.

Teaching Scientific Thinking

Hypothesis-driven assessment models scientific thinking for clients. RET teaches clients to think scientifically, that is, to evaluate their thoughts, and to test whether they are logically accurate and empirically consistent with reality. RET further emphasizes that one develops new ideas to replace ideas that have been proved to be false. This is exactly what the therapist is doing. Therapists demonstrate that they test their thoughts, give them up when data are wanting, and develop new thoughts in exchange.

Developing a Therapeutic Relationship

The hypothesis-driven assessment model is also helpful in establishing a therapeutic rapport. Once it is established, clients are more willing to reveal their true purpose for seeking help and to share more personal and possibly shameful information about themselves.

RET advocates that the best way to develop a therapeutic alliance (Ellis, 1985; Ellis and Dryden, 1987) is to attempt to solve the client's immediate problem. Usually, the therapist asks the client which problem he or she wishes to discuss. The therapist then interviews the client to identify the activating events, irrational beliefs, and emotional consequences in the problem identified by the client. The therapist does this for two or three sessions and then possibly suggests larger issues that the client may wish to work on. In this way, clients can reveal information at their own pace. They can see how the therapist uses the information they reveal, and they can develop a sense of trust and faith in the therapist's ability.

The client can see that the therapist not only is listening and empathizing with the client but is also actively thinking about the client and demonstrating his or her willingness to search for ways to understand and help the client. Offering hypotheses concerning the client's thoughts also demonstrates empathy. Not only does the therapist understand how the client feels, but the therapist also understands how the client is thinking. Cognitive therapy has always stressed the collaborative aspect of therapy and the importance of collaboration in building a therapeutic relationship (Beck et al., 1979). Asking the client directly for feedback on the accuracy of the clinician's hypotheses is the ultimate form of collaboration. The therapist's behavior demonstrates the importance of the client's cooperation in the process and the therapist's trust and respect for the client.

Limitations

Such a directive assessment strategy is not without its pitfalls, the most serious of which is narcissistic epistemology on the part of therapists. Therapist's hypotheses are what are normally referred to in psychotherapy as *interpretations*. Because interpretations result from the psychological induction of therapists, they can be wrong. Therapists have to be willing to accept that their brilliant hypotheses and interpretations may be false. If therapists continue to cling to false hypotheses, they not only pursue irrelevant lines of inquiry but may also impair the therapeutic relationship. A client's refusal to accept the interpretation of a therapist does not automatically mean that the client is resisting. The therapist may be wrong.

Testing hypotheses requires the feedback of the client. This can be honestly obtained only if the client perceives that the feedback is desired. To ensure that the client's participation will be forthcoming and to avoid the appearance (or reality) of closed-mindedness and authoritarianism by the therapist, it is recommended that hypotheses and interpretations be given in hypothetical language and not in declarative sentences: 'Could it be that you're feeling . . .?' or 'I have an idea I would like to share with you. Could you . . .?' or 'Other clients with your problem also seem to experience X. Could that be true of you?'

Assessing Irrational Beliefs

Assessing clients' irrational beliefs is the most important diagnostic task in rational-emotive therapy. Most therapists who come for training in RET usually attempt to discover the client's irrational beliefs by asking the client, 'What are you telling yourself?' This seems to be an appropriate strategy because irrational beliefs are cognitions, and cognitions are conscious. However, most clients respond to the questions concerning their conscious thoughts that precede or coexist with their disturbed emotions with inferences or automatic thoughts and not irrational beliefs.

A closer examination of rational-emotive theory suggests that irrational beliefs are not as transparent as many therapists initially think. Irrational beliefs are subconscious or tacit (Ellis, 1962, 1989a). By the term *subconscious*, Ellis does not imply the Freudian concept of *libidinal urges*. Ellis (1962) originally thought of irrational beliefs as preconscious. By that, he meant that they were outside the client's immediate consciousness but readily available to consciousness.

Beck (1976) and his colleagues (Beck and Emery, 1985; Beck et al., 1979) have a similar conceptualization. They refer to irrational beliefs as underlying schema or assumptions and also describe them as tacit cognitive constructs. They posit that the negative distortions are readily available in consciousness and therefore call them 'automatic thoughts'. These cognitions are what RET theory refers to as 'inferences' (DiGiuseppe, 1986a, 1986b, 1989; Huber and Baruth, 1989; Wessler and Wessler, 1980). It is most important that therapists learn to distinguish between automatic thoughts and inferences, on the one hand, and irrational beliefs, on the other. Below are six strategies for uncovering clients' irrational beliefs.

Inductive Awareness

The first strategy that therapists may use to uncover the core irrational beliefs I have labeled *inductive awareness*. In this strategy, the therapist asks clients what they are telling themselves when they feel upset. Therapists' queries concerning clients' thoughts, self-statements, or beliefs that precede or are linked to the clients' disturbed emotions frequently uncover clients' automatic thoughts or inferences, and not their irrational beliefs. The therapist then disputes the automatic thoughts. Each session proceeds in this way. Eventually, the client becomes aware that an underlying theme permeates all the beliefs that she or he and the therapist have been disputing. This underlying theme will be a schematic irrational belief. After the client has discovered this underlying irrational belief, the therapist switches the focus to disputing the irrational belief. This strategy appears to be the most common among people who have been exposed to RET and cognitive therapy by reading and workshop attendance, but who have had no formal training and supervision. RET would find nothing harmful in this strategy; however, it appears to be very inefficient. Therapists spend most of their time disputing inferences. Although this maneuver may be cognitive therapy, it is not RET (Ellis, Young and Lockwood, 1987). In fact, Dryden and DiGiuseppe (1990) identified the most common error of new rational-emotive therapists as disputing the first belief that clients report. This first belief represents the client's inferences, and therefore, in disputing the first belief, the therapist will not get to the underlying irrational beliefs.

Inductive Interpretation

A similar strategy involves the therapist's asking clients what they are thinking as they experience the disturbed emotion, thereby uncovering the inference, and subsequently disputing the inference. This strategy is followed for several sessions, perhaps five to ten. During these sessions, the therapist has to uncover numerous automatic thoughts or inferences that covary with the client's emotional disturbance. While examining these inferences, the therapist has been looking for a common theme among them. The therapist may collect more data before she or he is sure what the client's core schematic irrational belief is. Finally, the therapist shares with the client the underlying theme that appears to be a common thread throughout the automatic thoughts or inferences that the client has reported. If the client accepts the interpretation, the therapist starts challenging the validity of the core underlying theme.

This strategy is the one recommended by Beck and his colleagues (Beck and Emery, 1985). The decision to dispute automatic thoughts first, as a way to uncover core underlying irrational beliefs, versus immediately uncovering and disputing irrational beliefs appears to be the primary difference between general cognitive therapy and RET (DiGiuseppe and Linscott, 1990; Ellis, 1987). The inductive interpretation strategy also appears inefficient for several reasons. First, the therapist probably has a hypothesis concerning the client's core irrational belief long before he or she gives the interpretation. Holding the hypothesis in abeyance while collecting more data inductively allows the therapist to make some of the logical errors mentioned above. Second, the inductive interpretation strategy is inefficient because both Beck (1976) and Ellis (1987) believe that the automatic thoughts or inferences are caused by the underlying schematic irrational beliefs. So why not get to the core cognitions and challenge them as quickly as possible?

Inference Chaining

As it is common for clients to report automatic thoughts or inferences when asked what they are thinking, one can take the information that they give and use it to uncover the underlying core irrational beliefs. In inference chaining, the therapist socratically asks the client to assume that the inference is true. Then, the therapist follows with questions concerning what would happen if the first inference were true. This process is followed repeatedly until the client reports a different kind of thought, usually a schematic rule or core irrational belief. The therapists' questions might be the following: 'And if that were true, what else do you think would happen?' or 'Let us suppose X were true. What would that mean to you?' or 'If X were true, what would that mean about you?' In inference chaining, the therapist unravels layers of meaning that the client has connected to the automatic thought that first jumps into the client's consciousness.

Conjunctive Phrasing

Ellis has frequently been observed performing a variation of the inference chaining, which I have labeled *conjunctive phrasing*. In this strategy, Ellis asks his client what she or he was thinking when she or he got upset; the client is likely to respond with an inference. At this point, Ellis responds not with a question or a challenge, but with a conjunction or a conjunctive phrase. Some typical responses are 'and then . . .' or 'and that would mean . . .' or 'and if that were true . . .' or 'and that means I would be . . .'

The conjunctive phrase does not challenge or dispute the inference. It partially confirms its truth and is an invitation for clients to finish their thought. An advantage of this method is that it keeps clients focused on their thoughts. The less a therapist says, the less clients have to respond to the therapist's words or attend to whether the therapist has understood them. The conjunctive phrase focuses clients on the meaning of their statements. This strategy appears to be the most elegant and the most effective strategy for uncovering irrational beliefs.

Deductive Interpretation

Inference chaining and conjunctive phrasing both involve some degree of self-discovery on the part of the client. Even though the therapist guides the inquiry, the clients examine their own unconscious thought processes and are helped to uncover their core scheme or irrational belief. However, many times clients are unable to label their thoughts. As the therapist persists in asking open-ended or Socratic questions, clients feel frustrated by the long pauses and their inability to express their thoughts in words. Ellis almost always starts to assess clients' beliefs through inference chaining or conjunctive phrasing. It is best if clients can use self-discovery to become aware of their irrational beliefs. How long does a therapist pursue self-discovery and at what cost? How long does the therapist have to allow the client to explore and await self-discovery?

Usually, Ellis does not wait very long before he offers an interpretation, the interpretation being a hypothesis concerning what the client is thinking to cause his or her disturbance. Most clients respond to the early and frequent interpretation positively. They often comment that the therapist not only understands how they feel but also understands how they think. Although clients usually welcome therapists' hypotheses, they do not always accept them. If the therapist is off the mark, clients usually say this outright. More often, the hypothesis offered is close to, but not exactly, what the client is thinking. The interpretation may be close enough so that clients can put their thoughts into words themselves. On other occasions, therapists know that they are in the correct area and try to refine the hypothesis. This hypothesis testing frequently happens several times before the therapist and the client agree on the irrational belief that is underlying the client's emotional disturbance.

Disputing as Assessment

Once the client's irrational belief has been identified, the therapist usually moves on to disputing. However, clients' responses to the disputing questions may provide more information about the irrational beliefs that is at the core of their emotional disturbance. It is not uncommon for clients to respond to disputes of one irrational belief with another irrational belief to justify the first irrational belief. For example, a 38-year-old recently divorced man sought therapy for social anxiety about meeting women. He had identified his irrational belief as 'I can't stand being rejected by women.' After several attempts to dispute the client's LFT concerning female rejection, the therapist asked, 'Why do you think you could not stand being rejected by women?' The client responded that he could not stand rejection because that would mean (to him) that he was an unlovable person. If this were true, he certainly would be worthless. Although there is no logical connection between these two irrational beliefs, there was a psychological connection for this client. The fastest way to get to the most core irrational belief may be to dispute. Thus, the line between assessment and treatment is a fine line and may involve the same questioning.

This chapter has attempted to provide a model of assessment in rational-emotive therapy. I hope it clarifies some of the misconceptions about how RET is done. This model could be described as directive, hypothesis-driven, deductive and collaborative. It is my hypothesis that the general effectiveness and the short-term nature of RET result as much from this model of assessment as they do from the active disputing of irrational beliefs.

References

Achenbach, T. (1985) *The Assessment and Taxonomy of Child and Adolescent Psychopathology*. Newport Beach, CA: Sage.

Adams, J. (1972) The contribution of the psychological to psychiatric diagnosis, *Journal of Personality Assessment*, 36, 561–6.

American Psychiatric Association (1980) *Diagnostic and Statistical Manual of Mental Disorders* (3rd edn). Washington, DC: Raymond DiGiuseppe.

American Psychological Association (1985) Professional contributions to psychology as a profession – 1985: Albert Ellis.

Ayer, A.J. (1936) *Language, Truth and Logic*. New York: Dover.

Bachhuber, A. (1957) *Introduction to Logic*. New York: Appleton-Century-Crofts.

Barlow, D., Hayes, S. and Nelson, R. (1984) *The Scientist Practitioner*. New York: Pergamon Press.

Bartley, W.W., III. (1984) *The Retreat to Commitment* (2nd edn). New York: Knopf.

Beck, A. (1972) *Depression: Causes and Treatment*. Philadelphia: University of Pennsylvania Press.

Beck, A. (1976) *Cognitive Therapy and the Emotional Disorders*. New York: International Universities Press.

Beck, A. and Beck, R.W. (1972) Screening depressed patients in family practice: A rapid technique, *Postgraduate Medicine*, 52, 81–5.

Beck, A. and Emery, G. (1985) *Anxiety Disorders and Phobias: A Cognitive Perspective*. New York: Basic Books.

Beck, A., Rial, W.Y. and Rickels, K. (1974) Short Form of Depression Inventory: Cross validation, *Psychological Reports*, 34, 1184–6.

Beck, A., Rush, A., Shaw, B. and Emery, G. (1979) *Cognitive Therapy of Depression*. New York: Guilford Press.
Bernard, M. (1981) Private thought in rational-emotive therapy, *Cognitive Therapy and Research*, 5(2), 125–42.
Bernard, M. and DiGiuseppe, R. (eds) (1989) *Inside Rational-Emotive Therapy: A Critical Appraisal of the Theory and Therapy of Albert Ellis*. Orlando, FL: Academic Press.
Beutler, L. (1989) Differential treatment selection: The role of diagnosis in psychotherapy, *Psychotherapy*, 26(3), 271–81.
Beutler, L. and Crago, M. (1987) Strategies and techniques of psychotherapeutic intervention. In R.E. Hales and A.J. Frances (eds), *Annual Review of Psychology*. Vol. 6 (pp. 378–97).
Blatt, S.J. (1975) The validity of projective techniques and their research and clinical contribution, *Journal of Personality Assessment*, 39, 327–43.
Cook, T.D. and Campbell, D.T. (1979) *Quasi-experimentation Design and Analysis Issues for Field Settings*. Boston: Houghton Mifflin.
Cummings, N. (1986) The dismantling of our health care system, *American Psychologist*, 41, 426–31.
Daily, C.A. (1953) The practical utility of the clinical report, *Journal of Consulting Psychology*, 17, 297–302.
Daldrup, R.J., Beutler, L.E., Greenberg, L.S. and Engle, D. (1988) *Focused Expressive Psychotherapy: A Gestalt Therapy for Individuals with Constricted Affect*. New York: Guilford Press.
Diener, E., Emmons, R.A., Larsen, R.J. and Griffin, S. (1985) The satisfaction with life scale, *Journal of Personality Assessment*, 49, 71–5.
DiGiuseppe, R. (1986a) Cognitive therapy for childhood depression, *Psychotherapy and the Family*, 2(3/4), 153–72.
DiGiuseppe, R. (1986b) The implications of the philosophy of science for rational-emotive theory and therapy, *Psychotherapy*, 23(4), 634–9.
DiGiuseppe, R. (1989) Cognitive therapy with children. In A. Freeman, K. Simon, L. Beutler and H. Arkowitz (eds), *Comprehensive Handbook of Cognitive Therapy*. New York: Plenum Press.
DiGiuseppe, R. and Linscott, J. (1990) *Philosophical Differences Among Cognitive Behavioral Therapists: Belief in Rationalism, Constructivism, or Both?* Manuscript submitted for publication.
DiGiuseppe, R., Exner, T., Leaf, R. and Robin, M. (1988) The development of a measure of rational/irrational beliefs. Poster session presented at the World Congress on Behavior Therapy, Edinburgh, Scotland.
Dryden, W. and DiGiuseppe, R. (1990) *A Primer on Rational-Emotive Therapy*. Champaign, IL: Research Press.
DuPuy, H. (1984) A measure of psychological well-being. In N.K. Wenger, M.E. Mattson, C.D. Furberg and J. Elinson (eds), *Assessment of Quality of Life* (pp. 353–6). New York: Lecajq Publishing.
Ellis, A. (1957) Rational psychotherapy and individual psychology, *Journal of Individual Psychology*, 13, 38–44.
Ellis, A. (1962) *Reason and Emotion in Psychotherapy*. Secaucus, NJ: Lyle Stuart.
Ellis, A. (1973) *Humanistic Psychotherapy: The Rational-Emotive Approach*. New York: McGraw-Hill.
Ellis, A. (1985) *Overcoming Resistance: Rational-Emotive Therapy with Difficult Clients*. New York: Springer.
Ellis, A. (1987) A sadly neglected cognitive element in depression, *Cognitive Therapy and Research*, 11, 121–46.
Ellis, A. (1989a) Comments on my critics. In M.E. Bernard and R. DiGiuseppe (eds), *Inside Rational-Emotive Therapy: A Critical Appraisal of the Theory and Therapy of Albert Ellis* (pp. 199–233). New York: Academic Press.
Ellis, A. (1989b) *Is Rational-Emotive Therapy (RET) 'rationalist' or 'constructivist'?* Keynote

address to the World Congress of Cognitive Therapy, Oxford, England, June 29. Also in W. Dryden (ed.) (1990), *The Essential Albert Ellis*. New York: Springer.

Ellis, A. and Bernard, M.E. (eds) (1983) *Rational-Emotive Approaches to Children's Problems*. New York: Plenum Press.

Ellis, A. and Bernard, M.E. (eds) (1985) *Clinical Applications of Rational-Emotive Therapy*. New York: Plenum Press.

Ellis, A. and Dryden, W. (1987) *The Practice of Rational-Emotive Therapy*. New York: Springer.

Ellis, A., Young, J. and Lockwood, G. (1987) Cognitive therapy and rational-emotive therapy: A dialogue, *Journal of Cognitive Psychotherapy: An International Quarterly*, 1(4), 204–56.

Ellis, A., McInerney, J., DiGiuseppe, R. and Yeager, R. (1988) *Rational-Emotive Therapy with Alcoholics and Substance Abusers*. New York: Pergamon Press.

Ellis, A., Sichel, J., DiMattia, D., Yeager, R. and DiGiuseppe, R. (1989) *Rational-Emotive Couples Therapy*. New York: Pergamon Press.

Fodor, J. (1973) Some reflections on L.S. Vygotsky's thought and language, *Cognition*, 1, 83–95.

Freeman, A. (1986) Understanding personal, cultural and family schema in psychotherapy, *Journal of Psychotherapy and Family Therapy*, 2, 79–99.

Garfield, S.L. (1986) Research on client variables in psychotherapy. In S.L. Garfield and A. Bergin (eds), *Handbook of Psychotherapy and Behavior Change*. New York: Wiley.

Goldberg, D.P. (1972) *The Detection of Psychiatric Illness by Questionnaire: A Technique for the Identification and Assessment of Non-psychotic Psychiatric Illness*. Oxford: Oxford University Press.

Greenspoon, J. (1965) Learning theory contributions to psychotherapy, *Psychotherapy: Theory, Research and Practice*, 2(4), 145–50.

Hayes, S., Nelson, R. and Jarrett, R. (1987) The treatment utility of assessment: A functional approach to evaluating assessment quality, *American Psychologist*, 42, 963–74.

Hempel, C.G. (1966) *Philosophy of Natural Sciences*. Englewood Cliffs, NJ: Prentice-Hall.

Holland, J., Holyoak, K., Nisbett, R. and Thagard, P. (1989) *Induction: Processes of Inferences, Learning and Discovery*. Cambridge: MIT Press.

Huber, C. and Baruth, L. (1989) *Rational-Emotive Family Therapy*. New York: Springer.

Klerman, G.L., Weissman, M.M., Rounsville, B.J. and Chevron, E.S. (1984) *Interpersonal Psychotherapy of Depression*. New York: Basic Books.

Kuhn, T. (1970) *The Structure of Scientific Revolutions* (2nd edn). Chicago: University of Chicago Press.

Lakatos, I. (1970) Falsification and the methodology of scientific research programs. In I. Lakatos and A. Musgrave (eds), *Criticism and the Growth of Knowledge* (pp. 91–196). London: Cambridge University Press.

Luborsky, L. (1984) *Principles of Psychoanalytic Psychotherapy: A Manual for Supportive-expressive Treatment*. New York: Basic Books.

Meehl, P. (1960) The cognitive activity of the clinician, *American Psychologist*, 15, 19–27.

Millon, T. (1987) *Manual for the MCMI-II*. Minneapolis, MN: National Computer Systems.

Moore, G.H., Bobbitt, W.E. and Wildman, R.W. (1968) Psychiatric impressions of psychological reports, *Journal of Clinical Psychology*, 24, 373–6.

Nisbett, R.E. and Wilson, T.D. (1977) Telling more than we can know: Verbal reports on mental processes, *Psychological Review*, 84, 231–59.

Polanyi, M. (1958) *Personal Knowledge: Towards a Post-critical Philosophy*. Chicago: University of Chicago Press.

Popper, K.R. (1962) *Objective Knowledge*. London: Oxford.

Strupp, H.H. and Binder, J.L. (1984) *Psychotherapy in a New Key*. New York: Basic Books.

Tulving, E. (1972) Episodic and semantic memory. In E. Tulving and N. Donaldson (eds), *Organization of Memory*. New York: Academic Press.

Vygotsky, L.S. (1962) *Thought and Language*. Cambridge: MIT Press.

Walen, S., DiGiuseppe, R. and Wessler, R. (1980) *The Practitioner's Guide to Rational-Emotive Therapy*. New York: Oxford University Press.

Wessler, R.L. and Wessler, R.A. (1980) *The Principles and Practice of Rational-Emotive Therapy*. San Francisco: Jossey-Bass.
Wolpe, J. (1969) *The Practice of Behavior Therapy*. New York: Pergamon Press.
Woolfolk, R. and Sass, L. (1989) Philosophical foundations of rational-emotive therapy. In M.E. Bernard and R. DiGiuseppe (eds), *Inside Rational-Emotive Therapy: A Critical Evaluation of the Theory and Therapy of Albert Ellis*. Orlando, FL: Academic Press.

6

The Use of Chaining in Rational-Emotive Therapy

Windy Dryden

One of the drawbacks of the ABC[1] model of RET is that its simplicity obscures the fact that assessing and intervening in clients' problems can be quite difficult. For example, inferences are often chained together, inference and evaluative beliefs are connected in spiralling chains and these two types of cognitions interact with emotions and behaviours. In this chapter I shall outline and illustrate four types of chains that should preferably, when appropriate, become the focus for assessment and intervention during the course of RET.

Inference Chains

As noted above inferences are often chained together. The purpose of assessing these chains is to identify the major inference in clients' emotional episodes, that is, the one that triggers the irrational belief that creates their targeted emotional or behavioural problems at C. Moore (1983) advises that in inference chaining therapists initiate an enquiry based on 'then what?' and 'why?' questions in search of the client's most relevant inference. When clients report inferences,[2] 'then what?' questions are employed to uncover further inferences in the chain. However, when clients report emotional and/or behavioural consequences and these hold up research for relevant inferences, 'why' questions are used to help clients to continue their elaboration of inferential As. This process is exemplified in the following dialogue.

Client: So I get very scared when I think about going into the coffee bar.
Therapist: What do you think you are scared of?
Client: I'm scared of my hands shaking when I go to buy a cup of coffee.
Therapist: Because if it happens, then what?
Client: People will notice.
Therapist: And if they do notice, then what?
Client: Well, they'll bring it to each other's attention.
Therapist: And if they do, then what?
Client: I'd panic.
Therapist: Why? [The Client's previous response is treated as a C, hence the 'why?' question.]
Client: Because I'm sure I'd drop the cup.

Therapist: And if you do drop the cup, what then?
Client: They'd all start laughing.
Therapist: And if they did?
Client: Oh God! I couldn't stand that.

Inferences that trigger clients' irrational beliefs which, in turn, account for their targeted Cs are often expressed in close proximity to reports of these irrational beliefs (as in the above example). However, this does not always happen, in which case it is helpful to review the entire chain with clients and to ask them which inference in the chain is most relevant to the problem at hand.

It also happens that clients may report inferences that theoretically follow from 'then what?' questions, but which may not be implicated in their problems. Thus, the client in the above example might have reported the following inferences, in the chain after 'they'd start laughing'. 'I'd leave town and never come back' → 'I'd become a hermit'. To assess the relevance of such inferences to the client's problem, the therapist is advised to (1) review the entire chain with the client at the end of the sequence and (2) note the degree of affect expressed by the client when these inferences are reported. Clients often report theoretically possible, but clinically irrelevant, inferences with flat affect or halting puzzlement. Thus, it is important for therapists to realise that the most relevant inference is not necessarily the final inference in the chain, although it frequently is.

Finally, when clients find it difficult to respond to 'then what?' questions with further inferences, it is helpful to include some variant of the target emotion (C) as part of the assessment question. For example:

Client: People will notice.
Therapist: And if they do, then what?
Client: Er, I'm not sure.
Therapist: Well, what would be anxiety-provoking in your mind about them noticing?
Client: Oh. They'll bring it to each other's attention.

Inference-Evaluative Belief Chains

In inference chaining, as has been shown, the therapist assesses the way one inference leads to another. However, in reality, clients often hold implicit evaluative beliefs about each inference in the chain. These beliefs are bypassed in inference chaining, the purpose of which is to discover the most relevant inference in the chain, that is, the one that triggers the client's irrational belief which accounts for their targeted emotional or behavioural problem at C. However, there are occasions when it is important to assess these implicit evaluative beliefs. This is particularly so in the assessment and treatment of clients' problems where distorted inferences often stem from irrational beliefs (e.g., panic disorders). The principle that unrealistic inferences stem from irrational beliefs is an important but often neglected one in RET. As Ellis has noted:

> If you really stayed with desires and preferences, and virtually never escalated them into needs and necessities, you would relatively rarely make antiempirical statements to yourself and others. But just as soon as you make your desires into dire needs, such unrealistic statements almost invariably follow – and follow, frequently in great numbers. (1977: 9)

In inference-evaluative belief chaining, then, therapists are advised to assess both inferences and the irrational beliefs that are held about these inferences and which, in turn, produce further distorted inferences. This pattern is particularly observable in panic disorders. Clark (1986) has outlined a cognitive approach to panic that draws upon the work of Aaron Beck. In his model, Clark argues that people who are prone to panic attacks make increasingly catastrophic interpretations of their bodily sensations. However, he does not set out to distinguish between clients' interpretations (or inferences) and their irrational beliefs about these inferences, beliefs that are held at an implicit level. In the rational-emotive approach to panic disorders, these two types of cognitions are the targets for assessment and intervention. An example of inference-evaluative belief chaining is provided in Table 6.1 to illustrate this point.

Table 6.1 *An example of an inference-evaluative belief chain in panic disorder*

C	Feeling tense
Inference	I'm going to have trouble breathing
Irrational belief	I must be able to breathe more easily
Inference	I'm getting more anxious. I'm going to choke
Irrational belief	I must be able to control my breathing right now
Inference	I'm going to die
Irrational belief	I must not die in this fashion
C	Panic

While it is technically correct for RET therapists to dispute their clients' irrational beliefs about dying (see the end part of the chain in Table 6.1), the pragmatic purpose of this strategy, in such cases, is first to help clients to understand how their irrational beliefs which occur earlier in the chain actually produce their increasingly distorted inferences later in the chain and then to help them to dispute these evaluative beliefs. If this can be done in the session while the client is tense and beginning to experience the first signs of panic, then this can be a particularly powerful intervention.

At present, the relationship between distorted inferences and irrational beliefs awaits empirical enquiry and remains a fruitful area for future research in RET.

'Disturbance about Disturbance' Chains

One of the unique features of RET is the emphasis that it places on clients' tendencies to make themselves disturbed about their disturbances. This may involve exacerbation of a particular disorder (e.g., anxiety about anxiety; depression about depression) or it may involve several emotional and/or behavioural disorders within a single episode (e.g., guilt about anger; anxiety about procrastination). A typical sequence is illustrated in Table 6.2.

Table 6.2 *An example of a 'disturbance about disturbance' chain*

A	Sam treated me unfairly
B	He must not treat me unfairly
C	Anger
A	Anger
B	I must not get angry
C	Guilt
A	Guilt
B	There I go again experiencing needless guilt. I must not do this, I'm worthless
C	Depression

It is often quite difficult for novice RET therapists to select the most appropriate part of the 'disturbance about disturbance' chain to target for intervention with clients. My own practice is to keep three points in mind when making such treatment decisions. In general, I suggest that therapists work on the part of the chain that the clients want to start with and encourage their clients to do this for themselves outside the session. There are two exceptions to this general rule. The first occurs when clients actually experience in the session another inappropriate negative emotion that is part of the chain. In this case, I suggest that therapists offer their clients a plausible rationale for switching to that part of the chain (e.g., 'It seems as if right now you are experiencing guilt about your feelings of anger. Let's first work on this until you can give your full attention to working on your anger').

A second exception to the general rule occurs when clients experience outside the therapy session an inappropriate negative emotion that is also part of the chain (e.g., depression) as they attempt to work on overcoming the target emotion (e.g., guilt). In this case, I suggest that therapists encourage their clients to switch to the depression part of the chain, in the example given above, and give a plausible rationale for this (e.g., 'How can you work on your guilt when you are beating yourself over the head for feeling guilty?').

Complex Chains

Clients sometimes present problems that involve a number of cognitive, emotive and behavioural components linked together in a complex chain. I have found it quite helpful to assess such chains carefully in order to help clients (1) understand the process nature of their problems and (2) identify useful points in the chain at which they can intervene to prevent the build-up of these problems. In such cases, it is usually beneficial to encourage clients to intervene at or near the beginning of these complex chains for the following reason. Towards the end of the chain these clients are so overwhelmed by the intensity of their disturbed feelings or so caught up in their self-defeating behaviours that it is unrealistic for their therapist to anticipate that they will successfully initiate a disputing intervention. To illustrate these points, I present in Table 6.3 one example of a complex chain. This arose out of my work with a female client who sought help for what she described as 'uncontrolled binge-eating'.

Table 6.3 *An example of a complex chain*

A	Working on Master's thesis and experiencing difficulty with 'simple' statistics
B	I must be able to understand this. I'm a real idiot because I can't
C	Anger at self
A	Anger at self experienced as tension
B	I can't stand this tension
C	Anxious pacing around the room
A	Heightened anxiety
B	I've got to get rid of this feeling
C	Goes to the refrigerator and begins to eat a snack
A	Eating a snack
B	Oh God! What am I doing? I shouldn't be doing this
C	Guilt and increased eating (to try to get rid of the bad feeling)
A	Increased eating
B	What a pig I am. I must not binge again
C	Self-loathing and binge-eating

Two points are worth noting with reference to this example. First, when the client had reached the end of this complex chain, she reported that it is as if she is in an altered state of consciousness. While it is theoretically possible for her to intervene at this point and dispute her irrational belief that led her to feelings of self-loathing and binge-eating, in practice she found this enormously difficult. Thus, for pragmatic reasons, she needed to be helped to make a disputing intervention at a much earlier part of the chain. Second, the entire episode which has been detailed in Table 6.3 happened very quickly. The client barely noticed her tension before she headed towards the refrigerator, that is, she was not aware of her feelings of self-anger or of discomfort anxiety. Consequently, I helped her in the therapy session to review the entire process as if it were happening in slow motion. As a result she began to identify these implicitly felt emotions and associated irrational beliefs and began to see that psychological events (e.g., anger at self for not understanding 'simple' material) served as triggers for her subsequent irrational beliefs and more intense self-defeating emotions and behaviours.

She then began to anticipate these early signs and learned to dispute the related irrational beliefs that occurred at the beginning of the chain. She became very adept at doing this and virtually eliminated her binge-eating that was previously associated with such episodes. We could then deal with her irrational beliefs that occurred later in the chain. If I had started at the end of the chain I doubt whether she would have achieved as good a therapeutic outcome as she did in this case.

Outlining complex chains is particularly helpful then when clients are barely aware of disturbed emotions and self-defeating behaviours that occur at the start of the chain and when this non-awareness leads to more intense negative and self-defeating experiences later in the chain.

Therefore, as described above, chaining is a sophisticated skill and, when used sensitively, highlights the complexity that lies behind the simple ABC formulation of clients' problems.

Notes

1 In this chapter, 'A' refers to activating events and to inferences (i.e., interpretations that go beyond available data) about these events. 'B' is therefore reserved for evaluative beliefs.

2 It should be noted that 'Cs' can be treated as inferences and, when they are, 'then what?' questions are again employed to further the inference-based enquiry.

References

Clark, D.M. (1986) A cognitive approach to panic, *Behaviour Research and Therapy*, 24, 461–70.

Ellis, A. (1977) The basic clinical theory of rational-emotive therapy. In: A. Ellis and R. Grieger (eds), *Handbook of Rational-Emotive Therapy*, Vol. 1. New York: Springer.

Moore, R. H. (1983) Inference as 'A' in RET, *British Journal of Cognitive Psychotherapy*, 1(2), 17–23.

7
Thinking What to Feel

Raymond DiGiuseppe

In the present cognitive therapy zeitgeist, the cognitions seen as most important in determining emotional disturbance by theorists are inferences and evaluations about the self or external world (Beck, 1976; Ellis, 1979). Emotions are usually relegated to the role of dependent variables by cognitive therapists. Feelings are considered the result of cognitions and usually receive little other attention. This chapter will focus on the emotional aspects of cognitive therapies and will suggest the hypothesis that emotions are often the content of the cognitions that lead to excessive disturbed affect.

People have beliefs about the type and degree of emotions they are *supposed* to feel. People also have beliefs about which emotions are helpful or hurtful to themselves or to others. These cognitions, which I shall call *affective expectancies*, have received little attention in the cognitive therapy literature and as a result no systematic research has been carried out on the topic.

Ellis (1979) has frequently said that emotions, thoughts and behaviours are really interdependent processes. This view was recently restated by Schwartz (1982). However, the artificial division between these processes has persisted in the cognitive therapy literature. Thoughts and feelings are seen as being separate elements. However, they are experienced simultaneously. We do not have feelings as independent elements on a flow chart that come after thoughts. Feelings generate new thoughts that in turn maintain, intensify or change feelings. We evaluate those feelings and decide whether or not we like them and care to experience them again.

The evaluations we have about our emotions do not only arise from the sensory experiences with which emotions provide us. Cultural, familial and idiosyncratic attitudes exist which may influence evaluations of affect more than the sensory pain or pleasure they bring. Emotion which is disturbed and which may appear obviously unpleasant to therapists may be ambivalently or positively evaluated by clients. If either of these is the case, clients will not necessarily want to change that emotion. Disputing or challenging the irrational thoughts that elicit emotion is futile until clients recognize the advantages of changing the emotion. The following hypotheses will guide the remainder of this chapter:

1 Disputing irrational beliefs or automatic thoughts will be ineffective if the client maintains positive evaluations about his or her pathological emotion and is not committed to emotional change.
2 All clients have evaluative cognitions about their disturbed emotional experiences. Depressed clients have thoughts about their depression. They may like it, admire it, hate themselves for having it, or become resigned to it.
3 The evaluations clients have about their emotions are multiple and sometimes inconsistent.
4 Clients will also have expectancies of which emotions people in their situation are *supposed* to have. These expectancies will be based on implicit theories of behavior that the client holds, which are derived from cultural expectations.
5 Clients who cling to affective states which they label as negative may do so simply because they have difficulty construing alternative, more functional emotions.
6 Clients will not feel an emotion which they cannot conceptualize as an acceptable response to a situation.

Commitment to Emotional Change

The core element in cognitive therapies is challenging, disputing and changing dysfunctional or irrational thoughts. Disputing rests on three prerequisite assumptions: (1) the affective state being experienced is unpleasant, dysfunctional and a change is desired; (2) there is an alternative for the undesirable affect; and (3) thoughts mainly determine feelings. Clients who fail to share these assumptions are poorly motivated to change.

Rather than assume that clients have the three assumptions mentioned above, I suggest that therapists actively explore these areas and explicitly define the emotions to be changed and the alternatives to replace them.

The notion that beliefs mainly determine feelings is commonly taught to clients by cognitive therapists; assumptions 1 and 2 have received little formal attention in the cognitive therapy literature. Clinical experience suggests that clients' thoughts about their emotions or the alternatives available form the basis of many therapeutic failures. Clients will not be committed to changing their thinking unless they are committed to changing their feelings. A brief case vignette may help illustrate this point.

Joe, a 10-year-old boy, was referred because of his angry outbursts. During one session he reported being punished by his parents because he hit his brother. Since we were working on anger control we decided to analyse this situation. In previous sessions I explained to Joe how thoughts determine feelings and how he could change his feelings by disputing his irrational beliefs. Joe was angry at his brother for breaking his bicycle and independently identified his irrational beliefs. 'My brother should not have broken my bike; I can't stand not having my bike.' He was unresponsive to my challenge of his irrational beliefs, and responded: 'What's the matter with you, you want me to be happy about it?'

Joe knew that by disputing his irrational beliefs I was trying to change his anger. But if he were no longer to feel angry he saw only one alternative – to be happy, and that seemed 'crazy' to him. Joe's anger was maintained by his irrational beliefs but given that he perceived only one unacceptable alternative, Joe was not prepared to be unangry. To Joe, anger was the only *appropriate* emotion. Until Joe's thoughts about his anger could be changed, and a viable alternative emotion considered, disputing made no sense.

Disturbed yet Desired Emotions

Many cognitive therapists who present cases in supervision are at a loss when they confront clients who do not wish to change their disturbed emotions. Their first move is usually to keep disputing. When that does not work, they frequently attempt to shift to another theory. But it is not necessary to forgo the cognitive model when one meets such resistance. Ellis (1983) has outlined many cognitive explanations of resistance. One possibility is that clients might resist disputing because they still believe that the emotion, which causes them so much trouble, is actually desirable in some way. An alternative therapeutic strategy is to discuss with clients their rationale for believing that while the emotion in question is painful, it is beneficial in some way.

Some clients claim that the painful emotions they experience are desirable because they motivate or cue them to behave in a certain way. These clients may hold a false, unverified hypothesis, that their disturbed emotions are necessary to maintain desired behaviors. For example, clients may believe that they must feel guilty in order not to commit some moral or social transgression or that they must feel frightened of failure in order to assure achievement. Such anti-empirical beliefs may have developed from faulty learning, cultural messages or family experiences. Once the rationale is discovered, the stage is set to challenge. Therapists can proceed as they would in disputing any anti-empirical statement which is dysfunctional to clients. The discussion could focus on gathering empirical evidence for clients' hypotheses that disturbed emotions have provided the motivation for functional behavior. Reviewing the consequences of clients' behaviors when they experience disturbed emotions will usually bring up much disconfirming evidence. Clients can be shown models of others who behave in the desired manner but who do not experience the disturbed emotion in question. This will help clients believe that less disturbed emotions can lead to desired adaptive behavior. Clients who give up the ideas which maintain the emotion will be much more willing to dispute the irrational ideas that generate the emotion. Another brief case study may exemplify this point.

Mr X was seen in family therapy with his wife and 15-year-old daughter. The daughter was very distant toward her father. Mr X, however, claimed to love his daughter very much. He was the family disciplinarian. Whenever he played that role, he shouted in a deep loud voice at his children. His daughter interpreted his shouting as proof of his lack of affection for her. Mr X had trained himself to become angry at his children for minor transgressions. He readily admitted that his daughter should be perfect, should not answer back, should study hard, and never come home late. Initial attempts to dispute the irrational 'should' that elicited his anger were fruitless (Ellis, 1977). During these discussions Mr X seemed most uncomfortable. At one point he asked the therapist why it was so important that he give up his anger and his demandingness. Wasn't it good for his daughter to know that he was angry? Mr X was firmly committed to the belief that anger was necessary to convince his children that he disapproved of a transgression. If he were not angry they would think he approved of their actions and they would not change their behavior. Once this hypothesis was discovered, discussed and changed, Mr X could give himself permission to learn to control his anger. This allowed us to move on to disputing the irrational belief that his daughter must be perfect.

Negative Evaluations of Emotions

In the ABCs of RET, Cs often become As. As noted above, emotions are not experienced in a vacuum. They often become the source of new cognitions. Humans will almost always evaluate how they feel. This has been noted by Ellis (1978) and by Walen et al. (1980), who labelled it symptom stress. Depressed patients can become depressed over their present, past or future depression (Burns, 1980). Many anxious patients become afraid of their anxiety. In fact, this is believed to be a major element in the case of panic attacks and agoraphobia (Stampler, 1982; see Figure 7.1).

Ellis (personal communication) has suggested that clinicians should preferably change the symptom stress, or the emotion about the emotion first. The rationale for this is as follows. If clients experience additional depression (d2) whenever they become depressed (d1) about specific events, they will be distracted by the catastrophizing thoughts that lead to d2 whenever they discuss or dispute the thoughts leading to d1. The first goal of

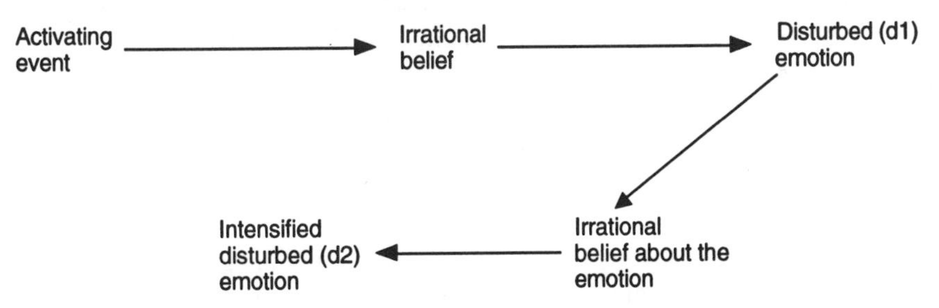

Figure 7.1 *Schematic diagram of symptom stress*

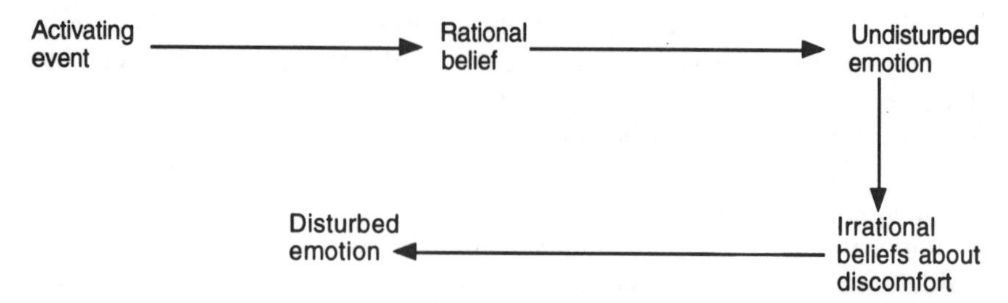

Figure 7.2 *Schematic diagram of normal emotion leading to discomfort anxiety*

treatment is to stop clients from exaggerating the pain of depression by helping them to evaluate it as unpleasant but bearable. Ironically, after one accepts one's emotional upset, one may be more likely to dispute and change the irrational belief that underpins it.

Many but not all clients will hold irrational beliefs about their disturbed emotional states. Rather than wait to have such cognitions interfere with therapy, therapists are advised to ask their clients how they feel about their feelings. Some typical questions might be: 'What do you think about what you feel?', or 'What are you thinking about yourself – for feeling it?' Some clients may even assume that their disturbed emotion is a sign of impending madness, phrenophobia (Walen, 1982).

In disputing the irrational beliefs that determine symptom stress, therapists try to convince clients that the symptom itself is not awful. Phrenophobia and concerns of prolonged incapacity can be alleviated by providing clients with information about the physiology and psychology of the emotion in question. For example, clients experiencing anxiety over divorce will be reassured to know their symptoms need not be the first step to schizophrenia. Clients with reactive depression to true losses will be relieved to find out that their emotional experience is common to individuals with similar activating events.

In addition to symptom stress, an attitude of low frustration tolerance concerning a normal emotional reaction may precipitate a truly pathological response (see Figure 7.2). Some clients believe that any kind of unpleasant emotion is 'too much'. Normal apprehension, disappointment, or grieving could become severe disturbance if clients hold beliefs such as:

- My life should be painless.
- Unpleasant emotions are unbearable.
- I don't deserve this.

These are all examples of what Ellis (1978) terms discomfort anxiety. It is important to teach clients that everyone experiences negative emotions as part of life. The elimination of these emotions is neither possible nor desirable.

Alternative Feelings

Emotional goals are just as important in therapy as behavioral goals. Knowing that one's present disturbed emotion is disadvantageous is one step toward change. The second, equally important step, is choosing an alternative. If a therapist and client have different emotional goals for the client, therapy is thwarted. Consensus concerning the emotional goals of therapy will be difficult to reach if the client has a limited conceptualization of what he/she could feel instead of the emotional pain that prompted the person to seek treatment. It is common knowledge that Ellis (1979) tries to change clients' thinking from believing that activating events are 'terrible' to believing that they are 'unfortunate.' In so doing, clients will no longer experience 'anxiety' but will feel 'concern.' How many clients can conceive of this emotional state when they start treatment? And if they do not understand the concept and experience of 'concern,' how can they work to feel an emotion they neither conceptualize nor understand? Clients may not know what to experience when they no longer feel depressed. The options are joy, neutrality, or some negative but not disturbed emotion.

Clients who have just experienced the loss of a valued lover may choose joy or neutrality as the goal of therapy to replace the pain of depression. In order to experience joy, they may change their irrational belief to 'I am much better off without that partner.' In order to experience neutrality they may replace the irrational belief with the idea 'It makes no difference that my partner has gone.' Both the joy and neutrality-producing thoughts seem rational, and in some instances may be true. But, if the loss is real, these ideas are mere rationalizations. Such thoughts will most readily be falsified by the person's experiences; and the irrational beliefs are likely to return with the depression. The rational belief which would be recommended by Ellis (1962) is that the event is disadvantageous, bad and painful, but bearable. This idea would be inconsistent with the goals of joy or neutrality. As a result, irrational beliefs would neither be sought nor maintained.

The goal which may be most difficult to conceptualize is a negative but less intense, non-disturbed emotion, for example, sadness, regret, concern, etc. Rational-emotive therapists strive to help clients experience such emotions in response to negative life events.

Clients will not fully participate in change-producing strategies if they do not conceptualize the alternatives or do not understand why their therapists believe that this is a desirable goal. My belief is that many clients do not conceptualize the emotional goals of RET.

Spivack et al. (1976) have presented a different view of cognitive therapy which they call Interpersonal Cognitive Problem Solving Skills (ICPS). Their main thesis is that pathology develops due to a deficit in cognitions which help solve social problems. Two of their ICPS skills are 'alternative solution thinking' (the ability to conceive alternative behavioral responses) and 'consequential thinking' (the ability to evaluate the effectiveness of those behavioral responses).

It is possible that similar skills exist for thinking of alternative emotional reactions to problem situations. I have postulated that such is the case with children (DiGiuseppe, 1981; DiGiuseppe and Bernard, 1983). My clinical experience suggests that adult clients also fail to conceptualize different emotional reactions and they cling to their disturbed emotions because they do not conceptualize an appropriate alternative.

There may be a number of reasons why people fail to conceptualize what to feel. First, they may have poor problem-solving ability for social problems in general. Second, the English language may help by failing to have specific words denoting meaning for variations in emotion. Americans, in particular, seem to use words for emotions with no regard for intensity. It would be interesting to see if other languages have more precision in their description of emotions. Third, clients may have had poor role models for the display of emotion in their families, that is, they may be hard pressed to imagine being annoyed rather than angry at a particular activating event because they have only observed people who have responded with anger. Finally, sex role stereotypes might contribute to what emotions people think they should feel, or what emotions they definitely should not feel in order to be manly or feminine.

Hochschild (1979), a sociologist, has pointed out that culture plays a large role in defining what emotions one can feel and how and when one should express a feeling. It may be most helpful for cognitive therapy to explore how such cultural norms are transmitted and whether pathological populations have failed to receive or incorporate the cultural norms on what to feel.

References

Beck, A. (1976) *Cognitive Therapy and the Emotional Disorders*. New York: International Universities Press.

Burns, D.D. (1980) *Feeling Good: The New Mood Therapy*. New York: Morrow.

DiGiuseppe, R. (1981) Cognitive therapy with children. In G. Emery, S. Hollon and R. Bedcrosian (eds), *New Directions in Cognitive Therapy*. New York: Guilford Press.

DiGiuseppe, R. and Bernard, M. (1983) Special considerations in working with children. In A. Ellis and M. Bernard (eds), *Rational-Emotive Approaches to Problems of Childhood*. New York: Plenum.

Ellis, A. (1962) *Reason and Emotion in Psychotherapy*. Secaucus, NJ: Citadel Press.

Ellis, A. (1977) *How to Live With and Without Anger*. New York: Reader's Digest Press.

Ellis, A. (1978) Discomfort anxiety: a new cognitive behavioral construct. Invited address to the Association for Advancement of Behavior Therapy Annual Meeting.

Ellis, A. (1979) Rational-emotive therapy. In R. Corsini (ed.), *Current Psychotherapies* (2nd edn). Itasca, IL: Peacock.

Ellis, A. (1983) Rational-emotive therapy (RET) approaches to overcoming resistance. 1: Common forms of resistance, *British Journal of Cognitive Psychotherapy*, 1(1), 28–38.

Hochschild, A. (1979) Emotive work, feeling rules, and social structure, *American Journal of Sociology*, 85, 551–75.

Schwartz, R. (1982) Cognitive-behavior modification: a conceptual review, *Clinical Psychology Review*, 2(3), 267–94.

Spivack, G., Platt, J. and Shure, M. (1976) *The Problem-solving Approach to Adjustment*. San Francisco: Jossey-Bass.

Stampler, F. (1982) Panic disorder: Description, conceptualization and implications for treatment, *Clinical Psychology Review*, 2(4), 469–86.

Walen, S. (1982) Phrenophobia, *Cognitive Therapy and Research*, 6, 399–408.

Walen, S., DiGiuseppe, R. and Wessler, R.L. (1980) *The Practitioner's Guide to Rational-Emotive Therapy*. New York: Oxford University Press.

PART 2
INTERVENTION

8
Comprehensive Cognitive Disputing in RET

Raymond DiGiuseppe

Disputing irrational beliefs has always been at the heart of RET. However, my 13 years' experience in teaching therapists to do RET has revealed that disputing is the art of the science and the hardest thing about RET to teach. Most new therapists learn how to identify the activating event, the emotional consequences, and then the irrational belief. Once the client reveals his or her irrational belief, the therapist asks, 'Where's the evidence?' The client looks confused and says, 'I guess there is none.' And the therapist assumes that the client has 'got it' and responds, 'What other problem would you like to discuss?' As therapists develop more experience, they spend more time disputing. They somehow develop a guide to all of the possible disputes that are available to use with a specific type of problem or a specific irrational belief.

Experienced RET therapists spend most of their time in therapy disputing clients' irrational beliefs. New therapists always appear perplexed by this fact and are not sure how one can spend so much time disputing. This confusion appears explainable if one examines the RET literature. Until now, most RET texts, (e.g., Bard, 1980; Ellis and Dryden, 1987; Grieger and Boyd, 1980; Maultsby, 1984; Walen et al., 1980; Wessler and Wessler, 1980) have attempted to teach disputing by providing specific disputational arguments that can be used to challenge specific irrational beliefs. Although such writings have been helpful, they do not provide a blueprint for the *process* of disputing, which allows therapists to generate new disputes.

This chapter attempts to expand and specify the possible disputing strategies that can be used in RET. First, I present an expanded model of an emotional episode, discuss the difference between what has been referred to as *philosophical* and *elegant disputing* versus *empirical* and *inelegant disputing*, and then focus on expanding the strategies that therapists can use in challenging and reconstructing clients' thoughts. The disputes are organized by four factors, each factor having two or more levels. The model allows therapists to move across levels of a factor and across factors. The factors are (1) the nature of the evidence – logical, empirical, heuristic, and so on; (2) the rhetorical style of the argument – didactic, Socratic, metaphorical, and so on; (3) the level of abstraction of the argument; and (4) the centrality of the client's irrational belief (i.e., disputing both the core and the derivative irrational beliefs).

An Expanded Model

Originally, Ellis (1958, 1962) presented his well-known ABC model. Wessler and Wessler (1980) expanded the original version. In their model, the B consists of two elements: inferences, which are statements, predictions, and conclusions about the world; and evaluations, which are the appraisals and meanings that people apply to the world. DiGiuseppe (1986) further revised the model to include an even finer distinction between different aspects of the B. According to this model, when clients encounter an activating event they produce inferences about the world; then, they evaluate the inferences that they have made. However, the evaluations and inferences that clients create are readily generated because of their core underlying personal paradigms or schemata. Irrational beliefs are of two types: evaluations of events or inferences, and core paradigms or schemata through which the client construes the world. Thus, the new model divides the beliefs into three components: inferences, evaluations, or appraisals, and core paradigm irrational beliefs.

DiGiuseppe (1986) theorized that irrational beliefs do not lead to disturbed emotions in a linear model; rather, he suggested that human beings think in a hypothetically deductive fashion. The inferences or automatic thoughts that one experiences are limited to those that are consistent with the underlying schema or worldview that one has. Kuhn (1970) argued that people draw only the inferences that they are prepared to make from their paradigm. Similarly, the evaluations one makes are logically derived from the same schema or worldview: the core irrational beliefs.

Disputing in RET is the process of challenging the truth of a client's beliefs and reconstructing new beliefs. Disputing follows a complicated, involved set of arguments that follow from the epistemological position taken in rational-emotive theory by Ellis. Most forms of cognitive-behavior therapy do not specify their epistemological assumptions. Beck's cognitive therapy (Beck and Emery, 1985; Beck et al., 1979) appears to rest on an empiricist or logical-positivist view of epistemology that posits that knowledge is accumulated by logical induction from empirically demonstrable facts. Most of the cognitive distortions that Beck and his colleagues believe lead to disturbed emotion are false inductions made from inadequate data. The approach in cognitive therapy of empirically testing automatic thoughts seems to this author to be a logical outgrowth of an unstated but implied epistemological position in favor of radical empiricism.

RET, however, is much clearer about its epistemological assumptions than cognitive therapy or most other forms of psychotherapy (Woolfolk and Sass, 1989). Ellis (1989a, 1989b; Ellis, Sichel, DiMattia, Yeager and DiGiuseppe, 1989) has put forth the notion that all humans think in a constructivist, hypotheticodeductive manner. People cannot help but create theories of the world, of their interpersonal relationships, and of themselves. These theories, schemata or paradigms may guide the person to cope adequately with the environment or may lead to poor coping and psychopathology.

Ellis has theorized that people think in a constructivist, hypotheticodeductive way and has posited that RET is based on a similar model of epistemology. Ellis (1962, 1973, 1985, 1989a, 1989b) has stated that RET is based on the scientific outlook and that disputing helps the client to think scientifically. However, he has not specified how such an assumption influences the disputing of clients' irrational beliefs. DiGiuseppe (1986) suggested that RET formally adopt a model of disputing that is based on a similar epistemological view. I propose here that Kuhn's model (1970) of scientific paradigms and his historical account of the types of evidence that lead scientists to forsake theories are helpful guides to disputing in psychotherapy to help clients relinquish their personal theories.

Kuhn's model suggests that scientists work from theories or paradigms that are broad schemata. A paradigm not only explains important variables but organizes one's view of the world, suggests which data one is prepared to select, suggests which inferences one is prepared to draw from the data, and suggests how various inferences will be evaluated. Kuhn indicated that scientists do not give up their paradigms easily. They do so only when either one or all of the following types of arguments are presented: (1) when there are considerable empirical data to suggest that the inferences that are deduced from the paradigm are false; (2) when there is considerable logical inconsistency within the paradigm; (3) when the paradigm lacks heuristic value, in that it fails to solve important problems; and finally, (4) when there is an alternative paradigm that is better at accounting for empirical findings and solving problems than the existing paradigm.

DiGiuseppe (1986) proposed that Kuhn's model (1970, 1977) of scientific thinking is generally accurate about human thinking and that the Kuhnian model of scientific epistemology can be considered a model of human epistemology.

The adoption of Kuhn's philosophy of science as a model of cognitive functioning has several advantages. First, it suggests that some specific relationships exist between different types of cognitive structures. For example, core schemata determine automatic thoughts and the type of evidence the person notices to support them. Second, we can look at the types of arguments and evidence that help humans change their thinking. Most of the criteria that Kuhn outlined as criteria that scientists use to evaluate theories correspond to the definitions of rational beliefs. Both Ellis (1962) and Maultsby (1975) have defined beliefs as irrational if they are (1) illogical, (2) inconsistent with empirical reality, and (3) inconsistent with reaching one's goal (not functional or heuristic).

The Target of the Dispute

The most frequent error made by new rational-emotive therapists is disputing the inference instead of the irrational beliefs (Dryden and DiGiuseppe, 1990). This happens for two reasons. First, most other forms of cognitive therapy specifically recommend that therapy begin in this manner (Beck et al., 1979). Second, clients often respond to therapists' inquiries about what they are thinking with inferences. Beck (1976), in fact, referred to inferences as automatic thoughts because they are quick to emerge into human consciousness. RET (Ellis, 1962, 1973, 1989a, 1989b; Ellis and Dryden, 1987; Walen et al., 1980) has always recommended that disputing of the inferences be a secondary goal. Disputing inferences has been referred to in RET jargon as *empirical* or *inelegant disputing*, whereas disputing the irrational beliefs has been referred to as *philosophical* or *elegant disputing*.

My supervisory experience over the years has suggested that the appellation *empirical disputing* for disputing the inferences has confused trainees. The term *empirical disputing* uses a description of a type of argument to refer to the object or target of the dispute. This is confusing because, as I point out below, one can and often does use empirical arguments directed at the irrational beliefs. Trainees and critics of RET are justifiably confused when they observe an empirical argument directed at an irrational belief and hear it referred to by Ellis as elegant and philosophical when Ellis at the same time refers to empirical arguments as inelegant. That confusion can be avoided if rational-emotive theory develops a consistent and organized way of categorizing the disputes used in therapy. Disputes can be labeled first by the target at which they are directed and, second, by the type of argument used in the dispute. Therefore, disputes leveled at the inferences or automatic thoughts of a client should be referred to as *inferential disputes*.

Disputes targeted at the irrational beliefs or underlying schemata of the client should be referred to as *philosophical disputes* to communicate that they are leveled at the client's core underlying philosophy.

Inferences themselves can be challenged on both logical or empirical grounds. Beck (1976) provided an extensive list of the types of cognitive distortions that usually account for the erroneous nature of inferences or automatic thoughts. If one studies this list it becomes evident that most of the cognitive distortion processes that Beck mentioned are errors of induction. A negative inference such as 'Because my spouse did not kiss me when I came home, my spouse does not love me' may be an error of false induction. Here, the client may be making an overgeneralized conclusion on insufficient data. Erroneous inferences can be challenged in a variety of ways. First, one can dispute the inference logically. Here, the therapist points out to the client that there are insufficient data to draw the conclusion she or he has reached. Second, one can search for more empirical data that will bear on testing the inference that the client reports she or he is thinking. The therapist could ask the client to search her or his memory for other examples of information relevant to the inference in question. Or the therapist can ask the client to collect specific data between sessions that can be a basis for testing the inference.

The point to be stressed here is that empirical disputing is a process or type of argument, not a target of an argument. Irrational beliefs or core schemata can also be disputed empirically, philosophically, or in other ways that are discussed below. Both inferences-automatic thoughts and irrational beliefs-core schemata can be disputed with the same types of arguments. Separating the target and the process of the dispute by the way we refer to them will make RET clearer and facilitate learning for new therapists and for clients.

The Nature of the Dispute

As I have suggested above, disputing can follow the model of paradigm change outlined by Kuhn (1970, 1977) in his philosophy and history of science. Kuhn suggested that scientists (and I would add people in general) change for several reasons: first, there are logical inconsistencies in the theory; second, substantial empirical evidence is accumulated that is inconsistent with the theory; third, the theory can not solve important problems and loses its practical or heuristic value; and finally, there is an alternative theory that is better. Since 1988, the fellows at the Institute for Rational-Emotive Therapy and I have been listening to Ellis's therapy tapes in an attempt to devise a content-analysis scoring system to determine what he actually does. Our informal impressions suggest that the disputing processes that Ellis uses correspond to the categories of evidence proposed by Kuhn.

General Considerations

Disputing strategy puts the responsibility on clients to prove that what they are thinking is correct. Often, there is no actual evidence for the irrational belief (that is why the beliefs are irrational). If left to dwell on this fact, clients may begin to become uncomfortable with their inability to defend what they are thinking. When clients cannot answer and hence feel uncomfortable, novice therapists usually rescue them from their discomfort and provide answers. This is fine. Clients may be motivated to think through the problem if they are uncomfortable about it. However, it may be more convincing for the client to continue to struggle to search for a proof and fail to find one.

Personal Epistemologies

Disputing clients' irrational beliefs involves teaching the client for the first time that humans usually have reasons for believing what they think. All people have some implicit epistemology for holding beliefs. The call for evidence helps clients become aware of what their personal epistemology may be. If the client does provide some sort of a rationale for the particular irrational belief, it is best for the therapist to take this rationale seriously, to attempt to evaluate its adequacy with the client, and if it is incorrect, to point out why.

As clients attempt to answer, the therapist's disputing questions may reveal the clients' implicit epistemology. That is the criterion the clients use to decide what to believe. We have noticed that clients may hold certain epistemologies that make it unlikely that they will cooperate or benefit from disputing because their epistemology is different from the scientific view inherent in RET.

Some examples of personal epistemologies are the following. First, *authoritarian epistemology*. Some clients believe that knowledge comes from a higher source, either spiritually or socially. A family member (i.e., a parent or a spouse) or a social or religious institution is believed to be the oracle of truth.

Second, *narcissistic epistemology*. Some clients believe that things are true just because they thought of them. That is, they take an extreme constructivist position and believe that whatever pops into their head must be true. This view may be held because the clients arrogantly believe that they are so smart that they must be correct, or because they have never evaluated why they believe things.

Third, *constructivist epistemology*. Some clients believe, like many constructivist social scientists (Mahoney, 1976, 1988; Polyani, 1966), that all views of reality are equally valid and that they are therefore entitled to believe what they think because it is right for them, even though the therapist has demonstrated that it is illogical.

Whenever clients hold any of these epistemological positions, it is advisable first to dispute the validity of the epistemology and convince them of the advantage of advocating a scientific epistemology before attempting to restructure any of their specific irrational beliefs.

Logical Disputing

The first criterion of rational thinking is that it is logical, and irrational beliefs usually do not meet this criterion. Clients can be shown that their beliefs are unsound on logical grounds. Logical arguments may focus on whether the irrational belief logically follows from the reasoning that the client uses to defend it. For example, when most clients are asked, 'Why must the world be the way you say it must be?' they proceed to explain that it would be more desirable for them if the world were the way they wanted it to be. Ellis's classic dispute points out that something's being more desirable does not logically lead to the non sequitur conclusion that the world must be constructed in a desirable way. Desirability and reality have no logical relation to each other. Other disputes may focus on the logical inconsistency of different aspects of a client's belief system. For example, a client who condemns himself or herself for not accomplishing a specific goal or aspiration may be asked if he or she would condemn others for either failing to reach that goal or failing to reach some other goal important to the person. Clients often respond 'no' to such a question. 'How,' one can ask, 'is it logical to condemn one person for a failing and not another?' The logical inconsistency of clients' evaluations can be repeatedly stressed.

Reality Testing of Irrational Beliefs

Irrational beliefs can also be challenged on empirical grounds. As noted above, therapists often miss this point because 'empirical disputing' in the RET literature has referred to disputing the inference. But one of the criteria of rational beliefs has always been that they are consistent with empirical reality. If a client's personal paradigm is correct, logical deductions from the paradigm will be consistent with reality. Just as scientists empirically test hypotheses that are logically deduced from their scientific paradigms, so, too, therapists can test the veracity of clients' personal paradigms by making deductions from the clients' paradigms and testing them against empirical reality. These are empirical disputes aimed at clients' irrational philosophies.

For example, suppose a client is angry at his spouse because he believes that she must love him and in fact she no longer does. The client's anger is generated by the irrational belief, 'She must love me.' The therapist could dispute this belief by pointing out to the client that, if his belief is correct his wife would in fact behave lovingly toward him. Then, the therapist and the client can review the evidence regarding her present or recent behavior. Failure to find loving behaviors by the wife toward the client disconfirms the prediction deduced from the irrational belief. Most demanding beliefs can be shown to be inconsistent with reality. No matter how strongly the client believes that the world 'must' be the way he or she wants it to be, the universe usually does not change to match the 'must.'

Our content analysis of Ellis's tapes indicates that he often uses this argument. He asks clients what reality is and then points out that it is not consistent with their 'must.' They have avoided noticing the reality and instead have clung to their demands.

Empirical disputes can also be constructed against the other three irrational belief processes. For example, clients who endorse low-frustration-tolerance beliefs can be shown that, even though they think that they can not stand the occurrence of an activating event, they have, in fact, stood it over and over again. Also, catastrophizing beliefs can be challenged with the argument that the activating agent did not result in a totally, 100 percent bad outcome. Self-downing beliefs can be challenged empirically by pointing out that an assessment of a person as totally worthless is almost always incorrect because all people do some things well and have some worth to some other people, even though that worth may be based on values that are very different from one's own.

Heuristic Disputing

The next criterion of rational beliefs is that the belief should help one attain one's goals. Scientists have always evaluated theories and beliefs on their heuristic or functional value. That is, does a particular idea help solve major important problems? Does it assist in accomplishing desired goals? Such functional disputes have long been advocated in RET (Walen et al., 1980). Clients can be asked to evaluate the consequences of holding their irrational beliefs. What are the emotions that the irrational beliefs elicit? What good do these emotions do? If the feelings are undesirable or troublesome, why would one want to hold a belief that makes her or him feel miserable? What are the behaviors that usually follow the irrational thoughts? Do these behaviors bring good or bad consequences? Do these behaviors help clients reach their long-term goals?

It is possible that heuristic disputes are the most influential, as they are the most closely linked to the behavioral notion of reinforcement. Heuristic disputes may help clients conceptualize or become aware of the actual reinforcement of holding irrational beliefs.

Constructing Rational Beliefs

Challenging irrational beliefs is not sufficient to change them. People frequently hold on to beliefs that they know are logically flawed and do not lead to accurate predictions of reality, but no alternative ideas are available to replace the flawed idea. The history of science is filled with such examples. People do not give up ideas, regardless of the evidence against the idea, unless they have an alternative idea to replace it.

Many forms of psychotherapy are based on consciousness raising alone (Prochaska and DiClemente, 1984). Consciousness-raising models of therapy assume that, once clients become aware of what their problem is or why they behave the way they do, their human potential for self-actualization will lead to their choosing an adaptive way of responding. In psychoanalysis, one becomes aware of the early conflicts that have led to one's development, and once this insight is conscious, the person will choose more adaptive behavior. In client-centered therapy, the therapist unconditionally accepts the client, so that the client becomes aware of and surrenders her or his conditions of worth. Again, once this is accomplished, it is assumed that the self-actualization drive will lead the individual to adjustment. Also, with Gestalt therapy, the therapist's role is to confront clients so that they become aware of their suppressed feeling and the 'phony' roles that they are playing. Again, consciousness raising is assumed to be sufficient for change, and it is assumed that the insight into one's emotions will free one to choose an adaptive life.

RET does not state that insight is sufficient for change. It is not sufficient to have the insight that one has irrational beliefs that are causing one's emotional disturbance, nor is it sufficient to have the insight that a particular irrational belief is irrational. Unless clients have new ideas to replace their old irrational beliefs, they are likely to cling to their irrational beliefs even though they are aware that the ideas are incorrect. Several lines of research support the importance of restructuring alternative rational beliefs. Wein et al. (1975) compared two forms of cognitive restructuring. In one treatment condition, clients were made aware of the reasons why their thinking was irrational, and in a second treatment condition, clients were taught alternative ideas. The second group improved significantly over the first. Also, DiGiuseppe et al. (1988) constructed a scale of both irrational and rational ideas. They found that although the irrational belief subscale significantly distinguished between disturbed clients and normal college students, the disturbed and normal groups differed more on the rational belief subscales than they did on the irrational belief scores. The authors concluded that, although disturbed groups do appear to endorse irrational beliefs, they are much less likely to endorse rational beliefs. This finding suggests that clients will not get better by just reducing their endorsement of irrational beliefs; they must also increase their endorsement of rational beliefs.

Even when clients become aware of the disputing arguments, which RET predicts will take both insight and lots of practice, clients have to learn new adaptive styles of thinking. For example, people are not always quick to come up with a self-accepting philosophy once they realize that their self-worth beliefs are irrational. Our content analysis of Ellis's therapy tapes indicates that he frequently suggests to clients that their irrational beliefs are wrong and that the rational alternative is better. New therapists frequently forget this part and dispute without emphasizing the new rational belief.

Rhetorical Disputing Styles of Therapists

Clients are not convinced only by the nature of the evidence against their irrational beliefs. Their beliefs are influenced by more than logic. The manner of presentation of the arguments is as important as the dispute itself. Ellis (1985, 1989a) has frequently argued that clients change when he disputes forcefully and vigorously. We have identified four different rhetorical styles that therapists can use in disputing irrational beliefs. They are didactic, Socratic, metaphorical and humorous.

Didactic and Socratic Styles

By far the most noticeable rhetorical strategy is the didactic dispute. When therapists observe Ellis performing one of his frequent demonstrations of RET, they notice that he teaches his client the difference between irrational and rational beliefs in a direct, didactic manner. RET has always been presented by Ellis (1962, 1973, 1985, 1989a, 1989b) as a psychoeducational intervention. As a result, the RET therapist frequently does a lot of direct education about the therapy, its theory, where emotions come from, and the reason why specific beliefs are irrational.

In addition to the direct, didactic presentation of material, RET therapists frequently use the Socratic method of questioning to help clients learn to dispute their irrational beliefs themselves. The term *Socratic questioning* comes from the Socratic Dialogues written by Plato of the conversations of the Greek philosopher Socrates. Socrates believed that people are more intelligent than they get credit for. He thought that the best way to teach people is to try to draw information out of them through a series of directive questions. In one of the most famous of the Socratic dialogues, the philosopher teaches a slave boy a geometric principle by asking questions.

Socratic disputing is probably the mainstay of interventions among most RET therapists. The therapist asks clients questions to get them to see for themselves that there is no evidence for their irrational beliefs. Some Socratic disputes are 'How does it follow logically that your spouse must love you because you really strongly desire her to?' or 'Can you tell me how it has helped you to think that your spouse must love you?' or 'Is there any evidence that your spouse behaves lovingly to you when you demand that she must?' These are examples of the logical, heuristic and empirical disputes using the Socratic style.

Didactic and Socratic interventions are the major strategies that RET therapists use in verbal disputing of clients' irrational beliefs. Some therapists prefer one over the other, but I suggest that each has its limitations and strengths in certain contexts.

Didactic disputing is probably essential to some degree for all clients in the initial sessions of therapy or when the therapy focuses on new problems. However, remaining in a didactic rhetorical mode can be inefficient. Although didactic interventions teach clients the arguments against their irrational beliefs and what the new rational beliefs are, didactic strategies do not involve the client in the actual *practice* of the disputes themselves. A therapist who relies too much on didactic intervention is doing all the work. The client is coasting. Once clients have learned some of the information from didactic interventions, they can put their skills to work by Socratic disputing and practice on their own.

Many therapists prefer Socratic disputing almost exclusively. They believe that knowledge is better acquired through self-discovery. The idea that learning occurs best through self-discovery has been a popular notion in American educational thought. It was probably best promulgated by the educational philosopher John Dewey and was strongly advocated by many progressive educators in the 1960s. Many therapists seem to take the preference for self-discovery learning to an extreme and believe that self-discovery is necessary for learning. Most forms of psychotherapy and counseling (except for behavior therapy) appear to share this view. It is frequently stated in the therapy and counseling literature that interpretations should not be given until clients have almost reached the same conclusion by themselves (Cormier and Cormier, 1985). Rational therapists do believe that Socratic dialogue is helpful and may even be preferable. But it is not the only way people learn.

Some clients of limited intelligence, limited creativity, or extreme emotional disturbance may not come up with an appropriate answer to a Socratic question. Letting them suffer because they have not thought of the solutions to their problems seems unnecessary or even unethical. It is recommended that therapists try Socratic questioning early in the session. However, if a client does not seem to be able to answer the questions after 5–10 minutes, the therapist can revert to the didactic style.

Another problem frequently encountered in therapy supervision is responding too quickly to clients' inability to answer Socratic questions. Socratic questioning requires clients to *think* about their answers, and Socratic disputing requires clients to defend their irrational beliefs. Because clients may never have thought through the issue in question and because their irrational beliefs may be indefensible, they may take some time to respond with an answer. Therapists frequently become impatient with the silences that occur while the client is thinking. Silences in social conversations are awkward events, and people often try to fill such pauses. Therapists are no different. They start talking to fill the pause and to rescue the client from the discomfort of this awkward social situation. This would be a mistake in therapy, as it interrupts the client's thought processes and disrupts the purpose of the Socratic question. There are several reasons that it may be better to let the pauses remain. First, clients often have nonlogical psychological reasons for holding irrational beliefs. For example, a client may believe that his wife must love him. When asked for the evidence for why she must love him, he responds that he needs a significant other in his life because he believes that he cannot stand to be alone. This is a psychological and not a logical reason for holding the irrational belief. Filling the pauses that occur in response to Socratic questions does not allow clients to search for, formulate, or explore the psychological reasons that support their irrational beliefs. In this way, Socratic disputing becomes a primary assessment strategy for uncovering clients' irrational beliefs.

If the client has already discovered his or her core irrational beliefs, it is also good to let the pauses remain. In that case, the client may be searching for the logical reasons for holding his or her irrational beliefs. And because the beliefs are irrational, there often is no good reason to hold the belief. This is not immediately apparent to the client, and he or she does not know that there is no evidence to support the core irrational belief. The experience of searching for the support and not being able to find it leads to some discomfort. This discomfort helps create cognitive dissonance with the irrational belief. It is wise to let the client feel the discomfort. Thirty seconds or so of silence in a therapy session may seem like an eternity, but it may be time well spent.

Clients often respond to Socratic disputes with illogical reasons for maintaining their core dysfunctional ideas. It is important for the therapist to know what the client is thinking so that these illogical reasons can be addressed. Finally, clients may be unable to answer Socratic disputes. They may feel discomfort about being unable to do so. However, they may not conclude that the reason they have failed to formulate an answer is that there is none. The therapist may have to interpret the client's failure to muster any evidence to support the irrational belief as stemming from the lack of support for the irrational belief.

Both didactic and Socratic interventions are used over the course of therapy and over the course of a session. As a general rule, didactic strategies are used more in the beginning of therapy and when the focus is switched to a new problem. Socratic questioning is used more as therapy progresses and as the therapist prepares clients to function more independently and to dispute on their own.

Metaphorical Disputing

RET has always advocated the use of metaphorical disputing strategies that work to shift clients' thinking (Walen et al., 1980). Metaphors and parables are part of the RET therapeutic armamentary. Metaphor use is extremely popular in psychotherapy and many therapists report using metaphors in therapy. Although metaphors are popular among therapists, there appears to be no well-developed theory or explanation of how metaphors operate in bringing about change. Most of the literature on metaphor use in psychotherapy has been generated from the work of Milton Erickson (see review by Muran and DiGiuseppe, 1990). Several problems emerge in following the metaphorical strategies recommended by the Ericksonian camp. The first problem is the assumption that the therapist need not (and had better not) communicate the meaning of the metaphor to the client. Muran and DiGiuseppe argue that this practice comes from a long theoretical history in psychotherapy dating back to Freud and Jung. Both of these seminal thinkers in psychotherapy believed that symbols had shared meaning among humans. This view, the foundation of Freud's theory, was based on a Lamarckian view of genetics and appears to be unfounded (Gould, 1988).

The contemporary theory that reflects the shared-meaning hypothesis is the work of Milton Erickson. The Ericksonian use of metaphor is subtle. The therapist does not teach the client how to use the metaphor, does not explain the metaphor, and assumes that the client understands the metaphor unconsciously.

DiGiuseppe and Muran (1992; Muran and DiGiuseppe, 1990) proposed that none of the hypotheses assumed in the Ericksonian use of metaphor are valid. They proposed that metaphor is a standard yet powerful form of language. One function of metaphor in psychotherapy is memory consolidation. Clients may not remember all of the things that go into the disputing process. Such information would include all the reasons why the irrational belief is erroneous, the new rational belief, the reasons why the rational belief is more correct, and the instructions that help to rehearse the disputing. When all this information is new and fresh and more difficult to recall, the metaphor may well function as an organizer. When the metaphor is recalled, all of the information consolidated around it is more accessible to memory.

DiGiuseppe and Muran (1992) provided guidelines for using metaphors in cognitive psychotherapies. The first step is for the therapist to clearly identify the idea they wish to communicate to the client. Next, the therapist explores a topic that the client is familiar with (e.g., art, literature, film, or sports). Then, the therapist searches for a concept in the content of the schema system that is analogous to the concept that the therapist wishes to teach. This analogous concept serves as the metaphor. The therapist then presents the metaphor to the client. Because it can not be assumed that the client will automatically (or inherently) see the analogous content in the metaphor, the therapist didactically or Socratically explores the client's understanding of the metaphor. Finally, the therapist asks clients how they can use the metaphor to help them dispute their irrational beliefs. Clients can be instructed to recall the metaphor when they experience emotional disturbances, and the metaphor can remind them to dispute.

Humor

Another rhetorical style of disputing is the use of humor. Ellis (1977) has long advocated the use of humor, and he usually considers it an emotive intervention (Ellis, 1985). A full theoretical discussion on the mechanism whereby humor leads to attitude change is beyond the scope of this chapter. Humor has long been ignored as both a psychotherapeutic intervention and a strategy of persuasion. At the Institute of Rational-Emotive Therapy, we try to teach all therapists to use humor. If the supervisors are bored listening to a therapy session, we assume that the client may be bored as well. In order to use humor effectively, there are only a few rules that the therapist can follow. Never make fun of a client; joke only about the client's behavior or thoughts. Ellis frequently isolates the thought that he is disputing before the humorous comment. He does this by careful use of pronouns to ensure that the target of the joke will always be clear and that no one could infer that the target is the client.

Level of Abstraction

Irrational beliefs can be stated in varying levels of abstraction. For example, if Ralph is angry at his spouse over her not behaving as he thinks she 'should,' several irrational beliefs can be identified as leading to his anger: (1) 'My wife must make dinner when I want her to make it'; (2) 'My wife must do chores the way I want her to do them'; (3) 'My wife must do things the way I want her to do them'; (4) 'Family members must do things the way

I want them to do them'; (5) 'People in my life must do things the way I want them to do them'; (6) 'All people must behave the way I want them to behave'; and (7) 'The world must be the way I want it to be.' These beliefs vary across a dimension of abstraction and generalizability. Fewer activating events would lead to emotional disturbance if the client believed only irrational belief Number 1. Successively, more activating events would be capable of activating emotional upset as the abstraction of the beliefs increases. The same also holds for rational beliefs: the more abstract the rational belief, the more activating events it can be associated with, and the more elegant and useful belief will be in helping the client to avoid emotional disturbance. The less abstract a belief is, the more it applies in a concrete, specific situation, and the more it resembles a self-statement than an unspoken philosophy.

Clients may be more likely to identify the concrete versions of the irrational beliefs in their therapy sessions. If we ask Ralph, 'What were you thinking the last time you got angry at your wife?' he is most likely to have thought the concrete version (1). Therefore, the concrete irrational belief will be the one that he most clearly experiences, is more ready to admit he is thinking, and is more motivated to change.

When therapists hypothesize clients' irrational beliefs or when they use didactic disputing strategies, they usually suggest abstract beliefs such as Number 5 or Number 6, rather than concrete irrational beliefs like Number 1. Again, the most abstract dispute is seen as the most elegant and the most likely to generalize to the widest number of stimuli.

Ellis (1962, 1973, 1985, 1989a, 1989b) has always credited general semantic theory and the work of Korzybski (1933) as providing some of the philosophical foundations for RET. Korzybski and other general semantic theorists have postulated the notion of the ladder of abstraction. They have posited that almost all words can be placed on a continuum of abstraction. As one goes up the ladder of abstraction, words express more general, abstract meaning and provide less information about specific cases. For example, we could refer to a specific client as Ralph, as a certain macho personality type, as a male humaniodae, as a primate, a mammal, or a vertebrate. Each step up the ladder of abstraction includes more cases under it, yet provides less information about Ralph. The general semanticists argue that communications are more clearly understood if the speaker goes up and down the ladder of abstraction. Communications that stay at only one level of abstraction are unclear. A communication including words only at the concrete level provides lots of specific information. However, listeners may fail to transfer the learning of new situations because they may not have grasped the abstract principle. Communications including only words at the top abstract level of the ladder may be able to express the abstract rule, but clients may fail to learn to apply the rule to specific situations, or they may never have seen (or heard) a specific application of the rule and may therefore misconstrue it.

The solution to this problem is to ensure that communications designed to teach or change attitudes include both concrete and varying levels of abstractions. Specifically, the therapist should move up and down the ladder of abstraction during the dialogue.

A question that needs more theoretical and research attention in RET is the relationship between the irrational beliefs held at one level of abstraction and those endorsed at another. Could a client lightly believe a concrete belief and more strongly hold an abstract one? I would think not. Holding an abstract irrational belief cannot lead to emotional upset unless the client holds the specific irrational belief associated with an activating event.

In supervision, we frequently hear therapists who provide elegant disputations of the most abstract version of the client's irrational belief, but the client does not appear to comprehend the point. The therapist has failed to present a concrete example that the client understands. Another problem can emerge if the therapist disputes only at the abstract level. Clients may verbally report that they comprehend the disputation but there is no resulting change in their emotion or behavior. These clients have not *applied* the change in their abstract belief to the particular irrational belief that they think when faced with the most provocative and/or frequent activating event. Other therapists dispute only the specific, concrete, irrational belief that the client presents when confronted with the activating event. Although clients may respond to treatment and not get upset when the same activating event occurs again, they become just as upset when a new troublesome activating event emerges on the horizon.

When disputing Ralph's irrational belief, it is recommended that therapists start disputing at the most concrete level with 'My wife must make dinner when I want her to.' By starting here, Ralph is likely to get some control over his emotions in the situation that offers the most problems. This strategy will provide some reinforcement for disputing and for continuing in therapy. Next, the therapist may want to teach Ralph that he tends to be demanding about other things as well and that the world does not have to be the way he wants it to be. By moving up and down the ladder of abstraction, the therapist ensures that Ralph will learn to deal with specific activating events, that he will be able to apply the RET solution to other similar events, and that he will understand the rule behind the reasoning and will be able to apply it to future aversive stimuli.

Multiple Irrational Belief Processes

Ellis (1958, 1962) originally identified 11 common irrational beliefs that he observed in his clients' thinking. Most research and writing in RET tended to center on these 11 irrational beliefs as the core of the theory and the therapy. Critics of RET (see Ellis and Whitely, 1979) thought that the 11 irrational beliefs were too content-specific. They argued that RET was overconcerned with the content of what clients thought. Beck (1976) in particular thought that the content of clients' dysfunctional beliefs is idiosyncratic in each case. He and other cognitive therapists thought it more helpful to focus on the process of clients' thinking. As rational-emotive theory has progressed, there has been more focus on such irrational thinking processes. Walen et al. (1980) categorized the 11 irrational beliefs into five process categories: demandingness, need statements, human worth statements, awfulizing, and low frustration tolerance. Later, Campbell and his associates (Burgess, 1990; Campbell, 1985) collapsed demandingness and need statements and proposed that all irrational beliefs fall within a four-by-three grid with four process variables (demandingness, human worth, awfulizing, and low frustration tolerance) and three content levels (approval, achievement, and comfort).

Ellis (1985, 1989a, 1989b) has gone on to hypothesize that demandingness is the core irrational belief that is responsible for human emotional disturbance. The newest version of rational-emotive theory posits that demandingness is always present in cases of emotional disturbance. Irrational beliefs concerning awfulizing, human worth, and low frustration tolerance are psychologically or logically deduced from holding a core demanding belief (Ellis, 1985, 1989a, 1989b). At issue is the number of irrational belief processes that the client may endorse around one content area.

Ralph could have any of four concrete irrational beliefs when he gets himself emotionally disturbed: 'My wife must make dinner when I want her to do it'; 'My wife is a worthless person when she does not make dinner when I want her to do it'; 'It is awful if my wife does not make my dinner when I want her to do it'; or 'I cannot stand it when my wife does not make dinner when I want her to do it.' If Ralph endorses one of these irrational beliefs, what is the likelihood that he will endorse them all? More important, if Ralph does endorse one or more of them, does his changing one automatically lead to change in the others?

Therapists in RET training often naively believe that clients have only one irrational belief. After all, it is an ABC model. Therefore, they forget to dispute all the irrational beliefs that clients think while they are getting upset. If a therapist fails to dispute the 'must' or demandingness belief and disputes only the derivative irrational belief that the client reports, the theory states that the client may remain upset and may deduce more beliefs from the core 'must'.

Our research experience suggests that, although therapists trained in RET may quickly and reliably differentiate between the four irrational belief processes, clients may experience them as similar (DiGiuseppe et al., 1989). When DiGiuseppe et al. (1989) created items for a new irrational belief scale, they wanted a separate subscale for each of the four irrational belief processes. Definitions were written for each of the four processes, and items were written to match the definitions. An item was used only if 13 psychologists, either staff or fellows at the Institute for Rational-Emotive Therapy, agreed that the item matched the definition. Although the resulting subscale yielded adequate internal consistency, clients who completed the inventory complained that the items were redundant; that is, they experienced the items as having the same meaning. A factor analysis of the scale did yield a very strong major general factor. Several other studies have found similar results. DiGiuseppe and Leaf (1991) found one general factor in Burgess's irrational belief scale (1986), and Demaria et al. (1989) found a large general factor in another measure of irrational beliefs (Kassinove, 1986). One could take this factor analysis literature to suggest that the four irrational belief processes are psychologically, if not logically, related. It seems that endorsing an item containing one of the irrational thought processes is related to endorsing items for all four processes.

We do not yet know whether disputing or changing thoughts about one irrational thought process will logically or psychologically cause change in the other irrational processes. There is always the possibility that the beliefs, once established, have functional autonomy. Allport (1955) suggested that personality constructs may persist well after the factors that created them cease. Traits take on a life of their own, so to speak, and continue even though the reasons for their emergence are no longer present.

The practical implications of the multiple irrational belief processes were spelled out by Dryden and DiGiuseppe (1990). They pointed out that, if Ellis's model is correct, clients usually have more than one irrational belief associated with an activating event for each emotional episode, that is, a core demandingness belief and one or more derivative irrational thoughts. Therapists cannot assume generalization across belief processes. If we successfully dispute Ralph's demandingness about his wife's behavior, there is no reason to assume that he has changed his low frustration tolerance beliefs about his wife's behavior. Dryden and DiGiuseppe argued that it is best to dispute all of the irrational thoughts that a client endorses. Therefore, the therapist would dispute the core 'must' and any other derivative irrational beliefs that have been assessed. In this way, they argued, generalization of change from disputing one irrational belief process to another is not assumed but planned for.

Although Ellis's new theory that demandingness is the core irrational belief remains to be confirmed, the advice by Dryden and DiGiuseppe (1990) remains sound whether Ellis's hierarchy is confirmed or not. Regardless of which irrational belief is found to be core, or of whether each client has his or her own core and derivative beliefs, it remains important to dispute all the irrational belief process that the client endorses. The factor-analytic data mentioned above strongly suggest that if a client holds to one irrational belief process, she or he will hold to another.

Comprehensive Cognitive Disputing in RET

The model presented above describes four factors in disputing strategies: the nature of the dispute, with four levels; the rhetorical style, with four levels; the level of abstraction, with at least two levels but probably more;

and the number of irrational processes that the client endorses with up to four levels. That gives at least 128 disputing statements that one can make to a client. Clearly, there is no reason for aspiring RET therapists not to have enough to say when the time comes to dispute!

It is recommended that, whenever possible, a therapist go through as many disputing strategies as possible. Kuhn (1977) suggested that scientists change their paradigms only when there is considerable challenge of their theory. If we are correct in believing that good scientific thinking results in mental health, should we not expect that clients will require just as much disputing of their paradigms before they surrender them? If people change their paradigms or belief systems only when considerable evidence has accumulated to show that the paradigms are not working, disputing only one factor or only one level of disputing may not be sufficient to move a person to change. Each of us may be susceptible to persuasion through different types of challenging strategies. Until we have a theory of personality or cognitive style that can predict which type of argument will be most influential with a particular client, it may be best to go systematically through the matrix of disputing strategies provided here to get clients to change.

Therapists can use the model systematically, starting in one cell of the matrix and working their way through as many cells of the model as possible. Having such a model in mind may remind new therapists to create disputes in cells that they have not covered yet. Experienced therapists can use the model to remind them to cover all disputes. Although this may sound like a mechanical recommendation for doing therapy, it is likely to force therapists to use all of the disputing strategies until they are familiar with them. It will ensure that considerable evidence will be mustered against clients' irrational belief systems and will ensure that clients will learn different rational beliefs to replace the irrational ones.

For an example, let us return to the client Ralph and show how the model can be applied. Once we are ready to dispute his irrational thinking, we would start with the concrete, core irrational belief: 'My wife must make dinner when I want her to do it.' We could also start with Socratic disputing. So what follows are Socratic, concrete, core disputes varying along the dimension of the nature of the evidence:

1 *Logical*: 'How does it follow, Ralph, that just because you want your wife to make dinner at a certain time, or that it would be more convenient for you if she made dinner at a certain time, she must behave in the way that would be to your liking?'
2 *Empirical*: 'It seems that you have told your wife when you want her to have dinner ready and you keep believing that she must do it when you want her to, but do we have any evidence that she has had to or has actually done what it is you demand of her?'
3 *Heuristic*: 'How has your marriage, or your home life, or your life in general benefited from believing that your wife must make dinner when you want her to?'

4 *Construction of a new rational belief*: 'Ralph, if you agree that your wife does not have to make dinner just when you want her to, what idea or thought could you tell yourself instead?'

If Ralph is unable to answer any of these Socratic disputes, the therapist can switch to didactic disputes. After the didactic interventions, the therapist can return to disputing socratically to see if Ralph has incorporated the disputes or understood them.

As therapy progresses, the therapist may want Ralph to generalize his disputing to other areas because it has been revealed that Ralph is just as demanding of his wife in many other areas. One possible strategy for generalizing the error of demandingness is to stay with the core 'must' belief and to dispute it at all possible levels of abstraction and then down the ladder again to all possible specific events that it is linked to:

1 *Didactic, abstract, logical dispute*: 'Ralph, there is no law of physics that says that your wife must do what you want her to do.'
2 *Didactic, abstract, empirical dispute*: 'You are frequently upsetting yourself about the fact that your wife *does not* do what you want her to do. That proves that she does not behave the way you want her to just because you decreed or demand it.'
3 *Didactic, abstract, heuristic dispute*: 'From the evidence that you have given me, it appears that your demanding philosophy toward your wife has resulted in several negative consequences for you: you feel depressed and angry when your wife does not behave as you demand; you have behaved obnoxiously toward your wife and as a result have reduced the goodwill between you and the pleasant parts of your relationship; and your kids are afraid to be with you because they fear your yelling. So you have lost many of the pleasures of your relationship with your family.'
4 *Didactic, abstract construction of an alternative rational belief*: 'Perhaps you can think instead, "I would like my wife to always do what I want, but there is no law of the universe that says that she must behave as I want nor that she should even want to behave as I want her to. She is her own person with desires of her own."'

Once the therapist has finished these didactic disputes she or he can do the Socratic version of each, again to assess whether Ralph has understood or incorporated them. If he has not, more time can be spent in the area of difficulty in a didactic mode. If Ralph does seem to understand the dispute on an abstract level, it is wise to test this out in a concrete mode: 'OK, Ralph, you seem to understand that neither the world nor your wife has to be the way you want them to be. Let us see if you can apply this new way of thinking to another problem. You said that you also get yourself upset when your wife talks on the phone with her friends. Now, what belief are you thinking then?' The therapist can then find the concrete belief and progress with Socratic or didactic concrete disputes along the nature-of-evidence dimension.

After disputing the core irrational beliefs that underlie Ralph's emotional disturbance, the therapist can also dispute the derivative beliefs that are deduced from the 'must.' Ralph has two such beliefs: first, that he cannot stand not to have things the way he wants them (low frustration tolerance; I can't stand it when my wife does not do things I want her to do) and, second, self-downing ('I am not a real man and therefore a worthless person if I can not command my wife').

The therapist can start on Ralph's LFT and first dispute using didactic, concrete disputes for all levels of the nature of the evidence. Then, the therapist can follow with Socratic concrete disputes for all types of evidence. The next step is abstract Socratic disputes for all types of evidence. Once all these interventions have been tried, the therapist can move on to the same sequence for the derivative irrational belief of self-downing.

The sequence of disputes used above is not mandatory. This is an actual example of a real therapy case. A therapist could have used a different sequence. For example, one could have started with concrete, core, didactic disputes and then moved on to concrete didactic derivative disputes. There are no rules about the sequence of moving through the model. However, I maintain that the more the cells in the model that the therapist follows, the more likely the client is to change.

Although the model provided here applies to verbal disputation strategies, there is no intention to downplay the use of imagery, emotive or behavioral interventions in RET. When one adds these interventions to the number of disputational interventions presented here, the therapist has a large armamentary to choose from.

References

Allport, G. (1955) *Becoming: Basic Considerations for a Psychology of Personality*. New Haven, CT: Yale University Press.

Bard, J. (1980) *Rational-Emotive Therapy in Practice*. Champaign, IL: Research Press.

Beck, A. (1976) *Cognitive Therapy and the Emotional Disorders*. New York: International Universities Press.

Beck, A. and Emery, G. (1985) *Anxiety Disorders and Phobias: A Cognitive Perspective*. New York: Basic Books.

Beck, A., Rush, A., Shaw, B. and Emery, G. (1979) *Cognitive Therapy of Depression*. New York: Guilford.

Burgess, P. (1986) Belief systems and emotional disturbance: an evaluation of the rational-emotive model. Unpublished doctoral dissertation, University of Melbourne, Parkville, Victoria, Australia.

Burgess, P. (1990) Towards resolution of conceptual issues in the assessment of belief systems in rational-emotive therapy: some preliminary results, *Journal of Cognitive Psychotherapy: An International Quarterly*.

Campbell, I. (1985) The psychology of homosexuality. In A. Ellis and M. Bernard (eds), *Clinical Applications of Rational-Emotive Therapy*. New York: Plenum.

Cormier, W. and Cormier, L.S. (1985) *Interviewing Skills for Helpers: Basic Skill and Cognitive Behavioral Interventions*. Monterey, CA: Brooks/Cole.

Demaria, T., Kassinove, H. and Dill, C. (1989) Psychometric properties of the survey of personal beliefs: A rational-emotive measure of irrational thinking, *Journal of Personality Assessment,* 53(2), 329–41.

DiGiuseppe, R. (1986) The implications of the philosophy of science for rational-emotive theory and therapy, *Psychotherapy*, 23(4), 634–9.

DiGiuseppe, R. and Leaf, R. (1991) Endorsement of irrational beliefs in a general clinical population, *Journal of Rational-Emotive and Cognitive-Behavior Therapy*.

DiGiuseppe, R. and Muran, C. (1992) The use of metaphor in rational-emotive therapy, *Psychotherapy in Private Practice*, 10, 151–65.

DiGiuseppe, R., Leaf, R., Exner, T. and Robin, M. (1988) The development of a measure of irrational and rational thinking. Poster session presented at the World Congress of Behavior Therapy, Edinburgh, Scotland.

DiGiuseppe, R., Robin, M., Leaf, R. and Gorman, B. (1989) A discriminative validation and factor analysis of a measure of irrational/rational thinking. Poster session presented at the World Congress of Cognitive Therapy, Oxford, England.

Dryden, W. and DiGiuseppe, R. (1990) *A Primer on Rational-Emotive Therapy*. Champaign, IL: Research Press.

Ellis, A. (1958) Rational psychotherapy, *Journal of General Psychology,* 59, 37–49.

Ellis, A. (1962) *Reason and Emotion in Psychotherapy*. Secaucus, NJ: Lyle Stuart.

Ellis, A. (1973) *Humanistic Psychotherapy: The Rational-Emotive Approach*. New York: McGraw-Hill.

Ellis, A. (1977) Fun as psychotherapy, *Rational Living*, 12(1), 2–6.

Ellis, A. (1985) *Overcoming Resistance: Rational-Emotive Therapy with Difficult Clients*. New York: Springer.

Ellis, A. (1989a) Comments on my critics. In M. Bernard and R. DiGiuseppe (eds), *Inside Rational-Emotive Therapy: A Critical Appraisal of the Theory and Therapy of Albert Ellis*. San Diego, CA: Academic Press.

Ellis, A. (1989b) Is rational-emotive therapy 'rationalist' or 'constructivist'? Paper presented at the World Congress of Cognitive Therapy, Oxford, England.

Ellis, A. and Dryden, W. (1987) *The Practice of Rational-Emotive Therapy*. New York: Springer.

Ellis, A., McInerney, J. F., DiGiuseppe, R. and Yeager, R. (1988) *Rational-Emotive Therapy with Alcoholics and Substance Abusers*. New York: Pergamon Press.

Ellis, A., Sichel, J., DiMattia, D., Yeager, R. and DiGiuseppe, R. (1989) *Rational-Emotive Couples Therapy*. New York: Pergamon Press.

Ellis, A. and Whitely, J. (1979) *Theoretical and Empirical Foundations of Rational-Emotive Therapy*. Monterey, CA: Brooks/Cole.

Gould, S.J. (1988) Freud's phylogenetic fantasy. *Natural History*.

Grieger, R. and Boyd, J. (1980) *Rational-Emotive Therapy: A Skills-Based Approach*. New York: Van Nostrand Reinhold.

Kassinove, H. (1986) Self-reported affect and core irrational thinking: a preliminary analysis, *Journal of Rational-Emotive Therapy*, 4(2), 119–30.

Korzybski, A. (1933) *Science and Sanity*. San Francisco: International Society for General Semantics.

Kuhn, T. (1970) *The Structure of Scientific Revolutions* (2nd edn). Chicago: University of Chicago Press.

Kuhn, T. (1977) *The Essential Tension: Selected Studies in Scientific Tradition and Changes*. Chicago: University of Chicago Press.

Mahoney, M. (1976) *The Scientist as Subject*. Cambridge, MA: Ballinger.

Mahoney, M. (1988) The cognitive sciences and psychotherapy: patterns in a developing relationship. In K. Dobson (ed.), *Handbook of the Cognitive-Behavior Therapies* (pp. 357–86). New York: Guilford.

Maultsby, M. (1975) *Help Yourself to Happiness*. New York: Institute for Rational-Emotive Therapy.

Maultsby, M. (1984) *Rational Behavior Therapy*. Englewood Cliffs, NJ: Prentice-Hall.

Muran, C. and DiGiuseppe, R. (1990) A cognitive formulation of the use of metaphor in psychotherapy, *Clinical Psychology Review,* 10(1), 69–88.

Polyani, M. (1966) *The Tacit Dimension*. New York: Doubleday.

Prochaska, J. and DiClemente, C. (1984) *The Transtheoretical Approach: Crossing Traditional Boundaries of Psychotherapy*. Monterey, CA: Brooks/Cole.

Walen, S., DiGiuseppe, R. and Wessler, R. (1980) *The Practitioner's Guide to Rational-Emotive Therapy*. New York: Oxford University Press.

Wein, K., Nelson, R. and Odom, J. (1975) The relative contribution of reattribution and verbal extinction to the effectiveness of cognitive restructuring, *Behavior Therapy*, 6, 459–74.

Wessler, R.A. and Wessler, R.L. (1980) *The Principles and Practice of Rational-Emotive Therapy*. San Francisco: Jossey-Bass.

Woolfolk, R. and Sass, T. (1989) Rational-emotive philosophy. In M. Bernard and R. DiGiuseppe (eds), *Inside Rational-Emotive Therapy: A Critical Appraisal of the Theory and Therapy of Albert Ellis*. New York: Academic Press.

9

Didactic Persuasion Techniques in Cognitive Restructuring

Thomas H. Harrell, Irving Beiman and Karen LaPointe

Therapeutic procedures that emphasize the role of cognitive variables have been increasingly employed in recent years. Unfortunately, the proliferation of cognitive treatment techniques has not, in general, been accompanied by systematic empirical evaluation of their effectiveness (Mahoney, 1974). This deficiency of controlled research may be explained, at least in part, by the relatively few attempts to specify the procedures found in the diversity of techniques and approaches encompassed by the label 'cognitive therapy'.

Attempts at specification have been notably limited and have not addressed all relevant aspects of cognitive treatment. Mahoney (1974) suggests at least the following components operative in Ellis's rational-emotive therapy (RET) approach: (1) didactic persuasion toward a belief system that recognizes the role of irrational thoughts in subjective distress and deficient performance, (2) training in the observation and discrimination of self-statements, (3) training in the logical and empirical evaluation of self-statements, (4) graduated performance assignments, (5) immediate social feedback, (6) instructions and selective reinforcement for alteration of self-statements, and (7) therapist modeling and role-playing of recommended cognitive mediation styles. Similar components have been delineated by authors attempting to integrate RET into a behavior therapy framework (Beck, 1970; Goldfried and Davison, 1976; Goldfried et al., 1974; Meichenbaum, 1972; Rimm and Masters, 1974). These latter proposals have resulted in specification of those techniques, such as graduated performance assignments and therapist modeling, that are most amenable to behavioral assessment.

Mahoney's (1974) recognition of didactic persuasion as one of the active components of RET is an important step, since many practitioners of RET, including Ellis himself, rely heavily on methods of verbal persuasion to help clients recognize the role of irrational thoughts in subjective distress and to facilitate the development of a more 'rational' belief system. Although the area has been recognized, the specific techniques involved in didactic persuasion have not been explicated in any systematic fashion. Consequently, didactic methods are noted as haphazard procedures (Goldfried et al., 1974), unsupported by empirical data substantiating their effectiveness. We believe the haphazard and empirically unverified state of verbal persuasion methods is a consequence of the failure to operationalize these procedures. Since many of the cognitive techniques previously mentioned occur within or along with various verbal persuasion methods, clear specification of the latter is essential if adequate teaching and implementation of cognitive therapy, and research in cognitive therapy, are to occur.

Explication of procedural components is an initial and essential step toward methodologically sound outcome research (Fiske et al., 1970; Paul, 1967). Without operationalized treatment procedures, the reliability and validity of therapist implementation of the procedures cannot be empirically verified. In turn, without evidence that those procedures were consistently and correctly employed, they cannot be specified as treatment variables responsible for the observed effects. Additionally, without clear specification of cognitive therapy procedures, the communicability of these strategies among therapists is reduced. This limits teachability, as well as the certainty of reliable implementation, of cognitive treatments.

The purpose of the present chapter is to specify verbal persuasion methods that may be utilized in cognitive therapy. Although verbal persuasion techniques may be found in such diverse areas as attitude change and persuasion, and argumentation and debate, as well as cognitive restructuring and self-control, only those procedures considered applicable within the context of a therapeutic relationship will be presented here. This explication of didactic persuasion techniques is intended to facilitate clinical application of cognitive therapy procedures, as well as future research efforts investigating their individual or collective effectiveness.

Didactic Persuasion Techniques

Explanation of Therapeutic Rationale

The basic assumptions, relevant theoretical considerations, and empirical support for the treatment procedure are explained to the client in clear, nontechnical terms. The persuasive value of this explanation lies in diminishing the client's unfamiliarity with the treatment methods and explicating his role in the therapy process. The rationale also prepares the client for acceptance of the appropriateness of the chosen treatment method(s) and avoids the 'contrarient idea' (resistive ideas elicited by presentation of conclusions without prior discussion or explanation) (McBurney and Mills, 1964).

Therapeutically, a number of elements are active in the presentation of the rationale. Cognitions are placed in a formal symbol system that enables the client to represent his cognitions tangibly and directs him to focus attention on both their content and consequences as critical elements in the therapeutic procedure (Mahoney, 1974). The formal paradigm and rationale allow a 'shared conceptual system' between therapist and client (Frank, 1961). By accepting the paradigm, the client essentially agrees to the overall therapeutic plan, increasing the probability of more extensive cognitive change.

The rationale stresses the client's personal responsibility for his thoughts and feelings, thus encouraging the client's perception that he, in fact, is responsible for and exerts control over his maladaptive cognitions. This element is essential to insuring the active participation of the client in the therapeutic plan, and to placing treatment within a self-control model (Kanfer and Karoly, 1972; Mahoney and Thoresen, 1974). An excellent example of a therapeutic rationale is presented by Bernstein and Borkovec (1973), although the procedure described is progressive relaxation training.

Logical Analysis and Evaluation

The principles of logic are applied by the therapist to the alteration of client maladaptive cognitions (Beck, 1976; Ellis, 1962, 1971, 1973). Logical discussion or formal argument can be directed toward two issues: (1) the logical validity of the client's premise (i.e., maladaptive belief or assumption); and (2) the incongruity, with his behavior, of the client's premise.

Ellis (1962) lists multiple reasons for the logical invalidity of common irrational premises. These reasons are used in logical argument to challenge the client's irrational premises.

When dealing with incongruity of belief and behavior, two forms of reasoning are applicable. In applying a generalization to a specific instance, deductive reasoning is used to show how the behavior does not follow from the basic premise. For example, 'Last week we discussed how it was not possible for anyone to live up to all the expectations others have for us. Yet today you seem to be degrading yourself as a mother because you weren't able to give your daughter all the attention she wanted while you were fixing dinner. It appears to be particularly hard for you realistically to accept your limitations in the relationship with your daughter. Is it possible for you to meet all of your daughter's demands on a daily basis?'

There are occasions when a client engages in adaptive behavior that is inconsistent with a maladaptive belief. In this case inductive reasoning, drawing a generalization from specific instances, is used to show how the belief does not follow from the behavior. For example, 'It sounds like you were able to handle that situation very well. You went into a crowded room and said to yourself, "I'm new here, and I feel a little nervous, but most people are somewhat apprehensive in a new situation, so my feelings are natural and to be expected." It seems to me that you're handling new social situations in a much more realistic manner.'

Reduction to Absurdity

The therapist appears to assume, for the moment, that the irrational premise of the client is accurate. Then, by carrying the faulty premise to its logical extreme, its absurdity is illuminated (Ellis, 1962, 1971, 1973). For example, 'You're telling me that you feel you really need to have other people's approval and can't stand it if you feel you've offended anyone. Let's assume that you actually can live your life without offending anyone and can gain everyone's approval. What would that take? Well, you'd have to dress in a way that everyone approved of, wear your hair in a way everyone approved of, eat what other people approved of, drink what other people approved of, say things that other people approved of, and always act in a way other people found acceptable. Of course, in order to know that you wouldn't offend anyone, you'd have to know all about what each person you were with liked. So you couldn't be with anyone until you knew them well enough never to offend them. And then you could never be with people who approved of different things because in order to be what one person approved of, you might offend another.'

Empirical Analysis and Evaluation

The cognition is compared with real-life observations and/or empirical evidence related to the content of the cognition. The comparison allows an evaluation of the degree to which the cognition is a realistic expression of the known facts of a situation (Beck, 1970, 1976; Ellis, 1962, 1971, 1973). For example, 'You seem to be saying that you have failed at everything you've ever tried in your life. It occurs to me that one way to determine if this is actually the case would be to look back over your life and see if you can't identify some accomplishments, as well as some failures. Let's try to be very objective as we do this and see if this examination really bears out your belief.'

This technique would seem to be particularly effective when supplemented by homework assignments arranged in such a manner that the client makes observations and collects information that indicate the degree to which the cognition realistically reflects everyday life experiences (Ellis, 1962).

Contradiction with Cherished Value

The therapist introduces a dissonant situation for the client by demonstrating that a particular cognition contradicts or is incongruent with a valued belief or quality (Crabb, 1971). For example, 'You're far too intelligent to believe that any one person could meet all your needs 100 percent of the time.' Acknowledging the incompatibility of the two cognitions can lead the client to reduce the resulting dissonance by modifying the maladaptive one. Unless the dissonance is resolved, a cognition that is inconsistent with a personally valued quality or belief will be maintained.

Incredulous Therapist Response

The therapist attempts to induce dissonance by simply expressing, in an incredulous manner, his disbelief that the client could actually maintain such a maladaptive or irrational cognition (Ellis, 1962, 1971, 1973). For example, 'You don't *really* expect her to respond to your every whim, do you?' Therapeutic utilization of this technique requires that the therapist direct incredulity toward the client's *attitude* and not toward the client; otherwise, the client is likely to respond with defensiveness and resistance.

Appeal to Negative Consequences

The client's maladaptive behaviors and the negative consequences of those behaviors are portrayed as resulting from maladaptive cognitions (Ellis, 1962, 1971, 1973). The technique involves specifying the negative consequences of the maladaptive cognition and encouraging the client to avoid or escape from the unpleasant consequences by modifying the problematic cognition. Affective consequences, such as depression and anxiety, as well as behavioral outcomes, such as poor performance on an exam or the continued avoidance of potentially pleasurable activities, are frequently specified. For example, a client's unfounded belief that he is much less competent in heterosexual relationships than his peers might be responded to in this manner: 'I know you really wanted to enjoy yourself when you went out on a date last weekend, but can you see how your constant self-evaluation of your performance prevented you from being relaxed and spontaneous? When you're constantly convincing yourself that you are incompetent and unable to do the right thing, you are making yourself so nervous that you're certain to look unsure of yourself and make mistakes.'

Negative Analogies

The therapist verbalizes an analogy that pairs the client's maladaptive cognition with a negative stimulus; that is, an unpleasant imaginal scene aroused by the analogy (Crabb, 1971). The analogy is designed to elicit negative feelings with respect to the cognition. For example, the client's belief that he needs his mother for security, which results in his lack of independent behavior when away at college, might be responded to in the following manner: 'Your behavior reminds me of a two-year-old kid walking down the street looking over his shoulder to see if Mom is still watching from the door. If she is, you'll go on, knowing that faithful Mom will pick you up if you fall. If she isn't, you'll run home and not attempt any independent activity.'

The analogy should be developed so that the client's negative feelings are associated with the maladaptive cognition and not directed toward himself as a person. Otherwise, the analogy is likely to increase defensiveness or elicit hostility.

Appeal to Positive Consequences of Change

The positive consequences of alternative, adaptive cognitions are developed by therapist and client (Brehm and Cohen, 1962). The therapist may specify the adaptive affective and behavioral consequences of cognitive change, focusing initially on the most apparent and immediate consequences and gradually developing those of a long-term nature. For example, 'Let's look at how things would be if you assumed that you were capable of being confident and relaxed in more varied social situations. For one thing, you could attend parties and meet new people; you could also start dating instead of staying home all weekend. As you gained greater confidence in your abilities, you could begin to take more initiative in determining your own social life by actively arranging those situations you enjoy most.'

The intent of the procedure is to induce the client to evaluate the positive consequences of more adaptive cognitions across a variety of situations. Successful application, however, is dependent upon insuring that the client perceives the relationship between cognitive change and the anticipated positive consequences. Graduated performance assignments in which the client experiences positive consequences contingent upon adaptive cognitive modifications should serve to exemplify the validity of this relationship and facilitate more permanent change. This method also should be more effective if used in conjunction with the techniques that stress negative aspects of maintaining maladaptive cognitions.

Conclusion

Despite the current proliferation of cognitive treatment techniques, those falling within the category of verbal persuasion procedures have generally remained unspecified. This lack of specification has led didactic persuasion techniques to be labeled haphazard and unverified (Goldfried et al., 1974). In order to increase communicability among therapists and facilitate research, various didactic persuasion techniques have been operationalized in this chapter. To facilitate clarity in the presentation, these techniques have been delineated without reference to additional therapeutic procedures. However, with respect to clinical application, these didactic procedures should be conceptualized as one of several components within a comprehensive cognitive behavioral treatment strategy (e.g., Beck, 1976; Goldfried and Davison, 1976; Mahoney, 1974).

A final point addresses the issue of how cognitive persuasion strategies can be most effectively implemented. A client–therapist relationship that embodies the qualities of respect, trust, empathy, and congruence is frequently noted as a prerequisite for successful implementation of therapeutic procedures (Frank, 1961; Goldstein, 1975). Although the importance of the client–therapist relationship is emphasized in almost every approach to psychotherapy, persuasive and logical evaluation techniques require particularly careful attention to the therapist's interpersonal style and ability to develop a therapeutic relationship. Specific pitfalls for inexperienced therapists include engaging in nonproductive argument, communicating disrespect for the client, and failing to maintain the distinction between the client as a person and the client's cognitions. Difficulties of this nature may be avoided most effectively by striving for a therapeutic relationship in which the client and therapist are working together to establish a more effective style of living for the client.

References

Beck, A.T. (1970) Cognitive therapy: nature and relation to behavior therapy, *Behavior Therapy*, 1, 184–200.

Beck, A.T. (1976) *Cognitive Therapy and the Emotional Disorders*. New York: International Universities Press.

Bernstein, D. and Borkovec, T. (1973) *Progressive Relaxation Training: A Manual for the Helping Professions*. Champaign, IL: Research Press.

Brehm, J.W. and Cohen, A.R. (1962) *Explorations in Cognitive Dissonance*. New York: Wiley.

Crabb, L.J. (1971) Sensible psychotherapy. Unpublished manuscript, University of Illinois at Champaign-Urbana.

Ellis, A. (1962) *Reason and Emotion in Psychotherapy*. New York: Lyle Stuart.

Ellis, A. (1971) *Growth Through Reason*. Palo Alto, CA: Science and Behavior Books.

Ellis, A. (1973) *Humanistic Psychotherapy: The Rational-Emotive Approach*. New York: Julian Press.

Fiske, D.W., Hunt, H.F., Luborsky, L., Orne, M.T., Parloff, M.B., Reiser, M.F. and Tuma, A.H. (1970) Planning for research on effectiveness of psychotherapy, *American Psychologist*, 25, 727–37.

Frank, J.D. (1961) *Persuasion and Healing*. Baltimore: Johns Hopkins University Press.

Goldfried, M.R. and Davison, G.C. (1976) *Clinical Behavior Therapy*. New York: Holt, Rinehart and Winston.

Goldfried, M.R., Decenteceo, E.T. and Weinberg, L. (1974) Systematic rational restructuring as a self-control technique, *Behavior Therapy*, 5, 247–54.

Goldstein, A.P. (1975) Relationship-enhancement methods. In F.H. Kanfer and A.P. Goldstein (eds), *Helping People Change*. New York: Pergamon Press.

Kanfer, F.H. and Karoly, P. (1972) Self-control: a behavioristic exploration into the lion's den, *Behavior Therapy*, 3, 398–416.

Mahoney, M.J. (1974) *Cognition and Behavior Modification*. Cambridge, MA: Ballinger.

Mahoney, M.J. and Thoresen, C.E. (1974) *Self-Control: Power to the Person*. Monterey, CA: Brooks/Cole.

McBurney, J.H. and Mills, G.E. (1964) *Argumentation and Debate* (2nd edn). New York: Macmillan.

Meichenbaum, D. (1972) Ways of modifying what clients say to themselves: A marriage of behavior therapies and rational-emotive therapy, *Rational Living*, 7, 23–7.

Paul, G.L. (1967) The strategy of outcome research in psychotherapy, *Journal of Consulting Psychology*, 31, 109–18.

Rimm, D.C. and Masters, J.C. (1974) *Behavior Therapy*. New York: Academic Press.

10

The Issue of Force and Energy in Behavioral Change

Albert Ellis

What I call the issue of force and energy in behavioral change is one that has been sadly neglected over the years. Although hundreds of psychotherapists utilize a great many forceful and energetic methods (Burton, 1969), they frequently do not acknowledge the concept of forcefulness in what they do, and sometimes they even deny it. The Freudians, for example, vigorously force their patients to fit themselves into the procrustean bed of their oedipal complexes, and they manipulate the 'transference' relationship with these patients so that they become very dependent on the analysts. Yet they often speak and write as if psychoanalysis mainly appeals to the scientific and reasoning aspects of humans and as if it finally wins out through the pure voice of reason (Freud, 1965). Other therapists, such as the Rogerians (Rogers, 1961) and the Gestalt therapists (Perls, 1969), consciously employ highly emotive methods with their clients, but they rarely talk about the *force* or *vigor* of their unsubtle techniques.

When the concepts of force or energy are employed in behavioral change, they are more commonly (and usually quite unscientifically) related to hypotheses about the central forces or energies of the universe; people are told that (1) such forces indubitably exist; (2) you can get in touch with them by various transpersonal and mystical approaches; (3) you can thereby tap these universal forces and use them to your own personal ends; and (4) you can consequently overcome virtually all your emotional problems and enormously increase your potential for actualizing yourself. This kind of devout belief in universal forces and of the human ability to tap these forces and acquire immense personal power from zeroing in on the 'energies' of the universe has been with us for literally thousands of years, but it is unfortunately becoming much more widespread in recent times. Innumerable books and articles state or imply that cosmic forces are there for the asking and that we can easily commune with them and thereby increase our own power of coping with ourselves and life (Albin and Montagna, 1977; Campbell, 1975; Harrell, 1976; Ingalls, 1976; Krippner et al., 1973; Ostrander and Schroeder, 1974; Pulvino, 1975; Schutz, 1971; Smith, 1976; Targ and Puthoff, 1977; Weil, 1973). Protesting against this mystical trend in psychology and psychotherapy have been relatively few recent writers, including Alperson (1976), Duffy (1975), Ellis (1972, 1977b, 1977c), Flew (1976), and Kurtz (1976).

The Basic Issue of Force and Energy in Behavioral Change

The real or basic issue of force and energy in behavioral change seems to have little or nothing to do with the mystical or transpersonal hogwash that presently abounds in the literature. It concerns the following question. Assuming that certain ideas or cognitions help individuals to change their basic personality structure (and rid themselves more temporarily and palliatively of certain psychological symptoms or disturbances), is it important that these ideas be conveyed by the therapists, or by the clients to themselves, in a pronouncedly vigorous, forceful, and dramatic manner? And if it is important that certain health-promoting ideas be forcefully invoked in therapy, what are some of the most effective ways of doing so?

As noted, little consideration has been given in the past to this particular problem of behavioral change. Many therapeutic writers have talked about intellectual insight and emotional insight and have held that the latter will lead to significant personality change, while the former will not (Alexander and French, 1946; Hobbs, 1962; Wolberg, 1967). Unfortunately, they have not been very precise in their definitions; I will discuss this problem shortly. I (and a certain number of other writers who have followed my lead) have defined emotion as 'nothing more or less than a certain kind – a biased, prejudiced, or strongly evaluative kind – of thought' (Ellis, 1962: 41), and I have consequently discussed the problem of changing behavior by utilizing powerful, vigorous thinking processes (Ellis, 1957, 1962, 1971, 1973, 1977a; Ellis and Grieger, 1977; Ellis and Harper, 1975). A few psychotherapists, such as Finney (1972), have not particularly discriminated between vigorous and blander thinking but have used what could be called vigorous counterpropagandizing methods in their therapy.

All told, however, surprisingly little has been done in this respect, in spite of the fact that methods of propaganda and counterpropaganda have been studied, mostly by social psychologists, for many years and that, in the course of these studies, considerable attention has been paid to the powerful or less powerful ways in which persuasion has been promulgated (Hovland and Janis, 1959). So I think that we might safely conclude that although therapists frequently *use* vigorous persuasion or 'brainwashing' methods in their encounters with clients, they have not been particularly keen on thinking about the concept of forcefulness or energeticness in their procedures; in fact, to some extent they may have even deliberately and defensively avoided this area of discussion and research.

The Problem of Intellectual and Emotional Insight

Clinical observers, as noted, have for many years noted the difference between intellectual and emotional insight and have pointed out that when clients are intellectually aware of their problems and understand the sources of these problems, they frequently make minor or minimal personality changes; when they have emotional insight into these same problems, they frequently make much more major changes. Unfortunately, the literature in this respect is quite vague as to what the real difference between emotional and intellectual insight is and as to why the former is presumably more effective than the latter.

I gave some fairly careful thought to this problem some years ago and came up with what I think is at least a partial solution to these questions (Ellis, 1963). First, I tried to define emotional and intellectual insight more precisely. In so doing, I noted that what we usually call emotional insight has several important characteristics. The first is that the client has some degree of intellectual insight – that is, admits that she or he is disturbed and that his or her behavior is irrational or self-defeating. Without this 'intellectual' acknowledgement or admission, emotional or 'fuller' insight will probably not occur.

Second, the client usually realizes that his or her present behavior has some antecedent causes and does not magically spring from nowhere. It does not 'just' occur but has tended to occur for quite a long period of time, and it occurs in conjunction with certain activating experiences or stimuli.

Third, the client assumes some kind of responsibility for the dysfunctional or self-defeating behavior, realizes that she or he has something to do with originating it and carrying it on. In the rational-emotive therapy A-B-C model of personality, the client realizes that A (an Activating Experience or Activating Event) does not directly or mainly cause C (an emotional or behavioral Consequence, such as anxiety or depression). Instead, B (the client's own Belief System) directly causes the feeling and the behavioral Consequence, and the client is responsible for having and carrying on this Belief System.

Fourth, the client realizes that even if she or he was significantly helped, usually during early childhood, to have certain irrational Beliefs (iBs) and to create self-defeating emotions with these Beliefs, she or he has now *chosen* to keep these Beliefs right now, in the present, and to keep affecting himself or herself by them.

Fifth, the client clearly and strongly 'sees' or 'acknowledges' that she or he can now do something *to change* his or her irrational Beliefs and thereby to change the habitual disturbed feelings and disordered behaviors that spring directly from these Beliefs. This Belief on the part of the client is firm or strong and is solidly held much or most of the time.

Sixth, the client feels determined to work at (yes, *work* at) changing his or her irrational Beliefs – to accept their falsity, acknowledge that they do not conform to empirical reality, to see their illogical or contradictory aspects, and to keep striving, because of the poor results they bring, to give them up and not return to believing them again. Working at changing Beliefs includes the client's (a) forcefully and repetitively disputing and challenging them, (b) forcing himself or herself to go through the pain and trouble of steadily contradicting them, (c) practicing feeling differently about them or their results (e.g., practicing feeling happy about giving up smoking instead of clinging to the idea that it is awful to go through the pain of giving it up), (d) directly and vigorously acting against the irrational Beliefs or against the actions to which they self-defeatingly lead (e.g., forcing oneself to put the lit end of a cigarette in one's mouth every time one takes a puff at the other end of it).

Seventh, the client not only feels determined to work at challenging his or her irrational Beliefs but actually does this kind of work and does it often and vigorously. Thus, if the client has a swimming phobia, she or he had better keep convincing himself or herself, over and over again, that swimming is not terribly dangerous, and also repeatedly plunge into a swimming pool until she or he gets rid of this self-defeating idea.

Eighth, this client fully realizes that his or her emotional disturbances are always under his or her own control and that she or he can continue to think and act his or her way out of them whenever they recur. This means continual determination and action, whenever a new emotional upset occurs, to conquer it as quickly as possible and to become convinced of some general Beliefs that will tend to prevent many kinds of future disturbances, Beliefs such as 'Nothing is awful or terrible,' 'I can always accept myself, no matter what faults I have,' 'Many things are hassles but not horrors,' and 'All humans, including myself, are incredibly fallible and will keep making fairly serious mistakes forever, and that is unpleasant and inconvenient but hardly the end of the world!'

Ninth, the client keeps admitting that there seems to be no other way to become and to remain undisturbed except by his or her continually working and practicing, in theory and action, against whatever disturbances may arise.

The preceding rules may be partially summarized by saying that people who have intellectual insight see how they create their own disturbances and what they can do about uncreating them, but tend to see these things lightly, occasionally and weakly; those who have emotional insight see the same things intensely, often, and strongly. Sometimes, more to the point, people with emotional insight normally work very hard, very often, and very powerfully at giving up their self-defeating Beliefs and acting against them, while people with intellectual insight do this kind of work mildly, seldom and weakly.

False Issues in Utilizing Force and Energy

If what I have just said about intellectual and emotional insight tends to be true, the main issue in utilizing force and energy to bring about behavioral change seems to be work and practice much more than it is an issue of mere insight or resolve to change. New Year's Resolutions are easy to make – but proverbially hard to keep. 'Willpower' is easy to invoke – but difficult to put into practice. Concepts such as motivation, determination, will, intention and resolve are all important in behavioral change, and it is possible that very little effective change takes place without people having a good degree of these 'feelings.' But just as bread is not enough for most people to live on and enjoy life, so willpower is not enough to incite and induce basic personality change unless we include, under willpower, not merely the resolve and determination to modify one's traits and behaviors but also the action, the work, the labor that one almost invariably must apply in order to back up this resolve.

That is why the transpersonal or mystical solutions just noted are usually false solutions. They assume the existence of general forces and energies as a central part of the universe; which probably has at least some partial validity, since human life seems unviable apart from a basic source of energy, such as that which we derive primarily from the sun. But they also assume some inert mass of such energy or force in some special or central place that can be easily tapped by humans and they can put to their own use – including their own psychological use. This hypothesis seems very questionable, especially when it assumes that we can *directly* zero in on universal forces and use them, at will, for our own pleasures and our own straighter thinking.

But perhaps the most foolish part of this kind of hypothesis is that *anyone* can *easily*, with a few simple mystical or religious instructions, focus on the universal reservoir of Mighty Energy and can use it for immediate personal satisfaction. This utopian view fairly obviously stems from the feelings of low frustration tolerance that many or most people have, and that constitutes one of their major disturbances! The idea that 'I must have things easy, and the universe must provide me quickly and effortlessly with immediate and immense gratification' is one of the most asinine *must*urbatory ideas with which humans victimize themselves and, as one would well imagine, it leads them far astray from the work and practice that they almost always use to bring about profound behavioral changes in themselves (Ellis, 1971, 1973, 1977a).

Ironically, some religious and mystical sects, such as the Zen Buddhists, refuse to take this easy way out to the heaven of vast resources of Universal Energy; instead they teach their members that they must discipline themselves, often in exceptionally rigorous and overzealous ways, if they are to get 'in touch with the infinite,' attain 'higher consciousness,' or otherwise acquire those Great Forces. Even though, as noted, such Energies and Forces probably do not exist, or have a nonexistent connection with human psychic abilities, the disciplined procedures that these sects advocate *do* often have a salutary effect on mental health. It is extremely difficult to maintain one's low frustration tolerance (LFT) when one is deliberately following rituals such as rising early in the morning, meditating in uncomfortable positions for hours on end, fasting a great deal of the time, wearing reasonable facsimiles of hair shirts, and so forth.

Although, therefore, the utopian, spiritualistic philosophies of these mystical sects are unverifiable and probably filled with errant claptrap, the disciplined procedures that lead to 'nirvana,' 'universal fulfillment,' 'higher consciousness,' or what you will, may themselves provide the kind of work and practice that help the devotees of these systems of thought (and they really are, for all the denials of the gurus of these religions, systems of *thought*) to achieve that aspect of emotional insight that includes work and practice. In other words, if you foolishly believe that when you rigorously diet, exercise and give up smoking, some kind of St Peter will reward you by permitting you to enter the pearly gates of Heaven after you have died, and you actually do consistently diet, exercise and refrain from smoking in accordance with this silly hypothesis, there is a good chance that you will, first, achieve much better physical health than you would otherwise achieve, and, second, learn how to discipline yourself and acquire confidence in your own self-controlling talents. These two beneficial results will occur in spite of the nonsense that you believe, but this nonsense will (partially by accident) motivate you to follow some sensible procedures that may well help you emotionally.

The following questions still remain, of course: How could you engage in the same kinds of useful self-discipline *without* believing devoutly in the mystical (and disturbance-creating) nonsense that goes with it? How can you validate the results of your high frustration tolerance in its own right, to discover what aspects of it are advantageous and what aspects are disadvantageous, so that you (and others) become more disciplined in more sensible ways and do not become disciplined for the sake of discipline (or for the sake of some imagined deity) itself?

An Operational Definition of Force and Energy in Behavioral Change

The hypothesis of rational-emotive therapy (RET) and of several other schools of psychotherapy is that emotional insight or intellectual insight, backed up by the individual's determination (will) to change and his or her consistent and hard work and practice at the process of actual change, will frequently result in pronounced and 'elegant' modification of some important personality traits and behaviors (Beck, 1976; Goldfried and Davison, 1976; Lembo, 1976; Mahoney, 1974; Meichenbaum, 1977). Another rational-emotive therapy hypothesis is that when elegant cognitive or philosophic restructuring occurs, the individual not only tends to minimize or lose his or her disturbed symptoms but also maintains increased emotional health in the future and automatically feels much less disturbed about 'traumatic' events when they occur in his or her later life (Ellis, 1977b, 1977c, 1978).

Assuming that these hypotheses have some validity, or that they are at least worth checking out, the following question arises. How may people specifically and concretely, forcefully and energetically change their disturbance-creating or irrational Beliefs so that they achieve a high degree of 'emotional' insight? To answer this, let me first try to define operationally the concepts of force and energy in psychotherapy or behavioral change, so that I thereby accurately lay out what individuals had better *do* to employ it.

To be more precise in this respect, I will start with the example of a very typical irrational Belief that many people seem to have and that leads them to feel anxious, depressed, needlessly inhibited, and inadequate; this is the Belief that 'I *must* perform adequately or well in this task and *have to* win the approval of others by doing so; if I significantly fail in these respects, it is *awful*, I *cannot stand* it, and I am a *rotten person (RP)* for behaving badly and for gaining the disapproval of others.' Let us assume that you (or one of your clients or associates) has this kind of irrational Belief and that it is leading to anxious and depressed feelings and to various kinds of dysfunctional behaviors. How, using an operational approach to defining force and energy, can you vigorously and effectively surrender this set of irrational Beliefs and change these self-defeating emotions and behaviors?

Let me list the specific things you may do in this connection to achieve emotional insight or elegant philosophic reconstruction. Some of the following tasks overlap with each other, but each may be important in its own right.

First, you had better actively and strongly Dispute (at point D in rational-emotive therapy) your irrational Beliefs *quite often*. To do this, you would *frequently* challenge and question these Beliefs, using the logico-empirical methods of science, and ask yourself nonrhetorical queries such as: 'Where is the evidence that I *must* perform adequately or well in this task? Why do I *have to* win the approval of others by doing so? What proof exists that it is *awful* (and not merely highly inconvenient) if I fail in these respects? Where is it written that I *cannot stand* failing and getting rejected? What data exist to show that I am truly a *rotten person* (instead of a person who may have *acted rottenly* on this occasion) if I fail and get rejected?'

The main essence here of gaining emotional and not intellectual insight (or, more accurately, of gaining *more complete* instead of *partial* insight) into the irrationality of your self-defeating Beliefs consists of your winding up with the new rational Effect (E in RET) or new empirically based philosophy more *commonly*, more *frequently*, and more *consistently* than you have done before. Even when you strongly or emotionally believe that you *must* perform well and win others' approval (or refrain from gaining their disapproval), you do not believe this 100 percent of the time. You *mostly* or *often* believe it. And if you get emotional or *forceful* insight into your Beliefs and their self-destructive qualities, you will come to believe this drivel only *occasionally* or much *less often* than you now do. Therefore you had better actively Dispute and surrender these crazy beliefs *quite often*.

Second, you had better acquire a *more total* or *more prevailing* belief that you don't have to perform well and win others' approval (or avoid their disapproval), and that you can fully accept yourself (i.e., your aliveness and potential for happiness) if you perform badly. Again, as a human you rarely believe anything *totally* or *completely* but have conflicting views about innumerable things. Thus you probably believe that overeating is bad for you, but you also believe that it is somewhat good for you; you also believe that it is horribly unfair when people treat you unjustly, but you also believe that that is the way the world is and that you can bear their unjust treatment.

Disturbance-creating beliefs, such as the idea that you *have to* perform well and be approved by others, tend to be totalistic or complete; you devoutly and fully believe them, at least at the moment when you feel depressed and destroyed about performing badly and gaining others' disapproval. In general, you do not believe them in a complete or 100 percent manner, but you tend to believe them in a basic, underlying, and 80 percent or 90 percent way. To *really* or *basically* disbelieve them, therefore, you had better keep working at believing them in a much less totalistic and less prevailing manner. Thus, if you have a 95 percent belief that the world is round and a 5 percent belief that it is flat, you will probably not get into any serious trouble and can take a long trip with minimum qualms; however, if you have a 95 percent belief that it is flat and a 5 percent belief that it is round, your travel will tend to be highly restricted or you will travel in an exceptionally anxious state! In the latter case, your problem is to work on your 95 percent belief that the world is flat until you make it into a 5 percent or less belief.

Third, you had better believe your rational Belief (rB) more strongly, intensely, or powerfully than your irrational Belief. Thus you can, if you wish, lightly or weakly believe that 'I must perform well and win others' approval,' but you had better more strongly and intensely believe that 'I really don't *have to* perform well and win others' approval, although it would be highly preferable if I did.' Exactly *how* you can measure the intensity of your beliefs is not entirely clear, since it overlaps with believing them often and totally, especially with the latter. But there does seem to be a power or intensity to beliefs, as Osgood (1971) has shown, and it is somewhat different from believing something often or totally.

Thus you can lightly or weakly believe that 'I had better not eat a lot of palatable food' and believe in a stronger manner that 'It would be better if I did eat a lot of palatable food.' If so, you would tend to *act* on the latter instead of the former belief. But there are probably also other indications of strength of a belief, such as your having, when you hold a strong or powerful belief, an intense feeling about its truth or (in more cognitive terms) an intense conviction that it is true and that you had better act as if it were true.

A strong belief, in other words, is one that you tend to hold (a) with firm conviction, (b) in a relatively fixed and unchanging manner, (c) with a high degree of probability or certainty, (d) without cavil or qualification, (e) dogmatically, (f) wholly or totally, (g) almost all of the time, (h) absolutistically, even when empirical evidence does not support it, and (i) perhaps in other ways that I have not quite specified here. Rationally, you may hold a strong belief because virtually all the evidence that you have seems to support it; irrationally, you may hold it because you 'feel' that it is true, even though there is little evidence to support it and much to refute it. In either instance, you tend to feel that the belief is quite true or valid, and you tend to act on it.

To make a strong irrational Belief weak and a weak rational Belief stronger, you can do several things. If, for example, you take the irrational Belief that 'I must perform well and be approved by so-and-so,' you could try to weaken it in these ways: (a) Ask yourself, 'Where is the empirical evidence that I *must* act in this manner and get these results?' Answer: 'There is no such evidence, since I obviously *can* (or have the ability to) perform badly and win disapproval.' (b) Ask yourself, 'Does it seem likely that a universal law exists that commands my performing well and winning the approval of others?' Answer: 'Obviously not, since if that law existed I would always and only have to perform well and win others' approval, and clearly I am able to perform badly and gain disapproval.' (c) Ask yourself: 'What horror or disaster will probably or possibly occur if I don't perform well and win the approval of others?' Answer: 'No horror or disaster! I will probably be quite inconvienced if I act badly and others don't like me, but I will still be able to live and enjoy my life in various ways.' (d) Ask yourself: 'Will I be a truly or totally rotten person if I do not perform well and get others' acceptance?' Answer: 'No, of course not. I will then be a person with, at worst, a rotten trait, poor performance, and a poor result, others' nonacceptance. But I will not be thoroughly rotten and can perform quite well in many respects in many other ways.' (e) Ask yourself: 'Will some force in the universe define me as undeserving and damn me, during my lifetime or some hypothetical afterlife, if I do not act well and get others' approval?' Answer: 'Not that I can see or prove! It is most unlikely that some force in the universe is personally interested in me, will spy on my poor performances and my unacceptability to others, and will utterly damn me and make me undeserving of any joy in the here and now or in some hypothetical afterlife if I behave poorly.' (f) You can vigorously and powerfully try to interrupt your irrational Beliefs and replace them by rational Beliefs. Thus you can ask yourself, in a vehement manner: 'Why the hell *must* I perform well, and where is the goddamned evidence that I *have to* win others' approval?' And you can answer, with equal vigor: 'There's *no* damned reason, no reason whatsoever why I must perform well! And if I do not win others' approval, hell, I do not! It will not kill me!' (g) You can dogmatically (and somewhat *irrationally!*) keep reindoctrinating yourself with a counterbelief that effectively gets you to give up your irrational, self-defeating Belief, for example, 'I am a perfectly lovely, special *person*, who deserves everything good in life just because I am I! Therefore I do not have to perform well, but am still noble and special! And if others disapprove of me, that is their problem, and they hardly deserve my acquaintance or friendship anyway. To hell with them!'

You can use still other methods of strongly uprooting your irrational Beliefs and coming to more rational Beliefs: (a) deliberately work at changing your beliefs from time to time so that virtually none of them remains fixed and invariant; (b) get yourself to believe, for instance, that 'I must perform well (or had better perform well) only in certain unusual situations, as when my life depends on it or I will truly cause some disaster to happen to me by performing poorly. I need others' approval only in special cases, as when I depend on them for life and limb'; (c) constantly interrupt your irrational Beliefs and replace them with rational Beliefs; and (d) work against your general absolutistic tendencies to believe devoutly in anything whatever and see that you only accept things skeptically, tentatively, and with a willingness to believe in the opposite. Practice keeping yourself open to new or contradictory beliefs.

Fourth, realize that having a belief system will not necessarily make you act on it (although it will distinctly help you to do so) and that determination to think, feel and act against it will tend to get you to carry it out. See that you can be firmly determined, mildly determined, or not determined to think or do something and work at being firmly or strongly determined to give up your irrational Beliefs and to act against them. Along these lines, talk to yourself as follows: 'I am utterly determined to accept myself even if I perform badly and people do not approve of me. If it is the last thing I do, I will work hard at unconditional self-acceptance. Knowing that I can live and enjoy myself no matter what others think of me is probably the most important view that I can ever have, and I *will* have it, I will, I *will*, I *will!*'

Fifth, strongly and determinedly push yourself into actions that will contradict your tendency to hold irrational Beliefs and will reinforce your tendency to have rational ones. Thus you could (a) risk failing at certain important tasks, instead of avoiding them; (b) deliberately fail at certain tasks to show yourself that you will not die of failure; (c) tell people whom you find significant bad things about yourself in order to risk their disapproval; (d) use rational-emotive imagery (Ellis, 1977a; Ellis and Harper, 1975; Maultsby, 1975; Maultsby and Ellis, 1974) to imagine yourself failing and to make yourself feel only disappointed and sorry instead of panicked and depressed when you imagine this.

Sixth, keep practicing and practicing at working against your irrational Beliefs, feeling healthy rather than unhealthy emotions (e.g., disappointment and sorrow instead of depression and feelings of worthlessness) when you fail, and acting in a risk-taking manner. Realize that it normally requires constant practice to make yourself *really* and *strongly* believe sane ideas and to act on them and that it requires still more practice, to some extent for the rest of your life, to get yourself to the point where you retain rational thinking and appropriate behaviors once you have initially attained them.

Seventh, accept the near inevitability of falling back on some or many occasions to your irrational Beliefs. As I have noted on several occasions (Ellis, 1962, 1973, 1976a, 1976b, 1977a; Ellis and Grieger, 1977; Ellis and Harper, 1975), humans not only have a strong tendency to think crookedly but to fall back to their crooked thinking once they temporarily overcome it. So, in all probability, do you! Accept the fact, therefore, that you most probably will return at times to silly ideas and self-defeating behaviors and that this is too bad, but not horrible; you are not a lesser person for falling back. At these times, merely focus on your behavior and how to change that instead of on your youness and how to condemn that. You can learn by most of your retrogressions, and you can have fewer and fewer of them as the years go by. But you most probably will not reduce them to zero, not as long as you are still human!

Eighth, accept the fact that no matter how many times you fall back to dysfunctional ways of thinking, emoting and behaving, you can just about invariably give them up again and return to more satisfying ways; you can work at strongly determining that you *will force yourself* to uproot your self-defeating behaviors and go back to less defeating pathways. Determine to keep rehabituating yourself to more efficient and more satisfying ways of living; work at this determination and at the actions required to actualize it.

Ninth, do not be afraid, at times, to use temporary or palliative techniques of changing yourself. You can, for example, learn relaxation methods (Benson, 1975; Jacobson, 1942; Lazarus, 1976), various kinds of pleasurable diversions (Ellis, 1976b; Masters and Johnson, 1970), yoga and meditation techniques (Shapiro and Zifferblatt, 1976), physical and body exercises (Lowen, 1970); emotive methods (Casriel, 1974; Janov, 1970; Lazarus, 1976, 1978), and other diversionary methods. You can also take tranquilizers, alcohol, marijuana, and various other types of drugs to help yourself be temporarily distracted and relaxed. But recognize that these methods usually do not lead to profound philosophical change, and sometimes interfere with it. They help you feel better but not get better. We might say, therefore, that they are often among the most dramatic forms of unforceful, unenergetic therapy; and that is why they tend to be so palliative and to leave you with an underlying shame-creating and hostility-instigating philosophy that will later rise to smite you. If you use distraction methods with the full knowledge that they usually bring temporary results and that they sometimes put you in a mood where you can *then* vigorously and determinedly work to change your underlying disturbance-creating assumptions, fine. If you employ them 'curatively,' they may well give poor results and ultimately lead you to more harm than good.

Discussion

Scientists are becoming more and more aware of the enormous importance of human perception, cognition and intention in world affairs. Psychotherapists have essentially said this for years (Adler, 1927/1968; Ellis, 1957, 1962, 1971, 1973, 1977a; Ellis and Harper, 1975; Maslow, 1962; Rogers, 1961). Now biological and physical scientists are also beginning to say it (Sperry, 1977).

When you want to have a significant effect, however, on your own life as well as the universe around you, it seems clear that your thinking clearly and rationally is often not enough – unless, under the heading of rational we also include an emotive element and acknowledge that efficient thinking involves a forceful, energetic and determined element. Mild-mannered thinking (the kind that you do when you merely observe that smoking or overeating has disadvantageous elements and that it would probably be better if you did not engage in such behavior) may be a necessary but not sufficient condition for basic personality change. It had better be accompanied or followed by a more vigorous, dramatic kind of thinking that goes one step further to include the determination to act and the actual action that backs up this kind of change-oriented cognition.

Overgeneralized or mystical-minded concepts of a universal force or energy and of how humans are to get in touch with and utilize such forces are again not enough; in fact, they can be pernicious and reactionary as far as instigating basic personality change is concerned. It therefore behoves social scientists to specify more operationally and practically the kinds of force or vigor that we can inculcate in our attempts at rationality and with which we can effectively implement these attempts. Peculiarly, little attention has yet been given to this problem in psychology or psychotherapy; this article is an attempt at specifying some of the more important elements in forceful, energetic thought and action and at harnessing some of these elements in the process of personality change. It is also an attempt to set up some hypotheses that can be experimentally investigated and either validated or rejected. Important therapeutic progress may well come out of such (*forceful* and *energetic*) thinking and acting!

References

Adler, A. (1968/1927) *Understanding Human Nature*. Greenwich, CT: Fawcett World (original work published 1927).

Albin, R. and Montagna, D.D. (1977) Mystical aspects of science, *Humanist*, 37(2), 44–6.

Alexander, F. and French, T.M. (1946) *Psychoanalytic Therapy*. New York: Ronald.

Alperson, B.L. (1976) On shibboleths, incantations, and the confusion of the I-thou and the oh-wow, *Humanist*, 36(1), 12–14.

Beck, A.T. (1976) *Cognitive Therapy and the Emotional Disorders*. New York: International Universities Press.

Benson, H. (1975) *The Relaxation Response*. New York: Avon.

Burton, A. (1969) *Encounter*. San Francisco: Jossey Bass.

Campbell, J. (1975) Seven levels of consciousness, *Psychology Today*, 9(4), 77–8.

Casriel, D. (1974) *A Scream Away from Happiness*. New York: Grosset and Dunlap.

Duffy, A. (1975) Esalen: slow death, *Village Voice*, 2 June, 8–9.

Ellis, A. (1957) *How to Live with a 'Neurotic'*. New York: Crown Publishers. [Revised edn, North Hollywood, CA: Wilshire Books, 1975.]

Ellis, A. (1962) *Reason and Emotion in Psychotherapy*. New York: Lyle Stuart.

Ellis, A. (1963) Toward a more precise definition of 'emotional' and 'intellectual' insight, *Psychological Reports*, 13, 125–6.

Ellis, A. (1971) *Growth Through Reason*. Palo Alto, CA: Science and Behavior Books; Hollywood, CA: Wilshire Books.
Ellis, A. (1972) What does transpersonal psychology have to offer to the art and science of psychotherapy, *Voices*, 8(3), 10–20.
Ellis, A. (1973) *Humanistic Psychotherapy: The Rational-Emotive Approach*. New York: Julian Press and McGraw-Hill Paperbacks.
Ellis, A. (1976a) The biological basis of human irrationality, *Journal of Individual Psychology*, 32, 145–68.
Ellis, A. (1976b) *Sex and the Liberated Man*. New York: Lyle Stuart.
Ellis, A. (1977a) *Anger – How to Live with and without it*. Secaucus, NJ: Citadel.
Ellis, A. (1977b) Religious belief in the United States today, *Humanist*, 37(2), 38–41.
Ellis, A. (1977c) Why scientific professionals believe mystical nonsense, *Psychiatric Opinion*, 14(2), 27–30.
Ellis, A. (1978) Rational-emotive therapy. In R.J. Corsini (ed.), *Current Psychotherapies* (rev. edn). Itasca, IL: Peacock.
Ellis, A. and Grieger, R. (1977) *Handbook of Rational-Emotive Therapy*. Vol. 1. New York: Springer.
Ellis, A. and Harper, R.A. (1975) *A New Guide to Rational Living*. Englewood Cliffs, NJ: Prentice-Hall; Hollywood, CA: Wilshire Books.
Finney, B.C. (1972) Say it again: an active therapy technique, *Psychotherapy*, 9, 128–31.
Flew, A. (1976) Parapsychology revisited: laws, miracles, and repeatability, *Humanist*, 36(3), 28–30.
Freud, S. (1965) *Standard Edition of the Complete Psychological Works of Sigmund Freud*. London: Hogarth.
Goldfried, M.R. and Davison, G.C. (1976) *Clinical Behavior Therapy*. New York: Holt, Rinehart and Winston.
Harrell, D.E., Jr. (1976) *All Things are Possible*. Bloomington, IN: Indiana University Press.
Hobbs, N. (1962) Sources of gain in psychotherapy, *American Psychologist*, 17, 741–7.
Hovland, C.I. and Janis, I.L. (1959) *Personality and Persuasibility*. New Haven, CT: Yale University Press.
Ingalls, J.D. (1976) *Human Energy: The Critical Factor for Individuals and Organizations*. Reading, MA: Addison-Wesley.
Jacobson, E. (1942) *You must Relax*. New York: McGraw-Hill.
Janov, A. (1970) *The Primal Scream*. New York: Dell.
Krippner, S., Davidson, R. and Peterson, N. (1973) Psi phenomena in Moscow, *Journal of Contemporary Psychotherapy*, 6, 79–88.
Kurtz, P. (1976) Gullibility and nincompoopery, *Religious Humanism*, Spring, 1–7.
Lazarus, A.A. (1976) *Learning to Relax* [Tape recording]. New York: Institute for Rational Living.
Lazarus, A.A. (1978) *In the Mind's Eye*. New York: Rawson.
Lembo, J. (1976) *The Counseling Process: A Rational Behavioral Approach*. New York: Libra.
Lowen, A. (1970) *Pleasure*. New York: Lancer.
Mahoney, M. (1974) *Cognition and Behavior Modification*. Cambridge, MA: Ballinger.
Maslow, A. (1962) *Toward a Psychology of Being*. Princeton, NJ: Van Nostrand.
Masters, W. and Johnson, V.A. (1970) *Human Sexual Inadequacy*. Boston: Little, Brown.
Maultsby, M.C., Jr. (1975) *Help Yourself to Happiness*. New York: Institute for Rational Living.
Maultsby, M.C., Jr. and Ellis, A. (1974) *Technique for Using Rational-Emotive Imagery*. New York: Institute for Rational Living.
Meichenbaum, D. (1977) *Cognitive Behavior Modification*. New York: Plenum.
Osgood, C.E. (1971) Exploration in semantic space, *Journal of Social Issues*, 24, 5–6.
Ostrander, S. and Schroeder, L. (1974) *Psychic Discoveries Behind the Iron Curtain*. New York: Bantam.
Perls, F. (1969) *Gestalt Therapy Verbatim*. Lafayette, CA: Real People Press.

Pulvino, C.J. (1975) Psychic energy: the counselor's undervalued resource, *Personnel and Guidance Journal*, 54(1), 28–32.
Rogers, C.R. (1961) *On Becoming a Person*. Boston: Houghton Mifflin.
Schutz, W.C. (1971) *Here Comes Everybody*. New York: Harper and Row.
Shapiro, D.H. and Zifferblatt, S.M. (1976) Zen meditation and behavioral self-control: similarities, differences, and clinical applications, *American Psychologist*, 31, 519–32.
Smith, R.F. (1976) *Prelude to Science*. New York: Scribner's.
Sperry, R.W. (1977) Bridging science and values: a unifying view of mind and brain, *American Psychologist*, 32, 237–45.
Targ, R. and Puthoff, R. (1977) *Mind-reach*. New York: Delacorte Press.
Weil, A. (1973) *The Natural Mind*. Boston: Houghton Mifflin.
Wolberg, L.R. (1967) *The Technique of Psychotherapy*. New York: Grune and Stratton.

11
Vivid Methods in Rational-Emotive Therapy

Windy Dryden

The fundamental goal of rational-emotive therapy is to enable clients to live effective lives by helping them change their faulty inferences and irrational evaluations about themselves, other people and the world. While there are many ways of achieving this goal, the purpose of this chapter is to highlight ways in which rational-emotive therapists can make the therapeutic process a more vivid experience for their clients, so that they may be stimulated to identify and change their faulty inferences and irrational evaluations more effectively. A number of rational-emotive and cognitive therapists have already written on the use of vivid methods in therapy (Knaus and Wessler, 1976; Ellis, 1979; Walen et al., 1980; Wessler and Wessler, 1980; Arnkoff, 1981; Freeman, 1981). However, a comprehensive account of the uses, advantages and limitations of such methods has yet to appear in the literature on rational-emotive therapy. In this chapter, attention will be given to the use of vivid methods in *problem assessment*, vivid *disputing methods*, and vivid ways in which clients may *work through* their emotional and behavioural problems.

Rationale for Vivid Methods in RET

Rational-emotive therapists aim to help clients achieve their goals through the systematic application of cognitive, emotive and behavioural methods. However, therapist and client rely heavily on verbal dialogue in their in-session encounters. The tone of such dialogue in rational-emotive therapy sessions can be rich, stimulating and arousing, but it is far too often dry and mundane (as supervisors of novice rational-emotive therapists will testify). While the role of emotional arousal in the facilitation of attitude change is complex (Hoehn-Saric, 1978), it is my contention that the majority of clients can be helped best to re-examine faulty inferences and irrational beliefs if we, as therapists, gain their full attention and make therapy a memorable experience for them. While there are no studies that address this point in the rational-emotive therapy literature, there is some suggestion from process and outcome studies carried out on client-centred therapy that vivid therapist interventions are associated with successful client outcome and with certain client in-therapy behaviours which have, in turn, been linked to positive outcome (Rice, 1965, 1973; Rice and Wagstaff, 1967; Rice and Gaylin, 1973; Wexler, 1975; Wexler and Butler, 1976). At present we do not know whether any client in-therapy behaviours are associated with successful outcome in RET. Yet, it is possible to hypothesise that such client in-session behaviours as attending to and being fully involved in the therapeutic process and making links between in-session dialogue and out-of-session activities will be associated with therapeutic gain in RET. If this proves correct, then it is my further contention that vivid methods in RET may effectively bring about such client behaviour.

Given the dearth of much-needed studies on these points, anecdotal evidence will have to suffice. This involves feedback from my clients, who have frequently related incidents of (1) how my own vivid therapeutic interventions helped them to re-examine a variety of their dysfunctional cognitions and (2) how they, with my encouragement, improved by making the working-through process a more stimulating experience for themselves.

It should again be stressed at the outset that, while there is a place for vivid methods in RET, these are best introduced into therapy at appropriate times and within the context of a good therapeutic alliance between therapist and client.

Problem Assessment

Effective rational-emotive therapy depends initially on the therapist gaining a clear understanding of (1) the client's problems in cognitive, emotional and behavioural terms and (2) the contexts in which the client's problems occur. To a great extent, the therapist is dependent on the client's verbal reports in gaining such an understanding. It is in this area that many obstacles to progress may appear. Some clients have great difficulty identifying and/or accurately labelling their emotional experiences. Other clients are in touch with and able to report their emotions but find it hard to relate these to activating events (either external or internal). Yet a further group of clients is easily able to report problematic activating events and emotional experiences but has difficulty seeing how these may relate to mediating cognitions. Vivid methods can be used in a variety of ways to overcome such obstacles to a valid and reliable assessment of client problems.

Vividness in Portraying Activating Events

With some clients, traditional assessment procedures through verbal dialogue do not always yield the desired information. When this occurs, rational-emotive therapists often use imagery methods. They ask clients to conjure up evocative images of activating events. Such evocative imagery often stimulates the client's memory concerning her or his emotional reactions, or indeed in some instances leads to the re-experiencing of these reactions in the session. While focusing on such images, the client can also begin to gain access to cognitive processes below the level of awareness that cannot be easily reached through verbal dialogue.

One particularly effective use of imagery in the assessment of client problems is that of bringing future events into the present. This is illustrated by the following exchange between myself and a client who was terrified that her mother might die, which led her to be extremely unassertive with the mother.

Therapist: So you feel you just can't speak up to her. Because if you did, what might happen?
Client: Well she might have a fit.
Therapist: And what might happen if she did?
Client: She might have a heart attack and die.
Therapist: Well, we know that she is a fit woman, but let's go along with your fear for the moment. Okay?
Client: Okay.
Therapist: What if she did die?
Client: I just can't think . . . I . . . I'm sorry.
Therapist: That's okay. I know this is difficult, but I really think it would be helpful if we could get to the bottom of things. Okay? [Client nods]. Look, Marjorie, I want you to imagine that your mother has just died this morning. Can you imagine that? [Client nods and begins to shake.] What are you experiencing?
Client: When you said my mother was dead I began to feel all alone . . . like there was no one to care for me . . . no one I could turn to.
Therapist: And if there is no one who cares for you, no one you can turn to . . .?
Client: Oh, God! I know I couldn't cope on my own.

Instructing clients to imagine vividly something that has been warded off often leads to anxiety itself. It is important to process this anxiety, as it is sometimes related to the client's central problem. Issues such as fear of loss of control, phrenophobia and extreme discomfort anxiety are often revealed when this anxiety is fully assessed. However, some clients do find it difficult to imagine events spontaneously and require therapist assistance.

While imagery methods are now routinely used in cognitive behaviour therapy (e.g. Lazarus, 1978), there has been little written on how therapists can stimulate clients' imagery processes. I have used a number of the following vivid methods to try and help clients utilise their potential for imagining events.

Vivid, Connotative Therapist Language One effective way of helping clients to use their imagery potential is for the therapist to use rich, colourful and evocative language while aiding clients to set the scene. Unless the therapist has gained prior diagnostic information, he or she is sometimes uncertain about which stimuli in the activating event are particularly related to the client's problem. Thus, it is best to give clients many alternatives. For example, with a socially anxious client I proceeded thus, after attempting without success to get him to use his own potential imagery.

Therapist: So at the moment we are unclear about what you are anxious about. What I'd like to suggest is that we use your imagination to help us. I will help you set the scene based on what we have already discussed. However, since we have yet to discover detailed factors, some of the things I say might not be relevant. Will you bear with me and let me know when what I say touches a nerve in you?
Client: Okay.
Therapist: Fine. Just close your eyes and imagine you are about to walk into the dance. You walk in and some of the guys there glance at you. You can see the *smirks* on their *mocking* faces and one of them *blows* you a kiss. [Here I am testing out a hypothesis based on previously gained information.] You start to *seethe* inside and . . .
Client: Okay, when you said I started to seethe, that struck a chord. I thought I can't let them get away with that but if I let go I'll just go berserk. I started feeling anxious.
Therapist: And if you went berserk?
Client: I couldn't show my face in there again.
Therapist: What would happen then?
Client: I don't know. I . . . It's funny – the way I see it, I would never go out again.

Here I was using words such as 'smirks', 'mocking', 'blows' and 'seethe' deliberately in my attempt to stimulate the client's imagination. It is also important for the therapist to vary his or her tone so that this matches the language employed.

Photographs I have at times asked clients to bring to interviews photographs of significant others or significant places. These are kept on hand to be used at relevant moments in the assessment process. I have found the use of photographs particularly helpful when the client is discussing an event in the past that is still bothering her or him. Thus, for example, one client who spoke without feeling about being rejected by his father who died seven years earlier, broke down in tears when I asked him to look at a picture of him and his father standing apart from one another. Feelings of hurt and anger (with their associated cognitions) were expressed, which enabled us to move to the disputing stage.

Other mementoes In a similar vein, I have sometimes asked clients to bring in mementoes. These may include pictures they have drawn, paintings that have meaning for them, and poems either written by themselves or other people. The important point is that these mementoes are to be related to issues that the client is working on in therapy. A road block to assessment was successfully overcome with one client when I asked her to bring in a memento that reminded her of her mother. She brought in a bottle of perfume that her mother was accustomed to wearing. When I asked her to smell the perfume at a point in therapy when the assessment process through verbal dialogue was again breaking down, the client was helped to identify feelings of jealousy towards her mother, which she experienced whenever her mother left her to go out socialising. Moreover, my client was ashamed of such feelings. This issue was centrally related to her presenting problem of depression.

Another of my clients was depressed about losing her boyfriend. I had great difficulty helping her to identify any related mediating cognitions through traditional assessment procedures. Several tentative guesses on my part also failed to pinpoint relevant cognitive processes. I then asked her to bring to our next session anyihing that reminded her of her ex-boyfriend. She brought in a record of a popular song that had become known to them as 'our song'. When I played the song at an appropriate point in the interview, my client began to sob and expressed feelings of abandonment, hurt and fear for the future. Again a vivid method had unearthed important assessment material where traditional methods had failed.

It should be noted from these examples that quite often such dramatic methods lead to the expression of strong affective reactions in the session. This is often an important part of the process, because such affective reactions are gateways to the identification of maladaptive cognitive processes that are difficult to identify through more traditional methods of assessment.

The 'Interpersonal Nightmare' Technique Rational-emotive and cognitive therapists sometimes employ methods originally derived from gestalt therapy and psychodrama to assist them in the assessment phase of therapy. These have been adequately described (Nardi, 1979; Arnkoff, 1981), and will not be discussed here. I would like to describe a related technique I have developed (Dryden, 1980), which I call the 'interpersonal nightmare' technique. This technique may be best used with clients who are able to specify only sketchily an anticipated 'dreaded' event involving other people but are able neither to specify in any detail the nature of the event nor to specify how they would react if the event were to occur. First the client is given a homework assignment to imagine the 'dreaded' event. He or she is told to write a brief segment of a play about it, specifying the exact words that the protagonists would use. The client is encouraged to give full rein to imagination while focusing on what he or she fears might happen. An example will suffice. The following scenario was developed by a 55-year-old woman with alcohol problems who was terrified of making errors at the office where she worked as a typist.

Scene: Boss's office where he sits behind a very large desk. He has found out that one of the typists had inadvertently filed a letter wrongly and sends for her. She comes in and is made to stand in front of her boss.

Boss: Have you anything to say in this matter?

Typist (me): Only that I apologise and will be more careful in the future.

Boss: What do you mean by saying you will be more careful in the future – what makes you think you have a future? [At this point he starts banging on the desk.] I have never yet met anyone less competent or less suited to the job than you are. You mark my words, I will make life so uncomfortable for you that you will leave. When I took over this job I intended to have the people I wanted working for me, and you are not on that list. I have already gotten rid of two typists, and I

> shall see that you are the third. Now get out of my office you stupid, blundering fool, and remember I shall always be watching you and you will never know when I shall be behind you.

I then read over the scene with the client, making enquiries about the tone in which she thought her boss would make these statements and asking her to identify which words the boss would emphasise. I then arranged for a local actor who was the same age as the boss to enact the scene realistically on cassette. In the next session I instructed my client to visualise the room in which the encounter might take place. She briefly described the room, paying particular attention to where her boss would be sitting and where she would be standing. I then played her the cassette, which evoked strong feelings of fear of being physically harmed and humiliated. Again, important data had been collected that traditional assessment procedures had failed to uncover.

These examples have shown how rational-emotive therapists can employ various visual, language and auditory methods to help clients vividly imagine appropriate activating events. This in turn helps them more easily identify maladaptive emotional experiences and related cognitive processes that are not readily identified through the verbal interchange of the psychotherapeutic interview. It is important to note that the use of such methods is not being advocated for its own sake. They are employed with specific purposes in mind.

Rational-Emotive Problem Solving

Knaus and Wessler (1976) have described a method that they call rational-emotive problem solving (REPS). This method involves the therapist creating conditions in the therapy session which approximate those the client encounters in her or his everyday life and which give rise to emotional problems. Knaus and Wessler contend that this method may be used either in a planned or impromptu fashion and is particularly valuable when clients experience difficulty in identifying emotional experiences and related cognitive processes through verbal dialogue with their therapists. I employed this method with a male client who reported difficulty in acting assertively in his life and claimed not to be able to identify the emotions and thoughts that inhibited the expression of assertive responses. During our discussion I began to search around for my pouch of pipe tobacco. Finding it empty, I interrupted my client and asked him if he would drive to town, purchase my favourite tobacco, adding that if he hurried he could return for the last five minutes of our interview. He immediately got up, took my money and walked out of my office towards his car. I rushed after him, brought him back into my office and together we processed his reactions to this simulated experience.

It is clear that this technique must be used with therapeutic judgement and that its use may threaten or even destroy the therapeutic alliance between client and therapist. However, because rational-emotive therapists value risk-taking, they are often prepared to use such techniques when more traditional and less risky methods have failed to bring about therapeutic improvement. It is further important, as Beck et al. (1979) have stressed, for the therapist to ask the client for the latter's honest reactions to this procedure, to ascertain whether it may have future therapeutic value for the client. When a client indicates that she or he has found the rational-emotive problem-solving method unhelpful, the therapist is advised to explain the rationale for attempting such a procedure and disclose that he or she intended no harm but was attempting to be helpful. Normally clients respect such disclosures, and in fact the therapist in doing so provides a useful model for the client, namely, that it is possible to acknowledge errors non-defensively without damning oneself. However, with this method, it is apparent that therapists cannot realistically disclose their rationale in advance of initiating the method, because this would detract from its potential therapeutic value.

Dreams

Although Albert Ellis has written a regular column for *Penthouse* magazine providing rational-emotive interpretations for readers' dreams, rational-emotive therapists are not generally noted for using dream material. However, there is no good reason why dream material cannot be used in RET as long as (1) it does not predominate in the therapeutic process and (2) the therapist has a definite purpose in mind in using it.

Freeman (1981: 228–9) has outlined a number of further guidelines for the use of dreams for assessment purposes:

1 The dream needs to be understood in thematic rather than symbolic terms.
2 The thematic content of the dream is idiosyncratic to the dreamer and must be viewed within the context of the dreamer's life.
3 The specific language and imagery are important to the meaning.
4 The affective responses to the dream can be seen as similar to the dreamer's affective responses in waking situations.
5 The particular length of the dream is of lesser import than the content.
6 The dream is a product of and the responsibility of the dreamer.
7 Dreams can be used when the patient appears stuck in therapy.

I inadvertently stumbled on the usefulness of dream material for assessment purposes when working with a 28-year-old depressed student who would frequently reiterate, 'I'm depressed and I don't know why'. I had virtually exhausted all the assessment methods I knew (including those described in this chapter) to help her identify depressogenic thoughts in situations when she experienced depressions, but without success. In a desperate last attempt, I asked her if she could remember any of her dreams, not expecting in the least that this line of enquiry would prove fruitful. To my surprise she said yes, she did have a recurring dream. In this dream she saw herself walking alone along a river bank, and when she peered into the river, she saw a reflection of herself as a very old woman. This image filled her with extreme sadness and depression. On further discussion she said that she believed that this dream meant that she had no prospect of finding any happiness in her life, either in love relationships or in her career and that she was doomed to spend her years alone, ending up as a sad, pathetic, old woman. This account of the dream and subsequent discussion of its meaning enabled me to help her identify a number of inferential distortions and irrational beliefs, which provided the focus for subsequent cognitive restructuring.

Daydreams may also provide important material for assessment purposes. For some people, particular daydreams occur in response to and as compensation for a negative activating event. Thus, one client reported having the daydream of establishing a multinational corporation after failing to sell insurance to prospective customers. The use of such daydreams by clients may not necessarily be dysfunctional but may impede them (as in the preceding example) from getting to the core of their problems. Often daydreams are an expression of our hopes and aspirations, and I have found it valuable to ask clients not only about the content of such material but also what would stop them from actualising their goals. Much important assessment material is gathered in this manner, in particular concerning ideas of low frustration tolerance.

In Vivo Therapy Sessions

Sacco (1981) has outlined the value of conducting therapy sessions in real-life settings in which clients experience difficulties. I have found moving outside the interview room to such settings particularly useful in gaining assessment material when traditional methods have failed to provide such data. For example, I once saw a male student who complained of avoiding social situations. He did so in case others would see his hands tremble. Traditional assessment methods yielded no further data. To overcome this treatment impasse, I suggested to him that we needed to collect more data and we eventually conducted a therapy session in a coffee shop where I asked him to go and get us both a cup of coffee. He refused because he feared that his hands might tremble, but I firmly persisted with my request. He was able to identify a stream of negative cognitions on the way from our table to the service counter. He returned without our coffees but with valuable information, which we processed later in my office. It is important for therapists to explain their rationale for conducting in vivo sessions in advance, in order to gain client cooperation. In addition, obtaining clients' reactions to these sessions is often helpful, particularly if in vivo sessions are planned for use later in the therapeutic process.

Disputing

In this section, various vivid disputing methods will be outlined. The purpose of these methods is (1) to help clients see the untenable basis and dysfunctional nature of their irrational beliefs and to replace them with more rational ones and (2) to help them make more accurate inferences about reality. These methods often demonstrate the rational message powerfully but indirectly, and they do not necessarily call upon the client to answer such questions as 'Where is the evidence . . .?'

It is important for the therapist to make certain preparations before initiating vivid disputing methods, because the success of such methods depends upon (1) the client clearly understanding the link between thoughts, feelings and behaviours and (2) the therapist ascertaining particular biographical information about the client.

Preparing for Vivid Disputing

The Thought–Feeling–Behaviour Link After the therapist has undertaken a thorough assessment of the client's target problem, the next task is to help the client see the connections among thoughts, feelings and behaviours. Here again vivid methods can be employed. Thus, the therapist, while speaking with the client, might pick up a book, drop it on the floor and continue talking to the client. After a while, if the client has made no comment, the therapist can ask for both affective and cognitive reactions to this incident. Thus, the client is given a vivid here-and-now example of the thought–feeling link.

Biographical Information Before initiating the vivid disputing process, I often find it helpful to gather certain information about the client. I like to find out about my client's *interests*, *hobbies* and *work situation*. I have found this information often helps me adapt my interventions, using phrases that will be meaningful to my client, given her or his idiosyncratic life situation. Thus, if my client is passionately interested in boxing, a message utilising a boxing analogy may well have greater impact than a golfing analogy.

I also find it helpful to discover *who my client admires*. I do this because later I may wish to ask my client how he or she thinks these admired individuals might solve similar problems. This prompts the client to identify with a model to imitate. Lazarus (1978) has employed a similar method with children. For example, I asked a male client to imagine that his admired grandfather experienced public speaking anxiety, and I enquired how he would have overcome it. This helped him identify a coping strategy that he used to overcome his own public speaking anxiety problem. This approach is best used if the client also can acknowledge that the admired individual is fallible and thus prone to human irrationality. In addition, it is important that the client sees the feasibility of imitating the model.

I find it invaluable to ask my clients about their *previous experiences of attitude change.* I try and discern the salient features of such a change for possible replication in my in-session disputing strategies. For example, one anxious female client told me she had changed her mind about fox-hunting after reading a number of personal accounts offering arguments against fox-hunting. As part of my disputing plan, I directed this client to autobiographies of people who had overcome anxiety. Another client claimed she had in the past received help from speaking to people who had experienced problems similar to her own. I arranged for this client to speak to some of my ex-clients who had experienced but overcome comparable problems.

I now propose to outline a number of ways in which rational-emotive therapists can vividly employ disputing techniques. The importance of tailoring interventions to meet the specific, idiosyncratic requirements of clients should be borne in mind throughout.

Vivid Disputing Methods

Disputing in the Presence of Vivid Stimuli In a previous section of this chapter, I outlined a number of ways of vividly portraying activating events to help clients identify their emotional reactions and the cognitive determinants of these reactions. I outlined various visual, language, auditory and olfactory methods. These same methods can be used as context material in the disputing process. For example, one client brought along a drawing of herself and her *mother.* She portrayed her mother as a very large, menacing figure and herself as a small figure crouching in fear in front of her mother. I asked the client to draw another picture where she and her mother were of the same height, standing face-to-face, looking each other in the eye. When she brought in this drawing, I enquired how her attitude towards her mother differed in the two pictures. This not only provided her with a demonstration that it was possible for her to evaluate her mother differently, but also led to a fruitful discussion in which I disputed some of her irrational beliefs inherent in the first drawing while having her focus on the second.

A similar tactic was employed using the 'interpersonal nightmare' technique with the 55-year-old woman mentioned earlier. After disputing some of the irrational beliefs uncovered when the technique was employed for assessment purposes, I repeatedly played the woman the tape while having her dispute some of the irrational beliefs it revealed. A similar method can be used when in vivo sessions are conducted. Earlier in this chapter I reported the case of a student who was anxious about his hands shaking in public. Both assessment and later disputing of his irrational beliefs were carried out in a coffee bar. Indeed he practised disputing his irrational beliefs while carrying two shaking cups of coffee back from the service counter to our table. Disputing in the presence of vivid stimuli enables the client to build bridges from in-session to out-of-session situations.

Imagery Methods One very effective imagery method that can be used in the disputing of irrational beliefs is that of time projection (Lazarus, 1978). When a client makes grossly exaggerated negative evaluations of an event, he often stops thinking about it and therefore cannot see beyond its 'dreaded' implications. The purpose of time projection is to enable clients to see vividly that time and the world continue after the 'dreaded event' has occurred. Thus, for example, a Malaysian student whose tuition fees were paid for by his village concluded that it would be terrible if he failed his exams because he couldn't bear to face his fellow villagers. I helped him to imagine his return to his village while experiencing shame. I then gradually advanced time forward in imagery. He began to see that it was likely that his fellow villagers would eventually come to adopt a compassionate viewpoint towards him and, even if they did not, he could always live happily in another part of the country or in another part of the world.

Imagery methods which focus on helping clients to think carefully and critically about 'dreaded' events are also extremely valuable. For example, another client who had a fear of other people seeing his hands shake was asked to imagine going into a bar, ordering a drink and drinking while his hands shook. He said that he would be extremely anxious about this because other people in the bar would stare at him. He was asked to imagine how many people would stare at him. Would they stare in unison or would they stare one at a time? He was asked to imagine how often they would stare at him, how long they would stare at him and how often in the evening they would resume staring at him. He concluded that everybody would not stare at him and those who did stare would possibly only stare for about 30 seconds and he could stand that. This and other methods illustrate that it is possible simultaneously to help clients dispute both their faulty inferences and irrational evaluations. Another technique I employed with this same client was 'imagery to exaggeration'. He was asked to imagine his hands shaking while consuming drink and with everybody in the bar staring at him continually for 3 hours. At this point he burst out laughing and realised the exaggerated nature of his inference.

Rational-emotive imagery is a frequently employed technique and has been fully described by Maultsby and Ellis (1974) and Ellis (1979). It often has dramatic impact and thus qualifies as a vivid method. It is worth while noting at this point that some clients have difficulty conjuring up images and may have to be trained in a stepwise fashion to utilise this ability. Furthermore, while helpful, it is probably not necessary for clients to imagine with extreme clarity.

The Rational-Emotive Therapist as Raconteur Wessler and Wessler (1980) have outlined the therapeutic value of relating various stories, parables, witty sayings, poems, aphorisms and jokes to clients. The important factor here is that the therapist modifies the content of these to fit the client's idiosyncratic situation. Telling identical stories to two different clients may well have two different effects. One client may be deeply affected by the story, while for another the story may prove meaningless. It is important that rational-emotive therapists become acquainted with a wide variety of these stories and be prepared to modify them from client to client, without introducing unwarranted distortions.

Active Visual Methods Active visual methods combine therapist or client activity with a vivid visual presentation. Young (1980) has outlined one such method, which he uses to help clients see the impossibility of assigning a global rating to themselves. He asks a client to describe some of his behaviours, attributes, talents and interests. Every answer the client gives Young writes on a white sticky label and sticks the label on the client. This continues until the client is covered with white sticky labels and can begin to see the impossibility of assigning one global rating to such a complex being. Wessler and Wessler (1980) outline similar active visual methods to communicate a similar point. For example, they ask their client to assign a comprehensive rating to a basket of fruit or a desk. Clients are encouraged to explore actively the components of the fruit basket or desk while attempting to assign a global rating to it.

Visual Models I have previously described the use of visual models I have devised, each of which demonstrates a rational message (Dryden, 1980). For example, I employ a model called the 'LFT splash'. In the model a young man is seated at the top of a roller coaster with a young woman standing at the bottom. I tell clients that the young man does not move because he is telling himself that he can't stand the splash. Clients are asked to think what the young man would have to tell himself in order to reach the woman. This model is particularly useful in introducing to clients the idea of tolerating acute time-limited discomfort which, if tolerated, would help them achieve their goals.

Flamboyant Therapist Actions A common disputing strategy that rational-emotive therapists use in verbal dialogue when clients conclude they are stupid for acting stupidly is to ask some variant of the question 'How are you a stupid person for acting stupidly?'. Alternatively, instead of asking such questions, the therapist could suddenly leap to the floor and start barking like a dog for about 30 seconds, resume her or his seat, and then ask the client to evaluate this action. Clients usually say that the action was stupid. The therapist can then ask whether that stupid action makes him or her a stupid person. Such flamboyant actions often enable clients to discriminate more easily between global self-ratings and rating of behaviours or attributes.

Rational Role Reversal Rational role reversal has been described by Kassinove and DiGiuseppe (1975). In this technique, the therapist plays a naive client with an emotional problem that is usually similar to the client's. The client is encouraged to adopt the role of the rational-emotive therapist and help the 'client' dispute his or her irrational belief. As Kassinove and DiGiuseppe point out, this technique is best used after the client has developed some skill at disputing some of his or her own irrational ideas. A related technique has been devised by Burns (1980), which he calls 'externalisation of voices'. In this technique which is again used after the client has displayed some skill at disputing irrational beliefs, the therapist adopts the irrational part of the client's personality and supplies the client with irrational messages. The client's task is to respond rationally to the irrational messages. When clients show a high level of skill at this, the therapist, in role, can try hard to overwhelm the client with a barrage of quick-fire irrational messages, thus helping the client to develop an automatic ability to respond to his or her own irrational messages. This method also can be used to help clients identify those negative thoughts to which they experience difficulty responding.

Therapist Self-disclosure Some clients find therapist self-disclosure an extremely persuasive method, while for others it is contraindicated. One way of attempting to ascertain a client's possible reactions to therapist self-disclosure is to include an appropriate item in a pre-therapy questionnaire. It may well be wise to avoid using therapist self-disclosure with clients who respond negatively to the item. In any case, the therapist had better ascertain the client's reaction to any self-disclosing statements she or he might make. The research literature on this topic indicates that therapists are advised not to disclose personal information about themselves too early in the therapeutic process (Dies, 1973). When therapists do disclose information about themselves, it is my experience that the most effective forms of self-disclosure are those in which they portray themselves as coping rather than mastery models. Thus, for example, it is better for the therapist to say to the client, 'I used to have a similar problem, but this is how I overcame it', rather than say, 'I have never had this problem, because I believe . . .'

Paradoxical Therapist Actions This method is often best used when clients, through their actions, communicate messages about themselves to the therapist that are based on irrational beliefs. For example, I once saw a female client who experienced a lot of rheumatic pain but had an attitude of low frustration tolerance towards it. Her behaviour towards me in sessions indicated the attitude, 'I am a poor soul, feel sorry for me'. This prompted me to adopt an overly sympathetic and diligent stance towards her. Thus, at the beginning of every session I treated her as if she could hardly walk and escorted her by arm to her chair and made frequent enquiries about her comfort. This eventually prompted her to make statements such as, 'Don't treat me like a child', 'I can cope', or 'It's not as bad as all that'. I then helped her to identify and dispute some of the original implicit irrational messages.

Whenever she began to lapse back into her self-pitying attitude, I began to behave in an overly solicitous manner again, which provided a timely reminder for her to attend to the behavioural components of her philosophy of low frustration tolerance and then to the philosophy itself.

Paradoxical Therapist Communications Ellis (1977) has written on the use of humour in RET, where the therapist humorously exaggerates clients' irrational beliefs. He points out the importance of using humour against the irrational belief, rather than as an *ad hominem* attack. Taking clients' beliefs and inferences to an absurd conclusion is another paradoxical technique that can be used. Thus, for 'shameful' acts or traits, therapists can take this to its illogical conclusion by saying, 'Well there is no doubt about it, they will find out, then they will tell their friends, some of whom will call up the local television station, and before you know it you will be on the six o'clock news'. Again, it is important that clients perceive that such communications are being directed against their beliefs rather than against them. Thus, feedback from clients on this matter had better be sought.

Rational Songs Ellis (1977) has written about the use of his now-famous rational songs in therapy. For example, the therapist can hand a client a song sheet and sing, preferably in an outrageous voice, a rational song that has been carefully selected to communicate the rational alternatives to the client's target irrational belief. Because Ellis tends to favour tunes that were written many years ago, it may be more productive for the therapist to rewrite the words to more up-to-date and popular songs, for clients not familiar with some of the 'old favourites'.

In-session Inference Tests Clients are likely to make faulty inferences about their therapist similar to those they make about other people in their lives. For example, one of my clients saw me talking to a fellow therapist at the end of one of our sessions. At our next session she told me that she was anxious about this because she was convinced I had been talking about her and laughing about what she had told me in the session (she was not in fact paranoid). I proceeded to pull out two pieces of paper, kept one for myself and gave the other one to her. I told her that I wanted to find out whether she indeed had extraordinary mind-reading powers. I thus wrote down the word 'chicken' on my piece of paper and asked her to concentrate very carefully for the next 3 minutes and to write down what she thought I was thinking about. I said that I would keep thinking about the word I had written down to make it a fair experiment. After the 3 minutes, she wrote down the word 'baseball'. This became known as the 'baseball-chicken' interview, which she recalled frequently when she made arbitrary inferences concerning the meaning of other people's behaviour.

Using the Therapist–Client Relationship Wessler (1982) has written that it is important for the rational-emotive therapist to enquire about the nature of his or her client's reaction to him or her, that is, to examine some of the client's here-and-now attitudes. Little has been written about this approach in the rational-emotive literature, and thus relatively little is known about its potential as a framework for disputing inaccurate inferences and irrational beliefs. Wessler (1982) also advocates that therapists give clients frank feedback about their impact on the therapist and explore whether clients have a similar impact on other people. Such generalisations must of course be made with caution, but such discussion is often a stimulus for clients to become more sensitive to their impact on other people and often leads them to ask other people about their interpersonal impact (Anchin and Kiesler, 1982).

The advantage of using the therapist–client relationship in this way is that it provides both parties with an opportunity to process the client's inferences and beliefs in an immediate and often vivid fashion. The outcome of such strategies is often more memorable for clients than the outcome of such traditional disputing methods where client inferences and beliefs about recent past events are processed.

Therapist Paralinguistic and Non-verbal Behaviour When rational-emotive therapists want to emphasise a point, one important way of doing so is for them to vary their paralinguistic and non-verbal behaviour. For example, Walen et al. (1980: 178) note that, when Ellis in his public demonstrations talks about something 'awful', he drops his voice several notes, stretches out the word and increases his volume, producing a dreary and dramatic sound, for example, 'and it's AWWWWWFUL that he doesn't like me'. Later, when he changes the word 'awful' to 'unfortunate' or a 'need' to a 'want', Ellis again pronounces the words now reflecting rational concepts in a distinct way. He says the key word slowly, enunciates very clearly, and raises the pitch of his voice as well as the volume. In addition, the therapist might associate some dramatic non-verbal behaviour with the paralinguistic clue. For example, when the word 'awful' is pronounced, the therapist might sink to the floor, holding his neck as if strangling himself.

Therapeutic Markers Another way of emphasising a point is to draw the client's attention to the fact that an important point is about to be made. For example, I might say to a client when I want to emphasise a point, 'Now I want you to listen extremely carefully to this point because, if you miss it, it would be awwwful' (therapist sinks to the floor again). I call such interventions 'therapeutic markers'. Another way of emphasising statements is to change one's body position. For example, by moving their torso forward towards clients, therapists can indicate the importance of their following statements. Whenever I want clients to become aware of important statements they have made, particularly when they make more rational statements at the beginning of the disputing process, I may, for example, pause and say, 'Excuse me, could you just repeat what you said – I really want to make a note of this'. If I am recording a session, I might say,

'Hold on a minute, I really want you to hear what you have just said, I can't believe it myself, I just want to check it out'.

Pragmatic Disputes One major way of encouraging clients to surrender their irrational beliefs in favour of more rational ones is to point out to them, and in this context in dramatic terms, the implications of continued adherence to their irrational beliefs. Ellis counsels that for particularly resistant and difficult clients this tactic is often the most effective (Ellis, 1985). Quite often I have heard Ellis tell clients something like, 'If you continue to cling to that belief you'll suffer for the rest of your life'. Here, as before, he changes his paralinguistic and non-verbal behaviour when he states the conclusion, 'You'll suffer for the rest of your life'. In similar vein, when clients state that they can't (or, rather, won't) change their beliefs, he points out to them the logical implications of not doing so when he says forcefully, 'So suffer!' In this regard it would be interesting to determine under what conditions pragmatic disputes are more effective than philosophical ones.

Working Through

This section focuses on how therapists can help clients to work vividly through some of their emotional problems. Ellis (1983) has criticised some popular behavioural techniques on the grounds that they do not necessarily encourage clients to make profound philosophical changes in their lives. In particular he criticises those methods that encourage the client to confront a dreaded event gradually. He posits that this gradualism may indeed reinforce some clients low-frustration-tolerance ideas. Whenever possible, then, rational-emotive therapists encourage their clients to act in dramatic and vivid ways because they believe significant attitude change is more likely to follow the successful completion of such tasks. I will outline the vivid methods that clients can put into practice behaviourally and cognitively in their everyday lives. First, however, rational-emotive therapists face a further problem, which has received insufficient attention in the RET literature: how to encourage clients to carry out their homework assignments.

Vivid Cues for Encouraging Clients to do their Homework

While some clients conscientiously do the homework assignments they and their therapists have negotiated, other clients do not. It is true that some clients do not follow through on these assignments because of low-frustration-tolerance ideas; still other clients do not follow through, particularly early on in the working-through process, because they require some vivid reminders to initiate this process. With such clients, I have found it particularly helpful to ask them what they generally find memorable in everyday life experiences. For example, some people find the printed word memorable, while others have visual images on which they cue. Yet others focus primarily on auditory stimuli. I find that it is profitable to capitalise on whatever channel the client finds memorable.

Vivid Visual Cues There are a number of ways clients can remind themselves to initiate the disputing process. A number of rational-emotive therapists encourage clients to carry around small cards 3 inches × 5 inches with rational self-statements written on them, to which clients can refer at various times. Other therapists have encouraged clients to write reminders to themselves either to initiate a homework assignment or to refer to a rational message. These clients are encouraged to pin such messages at various places around the home or in their work situation. I find it helpful to encourage those clients who find visual images powerful to associate a particular dysfunctional feeling with a visual image that would enable them to initiate the disputing process. Thus one client found it helpful to conjure up a sign in her mind that said 'dispute' when she began to feel anxious. Another client, who was depressed, began to associate the onset of depression with a road sign on which was written 'act now'.

Another strategy I have used is to ascertain from clients what, if any, in-session experiences they have found particularly memorable. I try to help them encapsulate some of these experiences as a cue either to initiate the disputing process or to remind themselves of the relevant rational principle to which this experience referred. One client who was prone to thinking of himself as an idiot for acting idiotically found it memorable when I made strange faces at him to help him get the point that concluding he was an idiot for acting idiotically was an overgeneralisation. Whenever he began to make such an overgeneralisation in everyday life, he would get the image of my making faces and quickly remembered to what this referred. This helped him accept himself regardless of any idiotic act he actually made or thought he might make in the future.

Another client who did virtually no cognitive disputing or behavioural assignments outside therapy sessions was helped in the following manner. First, this issue was made the focus of therapy. Instead of asking her traditional disputing questions, I asked her to imagine what I would say to her were I to respond to her irrational beliefs. She in fact had understood rational principles because her answers were very good. Her problem was that she would not employ these principles. I then asked her if there was any way she could conjure up a picture of me giving her rational messages at various emotionally vulnerable times in her everyday life. She hit on the idea of imagining that I was perched on her shoulder whispering rational messages into her ear. Additionally, she began to carry around a small card that said 'Imagine that Dr Dryden is on your shoulder'. This proved a particularly effective technique where all else had failed.

Vivid Language Wexler and Butler (1976) have argued in favour of therapists using expressive language in therapy. I have found that one of the major benefits of using vivid non-profane language is that clients remember these vivid expressions or catch-phrases and use them as shorthand ways of disputing irrational beliefs in their everyday lives. For example, in the case where I helped a client dispute a particular distorted inference by having her attempt to read my mind (the 'baseball-chicken' interview), whenever the client concluded that other people were making negative inferences about her without supporting data, she would remember the phrase 'baseball and chicken'. This served (1) as a timely reminder that she might be making incorrect conclusions from the data at hand, and (2) as a cue for her to start examining the evidence.

In a related technique, the therapist asks the client to give his or her own distinctive name to a faulty psychological process. Wessler and Wessler (1980) give such an example where a client came to refer to himself as 'Robert the Rule Maker', to describe his tendency to make demands on himself and other people. A knowledge of clients' subcultural values is particularly helpful here. I worked in a working-class area in Birmingham, England, and one word my clients frequently used, which was unfamiliar to me, was the word 'mather' (this is pronounced 'my-the' and means to be worried or bothered). I helped one client who was angry with her mother to see her mother as a fallible human being with a worrying problem, and that she could be accepted for this rather than be damned for it. My client suddenly laughed and said, 'Yes! I guess my mother is a matherer'. I encouraged her to remember this catchy phrase whenever she began to feel angry towards her mother.

Auditory Cues Rational-emotive therapists often make tape recordings of their sessions for clients to replay several times between sessions. This often serves to remind clients of rational principles they have understood in the session but may have since forgotten. Using personal recording systems, clients also can be encouraged to develop auditory reminders to initiate either cognitive or behavioural homework assignments. In addition, they can be encouraged to put forceful and emphatic rational statements on cassettes and play these while undertaking behavioural assignments. For example, I once saw a client who was anxious about other people looking at her for fear they might think her strange. I suggested that she do something in her everyday life which would encourage people to look at her so she could dispute some of her underlying irrational beliefs. She decided to wear a personal stereo system in the street, which she thought would encourage people to look at her. I suggested that while walking she play a tape on which she had recorded the rational message 'Just because I look strange doesn't mean that I am strange'.

The use of rational songs in therapy has already been described. Several of my clients have found that singing a particular rational song at an emotionally vulnerable time has been helpful for them. It has reminded them of a rational message they might not ordinarily have been able to focus on while being emotionally distressed. Another client told me that her sessions with me reminded her of a particular song and, whenever she hummed this song to herself, it helped bring to mind the fact that she could accept herself even though she did not have a man in her life. The song, ironically, was 'You're No One Till Somebody Loves You'. In fact, she rewrote some of the words and changed the title to 'You're Someone Even Though Nobody Loves You'.

Olfactory Cues It is possible for clients to use various aromas as cues to remind themselves to do a homework assignment or to initiate the disputing process. One client said that she found my pipe tobacco particularly aromatic and distinctive. Because we were both seeking a memorable cue, I suggested an experiment whereby she purchased a packet of my favourite tobacco and carried this around with her to smell at various distressing times. This aroma was associated in her mind with a particular rational message. This proved helpful, and indeed my client claimed that by saying to herself the phrase 'Pipe up' she now no longer has to take the tobacco out of her handbag to smell. Just the phrase is enough to remind her of the rational message.

The Working-through Process

From its inception, RET has strongly recommended that clients undertake 'some kind of activity which itself will act as a forceful counterpropagandist agency against the nonsense he believes' (Ellis, 1958). Ellis has consistently stressed that for clients who will agree to do them, dramatic, forceful and implosive activities remain the best forms of working-through assignments. Such assignments emphasise either cognitively based or behavioural activities.

Cognitive Assignments

In cognitive assignments, clients are encouraged to find ways in which they can convince themselves (outside therapy sessions) that rational philosophies which they can acknowledge as correct in therapy sessions are indeed correct and functional for them. Ellis has always urged clients to dispute their ideas vigorously, using aids as written homework forms (Ellis, 1979). Other vivid cognitive techniques that clients can use include the following.

Rational Proselytising (Bard, 1973) Here clients are encouraged to teach RET to their friends. In teaching others, clients become more convinced themselves of rational philosophies. This technique, however, had better be used with caution, and clients should be warned against playing the role of unwanted therapist to friends and relatives.

Tape-recorded Disputing In this technique, clients are encouraged to put a disputing sequence on tape. They are asked to play both the rational and irrational parts of themselves. Clients are further encouraged to try and make the rational part more persuasive and more forceful in responding to the irrational part.

Passionate Statements For those clients who are intellectually unable to do cognitive disputing in its classic sense, *passionate rational self-statements* can be used. Here client and therapist work together to develop appropriate rational self-statements that the client can actually use in everyday life. Clients are encouraged to repeat these statements in a very forceful manner instead of in their normal voice tone. Another variation of this technique is to have clients say rational self-statements to their reflection in a mirror, using a passionate tone and dramatic gestures again to reinforce the message.

Behavioural Techniques

Behavioural techniques which rational-emotive therapists particularly favour have clients do cognitive disputing in actual settings that vividly evoke their fears. The purpose is to enable clients to have the success experience of doing cognitive disputing while exposing themselves to feared stimuli. In addition, dramatic behavioural assignments are recommended to help clients overcome their low-frustration-tolerance ideas. Here the focus is oriented towards clients changing their dysfunctional attitudes towards their internal experiences of anxiety or frustration. Behavioural assignments include the following.

Shame-attacking Exercises Here the client is encouraged to do some act that she or he has previously regarded as 'shameful'. The client is encouraged to act in a way that will encourage other people in the environment to pay attention to her or him without bringing harm to self or other people and without unduly alarming others. She or he is encouraged to engage simultaneously in vigorous disputing, such as, 'I may look weird, but I'm not weird'. In my opinion, one of the drawbacks of encouraging a client to do shame-attacking exercises in a group is that the group serves to reinforce the client positively for doing the exercise. Doing shame-attacking exercises together can become a game that is not taken seriously. However, shame-attacking exercises are extremely valuable in promoting change and, while humour is an important component, my experience is that greater and longer-lasting change is effected when clients do shame-attacking exercises on their own as part of their individual therapy, without the social support of a group.

Risk-taking Assignments In risk-taking assignments clients are encouraged to do something they regard as being 'risky'. For example, a client may be encouraged to ask a waiter to replace a set of cutlery because it is too dirty. In preparing the client for risk-taking exercises, identification and disputing of faulty inferences and consequent irrational evaluations need to be done. The problem, however, is to get the client to prompt the aversive responses from others that he or she predicts will occur. In order for evaluative change to take place, the client is advised to be prepared to do such risk-taking experiences repeatedly over a long period of time so that he or she eventually encounters the 'dire' response. This is because such aversive responses from others occur far less frequently than the client predicts. Again the client is encouraged to undertake cognitive disputing along with the behavioural act.

Step-out-of-character Exercise Wessler (1982) has modified this exercise from Kelly (1955). Clients are encouraged to identify desired behavioural goals that are not currently enacted with frequency. For example, one group member chose the goal of eating more slowly, which for him was a desirable, non-shameful, non-risky exercise, but one that involved monitoring of eating habits and cognitive disputing of low-frustration-tolerance ideas.

In vivo Desensitisation These methods require clients to confront their fears repeatedly in an implosive manner. For example, clients with elevator phobia are asked to ride in elevators 20–30 times a day at the start of treatment, instead of gradually working their way up to this situation either in imagery or in actuality. Again, simultaneous cognitive disputing is urged. Neuman (1982) has written and presented tapes of short-term, group-oriented treatment of phobias. In his groups, clients are encouraged to rate their levels of anxiety. The most important goal is for the clients to experience a 'level 10', which is extreme panic. Neuman continually points out to people that it is important to experience 'level 10' because only then can they learn that they can survive and live through such an experience. Similarly, if in-roads to severe phobic conditions are to be made, it is important for rational-emotive therapists to work towards helping clients tolerate extreme forms of anxiety before helping clients to reduce this anxiety.

Stay-in-there Activities Grieger and Boyd (1980) have described a similar technique, which they call 'stay-in-there' activities, the purpose of which is to have clients vividly learn that they can tolerate and put up with uncomfortable experiences. One of my clients wanted to overcome her car-driving phobia. One of the things she feared was that her car would stall at a set of traffic lights and she would be exposed to the wrath of motorists who were stuck behind her. After eliciting and disputing her irrational ideas in traditional verbal dialogue, I encouraged her to turn off her engine at a set of lights and to stay there for about 20 minutes, thus creating the impression her car had broken down. Fortunately, the other car drivers did react in an angry fashion and she was able to practise disputing her dire needs for approval and comfort in a situation in which she remained for fully half an hour. (Caution needs to be exercised here because, in some parts of England, the police take a dim view of such behaviour.)

Some clients tend to do these dramatic exercises once or twice and then drop them from their repertoire. Therapists are often so glad and so surprised that their clients will actually do these assignments that they do not consistently show them the importance of *continuing* to do them. One of the reasons for continued practice has already been mentioned, namely, that clients are more likely to make inferential changes than evaluative changes by doing these assignments infrequently. This is largely because the 'dreaded' event has a far lower probability of occurring than clients think. However, sooner or later, if clients consistently and persistently put into practice these assignments, they may well encounter such events that will provide a context for disputing of irrational beliefs. Thus, if therapists really want to encourage clients to make changes at 'B' as well as 'A', they had better be prepared to encourage clients consistently to do these dramatic assignments over a long period of time.

Operant Conditioning Methods

Ellis (1979) has consistently employed operant conditioning methods to encourage clients to take responsibility for being their own primary agent of change. Here clients are encouraged to identify and employ positive reinforcements for undertaking working-through assignments, and apply penalties when they do not do so. While not all clients require such encouragement, difficult and resistant clients, whose resistance is due to low-frustration-tolerance ideas, can be encouraged to take full responsibility for not putting into practice assignments that would stimulate change. Thus, dramatic experiences, such as burning a £10 note, throwing away an eagerly awaited meal and cleaning a dirty room at the end of a hard day's work, are experiences that are designed to be so aversive that clients would choose to do the assignment previously avoided rather than undergo the penalty. Of course clients can, and often do, refuse to do the assignment and refuse to employ operant conditioning methods. However, many clients who have been resistant in the working-through process have, in my experience, begun to move when the therapist adopts this no-nonsense approach.

Limitations of Vivid Methods in RET

While the basic thesis in this chapter has been to show the possible efficacy of vivid RET, there are, of course, limitations to such an approach.

First, it is important for therapists to determine the impact on clients of introducing vivid methods into the therapeutic process. Thus, using the guidelines of Beck et al. (1979), it is perhaps wise for the therapist to ask the client at various points in the therapy to give frank feedback concerning the methods and activities used. While the therapist may not always agree not to use such techniques just because a client has a negative reaction to them we had better obtain and understand our clients' negative reactions to our procedures.

Second, it is important in the use of vivid dramatic techniques not to overload the client. One vivid and dramatic method carefully introduced into a therapy session at an appropriate time is much more likely to be effective than several dramatic methods employed indiscriminately in a session.

Third, it is important that rational-emotive therapists be clear about the rationale for using vivid methods and not to see the use of such methods as a goal in itself. The important thing to remember is that vivid methods are to be used as vehicles for promoting client attitude change and not to make the therapeutic process more stimulating for the therapist. It is also extremely important to ascertain what the client has learned from the vivid methods the therapist has employed. The client will not magically come to the conclusion the therapist wants. It is also important that therapists do not promote 'false' change in their clients. Change is 'false' when a client feels better as a result of some of these vivid methods but does not get better. Ellis (1972) has written an important article on such a distinction. Thus therapists should invariably ask questions such as, 'What have you learned from doing this vivid method? and 'How can you strengthen this learning experience for yourself outside of therapy?'

Fourth, dramatic and vivid methods are not appropriate for all clients. They are particularly helpful for those clients who use intellectualisation as a defence and/or who use verbal dialogue to tie rational-emotive therapists in knots. While there are no data at the moment to support the following hypothesis, I would speculate that dramatic and vivid methods had better not be used with clients who have overly dramatic and hysterical personalities. It is perhaps more appropriate to assist such clients to reflect in a calm and undramatic manner on their experiences than to overstimulate an already highly stimulated personality.

References

Anchin, J.C. and Kiesler, D.J. (eds) (1982) *Handbook of Interpersonal Psychotherapy*. New York: Pergamon.

Arnkoff, D.B. (1981) Flexibility in practicing cognitive therapy. In G. Emery, S.D. Hollon and R.C. Bedrosian (eds), *New Directions in Cognitive Therapy*. New York: Guilford.

Bard, J.A. (1973) Rational proselytizing, *Rational Living*, 8(2), 24–6.

Beck, A.T., Rush, A.J., Shaw, B.F. and Emery, G. (1979) *Cognitive Therapy of Depression*. New York: Guilford.

Burns, D.D. (1980) *Feeling Good: The New Mood Therapy*. New York: Morrow.

Dies, R.R. (1973) Group therapist self-disclosure: an evaluation by clients, *Journal of Counseling Psychology*, 20, 344–8.
Dryden, W. (1980) Nightmares and fun. Paper presented at the Third National Conference on Rational-Emotive Therapy, New York.
Ellis, A. (1958) Rational psychotherapy, *Journal of General Psychology*, 59, 35–49.
Ellis, A. (1972) Helping people get better: rather than merely feel better, *Rational Living*, 7(2), 2–9.
Ellis, A. (1977) Fun as psychotherapy, *Rational Living*, 12(1), 2–6.
Ellis, A. (1979) The practice of rational-emotive therapy. In A. Ellis and J.M. Whiteley (eds), *Theoretical and Empirical Foundations of Rational-Emotive Therapy*. Monterey, CA: Brooks/Cole.
Ellis, A. (1983) The philosophic implications and dangers of some popular behavior therapy techniques. In M. Rosenbaum, C.M. Franks and Y. Jaffe (eds), *Perspectives in Behavior Therapy in the Eighties*. New York: Springer.
Ellis, A. (1985) *Overcoming Resistance: Rational-Emotive Therapy with Difficult Clients*. New York: Springer.
Freeman, A. (1981) Dreams and imagery in cognitive therapy. In G. Emery, S.D. Hollon and R.C. Bedrosian (eds), *New Directions in Cognitive Therapy*. New York: Guilford.
Grieger, R. and Boyd, J. (1980) *Rational-Emotive Therapy: A Skills-based Approach*. New York: Van Nostrand Reinhold.
Hoehn-Saric, R. (1978) Emotional arousal, attitude change and psychotherapy. In J.D. Frank, R. Hoehn-Saric, S.D. Imber, B.L. Liberman and A.R. Stone (eds), *Effective Ingredients of Successful Psychotherapy*. New York: Brunner/Mazel.
Kassinove, H. and DiGiuseppe, R. (1975) Rational role reversal, *Rational Living*, 10(1), 44–5.
Kelly, G. (1955) *The Psychology of Personal Constructs*, 2 vols. New York: Norton.
Knaus, W. and Wessler, R.L. (1976) Rational-emotive problem simulation, *Rational Living*, 11(2), 8–11.
Lazarus, A.A. (1978) *In the Mind's Eye*. New York: Rawson.
Maultsby, M.C., Jr and Ellis, A. (1974) *Techniques for Using Rational-Emotive Imagery*. New York: Institute for Rational-Emotive Therapy.
Nardi, T.J. (1979) The use of psychodrama in RET, *Rational Living*, 14(1), 35–8.
Neuman, F. (Leader) (1982) *An eight-week treatment group for phobics* (Series of eight cassette recordings). While Plains, NY: F. Neuman.
Rice, L.N. (1965) Therapists' style of participation and case outcome, *Journal of Consulting Psychology*, 29, 155–60.
Rice, L.N. (1973) Client behavior as a function of therapist style and client resources, *Journal of Counseling Psychology*, 20, 306–11.
Rice, L.N. and Gaylin, N.L. (1973) Personality processes reflected in client and vocal style and Rorschach processes, *Journal of Consulting and Clinical Psychology*, 40, 133–8.
Rice, L.N. and Wagstaff, A.K. (1967) Client voice quality and expressive style as indexes of productive psychotherapy, *Journal of Consulting Psychology*, 31, 557–63.
Sacco, W.P. (1981) Cognitive therapy in-vivo. In G. Emery, S.D. Hollon and R.C. Bedrosian (eds), *New Directions in Cognitive Therapy*. New York: Guilford.
Walen, S.R., DiGiuseppe, R. and Wessler, R.L. (1980) *A Practitioner's Guide to Rational-Emotive Therapy*. New York: Oxford.
Wessler, R.L. (1982) Alternative conceptions of rational-emotive therapy: toward a philosophically neutral psychotherapy. Paper presented at the Twelfth European Congress of Behavior Therapy, Rome, 5 September.
Wessler, R.A. and Wessler, R.L. (1980) *The Principles and Practice of Rational-Emotive Therapy*. San Francisco, CA: Jossey-Bass.
Wexler, D.A. (1975) A scale for the measurement of client and therapist expressiveness, *Journal of Clinical Psychology*, 31, 486–9.
Wexler, D.A. and Butler, J.M. (1976) Therapist modification of client expressiveness, *Journal of Clinical Psychology*, 44, 261–5.
Young, H.S. (1980) Teaching rational self-value concepts to tough customers. Paper presented at the Third National Conference on Rational-Emotive Therapy, New York, June 8.

12
The Value of Efficiency in Psychotherapy

Albert Ellis

The issue of value in psychotherapy is exceptionally important, and the existential therapists in particular may be credited with highlighting this importance (Frankl, 1966; May, 1969). Some psychotherapeutic values, however, have often been neglected, and I shall stress in this chapter one of these: namely, that of efficiency, which I think is somewhat different from the value of effectiveness. Usually, we test the 'effectiveness' of a given form of therapy by showing that, in both controlled experiments and in clinical practice, it results in significant gains for clients when therapized groups are compared with placebo or nontherapized groups. But we rarely test the 'efficiency' of treatment methods to determine, on a cost-benefit basis, how much time and effort is normally spent by therapists and clients to achieve 'effective' results and how pervasive, thoroughgoing, and long-lasting these 'results' are. Yet, in view of pending efforts to establish suitable criteria for the setting of governmental and insurance company standards for reimbursing 'competent' therapists under existing and suggested mental health plans, a cost-benefit approach to psychotherapy looms as increasingly important (Hogan, 1980; Pottinger, 1980; Strupp, 1980).

What are some of the main goals to strive for in therapy that is 'efficient' as well as 'effective'? After giving this matter serious thought for more than a quarter of a century, and after experimenting in my own practice with several different methods of psychological treatment ranging from classical psychoanalysis to rational–emotive therapy, I have come up with the following hypotheses about 'efficient' psychotherapy.

Brevity in Psychotherapy

Although Freud (1965) himself usually practiced what today would be called brief psychotherapy and saw most of his analysands for only a matter of months (Jones, 1956), psychoanalysis turned to a longer period of treatment, usually taking a minimum of two years in its classic form and often much longer than that. In recent years, however, many analytically oriented therapists have espoused brief treatment (Small, 1979), and much of today's nonanalytic therapy is relatively short (Ellis and Abrahms, 1978). This obviously has its advantages: since most clients are in pain when they come for therapy, they function on a low level of competency; they enjoy themselves little; and the longer they take to overcome their disturbances, the more they and their associates are likely to suffer. Psychotherapy, moreover, is usually expensive and time-consuming; and if it is possible to achieve effective treatment in a short period of time, more clients will tend to come, stay in it, and benefit from it in various ways. Governmental and other agencies, moreover, will be more enthusiastic about reimbursing therapists for brief rather than for prolonged therapy.

Depth-centeredness in Psychotherapy

Many modes of therapy, especially psychoanalysis, advocate that psychotherapy be depth-centered (Freud, 1965; Jones, 1956; Kaplan, 1979). They assume that many symptoms, such as phobias, not only have an environmental and experiential core but that they also have some kind of deep-seated, underlying 'cause' and that this has to be thoroughly understood and worked through over a period of therapeutic time before it can really be resolved. In existential and philosophic therapies it is also assumed that a symptom has depth-centered roots. Thus, rational-emotive therapy (RET) holds that people's phobias largely stem from a basic absolutistic or *must*urbatory philosophy – for example, 'I *must* not suffer any form of severe discomfort or failure when I ride in elevators!' – and that it probably will not be resolved unless clients understand their self-invented 'needs' for certainty and unless they consistently think and act against these 'necessities.'

There are many advantages to therapists trying to help clients arrive at their fundamental disturbance-creating ideas and then to surrender these for less disturbing philosophies: (1) They can not only help reveal the sources of clients' current symptoms but also of prior and later ones, so that they obtain a more comprehensive and clearer knowledge of what they do to disturb themselves. (2) Clients may, in addition to eliminating their negative symptoms, show themselves how to lead a more joyous, creative, and fulfilled existence. (3) Depth-centered psychotherapy may promote a general understanding of human 'nature' that may be relevant to many aspects of living, including social and political relations, international understanding and artistic pursuits.

Pervasiveness in Psychotherapy

Pervasiveness in psychotherapy may be defined as the therapist's helping clients to deal with many of their problems, and in a sense their whole lives, rather than with a few presenting symptoms. Thus, a psychoanalyst who sees a woman who has poor sex with her husband will try to zero in not merely on that particular issue but also on her general relations with her mate and with other significant people in her life. And a rational-emotive therapist may first show this woman that she has great fear of failing sexually with her husband (because of her absolutistic philosophy, 'I *have to* do well sexually and *must* win his approval!') but *also* show her how her dire 'need' for success and love are interfering with her other marital and nonmarital functions.

Like depth-centeredness, the value of pervasiveness in psychotherapy has distinct benefits: (1) It shows clients how they can easily create several symptoms from the same underlying attitudes and feelings and how, by changing these attitudes, they can deal with or eliminate more than one or two presenting symptoms. (2) It helps them to understand and relate better to other people. (3) It may enable them, especially if they learn to apply a form of treatment like RET, to deal therapeutically with their close associates (Ellis, 1957).

Extensiveness in Psychotherapy

Extensiveness in psychotherapy means that clients can be helped not only to minimize their negative feelings (e.g., anxiety, depression, rage, and self-pity) but also to maximize their potential for happy living (e.g., to be more productive, creative and enjoying). Where 'intensive' therapy usually deals with pain, inhibition, panic and horror, 'extensive' therapy also deals with exploring and augmenting pleasure, sensuality and laughter. 'Efficient' psychotherapy, therefore, includes 'intensive' as well as 'extensive' treatment, provides self-actualizing as well as de-inhibiting procedures, and thereby tries to provide additional gains in the cost-benefit issues that are inevitably involved in therapy.

Thoroughgoingness in Psychotherapy

Since what we call 'thought,' 'emotion' and 'behavior' are processes that hardly exist in any pure state but significantly overlap and interact, and since 'emotional disturbance' has cognitive and behavioral as well as emotive aspects, 'efficient' psychotherapy had better consider and often include multimodal techniques (Ellis and Grieger, 1977; Ellis and Whiteley, 1979; Lazarus, 1971, 1976; Wachtel, 1978). This does not mean that it will unselectively use any and all available methods, but it will tend to be a comprehensive system that will explore several pathways and will test these to see which usually work best and which had better be used minimally with different clients. The more comprehensive a therapist's armamentary of techniques is, the more likely he or she is to find suitable procedures for especially unique or difficult clients.

Maintaining Therapeutic Progress

Symptom removal, as Wolpe (1973) has stated, may be quite valuable and may even lead to a real 'cure.' But it also has distinct limitations: (1) When a given symptom is removed or ameliorated, another may easily spring up later – not necessarily because of symptom substitution but as a derivative of the same basic self-defeating philosophy with which clients create their original symptoms. (2) Many clients feel so relieved by the temporary or partial removal of a painful symptom (e.g., depression) that they leave the core of it (or its close relatives) still standing. (3) Most clients have some degree of low frustration tolerance and therefore will welcome palliative procedures (e.g., tranquilizers or relaxation methods) to quickly alleviate their worst symptoms rather than working at more elegant philosophic changes that will result in more permanent changes.

For reasons such as these, 'efficient' therapy does not merely strive for symptom removal but for more lasting therapeutic gain; and, no matter how pleased clients may feel about their 'cures,' it does not accept these unless there is some evidence that they will be maintained for a period of time and, preferably, keep improving after formal therapy has ended. In rational-emotive therapy in particular, one of the hallmarks of 'elegant' or highly 'efficient' psychotherapy is for treated individuals to feel significantly better at the close of therapy than they did at the beginning – but also to keep improving for a considerable period of time after therapy has officially ended (Ellis and Whiteley, 1979).

Preventive Psychotherapy

Most modern systems of therapy strive to have their clients free of presenting symptoms at the close of treatment and still free of these same symptoms months or years after therapy has ended. Another fairly obvious efficiency goal is that of teaching clients to understand themselves so well, to see so clearly how they usually create their own emotional problems, and to understand so solidly what they can do to restore their own emotional equilibrium that they are able to approach the future with a basically un-upsetting philosophy. This is not easy, but it is presumably sometimes achievable. Just as medical patients can presumably learn from their physicians how to get over their current ailments and to prevent these from recurring, so can psychotherapy clients often learn from their therapists how to ward off future emotional ills and to keep themselves from returning to their old disturbed pathways. From a cost-benefit standpoint it seems obvious that any kind of treatment that provides this kind of preventive therapy will provide more gains than symptom-removal treatments (because the results are lasting and cumulative) and also entail less expense (because the nonrecurrence of the symptoms precludes future hours of therapy).

Illustrative Case Presentation

It is interesting to discuss 'efficiency' in psychotherapy abstractly, as I have just done, and to hypothesize about its advantages. Let me be more concrete by presenting a clinical case that illustrates how some of these principles may be practiced. Calvin R., a 40-year-old physician, was exceptionally depressed when he came for rational-emotive therapy. He damned himself for his medical errors and for his failings as a husband and father. He was extremely hostile toward his wife whenever she disagreed with him about some important matter. And he fumed and frothed about even the smallest un-niceties of his life, such as a leaky roof or a run in his socks.

In terms of brevity, Calvin was seen for four months on a once-a-week basis: first for one hour and during the last two months for half-hour sessions. His therapy made little inroads into his very busy medical schedule.

In regard to depth-centeredness, he was helped to zero in on three basic *musts*, or absolutistic philosophies, which permeated almost his entire life and largely created his depressed feelings: (1) 'I *must* do outstandingly well in my work and be approved by all my patients!' (2) 'My wife *must* never disagree with me about important things and *has to* do these things my way!' (3) 'Conditions under which I live *must* be easy and unhassled, and never frustrate me too badly!' Although Calvin was at first convinced that his depression was purely biological and endogenous (even though several self-prescribed antidepressants had not lifted it a bit), I was able to show him that every time he felt depressed he was invariably demanding (not wishing) that he do well and castigating himself when he did not perform outstandingly, and that he was frequently commanding that things be better than they were. He soon acknowledged that his *must*urbatory philosophy underlay his depressed and hostile feelings and that, with this Jehovian attitude, *he* was making himself disturbed.

In the area of pervasiveness, although Calvin at first only wanted to discuss his horror of failing at work, and occasionally his anger at his wife, he was shown that his self-downing and his low frustration tolerance invaded other areas of his life as well, including his sex activities and his social relations. In fact, he responded better at first in these two areas than he did in giving up his work perfectionism, and he was partly able to give up the latter by first surrendering the former.

Regarding extensiveness, Calvin was not only taught how to work against his presenting symptoms but to add interests and pleasures to his days – such as music and running – that enhanced his existence, distracted him somewhat from his incessant worrying, and gave him two more vital absorbing interests that made life more enjoyable.

In terms of thoroughgoingness, Calvin was not only treated with the highly cognitive methods of RET (Ellis, 1962) but given a number of emotive exercises and in vivo activity homework assignments as well. Thus, he especially seemed to benefit from shame-attacking exercises (Ellis, 1973), rational-emotive imagery (Maultsby, 1975), and deliberately staying in some painful situations (such as visiting with his boring in-laws) and showing himself that he could stand, if not like, the pain (Ellis and Abrahms, 1978).

Best of all, Calvin seemed remarkably able to maintain his therapeutic progress and to do preventive psychotherapy on his own and increase his gains. For he first, after four months of therapy, lost his depression, went back to a full schedule of work, and started getting along remarkably well with his wife and family in spite of some difficulties which they themselves presented. This seemed surprising, considering the brevity of his therapy. But even more surprising was what he reported when he returned to see me two years later to talk about his wife, who was severely panicked about driving a car (after she had previously driven one without trouble for twelve years) and who was going through a period of severe depersonalization. For Calvin was handling this situation remarkably well, in spite of the immense transportation and other difficulties it was causing his entire family.

To make matters worse, Calvin himself had become afflicted, for the past six months, with a rheumatic condition that handicapped him seriously in his practice; one of his sons turned out to be dyslexic and was behaving in a highly delinquent manner; both his parents were dying of cancer; and his economic situation, for a variety of reasons including some poor investments on his part, had deteriorated. In spite of all these adversities, this ex-client's spirits were unusually high. He had virtually no hostility or self-pity in the face of his family frustrations. He was not downing himself for his own economic blunders. And he was doing a reasonably good job in using some of the RET principles he had learned to help his wife, his children and his parents cope with some of the serious emotional troubles that they all were undergoing.

This is the kind of 'elegant' therapeutic result that I particularly strive for and like to see effected. Calvin not only overcame his presenting symptoms and maintained this change. Moreover, he improved significantly after therapy had ended and was at a stage, two years later, where virtually no normal kind of setback would he allow to disturb him too seriously – meaning, to make him depressed, panicked, hostile, or self-pitying.

Other Kinds of Efficiency in Psychotherapy

In addition to the ways just hypothesized, some other kinds of efficiency in psychotherapy may be obtained in the following ways. First, efficient therapy tends to be stated in clear and simple terms, so that it is relatively easily understood both by practitioners and their clients. Abstruse or esoteric modes of therapy may have desirable qualities, but they tend to have a limited appeal to therapists and, especially, to the people with whom they are used. Highly mystical and transpersonal forms of therapy, for example, are understood only by a minority of the populace, often aim at contradictory goals, and may easily lead their devotees up the garden path into questionably 'healthy' results (Ellis, 1972).

Second, efficient psychotherapy is fairly easily teachable to therapists and does not require them to undergo years of training and apprenticeship, not to mention years of personal therapy themselves.

Third, efficient therapy is often intrinsically interesting to therapists and clients, and motivates the latter to stay with it and to use it in their outside lives. This aspect of therapy may indeed have boomerang effects: for some of the most questionable and potentially harmful forms of psychological treatment – such as fanatical cult therapies like that promulgated by Jim Jones – are intrinsically fascinating to their followers and strongly motivate them to make changes in their lives. But assuming that a form of psychotherapy has healthy and lasting effects, it seems more efficient for it to be intrinsically interesting rather than dull and to be motivating rather than unmotivating.

Fourth, efficient psychotherapy helps clients achieve maximum good with minimum harm to themselves (and others). Many therapies, including some of the most esoteric and bizarre ones, help bring about healthy or beneficial results for clients (Frank, 1975). But it has also been shown that some of these forms of treatment have harmful results as well (Chapman, 1964; Garfield and Bergin, 1978; Gross, 1979; Hadley and Strupp, 1976; Lieberman et al., 1973; Maliver, 1972; Rosen, 1977). It may also be questioned whether some modes of cultist or mystical therapies (such as shamanism or exorcism) do not create, as well as alleviate, disturbance (Ellis, 1972, 1975). Behavioral or emotional change, when effected through psychotherapy, had better be conducive of human survival and happiness, including social as well as individual happiness; and if it leads to pernicious as well as beneficial social results, its efficiency had better be examined (Adler, 1964).

Fifth, efficient psychotherapy favors flexibility, lack of dogma, and provision and encouragement for its own change. It not only tends to help its clients be less absolutistic, rigid, unscientific, and devout but it also endorses scientific falsifiability; that is, it sets up its theories so that they are ultimately falsifiable; it views them skeptically and tentatively; and it constantly strives to check on their errors and invalidities (Popper, 1972; Russell, 1965). In this manner, it not only tries to achieve but does its best to maintain both effectiveness and efficiency.

Discussion

This chapter hypothesizes that therapy, even when it has been shown to have experimentally proven effectiveness, may still be inefficient, and it outlines several criteria of efficiency in psychotherapy and their presumed advantages. Psychotherapies, being humanistically oriented and somewhat allergic to hardheaded realities, often neglect the value of efficiency in their work. This is hardly in the best interests of their clients! Efficiency is a distinctly valuable concept for therapists, for their clients, and for the science of psychotherapy itself. Effectiveness is indeed an important aspect of psychological treatment, and we had better strive for therapy that works.

But efficiency includes, in addition to effectiveness, several other ingredients, such as depth-centeredness, pervasiveness, extensiveness, thoroughgoingness, maintaining therapeutic progress and preventive psychotherapy. It also encourages minimization of therapeutic harm and scientific flexibility and falsifiability. All these aspects of presumably efficient therapy can probably be concretized and measured. If this is done, it will probably be found that what we now call 'effectiveness' as measured in most contemporary outcome studies of therapy, is significantly correlated with 'efficiency' but that the latter involves important aspects of treatment that are commonly neglected in considering the former. Research along these lines would seem to be highly desirable.

References

Adler, A. (1964) *Social Interest: A Challenge to Mankind.* New York: Capricorn.

Chapman, A. H. (1964) *Psychiatry Digest*, September, 23–9.

Ellis, A. (1957) *How to Live with a 'Neurotic'*. New York: Crown.

Ellis, A. (1962) *Reason and Emotion in Psychotherapy*. Secaucus, NJ: Lyle Stuart.

Ellis, A. (1972) What does transpersonal psychology have to offer to the art and science of psychotherapy? *Voices*, 8(3), 10–20.

Ellis, A. (1973) *How to Stubbornly Refuse to be Ashamed of Anything* [Cassette recording]. New York: Institute for Rational Living.

Ellis, A. (1975) Critique of Frank's 'The limits of humanism', *Humanist*, 35(6), 33–4.

Ellis, A. and Abrahms, E. (1978) *Brief Psychotherapy in Medical and Health Practice*. New York: Springer.

Ellis, A. and Grieger, R. (1977) *Handbook of Rational-Emotive Therapy*. New York: Springer.

Ellis, A. and Whiteley, J. (eds) (1979) *Theoretical and Empirical Foundations of Rational-Emotive Therapy*. Monterey, CA: Brooks/Cole.

Frank, J.D. (1975) The limits of humanism, *Humanist*, 35(5), 40–52.

Frankl, V. (1966) *Man's Search for Meaning*. New York: Washington Square Press.

Freud, S. (1965) *Standard Edition of the Complete Psychological Works of Sigmund Freud.* London: Hogarth.

Garfield, S.L. and Bergin, A.E. (1978) *Handbook of Psychotherapy and Behavior Change*, 2nd edn. New York: Wiley.

Gross, M.L. (1979) *The Psychological Society*. New York: Simon and Schuster.

Hadley, S.W. and Strupp, H.W. (1976) Contemporary view of negative effects in psychotherapy, *Archives of General Psychiatry*, 33, 1291–302.

Hogan, D.B. (1980, September) *Defining what a Competent Psychotherapist does: Problems and Prospects*. Paper presented at the Annual Convention of the American Psychological Association, Montreal.

Jones, E. (1956) *The Life and Works of Sigmund Freud*. New York: Basic Books.

Kaplan, H.S. (1979) *Disorders of Sexual Desire*. New York: Brunner/Mazel.

Lazarus, A.A. (1971) *Behavior Therapy and Beyond*. New York: McGraw-Hill

Lazarus, A.A. (1976) *Multimodal Behavior Therapy*. New York: Springer.

Lieberman, M.A., Yalom, I.D. and Miles, M.B. (1973) *Encounter Groups: First Facts*. New York: Basic Books.

Maliver, B.L. (1972) *The Encounter Game*. New York: Stein and Day.

Maultsby, M.C., Jr. (1975) *Help Yourself to Happiness*. New York: Institute for Rational Living.

May, R. (1969) *Love and Will*. New York: Norton.

Popper, K. (1972) *Objective Knowledge*. London: Oxford.

Pottinger, P.S. (1980, September) *Certifying Competence not Credentials.* Paper presented at the Annual Convention of the American Psychological Association, Montreal.
Rosen, R.D. (1977) *Psychobabble.* New York: Atheneum.
Russell, B. (1965) *The Basic Writings of Bertrand Russell.* New York: Simon and Schuster.
Small, L. (1979) *The Brief Psychotherapies.* New York: Brunner/Mazel.
Strupp, H.H. (1980, September) *Toward the Measurement of Therapists' Contributions to Negative Outcomes.* Paper presented at the Annual Convention of the American Psychological Association, Montreal.
Wachtel, P. (1978) *Psychoanalysis and Behavior Therapy.* New York: Basic Books.
Wolpe, J. (1973) *The Practice of Behavior Therapy.* New York: Pergamon.

13

Rational-Emotive Therapy Approaches to Overcoming Resistance

Albert Ellis

Resistance to psychotherapy, even by those who strongly aver that they want to help themselves change and who spend considerable time, money and effort in pursuing therapy, has been observed for many years. Ancient philosophers – such as Confucius, Gautama Buddha, Epictetus, Seneca and Marcus Aurelius – recognized that people voluntarily pursuing personality change often resist their own and their teachers' best efforts. When modern psychotherapy began to develop in the nineteenth century, some of its main practitioners – such as James Braid, Hippolyte Bernheim, Jean-Martin Charcot, Auguste Ambroise Liebault and Pierre Janet – made the theory of resistance and the practice of overcoming it key elements in their psychotherapies (Ellenberger, 1970).

Early in the twentieth century, psychotherapeutic resistance particularly came into its own with the elucidation of the Freudian concept of transference (Freud, 1912/1965a) and with Freud expanding his earlier concept to include five main varieties of resistance: resistances of repression, of transference, and of secondary gain (all stemming from the ego), resistance of the repetition compulsion (arising from the id), and resistance of guilt and self-punishment (originating in the superego) (Freud, 1926/1965b). Since this time, psychoanalysis (and many related forms of therapy) have, we might say, almost been obsessed with problems of resistance.

As several recent writers have aptly noted (Wachtel, 1982), views on what resistance is and how it can best be resolved in therapy largely depend on one's definition of this fascinating phenomenon. Personally, I like Turkat and Meyer's definition: 'Resistance is client behavior that the therapist labels antitherapeutic' (1982: 158) since it is both simple and comprehensive; and, as its authors suggest, it can also be operationalized to each client's individual experience and be seen as that specific form of behavior that is observed when this particular client acts nontherapeutically according to his or her therapist in these particular situations.

However accurate such a definition of resistance may be, it is too general to be of much clinical use, and it hardly explains the main 'causes' of resistance, nor what can be done to overcome it. Rational-emotive therapy (RET), together with cognitive-behavioral therapy (CBT), assumes that when clients self-defeatingly and irrationally resist following therapeutic procedures and homework assignments, they largely do so because of their explicit and implicit cognitions or beliefs. RET, which tends to be more philosophical and more persuasive than some other forms of CBT – such as those of Bandura (1977), Mahoney (1980) and Meichenbaum (1977) – assumes that resisting clients have an underlying set of powerful and persistent irrational Beliefs (iBs), as well as an innate biosocial tendency to create new irrationalities, that frequently block them from carrying out the therapeutic goals and contracts that they overtly agree to work at achieving. Although RET does not agree with psychoanalytic and psychodynamic theory, which holds that client resistance is based on deeply unconscious, repressed thoughts and feelings, it does hypothesize that many – perhaps most – of the iBs that underlie client resistance are (1) at least partially implicit, unconscious, or automatic; (2) tenaciously held; (3) held concomitantly with strong feelings and fixed habit patterns of behavior; (4) to some extent held by virtually all clients; (5) difficult to change; and (6) likely to recur once they have been temporarily surrendered (Bard, 1980; Ellis, 1962, 1971a, 1973, 1976, 1979, 1983b; Ellis and Grieger, 1977; Ellis and Whiteley, 1979; Walen et al., 1980; Wessler and Wessler, 1980).

More specifically, RET assumes that clients who self-defeatingly resist therapy implicitly or explicitly tend to hold three main irrational Beliefs (iBs) or philosophies: (1) 'I *must* do well at changing myself, and I'm an incompetent, hopeless client if I don't'; (2) 'You (the therapist and others) *must* help me to change, and you're rotten people if you don't'; and (3) 'Changing myself *must* occur quickly and easily, and it's horrible if it doesn't!' Concomitantly with these irrational beliefs, resisters feel anxious, depressed, angry, and self-pitying about changing, and these disturbed feelings block their forcing themselves to change. Behaviorally, resisters withdraw, procrastinate, remain inert, and sabotage their self-promises to change. RET practitioners are largely concerned with helping resisters (and other clients) make a profound philosophic change so that they adopt a cooperative, confident, determined attitude toward self-change, rather than the self-blocking views that they hold. To effect this kind of cognitive restructuring, RET uses a wide variety of thinking, feeling, and activity methods.

Having said all of this, I shall spend the first part of this chapter trying to show, from an RET standpoint, what are the principal kinds of resistance, in what ways they usually arise, and what RET (and, hopefully, other) practitioners can do to understand and help themselves and their clients overcome therapy-sabotaging resistance. I shall first deal with common, 'normal,' or 'usual' resistance, and in the later sections with unusual or highly stubborn resistances.

Common Forms of Resistance

Some of the statistically common kinds of resistance that therapists encounter include the following:

'Healthy' Resistance

Clients sometimes resist change because therapists have their own fish to fry and mistakenly see these clients as having symptoms (e.g., hostility to their parents) or as having origins of their symptoms (e.g. oedipal feelings 'causing' their sexual inadequacy) that the clients view as figments of the therapists' imagination. Rather than allow these therapeutic 'authorities' to lead them up the garden path, such clients refuse to accept these interpretations and healthfully resist or flee from 'treatment' (Basch, 1982; Ellis, 1962; Ellis and Harper, 1975; Lazarus and Fay, 1982).

From a rational-emotive view, clients who resist for healthy reasons are explicitly or implicitly telling themselves rational beliefs (rBs), such as 'My therapist is probably wrong about my having this symptom or about the origins of my having it. Too bad! I'd better ignore his or her interpretations and perhaps get another therapist!' In the ABC theory of RET, at A (activating event) the clients experience their therapist's interpretations and directives (e.g., 'You think you love your mother very much but unconsciously you really appear to loathe her'). At B (belief system), the clients tell themselves the rational beliefs just noted, and at C (emotional and behavioral consequences) they feel appropriately sorry about their therapist's misperceptions about their disturbances and they actively resist these misperceptions. They are therefore acting rationally and sanely and, according to RET, their resistance is self-helping and healthy. The one who has the real problem in these cases – and is 'resisting' doing effective treatment – is their therapist!

Resistance Motivated by Client-Therapist Mismatching

Clients sometimes are 'naturally' mismatched with their therapists, that is, manage to pick or be assigned to a therapist whom they just do not like, for whatever reasons. Thus, they may have a therapist who, to their idiosyncratic tastes or preferences, is too young or too old, too liberal or too conservative, too male or too female, too active or too passive. Because of this mismatching, they don't have too much rapport with their therapist and therefore resist him or her more than they would resist a more preferable therapist. If this becomes obvious during the therapy (which it never may), the therapists may try to compensate for what these clients see as their 'flaws,' and may succeed in doing so by being extra-nice to or hardworking with such clients. Or the clients may naturally overcome their antitherapist prejudices as the course of therapy intimately proceeds (just as husbands and wives may become more attached to their physically unattractive mates as time goes by and more emotional intimacy is achieved). Or the clients and/or their therapists may (often wisely) bring the relationship to a close.

Resistance Stemming from Clients' Transference Disturbances

Following Freud (1912/1965a, 1900/1965c), psychoanalytic therapists assume that clients will unconsciously reenact with or transfer to their therapists the same kind of highly prejudiced relationships that they experienced with their parents during their early childhood. Thus, if a young woman has a middle-aged male analyst, she will strongly tend to fall in love with him (as she presumably once loved her father), will be jealous of his wife, will hate him when he refuses to go to bed with her, will try to control him as she tried to control her father, and so forth.

In RET, we take the view that these disturbed transference relations *sometimes* but not *necessarily* occur and that, when they do, they are usually sparked by some irrational beliefs (iBs). Thus, if this young woman strongly transfers her relationship from her father to her analyst, she is probably telling herself (and strongly believing) iBs like these: 'Because my analyst is helpful and fatherly to me in some ways, he *must* be a complete father to me, and he *must* love me dearly!' 'Because being loved by my father is enjoyable, I absolutely *must* be loved by my own father and by all fatherly people, including my therapist!' 'If my father and my therapist do not totally love me – as I utterly *need* them to do – I am a worthless person!'

If and when, then, disturbed transference relations occur in therapy, rational-emotive practitioners look for the irrational beliefs (iBs) *behind* these disturbances, show clients how to see and change these ideas, and thereby teach them how to surmount these kinds of relationship resistances.

Resistances Caused by Therapists' Relationship Problems

Therapists, like clients, also sometimes have their relationship difficulties. These may be of three major kinds. (1) Therapists may naturally not like some of their clients, particularly those who are nasty, stupid, ugly, or otherwise unprepossessing. (2) Therapists may have what the psychoanalysts call severe countertransference difficulties and may therefore be bigoted against their clients. Thus, if a therapist hates her mother and one of her clients looks and acts like this mother, she may unconsciously want to harm rather than help this client. (3) Therapists may not have personal negative feelings toward their clients but may be insensitive to these clients' feelings and may not know how to maintain good therapeutic relations with them (Goldfried, 1982; Lazarus and Fay, 1982; Meichenbaum and Gilmore, 1982).

If the first or third of these therapist problems exists, it can be met by therapists' becoming aware of their own limitations and by compensating for them. Thus, therapists who personally do not like their clients can still focus on suitable helpful procedures and thereby surmount this handicap. I particularly notice that in using RET I can focus so well on my clients' problems, and especially on showing them how to correct their thinking errors, that it hardly matters that I personally do not like some of them and would never select them as my friends (Ellis, 1971b, 1973).

RET therapists can also, especially with certain supersensitive clients, go out of their way to give these clients positive verbal reinforcement, to listen carefully and reflectively to their difficulties, to be open and honest with them, to give them active encouragement, to deliberately point out their good (as well as some of their self-defeating) characteristics, and otherwise to empathize with them in an almost Rogerian manner (Dryden, 1982; Ellis, 1977b; Johnson, 1980; Walen et al., 1980; Wessler and Wessler, 1980; Wessler, 1982). Although this kind of positive reinforcement has its distinct dangers (Ellis, 1983a; Turkat and Meyer, 1982), it can also at times be constructively used to overcome resistance.

If therapists are victims of countertransference and are negative of clients because of their own problems and bigotries, these can be resolved by looking for and disputing the irrational beliefs (iBs) creating their prejudices. Therapists who, for example, hate their clients who resemble the therapists' obnoxious mothers are irrationally telling themselves ideas like these: 'Because my mother treated me badly, I can't stand *any* person who has some of her traits!' 'This client *must not* behave the obnoxious way in which my mother acted! She's a horrible *person* for behaving in this crummy way!' Such irrational beliefs are fairly easily revealed if therapists use RET to probe their negative reactions to their clients. The kinds of overgeneralizations that lead to these beliefs are particularly uprooted through rational-emotive therapy (RET) and cognitive-behavioral therapy (CBT) (Ellis, 1962; Beck, 1976).

Resistance Related to Moralistic Attitudes of Therapists

In addition to the therapist-related resistances just mentioned, a common trait that many therapists possess and that blocks them in helping clients is their moralism: the profound tendency to condemn themselves and others for evil or stupid acts. Even though they are in the helping profession, they frequently believe that their seriously disturbed clients *should* not, *must* not be the way they are, especially when these clients abuse their therapists, come late, refuse to pay their bills, and otherwise behave obnoxiously or antisocially. Many therapists therefore overtly or covertly damn their clients for their wrongdoings and consequently help these clients damn themselves and become more, instead of less, disturbed. Naturally, many such clients often resist therapy.

RET practitioners particularly can combat this kind of resistance, since one of the key tenets of RET is that all humans, including all clients, merit what Rogers (1961) calls unconditional positive regard and what RET calls unconditional acceptance (Ellis, 1962, 1972a, 1973, 1976). This means that rational-emotive therapists look at their own (and others') moralism and the irrational beliefs (iBs) that underlie them, such as: 'My client *should* work at therapy! She *must* not sabotage my efforts! How *awful* if she does! I *can't stand* it!' And RET practitioners work hard at extirpating these ideas and giving all their clients, no matter how difficult they are, unconditional self-acceptance. In this manner they help minimize therapist-encouraged resistance.

Resistance Linked to Clients' and Therapists' Other Love–Hate Problems

Although the Freudians assume that love–hate problems between clients and their therapists are invariably sparked by and intimately involved with transference difficulties – that is, stem from clients' and therapists' early family relationships – this is questionable. Client-therapist difficulties, and the resistance to which they sometimes lead, may be based on reality factors that have nothing to do with anyone's childhood experiences. Thus, a young female client may just happen to have an exceptionally bright, attractive and kindly therapist who would be an ideal mate for her (or almost any other woman) if she met him socially; and she may quite realistically fall in love with him, even though he has virtually nothing in common with her father, her uncles, or her brothers. Similarly, her therapist may fall in love with her not because she resembles his mother but because, more than any other woman he has met and gotten close to in his entire life, she truly *is* charming, talented and sexy to him.

When nontransference, reality-based feelings occur in therapy, and when they lead to intense warm or cold feelings on the part of the therapists and/or clients, they can easily foment resistance problems. Thus, a female client who intensely loves her therapist may resist improving in order to prolong the therapy; and a therapist who intensely loves his or her client may also (consciously or unconsciously) foment resistance to ensure that the therapy indefinitely continues.

These nontransference relationship feelings that encourage resistance are sometimes difficult to resolve, since they are reality-based and therefore both therapists and clients may derive special gains (or pains) from them that may interfere with effective therapy. But they also may include iBs that can be disputed, such as: 'Because I love my therapist and it would be great to mate with him, I *can't bear* giving up therapy. So I'll refuse to change!' Or: 'Because I really care for my client and enormously enjoy the sessions with her, I *must* not help her improve and bring these sessions to an end!' These iBs can be sought out and disputed, until the client and/or therapist gives them up and thereby removes motivation for resistance.

Fear of Disclosure Resistance

One of the most common forms of resistance stems from clients' fear of disclosure. They find it uncomfortable to talk about themselves freely (e.g., engage in free association) or to confess thoughts, feelings and actions that they view as 'shameful' (e.g., lusting for their mothers or sisters). They therefore resist being open in therapy and getting at the source of some of the things they find most bothersome (Dewald, 1982; Freud, 1926/1965b; Schlesinger, 1982).

Where psychoanalysis finds this kind of resistance exceptionally common and attributes it to deeply unconscious and often repressed feelings of guilt,

RET holds that clients who resist therapy because they are afraid to reveal 'shameful' thoughts about themselves usually do so because they are quite aware of these feelings or else have them just below their level of consciousness (in what Freud called their preconscious realm of experience). Thus, if a male client resists talking about sex because of his incestuous feelings for his mother or sister, he usually (though not always) is consciously aware of these feelings but deliberately suppresses rather than expresses them. He resists talking about such feelings in therapy because he is usually telling himself irrational beliefs such as 'It's wrong to lust after my mother, and I *must* not behave that wrongly!' 'If I told my therapist that I lust after my sister, he would think I was a sex fiend and wouldn't like me. I *have to* be liked by my therapist and would be a shit even if he didn't like me!'

In RET, we help clients to reveal these iBs and, more important, to dispute and surrender them. We help them to see that their 'shameful' feelings may not even be wrong (for to lust after your mother is hardly to copulate with her!) and that even when they are self-defeating (as having continual obsessive thoughts about incest would be), human *behaviors* never make one a totally rotten *person*. By helping clients to give up just about *all* shame and self-downing, RET sees that they rid themselves of what Freud would call superego-instigated resistance and are considerably more open in therapy than they would otherwise be (Dryden, 1983; Ellis, 1957, 1962, 1971b, 1973; Ellis and Grieger, 1977; Ellis and Whiteley, 1979).

Resistance Created by Fear of Discomfort

Probably the most common and strongest kind of resistance in therapy is that motivated by low frustration tolerance or what RET calls discomfort anxiety (Ellis, 1979, 1980). Even psychoanalysis, albeit reluctantly, recognizes this form of resistance. Blatt and Erlich (1982) acknowledge it as broad and basic, a fundamental resistance to change and growth. They call it an expression of the basic wish to maintain familiar and predictable modes of adaptation, even though these are uncomfortable and painful in the long run. Dewald (1982) talks about strategic resistance, that is, clients' efforts to seek fulfilment of childhood wishes and to demand unrealistic or impossible goals.

In RET this important form of resistance is attributed to short-range hedonism – clients' shortsighted demands that they achieve the pleasure of the moment even though this may well defeat them in the long run. The main irrational beliefs that lead to low frustration tolerance (LFT) or discomfort anxiety are 'It's *too hard* to change, and it *shouldn't be* that hard! How *awful* that I have to go through pain to get therapeutic gain!' 'I *can't tolerate* the discomfort of doing my homework, even though I have agreed with my therapist that it is desirable for me to do it.' 'The world is a *horrible place* when it forces me to work so hard to change myself! Life *should be* easier than it is!'

RET shows clients how to dispute these grandiose ideas and to accept the realistic notion that no matter how hard it is for them to change in therapy, it's harder if they don't. It teaches them that there is rarely any gain without pain and that the philosophy of long-range hedonism – the seeking of pleasure for today *and* for tomorrow – is likely to result in therapeutic change. It shows them how to use their natural hedonistic tendencies by reinforcing themselves for therapeutic progress (e.g., overcoming procrastination) and penalizing themselves when they refuse to work at therapy (e.g., when they procrastinate) (Ellis and Knaus, 1977; Knaus, 1982). RET also stresses problem-solving skills that help clients to achieve more successful solutions to their problems with an expenditure of minimum unnecessary effort (D'Zurilla and Goldfried, 1971; Ellis, 1962, 1977a; Ellis and Harper, 1975; Ellis and Whiteley, 1979; Spivack and Shure, 1974).

Secondary Gain Resistance

Several nineteenth-century and early-twentieth-century therapists noted that many clients receive secondary gains or payoffs from their disturbances and that they therefore are very reluctant to give them up (Ellenberger, 1970). Thus, if a factor worker who hates his job develops hysterical paralysis of the hand, he may resist psychotherapy because if it succeeds he will have to return to the work he hates. Freud (1926/1965b) and some of his followers (Berne, 1964; Fenichel, 1945; A. Freud, 1936) emphasized the unconscious aspects of this defensive process and insisted that if clients have direct gains to make by improving but have important unconscious secondary gains to maintain by refusing to improve, they will stubbornly resist treatment for deeply unconscious, often repressed, reasons. Thus, a woman will refuse to lose weight or to have good sex with her husband because of her underlying hatred of her mother and the strong unconscious payoff she is receiving by spiting this mother (who wants her to be thin or to have a good marriage).

Although Freudians usually exaggerate the deeply unconscious (and very dramatic) element in secondary gains, it seems clear that many clients do resist change because the payoffs they are getting from their disturbances are (or at least *seem* to be) considerable. Goldfried (1982) puts this kind of resistance in behavioral terms by pointing out that when clients change for the 'better,' they sometimes discover hidden penalties. Women may overcome their unassertiveness, for example, only to find that assertiveness is often ill-rewarded in our society. Hence, they may 'logically' fall back again to being unassertively neurotic!

Using RET analysis, we often find that secondary gain resistance is spurred by several iBs, such as 'Because my mother *must not* try to make me lose weight, and is a *rotten person* for criticizing me for being overweight, I'll fix her wagon by remaining a fat slob!' Or 'Because macho men will put me down if I am an assertive woman, and I *can't stand* their put-downs, I'll give up my desire for assertiveness and remain fairly submissive for the rest of my life.' Using RET, we show clients how to dispute and surrender these iBs and thereby to be able to achieve the *greater* payoff of losing weight rather than the neurotic one of spiting their mother. And we may encourage women to achieve the *primary gain* of being assertive rather than the *secondary gain* of winning the approval of macho men.

Resistance Stemming from Feelings of Hopelessness

A sizable number of clients seem to resist therapeutic change because they strongly feel that they are *unable* to modify their disturbed behavior, that they are *hopeless* and *can't* change (Ellis, 1957, 1962; Turkat and Meyer, 1982). Such clients sometimes at first make good progress; but as soon as they retrogress, even slightly, they irrationally tend to conclude, 'My falling back like this proves that it's *hopeless* and that I'll *never* conquer my anxiety!' 'Because I *must* not be as depressed and incompetent as I now am, and am therefore a *complete depressive*, what's the use of my trying any longer to conquer my depression? I might as well give in to it and perhaps kill myself!'

Thoughts and feelings about the hopelessness of one's disturbed state are part of what RET calls the *secondary symptoms of disturbance*. As I have noted elsewhere (Ellis, 1962, 1979, 1980) these secondary symptoms tend to validate the RET or cognitive-behavior theory of neurosis. For on the level of primary disturbance, people desire to achieve their goals (such as success and approval), fail to do so, and instead of sanely concluding, 'It would have been nice to achieve what I wanted but since I didn't, too bad! I'll try again next time,' they irrationally conclude, 'I *should* have achieved success and approval, and since I didn't do what I *must* do, it's *awful* and I'm no damned good as a *person!*' They then become, or, in RET terms, *make* themselves, disturbed. But once emotionally upset, they *see* their upsetness and cognize about it in this vein: 'I *shouldn't* disturb myself as I am now doing! How *awful!* I am a *total fool* for acting this foolishly, and a fool like me *can't* change. It's hopeless!'

RET, because of its theory of secondary disturbance, particularly shows clients how they falsely *invent* their thoughts and feelings of hopelessness and how they can dispute and give them up. It uses many cognitive, emotive and behavioral methods of dispelling feelings of hopelessness that lead to resistance (Ellis and Abrahms, 1978).

Resistance Motivated by Self-punishment

Freud (1926/1965b) held that one of the main forms of resistance originates in the superego or in our guilt-creating tendencies. Thus, a female client who is jealous of her more accomplished sister and who may become more conscious of her hatred during therapy may strongly feel that she deserves to be punished for her meanness and may therefore resist giving up her self-defeating neurotic behavior (such as overeating or compulsive hand-washing). During my 40 years of clinical practice I have rarely found this kind of self-punishing resistance among neurotics (though I have found it a little more often in psychotics and individuals with severe personality disorders).

Assuming this kind of resistance does exist, it would seem to stem from irrational beliefs along these lines: 'Because I have done such evil acts, which I absolutely *should not* have done, I am a thoroughly *worthless individual* who *deserves* to suffer. Therefore, I deserve to be continually disturbed and will make no real effort to use therapy to help myself.' If clients actively have these ideas, RET would be most appropriate to show them how to combat their iBs. Psychodynamic therapies, on the other hand, might well be contraindicated, because, although they might show clients how self-punishing they are, they might not teach them how to eradicate the irrational beliefs behind this kind of masochism.

Resistance Motivated by Fear of Change or Fear of Success

Psychodynamic therapists, from Freud onward, have often held that resistance sometimes stems from fear of change, from fear of the future, or fear of success (Blatt and Erlich, 1982). This is probably true, since many disturbed people have a pronounced need for safety and certainty, and even though their symptoms are uncomfortable, at least they know and are familiar with their negative limits and may be afraid that if they lose them they may experience even *greater* discomfort. So they prefer to stick with the tried-and-true discomfort.

More important, perhaps, many symptoms (such as shyness and fear of public speaking) protect clients against possible failure (such as failing in love or giving a laughable speech). To surrender these symptoms would therefore mean to risk subsequent failure and disapproval, and many clients would find this much more 'catastrophic' or 'awful' than they find retaining their symptoms.

What has been labeled 'the fear of success' is almost never really that, but a fear of *subsequent* failure. Thus, if a withdrawn teenage boy stops withdrawing and begins to succeed at school, at sports, and at social affairs, he may (1) lose the comfort and indulgence of his overprotective parents, (2) gain the enmity of his siblings, (3) risk later failure at the activities in which he has now begun to succeed, and (4) be forced to take on much more responsibility and effort than he would like to assume. He may *view* his academic, athletic and social 'gains,' therefore, as actual 'dangers' or 'failures' and may resist or retreat from them. Does he, then, really have a 'fear of success' – or of failure?

When clients do resist psychotherapy because of fear of change or fear of success, RET looks for their iBs, such as 'I *must* not give up my symptoms, since change would be *too* uncomfortable and I *can't stand* such change!' 'I cannot change my neurotic behavior and do better in life because that would be too risky. I might encounter greater failure later, as I *must* not; for that would be *awful*!' These and similar iBs that underlie the fear of change or fear of success are revealed and eliminated during rational-emotive therapy, thus minimizing this kind of resistance to change.

Resistance Motivated by Reactance and Rebelliousness

A number of clinicians have observed that some clients react or rebel against therapy because they see it as an impingement on their freedom. Especially if it is active and directive, they perversely fight it, even when they have voluntarily asked for it (Brehm, 1976; Goldfried, 1982). Noting this form of resistance, several therapists have invented or adopted various kinds of paradoxical or provocative therapy to try to trick these perversely rebellious clients into giving up their resistance (Dunlap, 1928; Erikson and Rossi, 1979; Farrelly and Brandsma, 1974; Fay, 1978; Frankl, 1960; Haley, 1963; Watzlawick et al., 1974).

When clients resist therapy because of reactance, RET looks for their irrational beliefs, such as 'I *have to* control my entire destiny; and even though my therapist is on my side and is working hard to help me, I *must not* let him or her tell me what to do!' 'How *awful* if I am directed by my therapist! I *can't bear* it! I should have perfect freedom to do what I like, even if my symptoms are killing me!' RET reveals and helps clients rip up their iBs, but it also selectively (and not cavalierly!) makes use of paradoxical intention. For example, it gives some clients the homework assignment of failing at a certain task, to show them that failure is not world-shattering (Ellis and Abrahms, 1978; Ellis and Whiteley, 1979).

As can be seen by the foregoing survey of some of the common kinds of resistance, clients frequently come to therapy because they are plagued with symptoms of emotional disturbance, and yet they stubbornly resist the best efforts of their therapists to relieve their suffering. In many instances their 'resistance' is partly attributable to therapeutic fallibility – to the poor judgment, inept theories, and emotional rigidities of their therapists. But often (perhaps more often) they have their own reasons for resisting the therapist-directed procedures that they voluntarily seek. As noted, these reasons are varied and wide-ranging.

While some aspects of the rational-emotive approach to treating common resistances have already been briefly outlined, the next section will discuss RET's cognitive antiresistance techniques in considerably more detail.

Disputing Clients' Irrational, Resistance-creating Beliefs

RET employs a number of cognitive methods to interrupt, challenge, dispute, and change the irrational beliefs (iBs) that are found to underlie clients self-sabotaging resistances. These include the following techniques.

Cognitions that Underlie Resistance

Virtually all RET clients are taught the ABCs of emotional disturbance and dysfunctional behavior. Thus, when clients have a neurotic symptom or self-defeating consequence (C), such as depression and self-hatred, following their experiencing an unfortunate activating event (A), such as rejection by a significant person, they are shown that while A (rejection) probably contributes to and influences C (depression), it does not directly (as they tend to falsely 'see' or infer) *create* or *cause* C. Rather, the more direct (and usually more important) 'cause' of C is B, their belief system, with which they mainly 'create' or 'cause' C. Although they mistakenly believe that their depression and self-hatred directly and inevitably follow from their being rejected (A), they actually have a *choice* of Bs and Cs, and they foolishly *choose* to make themselves unhealthily depressed and self-hating (neurotic) at C, when they theoretically could have *chosen* instead to make themselves feel only healthily disappointed and frustrated (self-helping and unneurotic) (Ellis, 1957, 1962, 1973; Ellis and Harper, 1975).

According to the ABC theory of RET, when these clients want to be accepted and approved at A (activating event) and are unpleasantly, instead, rejected, they *can* choose to manufacture or resort to a set of sensible or rational beliefs (rBs) and *can* thereby conclude, 'How unfortunate that so-and-so disapproved of some of my traits and therefore rejected my friendship or love. Too bad! But I can still find significant others to approve of and accept me. Now how do I go about finding them?' If they rigorously create and stay with these rBs, these clients would, as stated, feel healthily disappointed and frustrated but *not* depressed and self-hating.

Where, then, do their unhealthy and disturbed feelings of depression and self-hatred come from? RET shows clients that these neurotic consequences (Cs) mainly or largely (though not exclusively) stem from their iBs. These iBs almost invariably consist of absolutistic, dogmatic, illogical, unrealistic beliefs. Instead of being expressions of flexible desire and preference (as rBs seem to be), they are inflexible, rigid commands and demands – absolutist and unconditional shoulds, oughts, musts and necessities. Thus, feelings of depression and self-hatred (at C) that follow disapproval and rejection (at A) are largely the result of iBs like (1) 'I *must* not be disapproved of and rejected by a person I deem significant'; (2) 'If I am rejected, as I must not be, it's *awful* and *terrible*'; (3) 'I *can't stand* being disapproved, as I *must* not be'; and (4) 'If I am rejected by a significant other, as must *never* under *any* conditions, occur, there has to be something horribly rotten about me, and that rottenness makes me a thoroughly *despicable, undeserving person!*'

RET, using its cognitively oriented ABC theory of human disturbance, first tends to show depressed and self-hating clients how they (and not their parents, teachers, society, or culture) unwittingly (and largely unconsciously) *choose* to *disturb themselves*; how they can therefore *decide* to change their iBs and thereby undisturb themselves; and how they can mainly (though not completely) acquire a realistic philosophy of *preference* rather than an absolutistic philosophy of *demandingness* and consequently rarely seriously disturb themselves in the future.

In combatting clients' self-defeating resistances, RET puts them into the

ABC model and shows them that when they promise themselves and their therapists that they will work at therapy at point A (activating event) and when they act dysfunctionally at point C and achieve the self-defeating consequence of resistance, they have both rational beliefs and irrational beliefs at point C. Their rBs tend to be 'I don't like working at therapy. It's hard to change myself! But it's hard*er* if I don't; so I'd damned well better push myself and do this hard work right *now* to make my life easier and better later.' If, says the theory of RET, they *only* believed and felt these rational beliefs at B, they would not be especially resistant at C.

No such luck! When clients seriously and self-injuriously resist they usually *also* create and indulge in irrational beliefs such as these: (1) 'It's not only too hard for me to work at therapy and change myself, it's *too* hard! It *should not, must not* be that hard'; (2) 'How *terrible* that I have to work so hard and persistently to change myself'; (3) 'I *can't stand* working at therapy that is harder than it *should be*'; and (4) 'What a *rotten therapist* I have, who makes me work harder than I *should!* And what *crummy methods* he or she inflicts on me! I'm sure there is some easier, more enjoyable method of changing, and until I find it I'll be damned if I'll make myself so uncomfortable with this one!'

These iBs of resistant clients, which mainly consist of a devout philosophy of low frustration tolerance (LFT) or discomfort anxiety (DA) (Ellis, 1979, 1980), can also be supplemented with a philosophy of self-downing or ego anxiety (EA). Resistant clients' iBs then tend to run along these lines: (1) 'I absolutely *must* work hard and succeed at therapy'; (2) 'If I don't change as much and as quickly as I *must*, it's *awful* and *terrible*'; (3) 'When I don't make myself change as well as I *must*, I *can't* stand it and life is *intolerable*'; and (4) 'Unless I do as well as I *must* in therapy, I am an inadequate, hopeless, worthless person!' One might think that these self-blaming iBs would help spur on clients to work at therapy and to overcome their resistance. Occasionally, this may be true, but usually these iBs sabotage clients, lead them to feel that they *can't* change, and result in still greater resistances.

RET's primary cognitive technique of combatting resistance, therefore, consists of showing clients that they do not 'just' resist and that they do not *merely* resist *because* they find it difficult to change, but that they *choose* to subscribe to a philosophy of low frustration tolerance and/or of self-depreciation which, in turn, largely 'causes' their resistance. The main cognitive message of RET, of course, is that they can instead choose to *dis*believe and to *surrender* their iBs and can exchange them for rBs that will help them work at rather than resist therapeutic change.

Disputing Irrational Beliefs

The basic disputing techniques of RET can be employed to show clients that the iBs behind their absolutistic *shoulds, oughts* and *musts*, and behind the inferences, attributions, overgeneralizations, non sequiturs, and other forms of crooked thinking that tend to stem from these *musts*, can be annihilated or ameliorated by vigorous scientific thinking (Ellis, 1958a, 1962, 1971a, 1973; Ellis and Becker, 1982; Ellis and Grieger, 1977; Ellis and Harper, 1975; Ellis and Whiteley, 1979). Thus resisters are challenged by the therapist and are induced to keep challenging themselves with scientific questions like 'Where is the evidence that I *must* succeed at changing myself?' 'Why is it *awful* and *horrible* that it is difficult for me to change?' 'Prove that I *can't stand* my having to work long and hard at therapy.' 'Where is it written that it's *too hard* to change and that it *should not* be that hard?' This kind of scientific disputing is persisted at, by both therapists and clients, until resisters start changing.

After A (activating event), B (rational and irrational beliefs), and C (emotional and behavioral consequences), RET goes directly (and often quickly) on to D: disputing. As just noted, D is the scientific method. Science accepts beliefs as hypotheses, constructs, or theories, not as facts. Furthermore, scientific theories are not dogmatic, inflexible, absolutistic, or devout. Otherwise they are religious rather than scientific (Ellis, 1983a; Rorer and Widiger, 1983). RET not only tries to be scientific about its own theories and to set them up so that they are precise and falsifiable (Bartley, 1962; Mahoney, 1977; Popper, 1972) but it is one of the new forms of cognitive-behavioral therapy that attempts to teach clients how to think scientifically about themselves, others, and the world in which they live. If, RET contends, people were consistently scientific and nonabsolutistic, they would rarely invent or subscribe to dogmatic *shoulds* and *musts*, would stay with their flexible wishes and preferences, and would thereby minimize or eliminate their emotional disturbances.

RET, therefore, encourages all clients, and particularly resistant ones, actively and persistently to dispute (at point D) their iBs and to arrive at point E, which is a new effect or effective philosophy. Where D consists of clients' disputing their iBs, E consists of the logical and empirical answers they then give to this disputing. Thus, to perform D and to arrive at E, a client's internal dialogue in regard to her or his resistance would go something like this:

iB: 'I *must* succeed at changing myself during therapy!'
D: 'Where is the evidence that I *have* to succeed?'
E: 'There is no such evidence! Succeeding at changing myself would have several distinct advantages and I'd definitely like to get these advantages. But I never *have* to get what I desire, no matter how much I desire it.'
iB: 'If I don't succeed in overcoming my resistance and working at therapy, I am an incompetent, hopeless person who can never stop resisting!'
D: 'Prove that I am an incompetent, hopeless person who can never stop resisting.'
E: 'I can't prove this, I can only prove that I am a person who has *so far* failed to stop resisting but not that I have, or always will have, *no* ability to do so in the future. Only my *belief* in my total incompetence to change myself will make me *more* incompetent than I otherwise would probably be!'
iB: 'It is *awful* and *horrible* that I have to work at therapy and to change myself.'
D: 'In what way is it *awful* and *horrible* to work at therapy and to change myself?'

E: 'In no way! It is distinctly difficult and inconvenient for me to work at therapy, and I'd rather it be easy. But when I label this work *awful* or *horrible* I mean that (1) it *should not* be as inconvenient as it is, (2) it is *totally* or 100 percent inconvenient, and (3) it is *more than* (101 percent) inconvenient. All these conclusions are wrong, since (1) it should be as inconvenient as it is because that's the way it is, (2) it virtually never can be 100 percent inconvenient because it invariably could be worse, and (3) it obviously cannot be 101 percent inconvenient because nothing can be *that* bad! Nothing in the universe is *awful* or *terrible* or *horrible*, since these are magical terms that go beyond reality and have no empirical referents. If I invent such antiempirical "descriptions" of my experience, I will thereby make my life *seem* and *feel* "awful" when it is only highly disadvantageous and inconvenient; and I will then make myself suffer *more* than I would otherwise suffer.'

iB: 'I can't *stand* my having to work long and hard at therapy.'

D: 'Why can't I stand having to work long and hard at therapy?'

E: 'I definitely *can* stand it! I don't *like* working that long and hard and wish that I could change myself easily and magically. But I *can* stand what I don't like, as long as (1) I don't die of it and (2) I can still in some ways enjoy myself and be happy. Fairly obviously I won't die because I work at therapy (though I may kill myself if I don't!). And even though this kind of work is often unenjoyable, it leaves me time and energy for other pleasures. In fact, in the long run, it helps me to achieve *greater* life enjoyment. So I clearly *can* stand, *can* tolerate the therapeutic work that I don't like.'

iB: 'Because there is no easy way for me to work at therapy and I'd better uncomfortably persist at it until I collaborate with my therapist and change myself, the world is a *horrible* place and life is hardly worth living. Maybe I'd better kill myself.'

D: 'Where is it written that the world is a horrible place and that life is hardly worth living because there is no easy way for me to work at therapy?'

E: 'It is only written in my self-defeating philosophy! It seems evident that, because of the way I am and because of the way the world is, I will often have trouble changing myself through therapy. Too bad! Really unfortunate! But if that's the way it is and that's the way I am, I'd better accept (though still dislike and often try to change) the world's limitations and my own fallibility, and I'd better attempt to live and to enjoy myself as much as I can with these undesirable realities. I can teach myself, as St. Francis recommended, to have the courage to change the unpleasant things that I can change, to have the serenity to accept those that I can't change, and to have the wisdom to know the difference between the two.'

RET's most famous and most popular technique is the one just outlined: that of teaching resistant clients to find their main irrational beliefs that significantly contribute to or 'cause' their resistances; to actively dispute these iBs by rigorously using the logico-empirical tools of the scientific method; and to persist at this disputing until they arrive at E, an effective philosophy that is self-helping rather than irrational and self-downing. As Kelly (1955) brilliantly noted, humans are natural predictors and scientists. RET, along with other cognitive behavioral therapies, tries to help them be better and more productive scientists in their personal affairs (Ellis, 1962, 1973; Ellis and Becker, 1982; Ellis and Grieger, 1977; Ellis and Harper, 1975; Ellis and Whiteley, 1979; Friedman, 1975; Mahoney, 1974, 1977).

Rational and Coping Self-statements

RET, following the leads of Bernheim (1886/1947) and Coué (1922), teaches resistant clients to say to themselves, repetitively, rational or coping statements and to keep actively autosuggesting these statements until they truly believe them and feel their effect. Thus, they can strongly say to themselves rBs such as 'Therapy doesn't *have* to be easy. I can, in fact, *enjoy* its difficulty and its challenge.' 'Sure it's hard to work at changing myself, but it's much harder if I don't.' 'Too bad if I am imperfect at changing myself. That only proves that I am still, and will continue to be, a highly fallible person. And I *can* accept myself as fallible!' Unlike positive thinking, however, RET encourages resisters to think through, and not merely parrot, rational and coping statements.

Referenting

RET uses the general semantics method of referenting (Danysh, 1974) and teahces resistant clients (1) to make a comprehensive list of the disadvantages of resisting and the advantages of working at therapy and (2) to keep regularly reviewing and thinking about this list (Ellis and Abrahms, 1978; Ellis and Becker, 1982; Ellis and Harper, 1975). Thus, under disadvantages of resisting, clients can list: '(1) It will take me longer to change. (2) I will keep suffering as long as I resist changing. (3) My refusing to change will antagonize some of the people I care for and will sabotage my relationships with them. (4) My therapy will become more boring and more expensive the longer I take to change myself. (5) Continuing to afflict myself with my symptoms will make me lose much time and money. (6) If I continue to resist, I may well antagonize my therapist and encourage him or her to put less effort into helping me. (7) My refusing to work hard at therapy and thereby continuing to remain irrationally fearful and anxious will force me to forego many potential pleasures and adventures and make my life much duller.' Similarly, using this referenting technique, clients are shown how to list the advantages of working harder at therapy and thereby abetting their own personality change. By reviewing and examining these disadvantages of resistance and these benefits of nonresistance, they are helped to resist considerably less.

RET often forcefully brings to clients' attention not only present but probable later disadvantages of resisting therapy. Thus, the RET practitioner can reward the client: 'Yes, you don't have to work right now at overcoming your low frustration tolerance, since your parents are still around to help support you economically. But how are you going to earn a decent living after they are gone unless you prepare yourself to do so now?' 'Of course, you may be able to get away with your drinking and staying up late at night at present, but won't it eventually sabotage your health? And do you really want to keep making yourself fat, tired and physically ill?'

Challenge of Self-change

RET tries to sell some resistant clients on the *adventure* and *challenge* of working at changing themselves. Thus, it gives clients the homework exercise of disputing irrational beliefs (DIBS) which helps them debate their iBs and to reframe some of the difficult things they do with therapy by asking themselves questions like, 'What good things can I feel or make happen if I work hard at therapy and still don't succeed too well?' (Ellis, 1974a; Ellis and Harper, 1975). Rational-emotive therapists also prod resistant clients with questions like 'Suppose you pick the wrong therapy technique and work hard at it with few good results. Why would that be great for you to do?' By these paradoxical questions they hope to help resisters see that (1) trying something and at first failing at it is usually better than not trying at all; (2) striving to change leads to important information about oneself that may result in later success and pleasure; (3) action can be pleasurable in its own right, even when it does not lead to fine results; (4) trying something and at first failing at it is usually better than not trying at all; (5) trying to change oneself and *accepting* delayed results increases one's frustration tolerance, and (6) the *challenge* of striving for therapeutic change (like the challenge of trying to climb Mount Everest) may be exciting and enjoyable in its own right.

Although ego-enhancing methods of therapy are seen by RET as having their distinct dangers (since if clients are led to think of themselves as good or worthy individuals when they succeed at therapy, they will also harmfully view themselves as bad or worthless individuals when they fail), some elements of verbal reinforcement can be used to combat resistance. Thus, therapists can show clients that *it* is good and desirable (and not that *they* are good or worthy) if they use their energy and intelligence to work at therapy. This technique can be combined with the challenging method. For example, the therapist can say to the client, 'Yes, many people are prone to sitting on their asses and to stupidly resisting changing themselves. But anyone who fortunately has *your* intelligence, talent and ability *can* overcome this kind of resistance and show how competent he or she is at changing. Not that you *have* to use your innate ability to change. But wouldn't you get much better results if you did?'

Proselytizing Others

One of the regular RET cognitive techniques that can be especially helpful with resistant and difficult clients consists of inducing them to use RET methods with others (Bard, 1980; Ellis, 1957; Ellis and Abrahms, 1978; Ellis and Harper, 1975; Ellis and Whiteley, 1979). If, using RET, you have clients who resist giving up anger, you can try to get them to talk others – relatives, friends, employees – out of *their* anger. If your clients refuse to do their RET homework, you can try to induce them to give homework assignments to others and to keep checking to see if these people actually do their homework.

Cognitive Distraction

Cognitive distraction frequently is used in RET to divert clients from anxiety and depression (Ellis, 1973; Ellis and Abrahms, 1978; Ellis and Whiteley, 1979). Thus clients are shown how to relax, to meditate, to do yoga exercises, and to use other forms of distraction when they upset themselves. Distraction, however, is often not that useful with resistant clients, since it only temporarily diverts them from rebelliously and defensively persisting with their disturbed behavior and they therefore soon return to it. One form of distraction that works well if you can get these clients to use it is in the form of a vital, ongoing interest that really absorbs them. Thus, if you can help them get absorbed in writing a book, being an active member of a self-help group, or volunteering to help others, they can sometimes find such constructive enjoyment as to minimize their need for self-defeating behavior like alcoholism, drugs, or stealing.

Use of Humor

Many resistant clients have little sense of humor, and that is precisely why they find it so hard to see how they are defeating themselves and how absurd their thoughts and behaviors are. But some, in spite of their severe disturbance, do have a good sense of humor that can be used to interfere with their resistance. Thus, I kept showing one of my stubborn clients how ironic it was that she railed and ranted against cold weather and thereby made herself suffer *more* from the cold. I also frequently tell resistant clients, 'If the Martians ever come to visit us and they're really sane, they'll die laughing at us. For they'll see bright people like you vainly insisting that they can do something they can't do – such as change your parents – while simultaneously saying they can't do something that they invariably can do, namely, change yourself. They won't be able to understand this and will probably fly back to Mars because we're so crazy!' RET frequently uses humor and rational humorous songs to combat therapeutic resistance (Ellis, 1977c, 1977d, 1981).

Paradoxical Intention

With highly resistant and negative clients, as Erickson (Erickson and Rossi, 1979), Frankl (1960), Haley (1963), and others have shown, paradoxical intention sometimes works and is therefore a cognitive method of RET (Ellis and Whiteley, 1979). Thus, you can tell depressed clients to loudly wail and moan about everything that occurs in their lives. Or you can have highly anxious people take the assignment of only allowing themselves to worry from 8.00 to 8.15 a.m. every day. Or you can insist that resistant clients refuse to do *anything* you tell them to do, such as refuse to come on time for their sessions and refuse to do any homework assignments. Perversely, resisters may then stop resisting. But don't count on this!

Paradoxical intention is a shocking but limited method that tends to work only occasionally and under special conditions.

Suggestion and Hypnosis

You may deliberately use strong suggestion or hypnosis with some difficult clients, even though these are inelegant techniques that somewhat interfere with clients' independent thinking. Resistant clients who *think* hypnosis works may allow themselves to change with hypnotic methods when they would not allow this without hypnosis. RET has included hypnosis methods from its inception in 1955 (Ellis, 1958a, 1962). Stanton (1977), Tosi (Tosi and Marzella, 1977; Tosi and Reardon, 1976), and other researchers and clinicians have shown how it can sometimes be used effectively with resistant clients.

Philosophy of Effort

The usual practice of RET is to explain to all clients, right at the beginning of therapy, that they have enormous self-actualization powers (as well as self-defeating tendencies) and that only with hard work and practice will they be able to fulfill these powers (Ellis, 1962; Grieger and Boyd, 1980; Grieger and Grieger, 1982; Walen et al., 1980; Wessler and Wessler, 1980). Clients are also shown that they can easily fall back to old dysfunctional patterns of behavior and that they therefore had better persistently keep monitoring themselves and working to change. With resistant clients this realistic message is often repeated with the aim of both prophylaxis and cure. A favorite RET slogan is 'There's rarely any gain without pain!' This philosophy is steadily promulgated to combat the low frustration tolerance of resisters (Ellis, 1979, 1980).

Working with Clients' Expectations

As Meichenbaum and Gilmore (1982) have shown, clients bring cognitive expectations to therapy and may see what is helping in their sessions with the therapist as disconfirming these expectations. Consequently, they may resist changing themselves. If so, you can accurately and empathically perceive and share your clients' expectations, make sense out of their unproductive resistant behavior, and thereby help overcome resistance. Using RET, you might well go one step further and, as you help your clients explore and understand the reasons for their resistance (and the iBs that often underlie this resistance), you can actively push, encourage, and persuade them to surrender their resistant ideas and behaviors.

Irrational Beliefs Underlying Primary and Secondary Resistance

Clients frequently have both primary and secondary resistance. Primary resistance stems largely from their three main musts: (1) 'I *must* change myself quickly and easily, and I'm an incompetent person if I don't'; (2) 'You *must* not force me to change, and I'll fight you to death if you do;' and (3) 'Conditions *must* make it easy for me to change, and I won't try to help myself if they don't!' Once humans resist changing themselves for any of these three (or a combination of these three) reasons, they *see* that they resist and have another set of irrational beliefs about this resistance, such as (1) 'I *must* not incompetently resist change, and I'm a pretty worthless person if I do'; (2) 'I *must* not resist change in a hostile or rebellious manner, and it's *awful* if I do'; and (3) 'I *must* not have low frustration tolerance that makes me resist change, and I can't stand it if I do!' Their secondary disturbance, that is, their guilt or shame *about* resisting, tends to tie up their time and energy and incite *increased* resistance. In RET, therefore, we look for and try to eliminate secondary as well as primary resistances, and we do so by showing clients their primary and secondary iBs and by disputing both these sets of iBs, just as we would dispute any other irrational beliefs. By helping them first to undo their disturbances *about* their resistance, we show them how to remove these secondary problems and then how to get back to changing the ideas and feelings that constitute the primary resistance.

Irrational Beliefs Underlying Avoidance of Responsibility

Resistance may sometimes stem from clients' trying to avoid responsibility for change and from their deliberately (though perhaps unconsciously) fighting the therapist's efforts to help them change. This form of childish rebelliousness can arise from ego irrationalities ('I must thwart my therapist and "win out" over him to show what a strong, independent person I am!') or from low frustration tolerance irrationalities ('I must not have to work too hard at therapy, because if I assume full responsibility for changing myself life becomes too rough and unsatisfying!'). When avoidance of responsibility and concomitant rebellion against the therapist or against working at therapy result in resistance, RET tries to show clients the irrational beliefs (iBs) behind this kind of avoidance and rebellion and teach them how to combat and surrender these iBs.

Use of Quick and Active Disputation

Although RET therapists may sometimes help create resistance by actively and quickly disputing their clients' irrational beliefs, they may also, by 'poorly' employing this technique, promptly smoke out clients' resistances, see exactly what kind of DCs (difficult customers) these clients are, and promote more efficient and effective therapy methods. Active disputing, though risky, may uncover resistances rapidly, save therapists and clients considerable time and effort, lead to vigorous countermeasures by the therapist, and sometimes lead to a suitable quick (and inexpensive!) end to therapy.

Some cognitive-behavioral therapists (e.g., Meichenbaum and Gilmore,

1982) recommend that resistance be overcome by graduating the change process into manageable steps and by structuring therapeutic intervention so that the therapist maximizes the likelihood of success at each stage. This will sometimes work but also has its dangers with those who resist because of abysmal LFT. With these individuals gradualism may easily *feed* their LFT and help them believe that it is *too* hard for them to change and that they *must* do so in a slow, gradual manner (Ellis, 1983c).

Disputing Impossibility of Changing

When clients contend that they *can't* change, RET can show them that this is an unrealistic, antiempirical view not supported by any facts (which merely show that *it is difficult* for them to change). But RET therapists do not use only this realistic, scientific refutation but also employ the more elegant anti*must*urbatory form of disputing. Clients usually tell themselves, 'I *can't change*' because they start with the basic proposition 'I *must* have an ability to change quickly and easily, and I'm incompetent and pretty worthless if I don't do what I *must*.' RET disputes this *must*urbatory, absolutistic thinking by showing them that they *never* have to change (though that would be highly desirable) and that they are *people who act incompetently* rather than *incompetent people*. This disputing of the idea 'I can't change' is therefore more profound and more elegant than the simple antiempirical disputing of Meichenbaum (1977), Beck (1976), Maultsby (1975), and other proponents of CBT.

Helping Clients Gain Emotional Insight

RET often shows resistant clients that they falsely believe they are working hard to improve and to overcome their own resistance, when they really aren't. Thus they frequently say,'I see that I am telling myself that therapy should be easy, and I see that that is wrong.' They then mistakenly think that because they have *seen* how they are resisting and have *seen* the error of their ways, they have worked at changing this error and thereby *overcome* their resistance. But they have usually done nothing of the sort. Their 'insight' has not been used to help them *fight* the idea that therapy should be easy. They can now be shown that they'd better see and fight this idea, that is, dispute it by asking themselves, '*Why* should therapy be easy?' and by vigorously answering, 'There's no damned reason why it should be! It often is – and should be – *hard!*'

RET tries to distinguish clearly between so-called intellectual and emotional insight (Ellis, 1963). Resistant clients often say, 'I have intellectual insight into my hating myself but this does me no good, since I still can't stop this self-hatred. What I need is emotional insight.' What these clients mean is that they hate themselves and may even see the irrational self-statements they make to bring about this feeling (e.g., 'I must always succeed at important tasks and I am worthless when I don't!'), but they do not know how to change their iBs or they know how to change them but refuse to do the persistent and strong disputing that is required to give them up.

In RET we try to show clients, particularly resistant ones, three main kinds of insight. First, people mainly disturb themselves rather than get upset by external conditions and events. Second, no matter when they first started to disturb themselves (usually in childhood) and no matter what events contributed to their early *disturbance*, people *now*, in the present, continue to make themselves upset by *still* strongly subscribing to irrational beliefs similar to those they held previously. They now keep their old disturbances alive by continually reindoctrinating themselves with these iBs. Third, since people are born with the tendency to accept iBs from others and to create many of their own, and since they consciously and unconsciously reinstill these iBs in themselves from early childhood onward, and since they easily, automatically and habitually actualize these ideas in their feelings and actions and thereby powerfully reinforce them over long periods of time, there is usually no simple, fast, easy and complete way to change them. Only considerable work and practice to challenge and dispute these irrational beliefs and only long, concerted *action* that contradicts the behavioral patterns that accompany them will be likely to minimize or extirpate them.

RET, then, teaches clients that insights 1 and 2 are important but not sufficient for profound philosophical and behavioral change and that they had better be accompanied by the most important insight of all – insight 3.

More specifically, RET shows resistant clients who say that they have intellectual insight into their symptoms (such as self-hating), but can't give it up because they don't have emotional insight, that they usually only have insight 1 – and even that, often, partially. Thus, a young woman may say, 'I see that I hate myself,' but may not see what she is irrationally believing to create her self-hatred (e.g., 'Because I am not as competent as I *must* be, I am a thoroughly *inadequate person*'). Even when she sees what she is believing to create her self-hatred, she only has achieved insight 1; and she may falsely believe that she obtained her self-hating belief from her parents and *that* is why she now hates herself.

In RET, we would therefore help her achieve insight 2: 'No matter how I got the irrational belief that I *should* be more competent and am an *inadequate person* if I'm not, *I* now continue to indoctrinate myself with it so that *I* am fully responsible for believing it today; and therefore *I* had better give it up.'

RET doesn't stop there, since she still might be left with only mild or 'intellectual' insight, but pushes her on to insight 3: 'Since *I* keep actively believing that I *should* be more competent and am an *inadequate person* if I'm not, and since I tend to keep recreating and newly inventing similar irrational beliefs (because it is my basic nature to do so), I had better keep steadily and forcefully *working and practicing* until I no longer believe this. For only by *continually* disputing and challenging this belief and only by *forcing myself* to keep acting against it will I be able *finally* to give it up and replace it with rational beliefs and effective behaviors.'

Insight 3, plus the determination to act on this level of understanding, is what RET calls 'emotional' insight or 'willpower.' It is this kind of cognitive restructuring or profound philosophical change that RET particularly employs with resistant clients.

Bibliotherapy and Audiotherapy

RET employs bibliotherapy with resistant clients and encourages them to read RET-oriented pamphlets and books, such as *Reason and Emotion in Psychotherapy* (Ellis, 1962), *A New Guide to Rational Living* (Ellis and Harper, 1975), *Humanistic Psychotherapy: The Rational-Emotive Approach* (Ellis, 1973), and *A Guide to Personal Happiness* (Ellis and Becker, 1982). RET practitioners also give a good many talks, courses, workshops, marathons and intensives that help clients understand theory and use the techniques of rational-emotive therapy. I have especially found that some RET cassette recordings, films and TV cassettes are useful with resistant clients, who are urged to listen to them many times until the presentations on these materials sink in. Notably useful in this respect are the cassette recordings *Conquering the Dire Need for Love* (Ellis, 1977b), *Conquering Low Frustration Tolerance* (Ellis, 1977a), *Overcoming Procrastination* (Ellis and Knaus, 1977), *I'd like to Stop, But . . .* (Ellis, 1974b), *Self-Hypnosis: The Rational-Emotive Approach* (Golden, 1982), *Twenty-One Ways to Stop Worrying* (Ellis, 1972b), and *How to Stubbornly Refuse to Be Ashamed of Anything* (Ellis, 1971b).

Imaging Methods

One of the main modes of human cognition is imagery, and RET frequently employs imaging methods. These are sometimes especially useful with resistant clients, since some of them resist because they see and feel things more incisively through pictoral than through verbal means (Coué, 1922; Lazarus, 1978, 1981). Consequently, when they block on or find difficulty with verbal self-statements and philosophical disputing of irrational beliefs, they can sometimes be reached more effectively by imagery methods. To this end, RET, following Coué (1922) and a host of his disciples, can teach resisters to use positive imagery to imagine themselves doing things that they negatively contend that they can't do (e.g., successfully giving a public talk), and it can help them imagine bearing up under frustrating conditions when they normally think that they absolutely can't bear such conditions. Also, RET frequently employs Maultsby's technique of rational-emotive imagery (Maultsby, 1975; Maultsby and Ellis, 1974), by which resistant (and other) clients are shown how to imagine one of the worst things that could happen to them, to implode their disturbed feelings about this happening, and then to work at changing these to more healthy negative feelings.

Modeling Techniques

Bandura (1969, 1977) has pioneered in showing how modeling methods can be used to help disturbed individuals, and RET has always used such methods (Ellis, 1962, 1971a, 1973; Ellis and Abrahms, 1978; Ellis and Whiteley, 1979). In the case of resistant and difficult clients, RET practitioners not only teach them how to accept themselves unconditionally and fully, no matter how badly or incompetently they behave, but they also model this kind of acceptance by displaying firm kindness to these clients and showing by their attitudes and demeanor (as well as their words) that they can fully accept such clients, even when they are nasty to the therapist, when they come late to sessions, when they fail to do their homework, and when they otherwise stubbornly resist the therapist's efforts (Ellis, 1962, 1973; Ellis and Whiteley, 1979). RET also sponsors public workshops, such as my famous Friday night workshops that are given regularly at the Institute for Rational-Emotive Therapy in New York, where live demonstrations of RET are given for large audiences, so that the members of the audience can see exactly how RET is done and can model their own self-help procedures after this model. Resistant clients who serve as volunteer demonstratees at these workshops are often particularly helped by the public session they have with me (or other RET therapists, when I am out of town) and by the feedback and the comments they receive from 15 or 20 members of the audience.

Recorded Playback of Therapy Sessions

Carl Rogers (1942) pioneered in using recordings of therapy sessions to help therapists understand exactly what they were doing and how to improve their techniques. RET, beginning in 1959, pioneered the use of audiotapes for two other purposes: (1) to show therapists throughout the world exactly how RET is done, so that they could model their own use of it after the practices of its originator and other RET practitioners (Elkin et al., 1971; Ellis, 1959, 1966a, 1966b; Wessler and Ellis, 1980), and (2) to give clients recordings of their own sessions so that they could listen to them several times and thereby hear and internalize some of the therapeutic messages that they would otherwise miss or forget. This second use of recordings, which also can be done with video equipment if this is available, has been found very useful with resistant clients. If they are given homework assignments of listening to their own taped sessions (and sometimes the taped session of others), they often get across to themselves some of the elements of RET that they otherwise easily miss (Ellis, 1979; Ellis and Abrahms, 1978; Ellis and Whiteley, 1979). One of my personality disordered clients, for example, who argued vigorously against almost every point I made about his needlessly upsetting himself, accepted these same points almost all the time when he listened to a cassette recording of each session several times during the week following this session.

Conclusion

As can be seen from the material just presented, RET cognitive methods, when carefully selected and employed with resistant and difficult clients, can often be effective. Also, RET often employs a variety of emotive and behavioral techniques, in addition to many cognitive methods, with resistant clients. Rarely, if ever, would it compulsively stick to one favored method. In fact, the more resistant a client is, the more cognitive, emotive and behavioral methods are usually employed. RET is designed to be not only effective but efficient and therefore to solve clients' problems as quickly as feasible, utilizing minimal therapist time and effort (Ellis, 1980). With average clients who are not resistant, it can therefore often employ a relatively small number of techniques and can help these clients to improve significantly in a fairly short period of time. It invariably uses some cognitive, emotive and behavioral modalities but doesn't have to utilize many of them compulsively, as is sometimes done in multimodal therapy (Lazarus, 1981) or in holistic psychotherapy. With resistant clients, however, RET is often done more comprehensively and intensively because that is what such clients may require.

References

Bandura, A. (1969) *Principles of Behavior Modification*. New York: Holt, Rinehart and Winston.

Bandura, A. (1977) *Social Learning Theory*. Englewood Cliffs, NJ: Prentice-Hall.

Bard, J. (1980) *Rational-Emotive Therapy in Practice*. Champaign, IL: Research Press.

Bartley, W.W. (1962) *The Retreat to Commitment*. New York: Knopf.

Basch, M.F. (1982) Dynamic psychotherapy and its frustrations. In P.L. Wachtel (ed.), *Resistance*. New York: Plenum.

Beck, A.T. (1976) *Cognitive Therapy and the Emotional Disorders*. New York: International Universities Press.

Berne, E. (1964) *Games People Play*. New York: Grove.

Bernheim, H. (1947) *Suggestive Therapeutics*. New York: London Book Company. (Originally published, 1886)

Blatt, S.J. and Erlich, H.S. (1982) Levels of resistance in the psychotherapeutic process. In P.L. Wachtel (ed.), *Resistance*. New York: Plenum.

Brehm, S.S. (1976) *The Application of Social Psychology to Clinical Practice*. Washington, DC: Hemisphere.

Coué, E. (1922) *My Method*. New York: Doubleday, Page.

Danysh, J. (1974) *Stop Without Quitting*. San Francisco: International Society for General Semantics.

Dewald, P.A. (1982) Psychoanalytic perspectives on resistance. In P.L. Wachtel (ed.), *Resistance*. New York: Plenum.

Dryden, W. (1982) The therapeutic alliance: conceptual issues and some research findings, *Midland Journal of Psychotherapy*, June, 1, 14–19.
Dryden, W. (1983) Vivid RET II: disputing methods, *Rational Living*, 1, 9–14.
Dunlap,K. (1928) A revision of the fundamental law of habit formation, *Science*, 67, 360–2.
D'Zurilla, T.J. and Goldfried, M.R. (1971) Problem solving and behavior modification, *Journal of Abnormal Psychology*, 78, 107–26.
Elkin, A., Ellis, A. and Edelstein, M. (1971) *Recorded Sessions with RET Clients (C2025)*. New York: Institute for Rational-Emotive Therapy.
Ellenberger, H.F. (1970) *The Discovery of the Unconscious*. New York: Basic Books.
Ellis, A. (1957) *How to Live with a 'Neurotic.'* New York: Crown.
Ellis, A. (1958a) Hypnotherapy with borderline psychotics, *Journal of General Psychology*, 59, 245–53.
Ellis, A. (1958b) Rational psychotherapy, *Journal of General Psychology*, 59, 35–49.
Ellis, A. (1959) *Recorded Sessions with Adolescent and Child RET Clients (C2011)*. New York: Institute for Rational-Emotive Therapy.
Ellis, A. (1962) *Reason and Emotion in Psychotherapy*. New York: Lyle Stuart.
Ellis, A. (1963) Toward a more precise definition of 'emotional' and 'intellectual' insight, *Psychological Reports*, 13, 125–6.
Ellis, A. (1966a) *Recorded Sessions with RET Neurotic Clients (C2004)*. New York: Institute for Rational-Emotive Therapy.
Ellis, A. (1966b) *Recorded Sessions with RET Severely Disturbed Clients (C2004)*. New York: Institute for Rational-Emotive Therapy.
Ellis, A. (1971a) *Growth Through Reason*. Palo Alto, CA: Science and Behavior Books; Hollywood, CA: Wilshire.
Ellis, A. (1971b) *How to Stubbornly Refuse to be Ashamed of Anything* [Cassette recording]. New York: Institute for Rational-Emotive Therapy.
Ellis, A. (1972a) *Psychotherapy and the Value of a Human Being*. New York: Institute for Rational-Emotive Therapy.
Ellis, A. (1972b) *Twenty-one Ways to Stop Worrying* [Cassette recording]. New York: Institute for Rational-Emotive Therapy.
Ellis, A. (1973) *Humanistic Psychotherapy: The Rational-Emotive Approach*. New York: Crown and McGraw-Hill Paperbacks.
Ellis, A. (1974a) *Disputing Irrational Beliefs (DIBS)*. New York: Institute for Rational-Emotive Therapy.
Ellis, A. (1974b) *I'd Like to Stop, But . . .* [Cassette recording]. New York: Institute for Rational-Emotive Therapy.
Ellis, A. (1976) RET abolishes most of the human ego, *Psychotherapy*, 13, 343–8.
Ellis, A. (1977a) *Conquering Low Frustration Tolerance* [Cassette recording]. New York: Institute for Rational-Emotive Therapy.
Ellis, A. (1977b) *Conquering the Dire Need for Love* [Cassette recording]. New York: Institute for Rational-Emotive Therapy.
Ellis, A. (1977c) *Fun as Psychotherapy* [Cassette recording]. New York: Institute for Rational-Emotive Therapy.
Ellis, A. (1977d) *A Garland of Rational Songs* [Songbook and cassette recording]. New York: Institute for Rational-Emotive Therapy.
Ellis, A. (1977c) *How to Live With – and Without – Anger*. New York: Reader's Digest Press.
Ellis, A. (1979) Discomfort anxiety: a new cognitive behavioral construct: 1, *Rational Living*, 14(2), 3–8.
Ellis, A. (1980) Discomfort anxiety: a new cognitive behavioral construct: 2, *Rational Living*, 15(1), 25–30.
Ellis, A. (1981) The use of rational humorous songs in psychotherapy, *Voices*, 16(4), 29–36.
Ellis, A. (1983a) *The Case Against Religiosity*. New York: Institute for Rational-Emotive Therapy.
Ellis, A. (1983b) Failures in rational-emotive therapy. In E. Foa and P.M. Emmelkamp (eds), *Failures in Behavior Therapy*. New York: Wiley.

Ellis, A. (1983c) The philosophical implications and dangers of some popular behavior therapy techniques. In M. Rosenbaum and C.M. Franks (eds), *Perspectives on Behavior Therapy in the Eighties*. New York: Springer.
Ellis, A. and Abrahms, E. (1978) *Brief Psychotherapy in Medical and Health Practice*. New York: Springer.
Ellis, A. and Becker, I. (1982) *A Guide to Personal Happiness*. North Hollywood, CA: Wilshire Books.
Ellis, A. and Grieger, R. (eds) (1977) *Handbook of Rational-Emotive Therapy*. New York: Springer.
Ellis, A. and Harper, R.A. (1975) *A New Guide to Rational Living*. Hollywood, CA: Wilshire; Englewood Cliffs, NJ: Prentice-Hall.
Ellis, A. and Knaus, W. (1977) *Overcoming Procrastination*. New York: Institute for Rational-Emotive Therapy; New York: New American Library.
Ellis, A. and Whiteley, J.M. (eds) (1979) *Theoretical and Empirical Foundations of Rational-Emotive Therapy*. Monterey, CA: Brooks/Cole.
Erickson, M.H. and Rossi, E.L. (1979) *Hypnotherapy: An Exploratory Casebook*. New York: Irvington.
Farrelly, F. and Brandsma, J.M. (1974) *Provocative Therapy*. Fort Collins, CO: Shields.
Fay, A. (1978) *Making Things Better by Making Them Worse*. New York: Hawthorn.
Fenichel, O. (1945) *Psychoanalytic Theory of Neurosis*. New York: Norton.
Frankl, V. (1960) Paradoxical intention: a logotherapeutic technique, *American Journal of Psychotherapy*, 14, 520–35.
Freud, A. (1936) *The Ego and the Mechanisms of Defense*. New York: International Universities Press.
Freud, S. (1965a) The dynamics of transference. In J. Strachey (ed. and trans.), *The Standard Edition of the Complete Psychological Works of Sigmund Freud*. New York: Basic Books. (Original work published 1912.)
Freud, S. (1965b) Inhibitions, symptoms and anxiety. In J. Strachey (ed. and trans.), *The Standard Edition of the Complete Psychological Works of Sigmund Freud*. New York: Basic Books. (Original work published 1926.)
Freud, S. (1965c) The interpretation of dreams. In J. Strachey (ed. and trans.), *The Standard Edition of the Complete Psychological Works of Sigmund Freud*. New York: Basic Books. (Original work published 1900.)
Friedman, M. (1975) *Rational Behavior*. Columbia, SC: University of South Carolina Press.
Golden, W. [Speaker] (1982) *Self-hypnosis: The Rational-Emotive Approach* [Cassette recording]. New York: Institute for Rational-Emotive Therapy.
Goldfried, M.R. (1982) Resistance and clinical behavior therapy. In P.L. Wachtel (ed.), *Resistance*. New York: Plenum.
Grieger, R. and Boyd, J. (1980) *Rational-Emotive Therapy: A Skills-based Approach*. New York: Van Nostrand Reinhold.
Grieger, R. and Grieger, I.Z. (eds) (1982) *Cognition and Emotional Disturbance*. New York: Human Sciences.
Haley, J. (1963) *Strategies of Psychotherapy*. New York: Grune and Stratton.
Johnson, N. (1980) Must the rational-emotive therapist be like Albert Ellis? *Personnel and Guidance Journal*, 59, 49–51.
Kelly, G. (1955) *The Psychology of Personal Constructs*. New York: Norton.
Knaus, W. (1974) *Rational-Emotive Education*. New York: Institute for Rational-Emotive Therapy.
Knaus, W. (1982) *How to Get Out of a Rut*. Englewood Cliffs, NJ: Prentice-Hall.
Lazarus, A.A. (1978) *In the Mind's Eye*. New York: Rawson, Wade.
Lazarus, A.A. (1981) *The Practice of Multimodal Therapy*. New York: McGraw-Hill.
Lazarus, A.A. and Fay, A. (1982) Resistance or rationalization? In P.L. Wachtel (ed.), *Resistance*. New York: Plenum.
Mahoney, M.J. (1974) *Cognition and Behavior Modification*. Cambridge, MA: Ballinger.

Mahoney, M.J. (1977) Personal science: a cognitive learning therapy. In A. Ellis and R. Grieger (eds), *Handbook of Rational-Emotive Therapy*. New York: Springer.
Mahoney, M.J. (1980) Psychotherapy and the structure of personal revolution. In M.J. Mahoney (ed.), *Psychotherapy Process*. New York: Plenum.
Maultsby, M.C., Jr. (1975) *Help Yourself to Happiness*. New York: Institute for Rational-Emotive Therapy.
Maultsby, M.C., Jr. and Ellis, A. (1974) *Technique of Using Rational-Emotive Imagery*. New York: Institute for Rational-Emotive Therapy.
Meichenbaum, D. (1977) *Cognitive Behavior Modification*. New York: Plenum.
Meichenbaum, D. and Gilmore, J.B. (1982) Resistance from a cognitive-behavioral perspective. In P.L. Wachtel (ed.), *Resistance*. New York: Plenum.
Popper, K.R. (1972) *Objective Knowledge*. Oxford: Clarendon.
Rogers, C.R. (1942) *Counseling and Psychotherapy*. Boston: Houghton Mifflin.
Rogers, C. (1961) *On Becoming a Person*. London: Constable.
Rorer, L. and Widiger, L. (1983) Personality assessment, *Annual Review of Psychology*, 34, 431–63.
Schlesinger, H.J. (1982) Resistance as process. In P.L. Wachtel (ed.), *Resistance*. New York: Plenum.
Spivack, G. and Shure, M. (1974) *Social Adjustment in Young Children*. San Francisco: Jossey-Bass.
Stanton, H.E. (1977) The utilisation of suggestions derived from rational-emotive therapy, *Journal of Clinical and Experimental Hypnosis*, 25, 18–26.
Tosi, D. and Marzella, J.N. (1977) Rational stage directed therapy. In J.L. Wolfe and E. Brand (eds), *Twenty Years of Rational Therapy*. New York: Institute for Rational-Emotive Therapy.
Tosi, D. and Reardon, J.P. (1976) The treatment of guilt through rational stage directed therapy, *Rational Living*, 2(1), 8–11.
Turkat, I.D. and Meyer, V. (1982) The behavior-analytic approach. In P.L. Wachtel (ed.), *Resistance*. New York: Plenum.
Wachtel, P. (ed.) (1982) *Resistance*. New York: Plenum.
Walen, S., DiGiuseppe, R. and Wessler, R.L. (1980) *A Practitioner's Guide to Rational-Emotive Therapy*. New York: Oxford.
Watzlawick, P., Weakland, J. and Fisch, R. (1974) *Change*. New York: Norton.
Wessler, R.A. and Wessler, R.L. (1980) *The Principles and Practice of Rational-Emotive Therapy*. San Francisco: Jossey-Bass.
Wessler, R.L. (1982, September) *Alternative Conceptions of Rational-Emotive Therapy: Towards a Philosophically Neutral Psychotherapy*. Paper presented at the Twelfth European Congress on Behaviour Therapy, Rome.
Wessler, R.L. and Ellis, A. (1980) Supervision in rational-emotive therapy. In A.K. Hess (ed.), *Psychotherapy Supervision*. New York: Wiley.

14

The Rational-Emotive Counselling Sequence

Windy Dryden and Joseph Yankura

Overview

This chapter provides a synthesis of the essential elements involved in the theory and practice of the rational-emotive counselling sequence, and illustrates the application of RET to an actual client problem.[1]

The rational-emotive counselling sequence consists of 13 important steps (Figure 14.1) that are typically part of the process of helping clients to overcome their emotional problems. In particular, it illustrates the manner in which RET's ABC model can be used as a vehicle for helping counsellor and client to assess and reach a common understanding of the client's problems before intervention (i.e., disputing of irrational beliefs) is attempted. The counselling sequence further specifies the importance of teaching clients the relationship between their thoughts and feelings, the central place of homework assignments within RET, and the desirability of helping clients to approach the goal of 'becoming their own therapists'.

The general format of this chapter is as follows: each step of the counselling sequence is described in detail, and then illustrated through presentation of actual case material, drawn from work that JY [Joseph Yankura] did with a 25-year-old female secretary who presented with work-related difficulties. In order to preserve this client's right to confidentiality she has been given a pseudonym ('Monica'), and identifying information has been omitted or altered.

The material that follows is used to demonstrate an orderly and organised implementation of the various critical components of RET. Counsellors are advised, however, that it is not always possible (or desirable) to adhere to the framework provided by the counselling sequence in such a neat, stepwise progression. As an example, early on in counselling a given client may appear to grasp the notion that her shoulds and musts are self-defeating; subsequent sessions, however, may reveal to the counsellor that the client is actually reluctant to surrender her absolutistic demands because she regards them as a source of motivation for impelling herself to higher levels of personal achievement. When this is the case, the counsellor may have to do considerable backtracking in order to resolve this issue so that counselling will be able to proceed in an effective manner. Hence the counselling sequence is perhaps best regarded as representing a set of guidelines for the effective and efficient practice of RET. Counsellors are cautioned against attempting to utilise these guidelines in a rigid, compulsive manner, and to watch out for their own perfectionistic demands that counselling *should* proceed in a tidy fashion!

Finally, it is noted that the counselling sequence material presented in this chapter focuses on the treatment of only one particular client problem. It does not deal with issues pertaining to case management and the entire *process* of rational-emotive counselling. Such issues will be discussed in Chapter 15, 'The Rational-Emotive Counselling Process'.

The initial step of the counselling sequence is presented below.

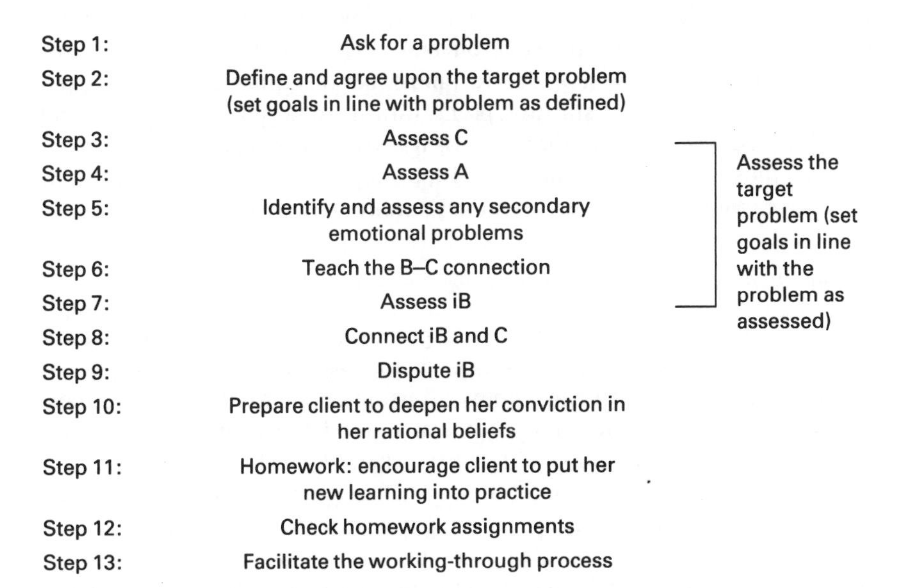

Figure 14.1 *The rational-emotive counselling sequence: A = activating event (and inference); B = belief; iB = irrational belief; C = emotional consequence*

Step 1: Ask for a Problem

After dealing with certain practicalities (e.g., determining a fee appropriate to the client's situation), counsellors are advised to establish a problem-solving orientation at the outset of counselling by immediately asking the client to describe the problem that she would like to discuss first. By doing so, counsellors can indirectly communicate a number of therapeutically important messages to the client. First, quickly requesting a problem helps to emphasise that counsellor and client are not meeting merely in order to socialise and have a pleasant conversation; rather, they are going to work together in order to assist the client in overcoming her emotional problems. Second, it can serve to highlight the fact that RET is a relatively efficient and focused approach to emotional problem solving. Finally, it conveys the message to the client that the counsellor is going to be quite active in the counselling process, and will tend to operate in such a way as to keep a problem-focused stance throughout this process.

Two Main Strategies: Client Choice versus Client's Most Serious Problem

Two basic strategies are recommended for counsellors to utilise when attempting to elicit a target problem from a client. The first of these relies upon client choice, and involves simply asking a question such as 'What problem would you like to work on first?' The client's response to this question may or may not be her most serious problem, but it can nevertheless provide a starting point for the counselling. The second strategy is somewhat more directive, as it involves asking the client to start with her most serious problem. Here, for example, the counsellor might ask, 'What are you most bothered about in your life right now?'

When Clients Fail to Quickly Identify a Target Problem

Occasionally, clients will appear to experience difficulty in identifying a target problem to focus on. When this is the case, there are a number of strategies that counsellors can employ to encourage such clients to describe a problem area. First, the counsellor can remind the client that it is not essential to choose a serious problem to work on. It can be made clear that it is perfectly appropriate to begin the counselling process with an issue that may be impeding the client in some slight way. Here, it can be helpful to point out that there is almost always something that individuals can work on in counselling, as human beings tend to operate at a less than optimal level.

Second, the client can be encouraged to identify feelings and behaviours she would like to either increase or decrease. This approach can be particularly useful for clients who are largely naive about the counselling process, and who may be in some confusion as to just how counselling might be of help to them. With respect to this issue, Dryden and Yankura (1993: 73–7) detailed the importance of attending to induction procedures within rational-emotive counselling as a means for mitigating client misunderstandings and eventual disillusionment with the counselling process.

Another, less direct, means of helping the client to identify a problem area involves making an inquiry as to what she would like to accomplish through counselling. After the client has stated a particular goal, the counsellor can then ask her to describe the ways in which she is failing to achieve this goal at the present time. In many instances, such questioning can lead to fruitful discussion of inappropriate feelings and behaviours that may serve as impediments to goal attainment. The counsellor can then explore these factors with the client, without necessarily labelling them as 'problems'. Some individuals (even after they have gone to the trouble of entering counselling) have difficulty owning up to the fact that they have problems; thus, they may be discouraged from becoming engaged in a problem-focused approach such as RET. When this appears to be the case with a particular client, the counsellor can attempt to identify and employ alternative terminology that may be more acceptable to the client.

Step 1: Monica

After greeting Monica and determining how she came to be referred to me, we discussed her expectations for counselling and agreed upon a fee appropriate to her circumstances. In order to quickly establish a problem-solving focus for the counselling, I then asked her what problem she would like to deal with first. She replied that she had started a new secretarial job in a small office approximately one month ago, and noted that her boss was quite demanding. She had, in fact, seen him yell at employees who made mistakes in their work. She related that she found herself constantly worrying about committing some error that would lead to her dismissal, as this would result in significant financial hardship. She stated that she felt particularly anxious and intimidated whenever in her boss's presence, and that she tended to avoid contact with him as a result.

Recently, Monica's boss had instructed her to learn how to operate the office's personal computer, which was used for billing and word-processing purposes. Monica was completely inexperienced with personal computers, and did not believe she was up to the task she had been assigned. Despite the fact that she had had numerous opportunities to read the operating manual, obtain assistance from fellow employees, and practise word processing and billing applications, she avoided this learning process and the machine that she had made her adversary. She lived in daily dread that her boss would learn of her failure to follow his directive and fire her on the spot. She described herself as 'computer phobic'.

It appeared that Monica had several problems that could be addressed in counselling, and I suggested that we list them so that they could be dealt with one at a time. Monica agreed to this suggestion, and together we generated the following problem list:

1 Avoidance of the task of learning how to operate the office computer.
2 Anxiety about being in the presence of her employer.
3 Worries about financial security.

I asked Monica which problem she would like to focus on first, and she decided she would like to work on overcoming her avoidance of the office computer. She picked this particular problem because she viewed it as having immediate relevance to her continued employment. Rather than questioning her view that she would immediately be fired for not following her boss's directive, I agreed to work on this problem with her.

Step 2: Define and Agree upon the Target Problem

Frequently, the nature of the client's problem will be clear after some initial discussion during the very first session of counselling. When this is the case, the counsellor may proceed to assess the problem as per steps 3, 4 and 5 of the RET counselling sequence. If, however, the nature of the client's problem remains unclear, it is desirable to reach an agreed definition of it prior to implementing the assessment stage. In addition, when a client discloses a number of problems in close succession, it is important to reach agreement as to which one will receive treatment first.

Arriving at a common understanding of a target problem and agreeing to work upon it together is an important component of rational-emotive counselling, as it helps to solidify the therapeutic alliance. Concurrence on these issues enables counsellor and client to function as a more effective team, and also helps the client to feel understood and to have confidence in the counsellor's expertise. In our experience as supervisors of counsellors in training, we have often reviewed audiotapes of counselling sessions in which counsellor and client seemed to drift along aimlessly, in large part because the novice counsellor failed to establish with the client a particular problem area to focus on.

Distinguish between Emotional and Practical Problems

It is useful to make a distinction with clients between *practical* problems (e.g., 'I might not have enough money to pay the rent') and *emotional* problems (e.g., 'I'm worried to death that I might not have enough money to pay the rent') when conducting rational-emotive counselling. Bard (1980) has noted that RET is an approach to counselling that is designed to assist clients in overcoming the latter type of problem; it is not designed to directly assist clients with problems falling in the former category. When clients have an emotional problem about a practical difficulty, however, this emotional problem may well become the focus of therapeutic exploration. In addition, as clients make progress in removing the emotional obstacles they create for themselves, they may experience greater success in resolving their particular practical issues (Ellis, 1985).

Target Unhealthy but Not Healthy Negative Emotions

Irrational beliefs will tend to lead an individual to experience unhealthy negative emotional responses when faced with negative life events. Rational beliefs, on the other hand, will usually lead an individual to experience healthy (although still negative) emotional responses to these same events.

Thus, feelings such as anxiety, hurt, anger, guilt and depression are considered to stem from irrational beliefs and to represent unhealthy negative emotions, whereas feelings such as concern, disappointment, annoyance, remorse, regret and sadness are viewed as the products of rational beliefs, and regarded as healthy negative emotions.

Rational-emotive counsellors do not encourage their clients to change their healthy negative emotions, as these are regarded as psychologically healthy reactions to negative events. Such emotions can motivate individuals to act on unfortunate or undesirable life circumstances in a constructive fashion, and are unlikely to impair adjustment to situations that may be largely unmodifiable. Clients *are* encouraged to change their unhealthy negative emotions, as these are more likely to stand in the way of healthy adjustment and goal attainment. In this vein, it is wise to make sure that clients understand the distinctions between healthy and unhealthy negative emotions. Asking the question, 'How is this a problem for you?' can often lead to a useful discussion which will help counsellor and client to identify and define a 'real' emotional problem.

Operationalise Vague Problems

Clients will sometimes discuss their target problems in vague or confusing terms. When this is the case with a particular client, it is important for the counsellor to help her to operationalise the problem. This involves defining the elements of the problem in terms that will assist the counsellor in applying RET to it.

To cite an example, a given client might state, 'My boss is a royal pain in the arse'. The counsellor can assist the client to specify the meaning of this statement by asking a question such as, 'What specifically does your boss do that leads you to this conclusion, and how do you feel when he acts this way?' This type of question can help the counsellor to begin formulating the client's problem according to RET's ABC model. The first part of the question may elicit descriptions of relevant activating events (As), while the second part may prompt the client to report on the emotional consequences (Cs) she experiences in the face of these As.

Focus on Helping Clients to Change C, not A

Clients may often wish to focus their counselling on a discussion of means to change A, rather than on their feelings (Cs) about A. Changing the A constitutes a practical solution, while changing C is the emotional solution. When counsellors encounter this situation, they can utilise certain strategies to encourage their clients to work at changing C before attempting to change A. First, they can attempt to show clients who already possess adequate practical problem-solving skills that they may be able to more effectively deploy these skills to change A if they are not emotionally disturbed at C. Second, they can attempt to show clients who lack an adequate repertoire of problem-solving skills that they will probably experience greater success in acquiring the skills needed to modify problematic As if they remove the emotional obstacles they have at C.

Dealing with Failure to Identify a Target Problem

When counsellors have reached this stage of the assessment process and have not yet reached agreement with the client as to the nature of the problem to be targeted for change, they can recommend that the client keep a *problem diary*. The client would utilise this to monitor and record disturbed feelings experienced between counselling sessions, with written notes concerning the types of feelings involved and when and where they were experienced.

Aim for Specificity in Assessing the Target Problem

It is important to be as specific as possible in defining and agreeing upon the target problem with clients. Clients experience emotional problems and hold related irrational beliefs in specific contexts, so that being specific will help the counsellor to obtain reliable and valid data about A, B and C. Providing clients with a sound rationale for specificity can aid this endeavour, particularly with those who tend to discuss their problems in vague terms. Clients can be taught that being specific about their target problem can help them to deal with it more constructively in the situations about which they disturb themselves. Counsellors can model specificity for clients by asking for a recent or typical example of the target problem (e.g., 'When was the last time A happened?').

In some cases, clients who remain unable to provide specific examples of their target problems may have secondary emotional problems about their primary emotional problem. When this appears to be the case, counsellors are advised to investigate further, as per Step 5 below.

Step 2: Monica

As stated earlier, Monica decided that she first wanted to focus on her avoidance of learning how to operate the office computer. I encouraged her to tell me a bit more about this problem, and the following dialogue ensued:

Monica: Well, I know I really should be making efforts to learn how to operate the computer, but it seems I've made the task into a monster. I've thumbed through the operating manual a bit, but that's about it. It's gotten so that I can't even stand to be in the same room with the bloody machine!

Joe: But let's suppose that you *were* in the same room with the computer. In fact, imagine that you're actually sitting in front of it, with the intent of turning it on and exploring its functions. What feelings do you think you might experience at that point?

Monica: I think I'd feel tense and jumpy. That's the way I feel whenever I even *think* about working on the computer.

Joe: Okay – so when you think about the computer and start to feel that way, what do you tend to do next?
Monica: [Humorously] Well, I certainly don't make a rush for the computer! I'll usually get myself busy doing some other task in the office. I feel better when my mind is on something else.
Joe: So you try to shy away from even thinking about the computer – right? Would it be safe to say that your busying yourself with other tasks represents a means by which you avoid experiencing the unpleasant feelings you described?
Monica: Yes, I think so.
Joe: Right. So in order to overcome your 'computer phobia', would it then make sense for us to focus on those negative feelings and help you come to terms with them so that you'll be better able to work on the task you've been assigned?
Monica: Yes – that sounds like a reasonable approach. If I could feel more comfortable about working on the computer, I probably wouldn't tend to avoid it so much.

Step 3: Assess C

A and C are typically assessed prior to B. At this stage of the counselling sequence counsellors may assess either A or C, depending upon which element of the target problem the client initially describes. For the purposes of this discussion, however, issues involved in the assessment of C will receive treatment first.

Re-check for an Unhealthy Negative Emotion

In assessing C, counsellors are advised to keep in mind that clients' emotional problems are conceptualised as unhealthy negative emotions, not as healthy negative emotions. Unhealthy negative emotions are targeted for change because they are strongly dysphoric, contribute to self-defeating behaviours, and block goal attainment.

On p. 217 we listed a number of feeling words to distinguish between healthy and unhealthy negative emotions. It is important to recognise, however, that clients may not tend to employ these terms in the same way as their rational-emotive counsellors. Thus, a given client may make reference to feelings of anger when she is really experiencing annoyance, or vice versa. Counsellors should take steps to ensure that they have identified an unhealthy negative emotion, and that they are using the same terminology as the client when referring to it (Dryden, 1986). Here, the counsellor can try to teach RET's 'emotional vocabulary' to the client, or may choose to adopt the client's own particular use of feeling language. Regardless of the alternative chosen, it is helpful for counsellors to be consistent in their vocabulary throughout the course of treatment.

Focus on an Emotional C

A client's C can be emotional or behavioural in nature. Dysfunctional behaviours often serve a defensive function, however, and may exist to help clients avoid experiencing certain unhealthy negative emotions. This discussion of the counselling sequence will therefore deal with the assessment of unhealthy negative emotions rather than the assessment of dysfunctional behaviours.

It is suggested that counsellors in training adopt the practice of attempting to identify (and treat) the unhealthy negative emotions that contribute to the dysfunctional behaviours that clients may present. Thus, if a given client states her desire to stop smoking, the counsellor can regard smoking as a defensive behaviour and encourage the client to identify the problematic emotions she might experience if she were to refrain from it.

Clarify C

A client's unhealthy negative emotions at C can provide valuable clues concerning the nature of the irrational beliefs to which she subscribes. It is therefore important for counsellors to gain clarification as to the Cs that clients experience.

If a client is vague or unclear in attempting to describe C, there are a number of specific techniques that can be used to clarify its nature. Gestalt exercises such as the empty-chair technique (see Passons, 1975) and Gendlin's (1978) focusing technique are sometimes helpful in this regard. In addition, imagery methods can be employed wherein the client is asked to imagine an example of her problem and to identify any associated feelings that are experienced. Albert Ellis will sometimes encourage his clients to 'Take a wild guess' when they have difficulty in identifying a specific emotion; surprisingly, this method can yield useful information about C in some instances.

Frustration is an A, not a C

Clients will sometimes refer to feeling frustrated at C. Here, it is important to note that some RET counsellors prefer to regard frustration as an activating event rather than a feeling (Trexler, 1976). As a C, frustration in RET theory is usually regarded as an appropriate negative emotion that clients experience when they are blocked from attaining their goals. When a given client reports feeling frustrated, however, it is possible that she is referring to an inappropriate negative emotion. Counsellors can often determine whether a client's reported feeling of frustration is a healthy or unhealthy negative emotion by asking if the feeling is bearable or unbearable. If the client responds to such an inquiry by describing the feeling as unbearable, she may well be experiencing an unhealthy negative emotion that could be targeted for change.

Assess Client Motivation to Change C

Clients sometimes experience unhealthy negative emotions that they are not motivated to change. This absence of motivation can occur when clients fail to recognise the destructive, self-defeating nature of the emotion in question. This situation arises most often in the case of anger; it may also occur with feelings of guilt and depression. As such, counsellors are advised to assess clients' understanding of the dysfunctional aspects of the target emotion (C). If a particular client does not understand why her disturbed emotion is unhealthy, it is beneficial to devote as much time as necessary to helping her see this point. This can be accomplished with the following three steps:

1 Assist the client to assess the consequences of the unhealthy negative emotion. What happens when she feels this way? Does she tend to act constructively or self-defeatingly?
2 Emphasise that the goal is to replace the unhealthy negative emotion with its healthy, more rational counterpart (e.g., replacing anxiety with concern). Making this point can be difficult, particularly if the client has rigidly entrenched ideas concerning the ways she is 'supposed' to feel when confronted with negative As (see DiGiuseppe, 1984, for a more extended discussion of this issue). If provided with healthy models, however, the client will usually be able to see that she can experience the healthy emotion in a given context. To cite an example, a client with public speaking anxiety can be helped to identify individuals she knows who experience feelings of strong concern, but not anxiety, prior to giving a lecture in front of an audience.
3 Finally, work with the client to assess the consequences that would occur if she experienced the corresponding healthy emotion when confronted with a problematic situation. As the client probably has not thought in these terms before, help her to imagine how she would behave and how the outcome might be different if she felt the healthy emotion in the face of a negative A. Then, compare the outcomes of experiencing healthy versus unhealthy emotions. As an example, a given client could be encouraged to imagine how he might act (and what types of results he might get) if he felt merely annoyed (instead of angry) when his teenage son breaks his evening curfew. This may help the client to better understand the advantages of the healthy emotion, and this insight may well increase his motivation to change C.

Avoid Potential Pitfalls in Assessing C

Counsellors may encounter a number of potential difficulties as they work to assess clients' problematic emotions at C. These difficulties may be avoided by implementing the following suggestions:

1 Avoid using questions that reinforce the notion that A causes C. Novice rational-emotive counsellors may make the error of asking clients questions such as 'How does the situation *make you* feel?' As an alternative, counsellors might ask 'How do you feel *about* the situation?'

This question can serve to elicit descriptions of problematic Cs, and does not implicitly convey the message that A *causes* C.

2 When clients respond to inquiries concerning their feelings about A with terms such as 'bad', 'upset', 'miserable' etc., do not attempt to work with these vague descriptions of emotions. Instead, work with clients to help them clarify exactly what feelings they experience at C. Also, do not accept statements such as 'I feel trapped' or 'I felt rejected' as descriptions of emotions occurring at C. Trapped and rejected are not emotions. These terms probably refer to combinations of A, B and C factors, and it is important to discriminate between these three and ensure that clients' C statements really do refer to feelings. To illustrate, if a client states 'I felt rejected', she can be helped to see that rejection is an A and then asked how she felt about the rejection at point C (e.g., hurt, ashamed, etc.).

Step 3: Monica

In Step 2, I established with Monica that her avoidance behaviour served as a means for warding off the unpleasant feelings she experienced whenever she thought about working on the computer. She seemed to understand that it made sense to target these feelings for change, and that a change in her feelings could help her to face the task her boss had given her. As such, my next task was to more fully assess the nature of her negative feelings:

Joe: You mentioned that you feel tense and jumpy whenever you think about working on the computer. Those terms – tense and jumpy – are usually used to describe *physical* feelings or sensations a person might experience. What type of *emotional* feelings do you think you experience when you think about working on the computer?

Monica: I have a bad case of nerves – I feel nervous.

Joe: Meaning you feel anxious?

Monica: No, not anxious – if I were anxious to learn the computer, I would have done it already!

Joe: Oh, I see. You're using the term 'anxious' to mean 'eager'. When I used the word 'anxious', I meant it in the sense of having anxiety. Behavioural scientists have done a lot of research which demonstrates that anxiety can interfere with a person's performance on complex tasks. Would it be correct to say that you experience anxiety with respect to the idea of working on the computer?

Monica: When you use the word that way – yes, that would be correct. That's what I feel.

Joe: So if we helped you to overcome your anxiety – which probably contributes to your feeling tense and jumpy and interferes with your getting down to the task – you would stand a better chance of becoming computer-proficient. Is that right?

Monica: Yes – I can see that.

Note that, as I worked with Monica to determine the precise nature of the feeling she experienced at C, it became apparent that she viewed the term 'anxious' as being synonymous with 'eager'. I thus took steps to clarify my use of the term, and obtained her agreement that 'anxiety' was an appropriate word to describe the uncomfortable emotion she felt with respect to learning to operate the office computer. As mentioned earlier, it is important to ensure that counsellor and client are employing language in the same way in order to avoid misunderstandings that may bog down the counselling process.

Step 4: Assess A

If C is assessed first, the next step in the counselling sequence is to assess A. As noted earlier, A can refer to activating events that may be regarded as confirmable reality (i.e., neutral observers could confirm a given client's descriptions of A). In this presentation, however, A will also be used to stand for clients' inferences or interpretations about the activating event.

As with assessments of C, aim for specificity when assessing A. This can be accomplished by asking the client to provide the most recent occurrence of A, a typical example of A, or the most relevant example the client can recall.

Identify the Part of A that Triggers B

In the process of assessing A, it is important to help the client to identify the most relevant aspect of A (i.e., the part that generally serves to trigger irrational beliefs at B). Identifying this trigger can sometimes be complicated by inferences the client makes about the situation. As these inferences are often linked (or chained) together, the technique referred to as *inference chaining* can be used to identify the particular inference in the chain that functions as the trigger.

By way of illustration, imagine a client who experiences anxiety at point C. Initial inquiry reveals that she is due to give a class presentation. Giving the class presentation thus represents an activating event, but the counsellor will wish to determine just what it is about the presentation that is anxiety-provoking in the client's mind. The following dialogue might then ensue:

Counsellor: What is it about giving the presentation that you are anxious about?
Client: Well, I'm afraid I may not do a very good job.
Counsellor: For the moment, let's just assume that you don't. What's anxiety-provoking in your mind about that?
Client: Well, if I don't do a good job in class, then my teacher will give me a poor grade.
Counsellor: Let's assume that as well. What would you be anxious about there?
Client: That I might flunk the course.
Counsellor: And if you did?
Client: Oh, my God, I couldn't face my father!
Counsellor: Imagine telling your father that you had failed. What would be anxiety-provoking about that in your mind?
Client: I can just picture his reaction – he would be devastated!
Counsellor: And how would you feel if that happened?

Client: Oh God, that would be terrible! I really couldn't stand to see my father cry – I'd feel so very sorry for him!

The class presentation was initially identified as A by the client. Through inference chaining, however, the counsellor has discovered the client's fearful anticipation of her father's upset upon hearing of her presumed failure.

To test whether a given inference in a chain genuinely represents the most relevant aspect of A in a client's emotional problem, the counsellor might write down the inference chain, review it with the client, and ask her to identify the point she thinks is most important. Another technique for confirming whether the newly identified aspect of A is central is to 'manipulate' A and then check the client's responses at C. Thus, for example, the counsellor could say to the client, 'Let's suppose you told your father that you flunked the course, and he wasn't devastated – in fact, he coped quite well with the news. Would that different turn of events have any impact on your anxiety about giving the class presentation?' If the client responds in the affirmative, the counsellor can be more confident that the problem has been accurately assessed. If the client indicates that she would still be anxious, this could indicate that the prospect of seeing her father cry (at A) is not the most relevant factor in her anxiety problem.

Once the most relevant aspect of A has been established, it is important to reassess any changes in the client's feelings at C since the initial analysis of the problem. Assuming that the new aspect of A revealed in the above illustration is indeed the central factor, it would be important to encourage the client to see that her anxiety is more closely associated with the overwhelming pity for her father she would feel at C, than with any general fears of failure she might have. Two alternative courses then present themselves in terms of treatment: the first would involve focusing on the client's feelings of anxiety at C about the future prospect of her father's emotional devastation. The second would involve asking the client to assume that the new A (the father's upset) had already occurred, and then dealing with the feelings of other-pity that would presumably occur at C.

A can Refer to Many Things

Rational-emotive counsellors generally agree that A can be a thought, an inference, an image, a sensation, or a behaviour, as well as an actual event in the client's environment that can be confirmed by neutral observers. In addition, a client's *feelings* at C may also serve as an A. A given client may, for example, experience guilt feelings at C. This guilt could then serve as a new A, and the client may feel ashamed (a new C) about feeling guilty. Here, the client has a secondary emotional problem about a primary emotional problem. Not all clients will present such secondary problems, but the process of determining whether or not they exist is an important part of assessment in the counselling sequence (see Step 5).

Assume (at least temporarily) that A is True

In the course of assessing A, it sometimes becomes apparent to counsellors that the client's most relevant A is a clear distortion of reality. When this is the case, it can be tempting to dispute A in order to correct the client's misinterpretations.

Generally, counsellors are advised to resist this temptation and to encourage the client to temporarily assume that A is correct. In the case previously described, for example, it is not essential to determine whether or not the client's father would truly be devastated upon hearing about her failure. Rather, it is important to treat A as if it is an accurate depiction of reality, in order to assist the client in identifying the irrational beliefs that lead to particular feelings at C.

Avoid Pitfalls in Assessing A

A number of potential pitfalls that counsellors may encounter in assessing A may be avoided by implementing the following suggestions:

1. Refrain from obtaining too much detail about A. Allowing clients to speak at length about A can turn counselling into a gripe session, which will make it difficult to maintain a problem-solving approach to overcoming emotional difficulties. With clients who tend to ramble or provide compulsive details concerning their As, counsellors can attempt to abstract the most salient theme, or what appears to be the major aspect of A. At times, it is appropriate to tactfully interrupt clients in order to re-establish a specific focus. A counsellor might say, for instance, 'I think you may be providing me with more detail than I require. Can you tell me what it was about the situation that you were most upset about?'
2. Discourage clients from describing A in vague terms. Attempt to obtain as clear and specific an example of A as possible. An example of a vague A would be, 'My husband was really on my case last night'. In contrast, a specific A would be, 'My husband told me I was lazy and inept for not having dinner ready and waiting for him when he arrived from work'.
3. Discourage clients from talking about several As at one time. Some individuals will jump from event to event within a given counselling session; in RET, it is important to work on one A at a time. Clients can be encouraged to deal with the A they consider to best illustrate the context within which they make themselves disturbed, and can be assured that their other As can be dealt with later on.
4. If at this point of the counselling sequence a given client still has not identified a clear A, encourage her to start a diary prior to the next session. This diary can be used to record examples of activating events about which she makes herself disturbed.

Agree on Goals

It has been emphasised that it is important for counsellor and client to develop a common understanding of the client's target problem. Likewise, it is desirable to reach agreement as to the client's goals for change, as this will facilitate the development of a sound therapeutic alliance between the two parties involved in the individual counselling process.

When to Agree on Goals

There are two main points at which counsellors will want to assess a given client's goals for change. The first point occurs when counsellor and client have defined and reached agreement concerning the client's target problem (Step 2). Here, it is recommended that the counsellor help the client to set a goal in line with the problem as initially assessed. Thus, if a particular client's problem relates to being overweight, an initial goal would be for her to achieve and maintain a specific target weight.

Counsellors may, however, wish to reconsider and reformulate the client's goal at the assessment stage (Steps 3, 4 and 5). For example, after agreeing that the client's goal is to achieve and maintain a specific weight, assessment may reveal that she becomes anxious and overeats when she is bored. At this point, the client's goal might be reformulated so that it focuses on her ability to deal more appropriately with boredom, so that she less often resorts to the (self-defeating) coping strategy of overeating. The client can be encouraged to work at feeling concerned (rather than anxious) about being bored, and to use that feeling of concern to deal with boredom in more constructive ways. Generally, it is helpful to encourage clients to select an appropriate negative emotion as a goal, and to assist them in understanding why such an emotion represents a realistic and constructive response to a negative activating event at A.

Help Clients Take a Long-term Perspective

When discussing goals with clients, it is useful to make them cognisant of the distinction between long-term goals and short-term goals. At times, clients may wish to settle upon a short-term goal that may in the long term be self-defeating and therefore irrational (e.g., in the case of a shoplifting client, the desire to steal without experiencing guilt feelings). Counsellors are advised to help clients adopt a broader perspective and to obtain their commitment to work towards productive long-term goals.

Avoid Pitfalls when Agreeing on Goals

Several potential difficulties may be encountered when working with clients to establish goals. The following suggestions may prove helpful in avoiding them:

1. Do not accept clients' goal statements when they express a desire to experience less of an unhealthy negative emotion (e.g., 'I want to feel less anxious', or 'I want to feel less guilty'). Rational-emotive theory maintains that the presence of an unhealthy negative emotion (such as anxiety or guilt) indicates that the client experiencing that emotion is subscribing to an irrational belief. As such, it is advisable to help clients to distinguish between the unhealthy negative emotion in question and its appropriate counterpart. Clients can be encouraged to set the latter type of emotion as their goal. They can therefore work at feeling concerned instead of anxious, or sorry rather than guilty and self-downing.
2. Do not accept client goals that express the wish to feel neutral, indifferent or calm with respect to events about which it would be rational to experience a healthy negative emotion. Emotions indicating indifference (e.g., calmness in the face of an unfortunate event) would mean that a given client did not have a rational belief about the event in question, whereas in reality the client would probably prefer that the event not occur. Acquiescing to the client's goal to feel calm or indifferent about a negative event may actually encourage her to deny the existence of her desires, rather than to think rationally.
3. For similar reasons, do not accept client goals that involve experiencing positive feelings about a negative A. It would be unrealistic for an individual to feel happy about a negative life event she would prefer not to encounter. Accepting the goal of feeling positive about a negative event may encourage clients to believe that it is good that a particular negative A occurred. This is undesirable, as it fails to promote rational thinking. To reiterate an earlier point, clients who become better able to experience a healthy (as opposed to unhealthy) negative feeling in the face of a negative life event may be more psychologically prepared to either accept it or modify it.
4. Do not accept vague goals, such as 'I want to be happy'. The more specific you can encourage your client to be in setting goals, the more likely it is that she will be motivated to do the hard work of changing her irrational beliefs in the service of achieving these goals.

Step 4: Monica

At this point I used inference chaining as a means of identifying the part of Monica's A that served to trigger her anxiety:

Joe: Okay – our next task is to figure out just what you're anxious about. Close your eyes and picture yourself actually sitting in front of the computer. You begin to feel very tense and jumpy. Now, what do you think you would be feeling anxious about?

Monica: I'd be anxious that I wouldn't be able to get it right – I'd make all sorts of mistakes. [Inference 1]

Joe: Okay. For the moment, let's assume that's the case – you try to operate the machine, and you make all sorts of errors. In your mind, what would be anxiety-provoking about that?

Monica: Well, I would regard it as evidence that I'd never be able to become proficient with it. [Inference 2]

Joe: That probably wouldn't be the case, but let's just assume that it is. Thinking about it now, what would be anxiety-provoking in your mind about that?

Monica: Well, it would mean that I'd be fired – and that would mean that I'd failed at my job. [Inference 3]

Joe: And if it were true that you had failed at your job . . .?

Monica: If I failed at my job . . . I'd feel like an incompetent.

Joe: So looking at it now, the real issue is not that you're afraid of making errors on the computer or of never being able to master it – what's *really* anxiety-provoking for you is the idea of failing at your job and having to regard yourself as an incompetent person. Does that sound accurate to you?

Monica: Yes, it does.

My next step was to establish a goal we would work on with regard to Monica's target problem and anxiety at C:

Joe: Okay – now, we've already touched on how anxiety can interfere with task performance, right? So we can be pretty sure that as long as you're anxious, you'll have difficulty getting yourself to work on learning how to operate the computer.

Monica: Right.

Joe: Now if anxiety gets in your way, what sort of feeling could you work at replacing it with that might help you in your learning process?

Monica: I wish I could be completely relaxed about it.

Joe: Well, at first glance that looks like a good alternative – but if you were *completely* relaxed, do you think you'd be very motivated to do a good job?

Monica: I think I see what you mean – I might just have an 'I don't care' attitude.

Joe: Right – that could be a possibility. How about aiming to feel *concerned* instead of anxious? Anxiety just gets in your way by contributing to avoidance behaviour, but a feeling of concern will very likely help you to face the difficulties involved in the task and motivate you to try your best.

Monica: I've never thought about it like that before – I could try to feel only concerned instead of anxious. That sounds reasonable, but how do I do it?

As sometimes happens, Monica expressed the desire to replace her feeling of anxiety at C with a feeling of being completely relaxed. This probably would not have proven to be a productive goal, for two reasons: first, it is unlikely that RET would be able to help Monica achieve such a feeling state given the circumstances with which she is faced; secondly, being 'completely relaxed' may have resulted in an apathetic approach to completing the task her boss had assigned her. As such, the goal of working to feel concerned rather than anxious was presented to her.

Step 5: Identify and Assess any Secondary Emotional Problems

Clients can frequently have secondary emotional problems about their primary emotional problems. If a particular client's primary problem is anxiety, for instance, the counsellor can check for the presence of a secondary emotional problem (such as shame about feeling anxious) by asking a question such as, 'How do you feel about feeling anxious?'

When to Attend to the Secondary Emotional Problem First

It is suggested that counsellors attend to the client's secondary problem if any of the following conditions are met:

1 The client's secondary problem significantly interferes with the work being done on her primary problem.
2 From a clinical perspective, the secondary problem appears to be the more important of the two.
3 The client can see the sense of working on her secondary emotional problem first.

It can be important to present clients with a plausible rationale for working on the secondary problem first. If the client still wishes to work on the primary problem first, even after a reasonable explanation has been provided, then it is advisable to do so. To do otherwise could jeopardise the therapeutic alliance between client and counsellor.

Check for an Emotional Problem about a Healthy Negative Emotion

In the course of assessing a client's *stated* primary problem, it may become evident that she is in fact experiencing a healthy negative emotion (e.g., sadness in the face of an important loss). If this is the case, check to see whether your client has a problem with this healthy emotion. A client may, for example, feel ashamed about feeling sad. Work to reach agreement that the secondary emotional problem (shame) will be the client's target problem and proceed to assess this agreed-upon problem.

Assess for the Presence of Shame

As noted above, clients who are reluctant to disclose an emotional problem may feel ashamed about having the problem, or about admitting it to a therapist. Counsellors can attempt to surmount this difficulty by asking such clients how they would feel if they *did* have an emotional problem about the activating event under discussion. With clients who provide indications that they would feel ashamed, the counsellor can attempt to reach agreement to work on shame as the target problem before encouraging disclosure of the original problem.

Step 5: Monica

Monica's question at the end of Step 4 suggested that she was ready to discuss the means by which she might change her anxiety to a feeling of concern. Prior to beginning such discussion, however, I briefly checked for the presence of a secondary emotional problem:

Joe: You've asked a good question, and we'll begin coming up with some answers in just a minute. But before we do, I wanted to check on something with you. Earlier, as you were describing your problems at work, I started to get the sense that you might be kicking yourself for having these difficulties. People will often do that to themselves – they'll give themselves a problem about having a problem. Is it possible that you're telling yourself you *shouldn't* have a problem?
Monica: No, I don't really think I'm kicking myself for having this problem. I think anybody who had to face the circumstances I deal with at work every day would feel anxious!

Monica's response appeared to indicate that she did not have a secondary emotional problem. It is noted, however, that she expressed the belief that any individual would experience anxiety if faced with circumstances similar to her own. As will be seen in Step 6, I was able to use this erroneous belief as a vehicle for teaching the B–C connection.

Step 6: Teach the B–C Connection

By this stage the A and C elements of a client's primary or secondary emotional problem have been assessed. The next step is for the counsellor to teach the client the *B–C connection*, that is, the concept that emotional problems are largely determined by beliefs rather than by the activating event that has previously been assessed. This step is critical, because unless the client understands that her emotional problems are determined by her beliefs, she will not understand why those beliefs are being assessed during the next step of the treatment process. Utilising an example unrelated to the client's problem can often be helpful in explaining this concept (see for example, the 'teaching dialogue' in Dryden and Yankura, 1993: 91–2). Alternative exercises and metaphors for conveying this idea are described in a number of the other available RET texts (e.g., Walen et al., 1980; Ellis and Dryden, 1987).

Step 6: Monica

As noted earlier, Monica voiced her belief that all individuals would feel anxious if they were in her position at work. I was able to utilise this misconception as a vehicle for teaching her the B–C connection:

Joe: Okay – it sounds like you're not putting yourself down for being anxious about learning how to operate the computer at work. That's good. I'm struck, however, by the fact that you seem to think that anxiety is inevitable under the circumstances you face. It sounds like you believe that those circumstances are *making* you feel anxious.
Monica: Well . . . they are, aren't they?
Joe: If that were true, then you'd *have* to continue to feel anxious at work until circumstances somehow changed for the better. I'd like to suggest that your

anxiety isn't caused by circumstances; it's caused by the way you *think* about those circumstances.

Monica: Hmm . . . the way I think? What do you mean?

Joe: Let me use an example to illustrate. Suppose we take two individuals who are strangers to each other, but happen to be going to the same party on a given Saturday night. Imagine that their circumstances are identical insofar as it's the same party, and neither of them knows any of the other partygoers except for their host. Are you with me so far?

Monica: Yes.

Joe: Okay. Now, Person A walks into the party with the following belief in mind: 'I *must* make a good impression on the people I'm going to meet, and it would be absolutely awful if I committed some faux pas and they disapproved of me'. Person B, on the other hand, enters the party with a different sort of attitude: 'I would certainly *like* to make a good impression, but if I commit some social error and they don't accept me, it's not the end of the world'. Now, which of these two people do you think will be more likely to experience anxiety at the party?

Monica: Um . . . . Person A.

Joe: Right – that will very likely be the case. Do you see why?

Monica: It's because of what he believes about making a good impression.

Joe: Right again. More specifically, it's because he's escalating a desire to the level of an absolute *must*. If he just stuck with his desire – like Person B – he would still feel concerned about making a good impression, but not anxious. Does that make sense to you?

Monica: Yes, it does seem to make sense.

Step 7: Assess Beliefs

In assessing B, it is important for counsellors to keep in mind the distinction between clients' rational and irrational beliefs, and to help clients understand the differences between these two types of thinking.

Assess Both Premise and Derivative Forms of Irrational Beliefs

Chapter 2 introduced the reader to the differences between rational and irrational beliefs, and Chapter 3 noted that irrational beliefs are often comprised of a premise and certain derivatives that tend to stem from that premise. To briefly review, the premise component of irrational beliefs embodies absolutistic shoulds, musts, have to's, etc.; these can be expressed as demands directed at self, others or the world and life conditions. The three main irrational derivatives are awfulising, I-can't-stand-it-itis and damnation.

At this stage of the counselling sequence, counsellors will want to carefully assess both the premise and the derivative components of their clients' irrational beliefs. With respect to irrational derivatives, counsellors may either teach and use the RET terms for these processes, or use clients' own language. If the latter alternative is chosen, however, it is advisable to make sure that the terms used by clients accurately reflect irrational beliefs.

This decision can be based upon client feedback concerning the strategy perceived to be most helpful.

Distinguish between Absolute Shoulds and Other Shoulds

Rational-emotive counsellors can become highly attuned to indications that clients are harbouring particular irrational beliefs in their thinking. It is important to bear in mind, however, that every client utterance of the word 'should' does not constitute evidence for the presence of an irrational belief. Most expressions of the word *should*, in fact, will be unrelated to a given client's emotional problems, as this word has multiple meanings in the English language. These include shoulds of preference (e.g., 'I *should* get to work on time'); empirical or probabilistic shoulds (e.g., 'When two parts of hydrogen and one part of oxygen are combined, you *should* get water'); and shoulds of recommendation.

Rational-emotive theory hypothesises that only *absolute shoulds* are related to emotional disturbance. When clients find the different meanings confusing, it can sometimes be useful to substitute the word *must* in cases where an irrational belief in its premise form may be operative (compare, for instance, 'I *should* be admired by my colleagues' and 'I *must* be admired by my colleagues'). Our own clinical experience (as well as that of Albert Ellis) suggests that the word *must* conveys the meaning of absolute demandingness better than the word *should*. In particular, clients can be helped to distinguish between absolute shoulds and shoulds of preference.

Use Questions to Assess Irrational Beliefs

Counsellors are advised to employ questions when assessing clients' irrational beliefs. An example of a standard question used by rational-emotive counsellors is 'What were you telling yourself about A to make yourself disturbed at C?' This type of *open-ended question* offers both advantages and disadvantages.

One advantage of such a question is that it embodies and may convey several important elements of the rational-emotive theory of emotional disturbance. In essence, it reinforces for the client the concept that A does not cause C: it is B that determines whether appropriate or inappropriate negative emotions are experienced at C. An additional advantage of the above type of enquiry is that it is unlikely to put words in the client's mouth concerning the content of her beliefs.

The main disadvantage of using this type of question is that clients (particularly those who are new to RET) will frequently not respond to it by articulating an irrational belief. Instead, they may respond by providing further inferences about A – and in some cases, these inferences may well be less relevant than the one previously selected at Step 4.

Imagine, for example, that a given client is particularly anxious that other people will think she is a fool if she stammers in public. If her counsellor asks, 'What were you telling yourself about other people's criticism to make yourself anxious at C?' she may conceivably respond by stating 'I thought they wouldn't like me'. Note that this response is actually an inference about A, and that it fails to reveal the client's irrational belief. Here, the counsellor would try to help the client see that her statement does not describe an irrational belief, and then educate her to look further for her anxiety-provoking irrational belief about A. This can be done by judiciously combining the use of open-ended questions with didactic explanation.

Walen et al. (1980) list a number of other open-ended questions that may be used to assess clients' irrational beliefs. These include: 'What was going through your mind?'; 'Were you aware of any thoughts in your head?'; 'What was on your mind then?' and 'Are you aware of what you were thinking at that moment?' Again, clients will not necessarily disclose irrational beliefs in response to these questions; they may require further help of a didactic nature.

Theory-driven questions represent an alternative to the use of open-ended questions for assessing irrational beliefs. Such questions are directly derived from rational-emotive theory, and are more specific with respect to identifying the type of response that is desired. As an example, a counsellor attempting to elicit a response concerning a client's operative must (i.e., a premise) might ask, 'What *demand* were you making about other people's criticism to make yourself disturbed at point C?' By way of further illustration, the following question could be used to assess for a particular derivative of an irrational premise: 'What kind of person did you think you were for stammering and incurring other people's criticism?'

Theory-driven questions are useful insofar as they orient the client to look for her irrational beliefs. In using them, however, the counsellor runs the risk of putting words in the client's mouth and encouraging her to look for irrational beliefs that she may not actually hold. This risk is minimised when careful assessment has already established that the client has an unhealthy negative emotion at point C.

Step 7: Monica

Joe: Okay – so it's not circumstances that determine whether a person feels anxious or not; it's the beliefs that a person holds about those circumstances. One's desires and preferences are unlikely to cause serious emotional trouble, but making those desires into absolutistic musts, shoulds and have-tos will often result in significant upsets and self-defeating behaviours. Now, as we go back to your own situation, see if you can keep in mind this distinction between desires and absolutistic musts. Okay?

Monica: Okay.

Joe: Now, with respect to the problem we've been discussing, what's your desire?

Monica: To overcome my anxiety and learn how to use the computer with a minimum of hassle.

Joe: Okay. And what *must* are you bringing to the situation that results in your feeling anxious?

Monica: I must succeed!

Joe: Right! And with that must in place, how will you tend to label yourself if you actually *don't* succeed?
Monica: As an incompetent loser.

Step 8: Connect Irrational Beliefs and C

After assessing clients' irrational beliefs in both premise and derivative form, counsellors should take care to ensure that clients grasp the connection between their irrational beliefs and their disturbed emotions at point C. This step should precede any attempts at disputing these beliefs.

A simple enquiry can be used to determine whether a given client understands this very important connection. Thus, a counsellor might say, 'Can you understand that as long as you demand that other people must not criticise you, you are bound to make yourself anxious about the possibility that this might occur?' With respect to an irrational derivative, the counsellor may ask, 'Can you see that as long as you believe that you are no good for being regarded by others as a fool, you will be anxious about being criticised?' If the client responds in the affirmative, the counsellor can then attempt to elicit from the client the B–C connection: 'So, in order to change your feeling of anxiety to one of concern, what do you need to change first?' Eliciting this connection is likely to be more productive than simply telling the client that such a connection exists. If the client fails to see the connection, it is strongly advised that the counsellor spend time helping her to understand it before proceeding to dispute her irrational beliefs.

Step 8: Monica

Joe: So, do you see that as long as you believe that you *must* succeed and that you would be an incompetent loser if you didn't, you'll tend to feel anxious and avoid working on the computer?
Monica: Yes, that connection seems to make sense.
Joe: Right. So, if you want to change your feeling of anxiety to a feeling of concern and stop avoiding – assuming that circumstances remain the same – what do you need to change?
Monica: My belief that I must succeed.
Joe: Right – and also, the idea that not succeeding would mean you're an incompetent loser.

Step 9: Dispute Irrational Beliefs

After conducting a thorough assessment of the target problem, identifying and assessing any secondary emotional problems, and teaching the B–C connection, the next step in the counselling sequence is to begin the process of disputing clients' irrational beliefs.

The Goals of Disputing

A major goal of disputing at this point is to help clients to understand that the irrational beliefs to which they subscribe are unproductive (in the sense that they lead to self-defeating emotions and behaviours), illogical and inconsistent with reality. Counsellors attempt to teach clients that the alternatives to these beliefs (i.e., rational beliefs) are productive, logical and consistent with reality.

Even if a given client provides evidence that she has reached such an understanding, it would probably be an error for the counsellor to assume that her conviction in the alternative rational belief will be strong. In this vein, it can be helpful to teach the client the distinction between *light conviction* and *deep conviction* in a rational belief. The former state is considered characteristic of intellectual rational insight, while the latter state is characteristic of emotional rational insight. Clients can be encouraged to view even a light conviction in an alternative rational belief as a sign of progress, albeit usually insufficient in itself to promote emotional change.

With specific regard to the target problem, the goals of disputing are to help the client to understand the following:

1. Preferences versus musts: human beings quite frequently change their preferences into absolute demands (i.e., irrational beliefs). It is very likely that there is no evidence in support of the absolute demands embodied in irrational beliefs, whereas evidence can be found to support preferences.
2. Awfulising: individuals experiencing emotional disturbance are often defining their negative As as being absolutely awful (i.e., 101 per cent bad). This constitutes magical nonsense, since in reality all experience lies within a 0–99.9 per cent range of badness.
3. I-can't-stand-it-itis: human beings can virtually always tolerate and survive that which they think they cannot stand, and can find some degree of happiness even if their negative As persist.
4. Damnation: this is a concept that is illogical and inconsistent with reality and will lead to emotional trouble. The preferable alternative to damnation is for human beings to accept themselves, other people and the world as imperfect and complex – too complex to be given a single global rating.

As treatment proceeds, counsellors can pursue the goal of helping clients to internalise a broad range of rational beliefs so that they become part of a general philosophy of rational living. This process, however, is beyond the scope of the present chapter.

Use Questions during Disputing

In the first stage of the disputing sequence, counsellors typically ask clients to provide evidence in support of their musts. Standard questions used for this purpose include, 'Where is the evidence that you *must* under all conditions?'; 'Where is the proof?'; 'Is it true that you absolutely *must*?'; and 'Where is it written that you *must*?'

It is important for counsellors to ensure that clients actually answer the disputing questions asked of them. For example, in response to the question 'Why *must* you succeed?' a given client might answer, 'Because succeeding will bring me certain advantages'. Note that the client has really not addressed herself to the question that was asked; rather, she has actually provided a response to the question, 'Why is it *preferable* for you to succeed?' Generally, it is good practice to anticipate that clients will not immediately provide correct responses to initial disputing questions.

As per RET theory, the only valid answer to the question 'Why *must* you succeed?' is 'There is no reason why I absolutely *must*, although it would be preferable'. When clients provide any other answer, it is likely that they need to be educated as to why their answer is (1) incorrect with respect to the question that was asked, or (2) a correct answer to a different question. During this process a combination of questions and short didactic explanations may be used to help clients attain an understanding of the correct answer.

It is usually helpful at this point to assist clients in distinguishing between their rational and irrational beliefs. One means for accomplishing this is to write down two questions, such as the following:

1 Why *must* you succeed?
2 Why is it preferable but not essential for you to succeed?

When clients attempt to answer these questions, it is often the case that they will give the same answer to both. When this occurs, they can be helped to see that the reasons they provided in their response constitute evidence for their rational belief, but not for their irrational belief. Here, the goal is to help clients to comprehend that the only answer to a question concerning the existence of musts is – to paraphrase Ellis – 'There are probably no absolute musts in the universe'.

Persistence in Disputing

As noted earlier, it is important to dispute both the premise and the derivative forms of a given client's irrational beliefs. If, however, the counsellor has started this process by disputing the irrational premise, it is important to persist in this endeavour until the client is able to see that there is no evidence in support of this premise before beginning to dispute a derivative from the premise.

Switching too quickly from premise to derivative (and vice versa) during disputing can be confusing for the client. If, however, disputing is initially aimed at an irrational premise and it becomes clear that the client is not finding this helpful, it can make sense to redirect the focus toward a derivative and monitor the client's reactions. Some clients appear to have an easier time understanding why their derivatives are irrational than why their musts are irrational.

Use a Variety of Disputing Strategies

There are three main foci for disputing irrational beliefs. It is probably preferable to use all three of these strategies whenever possible:

1 *Focus on illogicality*: here, clients are helped to understand why their irrational beliefs are illogical. They are shown, for instance, that simply because they may *want* something to happen, it does not logically follow that it absolutely *must* happen. Counsellors can show clients that their irrational beliefs often represent illogical non sequiturs.
2 *Focus on empiricism*: the goal of this strategy is to demonstrate to clients that their musts and irrational derivatives are almost always inconsistent with reality. To accomplish this goal, counsellors use questions which ask clients to provide evidence in support of their irrational beliefs (e.g., 'Where is the evidence that you *must* succeed?'). A given client could be helped to see that if there were evidence to support her belief that she *must* succeed, then she would have to succeed no matter what she believed. If she is not succeeding at present, that fact constitutes evidence that her irrational belief is empirically inconsistent with reality.
3 *Focus on pragmatism*: with this strategy, counsellors focus on showing clients the pragmatic consequences of holding irrational beliefs. The goal is to help clients see that as long as they subscribe to their irrational musts and their derivatives, they will remain disturbed. Here, questions such as, 'What is believing that you *must* succeed going to get you other than anxious and depressed?' are used.

After disputing an irrational belief, clients need to learn how to replace their irrational belief with a new, rational belief. Counsellors work together with clients to construct a rational belief that appears to be most adaptive with respect to A. After an alternative rational belief has been formulated, the three disputing strategies described above can be applied to it in order to demonstrate to clients that rational beliefs are in fact rational. It is much better for clients to see for themselves the evidence that rational beliefs are more valid and helpful, than for counsellors to simply tell them that this is so.

Use a Variety of Disputing Styles

While seasoned practitioners of rational-emotive counselling tend to develop their own individual disputing styles, four basic styles for disputing irrational beliefs will be emphasised here. These four styles are termed Socratic, didactic, humorous and self-disclosing.

Socratic Style When utilising the Socratic style of disputing, counsellors set themselves the task of asking clients questions concerning the illogical, empirically inconsistent and dysfunctional aspects of their irrational beliefs. Such questions are intended to prompt clients to think for themselves, as opposed to simply accepting the counsellor's viewpoint because it stems from a background of expertise. Although the Socratic style emphasises the use of questions, it can be supplemented with brief explanations designed to quickly correct client misconceptions that may arise along the way.

Didactic Style Although a good number of rational-emotive counsellors seem to prefer using the Socratic style, it is acknowledged that the use of questions does not always prove productive. When this is the case, counsellors can shift to utilising direct, didactic explanations as to why irrational beliefs are self-defeating and rational beliefs are more productive. It is quite likely that almost all counsellors find it helpful to use didactic explanations at various points in the treatment process.

When didactic explanations are employed, it is good practice to check whether clients have understood the message conveyed. One means of doing this is to request that they paraphrase the points made. Here, the counsellor might make a statement such as 'I'm not quite sure I'm making myself clear to you – perhaps you could put into your own words what you think I've been saying to you'. It can be a mistake to accept clients' non-verbal and paraverbal signs of understanding (e.g., head nods, mm-hmms) without questioning them. Clients will sometimes evince understanding even when they actually have not understood a word the counsellor has said (Dryden, 1986).

Humorous Style With some clients, the use of humour or humorous exaggeration can present a productive vehicle for making the point that there is no evidence to support irrational beliefs. The use of humour as a disputing strategy, however, is advised only when the following conditions are met: (1) the counsellor has established a good working relationship with the client; (2) the client has already provided some evidence that she has a good sense of humour; and (3) the humorous interventions are directed at the irrationality of the client's belief and *not* at the client as a person. In addition, Ellis (1985) has noted that it is important for counsellors to refrain from overusing techniques that they find enjoyable at clients' expense.

Self-disclosing Style Counsellor self-disclosure can represent another useful means of disputing clients' irrational beliefs. Generally, the coping model (as opposed to the mastery model) of self-disclosure is viewed as having features which are likely to be helpful to clients. In using the coping model, counsellors reveal that: (1) they have experienced a problem that in some sense is similar to the client's problem; (2) they once held an irrational belief that is similar to the one the client maintains; and (3) they worked at changing this belief and thus no longer have the problem.

In contrast to the coping model of self-disclosure, the mastery model would involve telling the client that the counsellor has never experienced a problem similar to the client's because he or she has always thought rationally about the issue at hand. Although this approach can highlight the fact that rational thinking helps an individual to avoid particular emotional problems, it can be disadvantageous insofar as it accentuates the differences between counsellor and client. In our experience, the mastery model is less productive than the coping model in encouraging clients to challenge their irrationality. We would note, however, that some clients will not even find the coping model useful. Particular clients, for instance, will tend to condemn the counsellor when the latter displays any signs of 'weakness'. If it becomes apparent that attempts at self-disclosure are failing to benefit the client (and are perhaps damaging the therapeutic alliance), other disputing strategies may be used instead.

Creative Disputing

As noted earlier, counsellors tend to develop their own individual styles as they gain experience in disputing clients' irrational beliefs. Typically, they build up a repertoire of stories, metaphors, aphorisms and examples which are used to demonstrate why irrational beliefs are indeed irrational, and why rational beliefs will tend to promote psychological health. As these various vehicles can serve to increase counselling's impact on the client, it is desirable for counsellors to work at accumulating their own repertoire of creative disputing strategies.

The 'Terrorist Dispute' (see Dryden and Yankura, 1993: 109–10) can be considered as an example of a creative approach to working with clients who believe that they absolutely cannot stand the discomfort involved in changing long-standing patterns of self-defeating emotions and behaviours. Another creative disputing strategy, termed the 'Friend Dispute', can be useful for pointing out the existence of irrationally demanding self-standards. If, for example, a given client has failed at an important endeavour and is engaging in self-damning (stemming from the irrational belief 'I *must* do well and I'm no good if I don't'), she can be asked if she would condemn a close friend for a similar failure in the same manner that she condemns herself. When she responds in the negative, she can be shown that she has one set of standards for herself and another set of quite different standards for her friend. She can then be helped to see that if she were as accepting of herself as she is of her friend, she would be less prone to emotional disturbance.

Additional creative strategies for disputing clients' irrational beliefs can be found in the discussion of vivid disputing methods presented in Chapter 11. Counsellors are cautioned, however, to work toward mastery of basic disputing skills before attempting to be too creative.

Step 9: Monica

Joe: Okay – we've identified two beliefs that result in your feeling of anxiety and your avoidance of the task of learning to operate the computer. The first belief is, 'I *must* succeed'. The second belief, which stems from the first one, is 'I'm an incompetent loser if I don't succeed'. Now, in order to change those beliefs we have to question and challenge them through a process called *disputing*. Let's dispute these beliefs one at a time – even though they're really linked to each other – because that way we can be more sure we're not missing anything. Okay?

Monica: Okay – how do we proceed?

Joe: Let's start with the first belief: 'I *must* succeed'. There are basically three ways we can challenge this belief. First, we can ask whether or not it's logical. Second, we can put it to the test to see whether it's consistent with reality. Finally, we can consider the consequences of holding the belief – does it help you or hinder you?

Let's look at the logical argument first. Now, your desire, or preference, is to be able to learn how to operate the computer with a minimum of difficulty. That's how you would define succeeding at the task – right?

Monica: Right.

Joe: But – is it sound logic to conclude that because you would prefer to succeed, you *must* succeed?

Monica: No . . .

Joe: Why not?

Monica: Well . . . it sort of reminds me of the old saying: 'If wishes were horses, then beggars would ride'. Just because I might prefer a particular outcome, that doesn't mean that that outcome must occur.

Joe: That's right – demanding that a particular outcome *must* occur because we want it to occur is equivalent to believing in magic.

Monica: And magic doesn't really exist – I've never believed in it, anyway!

Joe: Right! Now, let's see if your belief is consistent with reality. Do you believe that the universe is governed by particular laws and principles? I'm making reference here to the kinds of 'laws' that physicists and other scientists are interested in studying.

Monica: Yes, I believe that.

Joe: Okay – these 'laws' generally state that if a particular set of conditions exists, then a particular outcome will follow. If there were a law of the universe that stated, 'You *must* succeed', then what outcome would have to follow?

Monica: I would succeed! But of course, there really is no guarantee that I'll succeed – so my belief amounts to demanding an outcome that could possibly not occur.

Joe: Right – if it were true that you *must* succeed, then you would have no choice but to succeed. And that isn't consistent with reality, is it?

Monica: No, it's not.

Joe: Now let's take the third way of challenging this belief. Let's examine the consequences of holding it, and determine whether those consequences are useful to you or not. As long as you maintain the belief, 'I *must* succeed', what are you going to experience?

Monica: Anxiety and avoidance, which aren't going to help me.

Joe: That's correct – the 'must' will create emotional and behavioural difficulties for you. Now, we've challenged your belief by asking, 'Is it logical?'; 'Is it consistent with reality?'; and 'Will it get me good results?' As we've seen, the answer to all three of these questions is 'no'. It's important, however, for you to continue thinking this through for yourself – you can practise challenging your must on your own. Also, it's a good idea to apply these three questions to your non-absolute preference as well – that way, you can show yourself that your preference is more logical, consistent with reality and useful than the absolute must.

Monica: Right – I can see that it would be good for me to review what we've gone over here.

Joe: That will really be helpful. Now, let's use the same three questions to challenge your second belief: 'I would be an incompetent loser if I didn't succeed'.

First, is it logical to conclude that you would be an incompetent loser if you failed at this particular task?

Monica: Well, it *feels* that way – I mean, I could lose my job if I don't succeed.

Joe: But let's suppose that came to pass – you actually did lose your job. How could that one failure make you an incompetent loser? Does failing at something logically make you a failure?

Monica: I think I see what you mean now – I would be condemning my entire self because of one screw-up.

Joe: That's right – you would be negatively rating the whole on the basis of just one part. Now, is that logical?

Monica: No, certainly not.

Joe: That's right – in fact, it's a good idea to work at giving up the idea of trying to place one all-encompassing rating on your*self*. You can rate parts of the whole, but as a human being you are far too complex to be subsumed under any one label. You're made up of thousands – maybe millions – of parts!

Now, let's look at the second argument. If the belief 'I'm an incompetent loser' were consistent with reality, what would that mean about your ability to succeed at other endeavours?

Monica: I'd be doomed to fail at everything – and that's not true! Even with my present job, I'm able to handle most of my responsibilities quite well.

Joe: That's right – but if you were truly an incompetent loser, you would fail at everything you attempted. Now, what's more true – that you're an incompetent loser if you fail, or that you're a fallible human being with both strong points and weak points – too complex to be given a single rating?

Monica: The second is definitely more true!

Joe: Right. Now let's move to the third point – if you continue to believe that failing to learn how to operate the computer means you're an incompetent loser, what kinds of emotional and behavioural consequences will you get?

Monica: Well, if I'm basing my entire view of myself on how I do with this one task, I'll be terrified to even try! I'll continue to feel anxious and to avoid getting down to business with the computer.

Joe: That could very well be the outcome. If, on the other hand, you hold the view that you're a fallible, unratable human being, what types of consequences will you be more likely to experience?

Monica: Going back to what we discussed earlier, I'd still feel concerned – but not anxious. And if I did away with my anxiety, I'd probably stand a better chance of getting down to task.

Step 10: Prepare Clients to Deepen their Conviction in Rational Beliefs

Once clients have acknowledged that (1) there is no evidence in support of irrational beliefs, but rational beliefs can be supported by evidence; (2) it is more logical to think rationally; and (3) rational beliefs will lead to more productive emotional results than irrational beliefs, counsellors are in a position to help them deepen their conviction in their new, alternative rational beliefs.

Emphasise that Weak Conviction in a Rational Belief is Unlikely (on its Own) to Promote Change

Intellectual rational insight is usually insufficient to bring about meaningful emotional and behavioural change. As such, at this stage of the counselling sequence, counsellors help their clients to see that weak conviction in rational beliefs – although important – is unlikely to help them reach their counselling goals. This can be accomplished with brief discussion of the rational-emotive view of therapeutic change. Through the use of Socratic questioning and brief didactic explanations (as per Step 9), clients can be helped to understand that they will strengthen their conviction in their new rational beliefs by disputing irrational beliefs (and replacing them with their rational alternatives) within and between counselling sessions. Clients should also understand that this process will require them to *act* against their irrational beliefs as well as to dispute them cognitively. Teaching this concept now will make it easier for counsellors to encourage clients to put their new learning into practice (Steps 11 and 12) and to facilitate the working-through process (Step 13).

Dealing with the 'Head–Gut' Issue

As clients learn to think more rationally, they may sometimes make statements such as, 'I understand that my rational belief will help me to achieve my goals, but I don't really believe in it yet'. Counsellors can anticipate that clients will often experience some difficulty in crossing the bridge between intellectual and emotional insight, and can initiate discussion on this point as a prelude to consideration of ways to deepen conviction in rational beliefs and weaken conviction in irrational ones. As an example, a counsellor might ask a client, 'What do you think you'll have to do in order to get your new rational belief into your gut?'

It is good practice to encourage clients to commit themselves to a process of therapeutic change that will require repeated and forceful disputing of irrational beliefs, as well as efforts to practise rational thinking within relevant life contexts. Here, clients are helped to design and undertake a variety of homework assignments, as described in Step 11.

Step 10: Monica

Joe: Now, how often do you think you'll have to challenge your self-defeating beliefs in order to more strongly subscribe to their alternatives?

Monica: Quite often, I suppose.

Joe: I would agree – but why do you see it that way?

Monica: Well, because it probably takes a lot of work to change the way you're accustomed to thinking about something.

Joe: Right. Let's consider an example – you have secretarial skills, right?

Monica: Right.

Joe: Okay. Imagine that when you were learning how to type, you had a teacher who taught you all wrong. Nevertheless, you eagerly practised the incorrect technique because you didn't realise that it was wrong. As time went on, you noted that your typing speed was not improving, and that you were indeed much slower than other typists. As a result, you decided to consult with a second teacher who was able to diagnose your problems and show you the correct way to type. Now, would that be all you needed to improve your typing?

Monica: No . . .

Joe: Why not?

Monica: I'd have to keep practising the correct technique.

Joe: That's right – but would the new technique feel comfortable to you at the start?

Monica: I guess not.

Joe: Why is that?

Monica: Because I'd developed some bad habits. The incorrect way would still feel more comfortable.

Joe: Right – the incorrect technique would feel more natural to you. But would that 'natural feeling' have to stop you from correcting your technique once you realised it was wrong?

Monica: No.

Joe: That's right. It's the same thing with your beliefs. The next time you think about sitting down to try and learn how to operate the computer, it's quite likely that your beliefs, 'I must succeed; to do otherwise would prove I'm an incompetent loser', will still be operative. That's because you've subscribed to those beliefs for some time, and at this point they're fairly natural to you. But if you resist that natural feeling you can work at identifying, challenging and changing these beliefs until the new, alternative way of thinking comes more naturally to you. Also, the more you *act* in accordance with your new beliefs, the more likely it is that you'll become convinced of their validity and usefulness. Does that make sense to you?

Monica: Yes, it does. It's important for me to continually challenge my old way of thinking, and to act as if I subscribed to the new beliefs.

Joe: That's it. Keep practising the new beliefs until you've really internalised them. It's a process of moving beyond intellectual understanding to a point where you can really feel the truth of the new beliefs in your gut. Once they're at that gut level, you'll be better able to act spontaneously on them.

Step 11: Encouraging Clients to Put New Learning into Practice

At this point, clients should be ready to put their rational beliefs into practice. They can be reminded that, as per the rational-emotive theory of therapeutic change, they will have greater success in deepening conviction in their rational beliefs if they work at disputing irrational beliefs and strengthening rational ones in situations that are the same or similar to the activating event previously assessed. RET advocates a variety of homework assignments for accomplishing this end. These assignments can be categorised according to whether they have a cognitive, behavioural or imagery focus. In using homework assignments with clients, counsellors should bear in mind the following important points:

1 *Ensure that homework assignments are relevant*. Counsellors are advised to develop homework activities that are relevant to the irrational belief targeted for change. Enacting the homework assignment will help the

client to weaken conviction in this irrational belief and deepen conviction in the alternative rational belief.

2 *Collaborate with clients*. It is good practice to enlist clients' active collaboration when discussing appropriate homework assignments. In order to increase the likelihood that a particular assignment will be enacted, the counsellor should ensure that the client (a) sees the sense of doing the homework assignment; (b) agrees that carrying out the assignment will help in the attainment of desired goals; and (c) has some degree of confidence in her ability to carry out the assignment. The probability of client compliance with homework assignments can be further maximised by establishing when, where and how often the particular activity will be implemented.

3 *Be prepared to compromise*. Ideally, homework assignments involve having clients actively and forcefully dispute their irrational beliefs in the most relevant life contexts possible. If this is not feasible, however, clients can be encouraged to (a) dispute their irrational beliefs in situations that approximate the most relevant A, or (b) use imagery to dispute irrational beliefs while vividly imagining A. Doing these less-than-ideal assignments can sometimes increase the likelihood that clients will eventually take on more challenging homework activities.

4 *Assess and troubleshoot obstacles*. Counsellors can work with clients to specify in advance any obstacles that may serve as impediments to homework completion. Clients can be encouraged to find possible ways of overcoming these obstacles before carrying out the assignment.

5 *Use homework at different times during counselling*. The present discussion has focused on homework assignments that help clients to strengthen conviction in their rational beliefs. It should be noted, however, that homework assignments can be useful at various points and for various purposes throughout the treatment sequence. Thus, homework assignments can be designed to help clients (a) specify their problematic emotions at C; (b) detect their irrational beliefs at B; and (c) identify the most relevant aspect of A about which they have made themselves disturbed. In addition, homework assignments can also be used as a means for educating clients about the ABCs of RET. Clients can be encouraged to read particular books (bibliotherapy), or to listen to RET lectures on audio tape. When suggesting such assignments, it is wise to select material that is relevant to the target problem and readily understandable. Counsellors can consider creating their own written materials or audio tapes to use with particular clients when appropriate material is not available.

Step 11: Monica

Joe: Now, since changing your beliefs usually takes a lot of effort, it's desirable to practise between sessions what you learn within sessions. Does that idea make sense to you?

Monica: Yes, it does.

Joe: Okay, good. What do you think you could do along those lines?
Monica: I'm not sure – I suppose I could practise applying the three arguments we went over to my self-defeating beliefs.
Joe: That sounds like a good idea. Specifically, you could use those arguments to challenge the idea that 'I *must* succeed; failing would prove that I'm an incompetent loser'. Also, you can apply those same three points to the more constructive, alternative beliefs we've discussed: 'I would prefer to succeed, but that doesn't mean that I must' and 'If I don't succeed I'm not an incompetent loser, I'm a fallible, unratable human being who happened to fail at a particular task'. Again, the idea is to weaken your conviction in your old beliefs, and strengthen your conviction in your new beliefs.
Monica: Right.
Joe: Now, how often would you like to review those arguments?
Monica: Oh . . . I think once in the morning – before going to work – and once in the evening.
Joe: That sounds fine. Do you anticipate any obstacles to doing this?
Monica: No, it sounds quite manageable.
Joe: Good. Why don't we just make some written notes on the three types of arguments that you can refer to as you practise?

Step 12: Check Homework Assignments

It is good practice to review previously negotiated homework assignments at the start of each session. Failure to do so may inadvertently communicate to clients that the counsellor does not consider these assignments to be an integral part of the change process. This is undesirable, as homework assignments are central to helping clients achieve their counselling goals.

Confirm that Clients Faced A

Unfortunately, clients can be quite creative in developing strategies to avoid problematic As. As such, it is advisable for counsellors to ascertain that clients actually faced the As they committed themselves to confronting. When clients genuinely *have* faced their As, they typically report that they first made themselves disturbed and then managed to become undisturbed (without simply escaping from the situation) by utilising the disputing techniques discussed in counselling. When clients fail to carry out their homework assignments in this manner, counsellors can help them to identify and deal with any obstacles that may have been involved. They can then encourage clients to again confront their troublesome situations and use vigorous disputing to make themselves undisturbed within that context. As necessary, appropriate disputes can be modelled and rehearsed in the session before clients make another attempt to confront the A in question.

Verify that Clients Changed B

When clients report success in implementing homework assignments, it is good practice to determine whether this success can be attributed to (1) changing an irrational belief to its rational alternative; (2) changing either A itself or inferences about A; or (3) the use of distraction techniques. If enquiry reveals that a given client utilised the latter two methods, the counsellor can acknowledge the client's efforts but then point out that these strategies may not be helpful in the long term. Practical solutions (i.e., changing A) or distractions are merely palliative, as they do not require clients to change the irrational beliefs that produce inappropriate negative emotions when A is faced. Many As are unavoidable; as such, the emotional problem will tend to reassert itself again and again. Counsellors can attempt to convey these points to clients, encourage them to again face the situation at A, and elicit their commitment to dispute their irrational beliefs and practise acting on the basis of the new rational beliefs.

Deal with Failure to Complete Homework Assignments

When clients fail to execute agreed-upon homework, rational-emotive counsellors accept them as fallible human beings and help them to identify the reasons the assignment was not carried out. The ABC framework can be used to help clients identify possible irrational beliefs that interfered with homework completion. In particular, counsellors will want to assess for irrational beliefs that contribute to low frustration tolerance (e.g., 'I shouldn't have to work so hard at changing – it's too damn hard!'). When clients hold such beliefs, they can be helped to challenge and change them prior to reassignment of the homework.

Step 12: Monica

The following exchange occurred one week later, during Monica's next session:

Joe: So, how did you make out with your homework assignment? You were going to work at challenging your self-defeating beliefs twice a day . . .

Monica: Well, I did okay at first, but as the week wore on I became rather inconsistent. I'd miss a morning, or an evening, or maybe even an entire day.

Joe: So you were doing well at first – let's give you some credit for that! But let's take a closer look at how you got yourself off track. When was the first morning when you didn't do your homework exercise?

Monica: Um . . . Thursday, I think.

Joe: Okay, imagine it's Thursday morning once again. What were you telling yourself at that time to make yourself miss your practice?

Monica: 'This is getting sort of boring'.

Joe: Well, wait a minute – that wouldn't be enough to stop you from practising. After all, you could have told yourself, 'This is getting boring. Too damn bad – I'll push myself to do it anyway, because I know that it will benefit me'. You then probably would have gone on to do the exercise.

Since you didn't do the exercise, you were probably telling yourself something *about* the boredom that dissuaded you from practising. What do you think that might have been?

Monica: Oh! Now I see it: 'It must not be boring!'

Joe: Right – that belief may well have been in operation. Also, you may have been adding this: 'I *can't stand it* if it's boring!' How could you challenge those two beliefs?

Monica: Well, I could make use of the same sorts of challenging questions we discussed last week.

Joe: Right! 'Is it logical?' 'Is it consistent with reality?' 'Does it produce helpful outcomes for me?' You can show yourself that it doesn't *have to* be stimulating, and that even if it isn't, you can still stand it.

Monica: That second part sounds important to me – I can tolerate the practice even if I do find it boring.

Joe: And perhaps you can experiment with ways to make it more interesting for yourself. Want to try the assignment again during the coming week?

Monica: Yes – I'm determined to keep working at it.

The session continued with further discussion of Monica's work-related problems and consideration of activity-oriented exercises that she could undertake to challenge her irrational beliefs.

Step 13: Facilitate the Working-through Process

It is unlikely that clients will achieve enduring therapeutic change unless they repeatedly and forcefully challenge their irrational beliefs in relevant contexts at A. By engaging in this process, they will further strengthen their conviction in rational beliefs and continue to weaken their conviction in irrational ones. The working-through process represents a means by which clients integrate rational beliefs into their emotional and behavioural repertoires.

Suggest a Variety of Homework Assignments Targeted at the Same Irrational Belief

When clients have experienced some success in disputing particular irrational beliefs in relevant situations at A, they can be encouraged to use different types of homework activities to further erode the degree to which they subscribe to these same beliefs. Doing so teaches clients that a variety of methods can be used to dispute their targeted irrational beliefs, as well as others. In addition, introducing this sort of variety can help to sustain clients' interest in the change process.

Discuss the Non-linear Model of Change

Counsellors can explain that change is a non-linear process in order to prepare clients for the difficulties they may encounter as they try to dispute irrational beliefs within a wide variety of contexts. Potential setbacks can be identified, and clients can be helped in advance to develop ways of dealing with them. Specifically, clients can be given assistance in identifying and challenging the irrational beliefs that might underpin their relapses.

In addition, counsellors can teach clients to evaluate change on the following three major dimensions:

1 Frequency: are unhealthy negative emotions experienced less often than before?
2 Intensity: when unhealthy negative emotions *are* experienced, are they less intense than before?
3 Duration: do unhealthy emotional episodes last for shorter periods than before?

Clients can be encouraged to keep records of their unhealthy emotions at point C, using these three criteria for change. In addition, clients may find it helpful to read the booklet, *How to Maintain and Enhance your Rational-Emotive Therapy Gains* (Ellis, 1984). This publication (which is reproduced in Chapter 15) contains many useful suggestions that clients may use to facilitate the working-through process.

Encourage Clients to Take Responsibility for Continued Progress

At this stage, clients can be helped to develop their own homework assignments to change their target beliefs and to change other irrational beliefs in different situations. If, for example, a given client has been successful in disputing an irrational belief about approval in a work-related situation that involves criticism, she might be encouraged to dispute this belief in other situations in which criticism is encountered (e.g., with family members or friends). As clients develop confidence in designing and carrying out their own homework assignments, they are likely to experience increasing success in acting as their own therapists. This accomplishment is most important, as the long-term goal of rational-emotive counselling is to encourage clients to internalise the RET model of change and to take responsibility for further progress after therapy has ended.

Step 13: Monica

At the close of her second session, Monica agreed to take on the activity-oriented assignment of getting to work a half-hour earlier in order to have time to develop her skills on the office computer. She took on this assignment in addition to the cognitive exercise of challenging her irrational beliefs with the three types of disputing arguments she had learned in session. It was emphasised that she could utilise these arguments if she began to feel anxious while working with the computer.

With respect to working to overcome her 'computer phobia', Monica was generally more consistent in implementing her activity-oriented disputing exercises than her cognitive disputing exercises. Nevertheless, she did continue to use and benefit from the latter. As she progressed in therapy she began to tackle some of her other problem areas, including her fear of being criticised by her employer and her worries about financial security. With regard to the former, she successfully utilised rational-emotive imagery to help herself reach a point where she could remain in her boss's presence without experiencing anxiety. With respect to the latter issue, she was able to take steps toward internalising a personal philosophy wherein the possibility of temporary unemployment (with its attendant financial hardships) was regarded as a definite inconvenience, but certainly not a horror.

Monica also followed up on some of my suggestions for bibliotherapy assignments, and as a result sharpened her awareness of the broad range of emotional and behavioural problems to which RET can be applied. It seemed apparent that she was taking important steps towards becoming her own counsellor, as she often spontaneously reported instances in which she had utilised rational-emotive techniques to deal with upsets other than those that were included on her original problem list. We jointly decided that it was appropriate to end regularly scheduled contacts after we had met for a total of 14 sessions. Monica seemed pleased with the progress she had made in counselling, and understood that she could return for additional sessions if she encountered difficulty in coping on her own.

Note

1 In Chapters 14 and 15 for simplicity the client is referred to throughout as 'she'.

References

Bard, J.A. (1980) *Rational-Emotive Therapy in Practice*. Champaign, IL: Research Press.

DiGiuseppe, R. (1984) Thinking what to feel, *British Journal of Cognitive Psychotherapy,* 2(1), 27–33.

Dryden, W. (1986) Language and meaning in rational-emotive therapy. In: W. Dryden and P. Trower (eds), *Rational-Emotive Therapy: Recent Developments in Theory and Practice.* Bristol: Institute for RET (UK).

Dryden, W. and Yankura, J. (1993) *Counselling Individuals: A Rational-Emotive Handbook* (2nd edn). London: Whurr.

Ellis, A. (1984) *How to Maintain and Enhance your Rational-Emotive Therapy Gains*. New York: Institute for RET.

Ellis, A. (1985) *Overcoming Resistance: Rational-Emotive Therapy with Difficult Clients*. New York: Springer.

Ellis, A. and Dryden, W. (1987) *The Practice of Rational-Emotive Therapy*. New York: Springer.

Gendlin, E.T. (1978) *Focusing*. New York: Everest House.

Passons, W.R. (1975) *Gestalt Approaches in Counseling*. New York: Holt, Rinehart and Winston.

Trexler, L.D. (1976) Frustration is a fact, not a feeling, *Rational Living,* 11(2), 19–22.

Walen, S.R., DiGiuseppe, R. and Wessler, R.L. (1980) *A Practitioner's Guide to Rational-Emotive Therapy*. New York: Oxford University Press.

15

The Rational-Emotive Counselling Process

Windy Dryden and Joseph Yankura

Overview

In Chapter 14 we presented the rational-emotive counselling sequence, which provides guidelines for helping clients to deal with a specific problem area. In this chapter we review the rational-emotive counselling *process*, and review treatment issues relevant to the beginning, middle and ending stages of counselling. Of particular note, we discuss issues pertaining to the formation of a sound therapeutic alliance, assisting clients in dealing with multiple problem areas, dealing with obstacles to therapeutic change, and encouraging clients to become their own counsellors. We conclude by presenting a brief account of a typical case in rational-emotive counselling.

It is noted that dividing the counselling process into beginning, middle and ending phases is a somewhat artificial convention we have chosen to employ in order to provide structure for the material presented in this chapter. Actually, it is impossible to differentiate so clearly between the various components of the counselling process. Issues pertaining to the therapeutic alliance between counsellor and client, for instance, will have importance throughout a course of treatment, and in reality are not restricted to the beginning stage of counselling. As such, we would advise the reader to approach the material that follows with a flexible frame of mind.

THE BEGINNING STAGE

Establishing a Therapeutic Alliance

Within the counselling field, the quality of the therapeutic alliance between counsellor and client is generally regarded as an important determinant of treatment outcome. Bordin (1979) provides a useful framework for conceptualising the therapeutic alliance by breaking it down into three major components: bonds, goals and tasks. The *bond* between counsellor and client refers to the nature and quality of the interpersonal relationship that exists between the two individuals. *Goals* are the purposes that counsellor and client would like to see achieved through counselling. *Tasks* are the respective activities that counsellor and client take responsibility for in the service of approaching counselling goals.

Bonds

If a productive bond fails to form between counsellor and client, the likelihood of therapeutic failure may be increased. In the service of promoting a productive bond, rational-emotive counsellors will attempt to identify the style of interaction most suitable for a given client. At the outset of counselling, for instance, counsellors can make enquiries concerning the client's view of what constitutes helpful versus unhelpful counsellor behaviour. Here, questions concerning the client's experiences with any previous counsellors can be particularly helpful. Some counsellors like to employ Lazarus's (1981) 'Life History Questionnaire', which contains the following questions:

1 In a few words, what do you think counselling is all about?
2 How do you think a therapist should interact with his or her clients?
3 What personal qualities do you think the ideal therapist should possess?

It is important to recognise that certain qualifications apply to the issue of counsellors modifying their interactional style to suit the client. Rational-emotive counsellors are willing to be flexible concerning the manner in which they relate to clients, but only insofar as this does not interfere with the attainment of counselling goals.

First, it may be wise for counsellors to take the client's own personality style into account when trying to identify an optimal style of therapeutic interaction. It may be best, for example, to avoid an overly cognitive, intellectualised style when working with clients who appear to have obsessive-compulsive personality traits. Alternatively, some variant of this sort of style may prove quite suitable with clients who tend to be excitable and histrionic. As RET is a psychoeducational approach to counselling, a good rule of thumb is to find an interactional style that promotes an optimal learning environment for the particular client.

Second, some clients – either because of their own personality make-up or their prior experiences with counselling – may strongly prefer that their counsellor adopt a passive role within sessions. They may convey this preference directly through verbal statements, or indirectly through passive-aggressive responses to the counsellor's ministrations. It is important to bear in mind, however, that an active-directive counsellor style tends to be the preferred vehicle for implementing the problem-solving approach to counselling which is characteristic of RET. Thus, with clients who prefer counsellor passivity, rational-emotive counsellors would attempt to structure therapeutic conditions such that these clients become more receptive to a high degree of counsellor activity and directiveness. Initially, this could mean overtly presenting clients with a sound rationale for the counsellor's active-directive stance. If this fails, less direct strategies can be employed.

These might include a gradual increase in the counsellor's verbal activity level over the course of the beginning stage of counselling, or the use of well-chosen, well-timed questions which promote a high degree of *client* verbal activity, while structuring sessions in a productive way. A minority of clients will remain 'allergic' to active-directive counsellor behaviour; for such individuals, a judicious referral to a practitioner who utilises a more passive approach to counselling may be in order.

It is noted that rational-emotive counsellors attempt to put into practice a philosophy of unconditional acceptance in their work with clients; this can also contribute to the formation of a good bond between counsellor and client. Translated into actual behaviour, a philosophy of unconditional acceptance means that counsellors refrain from responding in a judgemental, condemning fashion when clients report acts that society would consider unethical or morally wrong, or when clients behave inconsiderately toward their counsellor. When confronted with such things, rational-emotive counsellors generally attempt to respond to clients in a reasoned, matter-of-fact and objective manner. This can promote an air of trust and openness within counselling, and can indirectly convey to clients that they do not have to condemn themselves for their 'bad' acts. Counsellors will, however, sometimes opt to bring obnoxious behaviour to a client's attention, as when it appears that the client's negative behaviour toward the counsellor is representative of a larger pattern that impairs her ability to form good relationships with others.

Goals

It is important for counsellor and client to be working mainly towards the same goals within counselling. Failure to agree upon goals can lead them to operate at cross-purposes with each other, which will probably result in eventual dissolution of the therapeutic alliance.

Assessment of Client Attitudes about Counselling At the start of counselling, counsellors can promote congruence in the goal domain by initiating a discussion on the client's views as to whether and how counselling might be helpful to her. Just because a given client has presented herself at the counsellor's office, it should not be assumed that the client regards counselling as a potentially useful endeavour. Some clients, for instance, are pushed into counselling by significant others or the judicial system. Needless to say, special steps need to be taken to engage reluctant clients in the counselling process. Sociopathic individuals, for example, may not be open to counselling until the counsellor has presented strong arguments that it can help them to more effectively avoid legal problems and attain desired ends.

A number of clients willingly enter into counselling, but harbour misconceptions concerning how it might assist them. It is often advisable for counsellors to educate clients as to what counselling can and cannot provide. Clients should, for instance, understand that rational-emotive counselling is focused upon helping them with their psychological problems, as opposed to their practical problems. They can be helped to see, however, that improved psychological functioning may facilitate their ability to resolve practical issues. Counsellor utilisation of induction procedures can be a worthwhile investment of session time with clients who are largely naive about the ways in which counselling works.

Use of a Problem List Congruence in the goal domain can be further enhanced by encouraging clients to generate a 'problem list'. This is an inventory of problems for which the client is seeking help during counselling. It can be suggested to clients as an initial homework assignment to be completed prior to the next scheduled appointment, although it can be perfectly legitimate to devote session time to its production. Ideally, the list should exist in written form with copies for both counsellor and client to keep.

When counsellor and client are ready to start focusing on a problem, the client is invited to choose an item from the problem list. This item may be the client's most pressing problem, the problem which is easiest to solve, or one which – if progress is achieved – engenders most hope for the client. The guiding principle here is that counsellor and client work together on problem selection and agree on the chosen issue, which, in practice, usually tends to be the client's most pressing problem.

When a client chooses an item from her problem list to focus upon, it will often be necessary for the counsellor to work with the client on translating that problem into an appropriate goal for rational-emotive counselling. Counsellor/client collaboration in this venture also helps to ensure that both individuals are working together to achieve the same outcome in counselling.

It is noted that allowing the client to choose the problems to be dealt with in counselling can enhance the therapeutic alliance by indirectly conveying that the counsellor is sensitive to the client's concerns and priorities. In addition, encouraging client choice can serve to set the stage for the client's active involvement in the counselling process. On occasion, however, it will be evident to the counsellor that the client's choice of a problem area to focus upon is not entirely appropriate. Such a situation can arise when the counsellor obtains evidence (through enquiry and observation) that the client has a secondary problem *about* the chosen problem. In such cases, it is generally good practice for the counsellor to bring the secondary problem to the client's attention and to present a rationale for dealing with it first. If, however, the client expresses a strong preference to work on the chosen problem rather than the secondary problem, it may be wise for the counsellor to assent to this wish. To do otherwise could compromise the therapeutic alliance.

Use of a Session Agenda When counsellors work with clients to establish a session agenda (see Beck et al., 1979) at the start of each counselling contact, they can help to promote goal congruence on a per session basis. A session agenda constitutes an agreement between counsellor and client as to what will be discussed during a particular session, and can serve as a means for structuring the proceedings. It can, for example, discourage either counsellor or client from jumping unhelpfully from problem to problem without making significant progress on any given one.

The following excerpt from *Daring to be Myself* (Dryden and Yankura, 1992) illustrates how WD [Windy Dryden] introduced the concept of establishing session agendas to his client, Sarah:

Dr Dryden: What I usually like to do at the beginning of every interview is to set up an agenda with you. I'll make suggestions about any items I might want to bring up, but it's mainly for any items that you want to talk about. This way, we can actually get the sense that we're working together on the same agenda. Okay?
Today, I'd like to discuss the problem list you were going to do – did you bring it with you?
Sarah: I did it very quickly last night.
Dr Dryden: Okay. Also, did you research any places to go [for social contacts]?
Sarah: Well, I phoned up social services.
Dr Dryden: Okay – we'll go into that in a minute. But first, what would you like to spend the bulk of today's session talking about? What particular issue or problem?
Sarah: Well, to put it in a nutshell, I'd like to talk about why I'm sort of frightened to get on with people.
Dr Dryden: So it's mainly your fear with other people?
Sarah: Mostly people I know, funny enough.
Dr Dryden: Okay. (Writing) 'People I know . . .' Do you think that will take up the whole of the session?

[The session proceeds with review of the client's reactions to the last session and discussion of current agenda items.]

It is advisable for counsellors to exercise flexibility in using session agendas, and to avoid conveying the impression that an agenda *must* be thoroughly covered in any particular session. In this vein it is usually wise to avoid agendas that contain a long list of items, especially when it seems likely that one item will require a large portion of session time.

Tasks

Counsellors can avoid a particular threat to the therapeutic alliance by taking steps to ensure that clients understand the respective tasks of counsellor and client within rational-emotive counselling. Generally, rational-emotive counsellors will take the role of active-directive problem-solvers, and will collaborate with clients to dispute their irrational beliefs and design potentially helpful homework assignments. Clients, on their part, will ideally become active participants in their counselling and accept the task of working with counsellors to identify and challenge their irrational beliefs. Hopefully, they will also take an active hand in designing homework assignments for themselves and take responsibility for enacting these homework assignments between sessions.

Counsellors can utilise both direct and indirect means to educate clients as to the respective tasks of counsellor and client. With respect to direct means, counsellors can make statements early on in counselling (and at various points later on, as appropriate) which describe the tasks for which they will take responsibility. These statements may take a form such as the following: 'Okay – as you've already noted, we've spent much of our first session together discussing your *attitudes* about your current job. As you've seen, some of these attitudes are causing you to experience feelings of anxiety and depression. As your counsellor, I propose to help you by sharpening your awareness of the attitudes that contribute to your upsets, and by showing you how you can *change* those unhelpful attitudes to more helpful ones. If you agree, we'll get down to working on that the next time we meet.' Similarly, counsellors can make direct statements that outline the tasks that clients are encouraged to take on.

Indirect means for communicating counsellor and client tasks include the following:

1 The counsellor's stance as an active-directive problem-solver throughout the course of counselling, conveyed through a high level of focused verbal activity.
2 The use of techniques such as Socratic questioning which prompt the client to engage in the task of actively examining and questioning her beliefs.
3 The use of prompts which encourage the client to play an active role in the design of relevant homework assignments (e.g., 'What do you think you could do during the coming week to put your new philosophy of self-acceptance into practice?').
4 Counsellors consistently devoting session time to designing and then subsequently following up on homework exercises.

The activities listed here are probably best viewed as vehicles for supplementing more direct communications concerning counsellor/client tasks. Conceivably, clients could fall into confusion and doubt if these activities are introduced into counselling sessions without direct verbal statements describing their purpose.

It is important to note that counsellors' and clients' respective tasks will change somewhat over the course of rational-emotive counselling. Counsellors attempt to gradually decrease their activity level such that clients are encouraged to take on more of the responsibility and effort involved in making progress and maintaining gains. This issue is dealt with again in the forthcoming section on the middle stage of counselling.

Monitoring Clients' Reactions As an additional means of promoting a sound therapeutic alliance, we have found it helpful to monitor clients' reactions to counselling throughout the course of treatment. Thus, we will routinely ask clients at the end of a given session if they found any of our statements or suggestions particularly helpful or unhelpful. At the start of the next scheduled session, we enquire of clients whether they had any additional reactions to the preceding session. The feedback resulting from these enquiries allows us to identify and correct any misunderstandings or misconceptions which clients may have developed, and helps us to modify our strategies and interventions so that they are more likely to promote beneficial change for individual clients.

Some clients will be reluctant to provide their counsellor with negative feedback, as they are afraid of losing the counsellor's approval and acceptance. When a given client only provides glowing responses to counsellor enquiries concerning her reactions to sessions, it may be appropriate to consider the hypothesis that this individual has a self-created need for the counsellor's approval. If this appears to be the case, it is generally good practice for the counsellor to directly (but tactfully) broach this issue and devote session time to exploring it with the client. In doing so, the counsellor may be able to identify and dispute any irrational beliefs (e.g., 'I *must* maintain my counsellor's approval; to lose this approval would *really* prove that I'm a worthless and unlovable person!') that could interfere with the counselling process.

Teaching the ABC Model

In order for clients to make sense of their rational-emotive counsellor's approach to helping them overcome emotional problems, they will require a foundation in rational-emotive concepts and techniques. Thus, during the beginning stage of counselling, counsellors need to teach clients the three main insights of RET and the means by which emotional problems can be analysed and remediated with the ABC model.

With respect to RET's first main insight, it is important for clients to understand that their emotional problems are largely determined by their irrational beliefs, and not directly by the troublesome life events that they have experienced. This should be considered a fundamental point for counsellors to convey to clients; if clients do not attain this understanding then they will probably fail to grasp why their counsellors focus so much attention on their thinking. As a result, they may make continued efforts to focus discussions upon the details of the current negative circumstances that they face, and may be put off by the counsellor's limited interest in this material.

RET's second major insight holds that individuals remain disturbed by continually reindoctrinating themselves in the *present* with the irrational beliefs to which they subscribe. Thus, detailed exploration of the historical antecedents of a client's irrational beliefs is eschewed within rational-emotive counselling, and a focus is placed upon identifying currently held musts, shoulds and have to's. It is important for clients to understand that it is not essential for them to determine precisely where their irrational beliefs came from, as long as they see that continuing to hold these beliefs will increase their vulnerability to emotional upsets and dysfunctional behaviour.

RET's third main insight emphasises that clients will need to work consistently and diligently at challenging and replacing their irrational beliefs if they are to derive significant, lasting benefits from counselling. Clients who possess this understanding are in a position to be active participants within their counselling, and will be able to see the desirability of putting into practice the knowledge they gain during counselling sessions.

Clients are taught both directly and indirectly to utilise the ABC model as a means for analysing and understanding their emotional upsets. Didactic explanations represent a direct means for teaching clients about the model's components, and can be useful at various points throughout the course of counselling. The model can also be conveyed indirectly through the Socratic questioning technique, which can be used to prompt clients to identify the relevant activating events, consequent emotions and behaviours, and operative irrational beliefs involved in their emotional episodes. Brighter clients may often be able to learn how to independently analyse their upsets through the counsellor's use of Socratic questioning, and may require fewer didactic explanations. In our own practices, however, we will generally employ a didactic presentation of the ABC model at some early point in the counselling process, rather than assuming that clients will pick it up indirectly.

Given that rational-emotive counselling has a psychoeducational focus, it is important for counsellors to take steps to ensure that clients grasp the material they are trying to teach them. One way to accomplish this is to ask clients periodically to convey their understanding of critical points that have been covered. This can be tactfully done when counsellors use questions such as the following: 'We've been discussing how you don't have to rate yourself as either a good or a bad person, but I want to be sure I've been expressing myself clearly. Can you restate to me – in your own words – what you've understood me to be saying?'

In addition to utilising periodic checking, counsellors are advised to avoid jumping from problem to problem within any given counselling session. Remaining focused on one problem at a time (and covering the essential steps of the counselling sequence) is usually the best means for teaching clients the elements of rational-emotive problem-solving.

By the end of the beginning stage of counselling, clients should have learned the three main insights of RET. They will also have had some initial experience in identifying and disputing the irrational beliefs that underpin their emotional problems. Counsellors will also have introduced clients to the concept of homework assignments, which will serve as an important vehicle for facilitating client movement from intellectual to emotional rational insight as counselling continues. Bibliotherapy assignments (which involve suggesting that clients obtain and read some of the relevant RET self-help texts) given at an early point in counselling can often help clients to become accustomed to the idea of devoting time and effort to working on their problem areas between sessions.

Dealing with Client Doubts

During the beginning stage of counselling, some clients may express doubts as to whether the rational-emotive approach will be able to help them solve their own particular set of emotional problems. In responding to these expressed doubts, the counsellor is advised to first assess and correct any misunderstandings about the approach that a given client may have. If the client still appears doubtful after this intervention, the counsellor can suggest that she try a brief 'trial' of counselling (consisting of five or so sessions) as a means for determining through direct experience whether she finds the rational-emotive approach helpful. At the end of this trial counsellor and client can review and discuss any remaining doubts that the client may have. If the client still maintains strong doubts at this point, it may be wise to make a judicious referral to another mental health professional who practises an alternative form of counselling. Such a referral would take into account the client's views concerning the type of counselling approach most likely to promote therapeutic gains.

It should be noted that some clients may harbour doubts about counselling because they are confusing the rational-emotive approach with the counsellor's interactional style. Thus, it can be important for counsellors to make enquiries which will help them to determine whether client objections are focused on issues pertaining to the counselling or the counsellor. If a given client is having a negative reaction to the counsellor's style of interaction within sessions, an appropriate modification in style may resolve this issue so that counselling may proceed.

THE MIDDLE STAGE

As clients move into the middle stage of counselling, they may experience some initial success in disputing their irrational beliefs and dealing with particular episodes of emotional disturbance. At the same time, however, they may begin to see that their irrational beliefs are deeply entrenched and that they adversely affect a number of different areas of their functioning. In a related vein, they may find that it is difficult to work in a consistent and determined manner at modifying the thinking habits that contribute to their psychological problems. Thus, the middle stage of counselling presents the rational-emotive practitioner with a number of significant challenges germane to promoting continued therapeutic progress. The sections that follow will provide guidelines for counsellors to follow as they attempt to facilitate client movement from intellectual to emotional rational insight.

Dealing with Multiple Problem Areas

Typically, clients present more than one problem area during a course of counselling. In some cases these multiple problem areas will be identified and targeted for change at an early point in the counselling process. Frequently, however, new problem areas will emerge as counselling proceeds. This can occur for several reasons:

1 The client develops a level of trust in the counsellor such that she becomes comfortable in disclosing problems previously considered 'too embarrassing' for discussion.
2 The client develops an awareness of how particular irrational beliefs are adversely affecting a number of different areas of her life.
3 The client experiences additional unfortunate activating events during the course of counselling (such as the loss of a job) that serve to trigger 'new' upsets.

Rational-emotive counsellors prefer to deal with a particular problem area until the client is able to cope with it reasonably well. It will sometimes happen, however, that during the course of working on one problem area, the client wishes to change the focus to another problem area that is experienced as more pressing or important. Alternatively, circumstances may arise which lead the counsellor to wonder whether a change in tack would be desirable from a therapeutic perspective. When confronted with such situations, counsellors will find it useful to have a set of guidelines to which they can refer in deciding whether to switch to discussion of the new problem area.

First, it is important to consider the effect that persisting with treatment of the original problem area will have on the therapeutic alliance. If a client maintains a strong desire to switch to a new problem area after the counsellor has presented a rationale for staying with the original problem until it is resolved, it may be wise to accede to the client's preference and begin to work on the new problem. To do otherwise could communicate the unfortunate message that the counsellor is more interested in following his or her own agenda than in responding to the client's concerns. This, of course, could damage the working relationship between counsellor and client.

Second, clients will sometimes experience crisis situations during the course of counselling which serve as triggers for new, additional upsets. When this occurs, efforts to resolve the original targeted problem may temporarily become irrelevant until the new upset has been dealt with. To cite an example, a given counsellor/client dyad may have been working to help the client overcome the feelings of anger and hurt he typically experiences in the face of his wife's harsh criticisms. While attending to this problem area, the client loses his job and makes himself depressed through negative self-rating and self-pity. As this depression significantly interferes with a number of areas of this client's functioning (including his ability to engage in the immediate task of job-hunting), it is appropriate for the counsellor to shift attention away from the original problem in order to focus attention to the new problem area. When the new problem area has received adequate treatment (such that the client is able to manage his depressed moods and function more effectively), counsellor and client may decide to return to their work on the original problem area.

Third, counsellors may see that it is advisable to switch attention to a 'new' emotional problem that the client is experiencing when it becomes apparent that this upset is impeding the client's ability to concentrate on the original problem area under consideration. In such a situation it would make little sense to continue working on the original problem area, as the client is not in a state to benefit from such efforts. Again, counsellor and client may decide to put aside their work on the original problem until the client is able to cope reasonably well with the new one.

Finally, there may be some circumstances in which it becomes evident to the counsellor that the client has an ongoing problem – currently not the focus of treatment – that pervades numerous areas of her life. Here, the counsellor may wish to suggest to the client that they shift their attention to this other problem area. A given client may, for instance, exhibit problematic drinking behaviour that interferes with her functioning at work and within her interpersonal relationships. Conceivably, however, she might not regard her drinking as being central to many of the difficulties she encounters and could express a preference to work on a more circumscribed area of her functioning (e.g., being more assertive with co-workers). It would be wise in such a situation for her counsellor to bring to her attention the way in which her drinking negatively affects numerous areas of her life, and to present a rationale for working to modify this behaviour. In this scenario, counsellor and client could proceed to work at identifying and disputing the irrational beliefs that contribute to episodes of overdrinking, and later attend (if necessary) to other, more circumscribed problem areas of concern to the client.

Whenever counsellor and client switch from one problem area to another, it is important for the counsellor to encourage the client to maintain a focus on this new problem until a coping criterion has been attained. Frequent jumping from problem to problem is likely to interfere with the counselling process, as it will make it difficult for clients to learn the emotional problem-solving techniques that are part and parcel of RET.

Occasionally, counsellors will encounter a client who tries to touch upon numerous problem areas during any given session, as opposed to focusing on only one or two. If a counsellor presents a rationale for dealing with one problem at a time but the client persists in this pattern, it may be appropriate for the counsellor to exercise flexibility on this issue in order to avoid endangering the therapeutic alliance. In some cases, however, the client's frequent switching can represent avoidance behaviour. Some individuals, for instance, will try to get on to a different topic when they begin to experience strong negative emotions during the course of discussing a particular problem area. If this occurs frequently, the counsellor may choose to bring it to the client's attention as another problem area to work on. Again, it is incumbent upon the counsellor to exercise an appropriate degree of flexibility with respect to the issue of switching problems, and to recognise that it may be quite difficult for some clients to face and deal with their dysfunctional avoidance of upsetting feelings.

Identifying Core Irrational Beliefs

As counsellors work with clients on the various problem areas targeted for intervention within counselling, they are advised to watch for common themes among the irrational beliefs that underpin these problems. By looking for common themes, counsellors can often identify core irrational beliefs to which clients subscribe. When core irrational beliefs are identified, it becomes possible to show clients that various problem areas (perhaps previously regarded by clients as being largely independent of one another) have similar underlying cognitive dynamics. During the middle stage of counselling, these core irrational beliefs – as opposed to specific problems – can receive more attention with respect to therapeutic exploration.

To illustrate the usefulness of identifying and dealing with core irrational beliefs, consider the case of a client who presents for counselling with complaints of non-assertiveness with friends and family, anxiety in social situations, and an unsatisfying marital relationship. As counselling with this individual proceeds, it is possible that her counsellor will identify the following irrational belief as being central to her problem areas: 'I *must* have the approval of others in order to consider myself a worthwhile person'. With respect to her non-assertiveness with friends and family, this irrational belief may make it difficult for her to refuse unreasonable requests for favours out of fear that significant others will reject her. With regard to her social anxiety, her *must* may result in worries about saying or doing 'the wrong thing' in interpersonal situations. As concerns her unsatisfying relationship with her husband, her irrational belief may cause her to make unreasonable efforts to please him while sacrificing her own set of wants and preferences.

Once this client's counsellor has assembled a reasonable body of evidence to support the hypothesis that a particular irrational belief is at the root of many of her interpersonal difficulties, she can be shown the common theme that runs through her problem areas. This insight can help the client to have a better understanding of her own individual psychology, and can simplify the work of counselling for her to a considerable degree. Now, instead of working on the 'separate' areas of non-assertiveness, shyness and an unsatisfying marriage, she can focus her efforts on overcoming her self-created need for others' approval.

With respect to the process of identifying themes across problems, counsellors are cautioned to guard against assuming that all of a client's problems can be explained with reference to a single irrational belief. In our experience, it is more typically the case that clients will subscribe to two or three core irrational beliefs. As a potentially helpful rule of thumb, counsellors are advised to bear in mind that RET identifies two broad categories of disturbance: ego disturbance and discomfort disturbance.

Since it is relatively rare for clients to present for counselling with only one of these two categories of disturbance, counsellors can remain alert to manifestations of both forms. They can then work to identify the central irrational beliefs that underpin the manifestations of these two forms of disturbance for a particular client.

Encouraging Clients to Engage in Relevant Tasks

A primary task for counsellors during the middle stage of counselling is to assist clients in approaching emotional rational insight by encouraging them to strengthen their conviction in their rational beliefs. As noted previously, emotional rational insight – as opposed to intellectual rational insight – is likely to lead to significant emotional and behavioural changes for clients.

There is a variety of cognitive, behavioural and imagery techniques used within rational-emotive counselling to help clients move from intellectual to emotional rational insight. Although counsellors may initiate the use of some of these techniques, it is important that by the middle stage of counselling clients see the role that *they* can play in promoting the change process. In particular, they need to see the usefulness of working hard to overcome their problems outside counselling sessions via homework assignments. Thus, by this stage of counselling, counsellors should have presented clients with a plausible rationale for homework assignments and should also have dealt with any objections or questions that clients may have had about undertaking such assignments.

Some clients will show that they understand the importance of their own efforts and homework assignments within counselling, but will harbour doubts about their ability to execute relevant tasks (i.e., those that will promote emotional rational insight) outside sessions. Counsellors can respond to these doubts in a number of different ways.

First, counsellors can work collaboratively with clients to design homework assignments that they are willing to do. Novice rational-emotive counsellors will sometimes make the error of pushing behavioural 'flooding' homework assignments on clients, since they know that RET views such assignments as representing the most efficient vehicle for promoting swift and meaningful modifications of irrational beliefs. Many clients will, however, make themselves anxious when they think about enacting flooding assignments, and will thus avoid doing them. As an example, a counsellor might insist that an agoraphobic client take on the exercise of spending an afternoon alone at a shopping mall, as a means for powerfully countering the client's self-created needs for security and comfort. The client may very well avoid implementing this assignment because the mere image of being in a crowded store (in combination with the irrational belief, 'I *must* feel emotionally comfortable at all times') leads to anxiety. Rather than suggesting assignments that clients are unlikely to implement because of the emotional obstacles they create for themselves, counsellors can work with them to design homework activities that are 'challenging but not overwhelming'. Here, clients are encouraged to take on assignments involving behaviours not currently engaged in with frequency or complete ease (that are thus 'challenging'), but that are not regarded as too difficult or threatening (i.e., 'overwhelming'). With reference to the example described above, the counsellor could work with the client to design a homework assignment – such as going to a neighbourhood shop to complete a quick errand – that may stand a better chance of being completed. In the process of designing this assignment the counsellor can explain that tasks involving some degree of difficulty are more likely to facilitate the process of belief change.

As a second means of dealing with clients' doubts concerning their ability to execute homework assignments, counsellors can help clients to practise implementation of these assignments within counselling sessions. Certain behavioural assignments can be readily rehearsed within sessions, such as assertively requesting a rise in pay from one's employer. With other types of assignments – such as certain shame-attacking exercises – rehearsal of the behaviours involved would be more difficult. In such cases, however, the counsellor can help the client to rehearse the assignment in imagery. Whether an assignment is practised through overt behaviour or imagery, the counsellor can use the rehearsal to assist the client in identifying emotional 'trouble spots' (i.e., points at which the client might create anxiety or some other upset for herself) in advance of actual implementation, and can then devote time to dealing with the irrational beliefs responsible for these upsets.

A third way of increasing the likelihood of homework enactment is for counsellors to work with clients to identify when, where and how particular homework assignments will be implemented. Although this would seem to be a rather minimal standard of practice in the design of homework assignments, our experiences as counselling supervisors suggest that it is often neglected by even the more experienced RET practitioners. A fairly large number of clients (particularly those who have difficulty in keeping themselves organised) will fail to do homework assignments because they do not plan when they will fit them into their weekly schedules. Counsellors can prompt clients to do such planning by simply asking them on what days, and at what times of day, they will engage in homework activities. In addition, counsellors can establish with clients the place or context within which homework assignments will be implemented, and can make sure that they are aware in advance of all the component steps that may be involved in the completion of a particular assignment.

It is also important that homework assignments be of a practical nature, meaning that clients are able to implement them without experiencing a great deal of inconvenience. Many individuals in counselling may be highly motivated to work at overcoming their disturbance; the fact remains, however, that they also have daily lives to attend to. The tasks of daily living can take up a good part of the day, and will impose limits on the amounts of time and effort that clients will be able (and willing) to devote to counselling-related activities. As such, homework assignments that require extraordinary investments of time, money or energy will stand a much lower chance of completion.

Given the central place of homework assignments within rational-emotive counselling, it is important for counsellors to check up on clients' experiences in executing them. Failure to follow-up on homework assignments may indirectly communicate the unfortunate message that such activities are not so significant a part of the change process.

With respect to thoroughgoing follow-up on homework assignments, counsellors will want to keep the following suggestions in mind:

1 Make an enquiry as to what the client learned through enactment of the assignment. Is this learning beneficial in terms of countering an irrational belief that the client holds, or will it serve to somehow reinforce the client's irrational thinking?
2 Reinforce the client's success in enacting the homework assignment. If the assignment was not successfully implemented (e.g., the client did only part of it), then recognise and reinforce any efforts that *were* made to complete it.
3 Identify and deal with the client's reasons for not attempting or completing the homework assignment (see Appendix I). Help the client to identify and dispute any irrational beliefs that may have been involved here.
4 If appropriate, encourage the client to try the assignment again if she was not fully successful with it. Even if the criterion for success was attained, bear in mind that repetition of particular homework activities can be helpful.

As a final note, it is recommended that counsellors assess the reasons for the apparently therapeutic changes that clients may report. In some cases, clients may enact homework assignments and describe seemingly positive changes in their usual patterns of behaviour that occur for the 'wrong' (i.e., non-therapeutic) reasons. As an example, a young male client seen by JY [Joseph Yankura] reported at one point during his counselling that he was no longer fearful about approaching and starting conversations with women. Upon enquiry, it was learned that he had adopted the following attitude as a means for countering his approval anxiety: 'If they reject me, it doesn't mean that I'm a loser, it means that *they* are losers'. Although the first part of this statement may be logically and empirically correct, the second part is irrational as it embodies a person-rating philosophy. Conceivably, such a philosophy could lead this individual to reject other people too readily.

Dealing with Obstacles to Change

A number of significant obstacles to change may be encountered during the middle stage of counselling. Clients may, for instance, have had some success at this point in terms of disputing their irrational beliefs, but will typically experience recurrences of their emotional problems. This is because they are still in the process of approaching emotional rational insight. When clients bring a philosophy of low frustration tolerance (LFT) to bear upon their failure to remain free of upsets, they may block themselves from persisting with their efforts to internalise a new rational philosophy. Here, it is important for counsellors to help their clients to identify and dispute the beliefs that produce their LFT. Such beliefs may take numerous forms, including 'Change must not be difficult' and 'I shouldn't have to work so hard in counselling'.

Also, it is important to note that change itself can be an uncomfortable experience for clients. Maultsby (1984) has described a state which he refers to as *cognitive-emotional dissonance*, in which clients experience feelings of 'strangeness' as they work to strengthen their conviction in their irrational beliefs. Counsellors can encourage their clients to accept such feelings as being a natural part of the change process, and if necessary can dispute their irrational demands to feel natural and comfortable all of the time.

A minority of clients will develop a state of 'pseudo-rationality', which can interfere with their ability to effect meaningful emotional and behavioural changes in their lives. Such clients become avid consumers of rational-emotive books and audiotapes, and make themselves extremely knowledgeable about RET's theory and practice. They can quote extensively from the RET literature and are able to give all the 'right' answers to counsellors' disputing questions during sessions, but fail to put their knowledge into practice between sessions. Such lack of effort may again be attributable to a philosophy of low frustration tolerance; alternatively, it may stem from the erroneous belief that intellectual insight is sufficient to bring about lasting changes. In either case, counsellors need to help clients to challenge and change the attitudes that block them from working to approach emotional rational insight.

Counsellors may sometimes encounter bright, achievement-oriented clients who are able to understand the B–C connection, but who nevertheless evince a reluctance to surrender their musts. With such clients, an enquiry may reveal that they view their musts as an important source of motivation for achieving their goals, and that they worry that giving up their musts will lead them into apathy and inertia. Counsellors can emphasise the distinction between strong desires and absolutistic demands with these clients, and can show them that their strong desires will provide sufficient motivation for working towards attainment of the goals they value. Further, they can be shown particular ways in which their musts create emotional obstacles that may function to block goal attainment.

The material presented in this section is intended to highlight some of the obstacles to client progress that are particularly germane to the middle stage of counselling.

Encouraging Clients to Maintain and Enhance their Gains

It is usually the case that clients will display the greatest variability in their rates of progress during the middle stage of counselling. They will at times appear to make significant gains with respect to approaching emotional rational insight; they will, however, also experience periodic backsliding. During this stage, counsellors need to help their clients to deal with set-backs, maintain the progress they have made, and explore ways to enhance their therapeutic gains. Ellis (1984) has written an excellent pamphlet on these issues which is reproduced below, with minor modifications. It can be helpful for counsellors to provide clients with a copy of this handout when the issues it covers become salient during the course of counselling.

How to Maintain your Improvement

1 When you improve and then fall back to old feelings of anxiety, depression, or self-downing, try to remind yourself and pinpoint exactly what thoughts, feelings, and behaviours you once changed to bring about your improvement. If you again feel depressed, think back to how you previously used rational-emotive principles to make yourself undepressed. For example, you may remember that:
   (a) you stopped telling yourself that you were worthless and that you couldn't ever succeed in getting what you wanted;
   (b) you did well in a job or in a love affair and proved to yourself that you did have some ability and that you were lovable;
   (c) you forced yourself to go to interviews instead of avoiding them and thereby helped yourself overcome your anxiety about them.

   Remind yourself of thoughts, feelings and behaviours that you have changed and that you have helped yourself by changing.
2 Keep thinking, thinking and thinking rational beliefs or coping statements, such as: 'It's great to succeed but I can fully accept myself as a person and enjoy life considerably even when I fail!' Don't merely parrot these statements but go over them carefully many times and think them through until you really begin to believe and feel that they are true.
3 Keep seeking for, discovering, and disputing and challenging your irrational beliefs with which you are once again upsetting yourself. Take each important irrational belief – such as, 'I have to succeed in order to be a worthwhile person!' – and keep asking yourself: 'Why is this belief true?', 'Where is the evidence that my worth to myself, and my enjoyment of living, utterly depends on my succeeding at something?', 'In what way would I be totally unacceptable as a human if I failed at an important task or test?'

   Keep forcefully and persistently disputing your irrational beliefs wherever you see that you are letting them creep back again. And even when you don't actively hold them, realise that they may arise once more, bring them to your consciousness, and preventively – and vigorously! – dispute them.

4 Keep risking and doing things that you irrationally fear – such as riding in elevators, socialising, job hunting or creative writing. Once you have partly overcome one of your irrational fears, keep acting against it on a regular basis. If you feel uncomfortable in forcing yourself to do things that you are unrealistically afraid of doing, don't allow yourself to avoid doing them – and thereby to preserve your discomfort for ever! Often, make yourself as uncomfortable as you can be, in order to eradicate your irrational fears and to become unanxious and comfortable later.

5 Try to see clearly the difference between rational negative feelings – such as those of sorrow, regret and frustration, when you do not get some of the important things you want – and unhealthy negative feelings – such as those of depression, anxiety, self-hatred and self-pity, when you are deprived of desirable goals and plagued with undesirable things. Whenever you feel *over*concerned (panicked) or *unduly* miserable (depressed) acknowledge that you are having a statistically normal but a psychologically unhealthy feeling and that you are bringing it on yourself with some dogmatic *should*, *ought* or *must*. Realise that you are invariably capable of changing your irrational (or *must*urbatory) feelings back into rational (or preferential) ones. Take your depressed feelings and work on them until you *only* feel sorry and regretful. Take your anxious feelings and work on them until you *only* feel concerned and vigilant. Use rational-emotive imagery to imagine unpleasant activating events vividly even before they happen: let yourself feel unhealthily upset (anxious, depressed, enraged or self-downing) as you imagine them; then work on your feelings to change them to healthy emotions (concern, sorrow, annoyance or regret) as you keep imagining some of the worst things happening. Don't give up until you actually do change your feelings.

6 Avoid self-defeating procrastination. Do unpleasant tasks fast – today! If you still procrastinate, reward yourself with certain things that you enjoy – for example, eating, vacationing, reading and socialising – only *after* you have performed the tasks that you easily avoid. If this won't work, give yourself a severe penalty – such as talking to a boring person for 2 hours or burning a $100 bill – every time that you procrastinate.

7 Show yourself that it is an absorbing challenge and something of an adventure to maintain your emotional health and to keep yourself reasonably happy no matter what kind of misfortunes assail you. Make the uprooting of your misery one of the most important things in your life – something you are utterly determined to steadily work at achieving. Fully acknowledge that you almost always have some choice about how to think, feel and behave: and throw yourself actively into making that choice for yourself.

8 Remember – and use – the three main insights of rational-emotive counselling:
Insight no. 1: you largely *choose* to disturb yourself about the unpleasant events of your life, although you may be encouraged to do so

by external happenings and by social learning. You mainly feel the way you think. When obnoxious and frustrating things happen to you at point A (activating events), you consciously or unconsciously *select* rational beliefs that lead you to feel sad and regretful and you also *select* irrational beliefs that lead you to feel anxious, depressed and self-hating.

Insight no. 2: no matter how or when you acquired your irrational beliefs and your self-sabotaging habits, you now, in the present, *choose* to maintain them – and that is why you are now disturbed. Your past history and your present life conditions importantly *affect* you; but they don't *disturb* you. Your present *philosophy* is the main contributor to your *current* disturbance.

Insight no. 3: there is no magical way for you to change your personality and your strong tendencies to needlessly upset yourself. Basic personality change requires persistent *work and practice* – yes, *work and practice* – to enable you to alter your irrational beliefs, your unhealthy feelings and your self-destructive behaviours.

9 Steadily – and unfrantically! – look for personal pleasures and enjoyments – such as reading, entertainment, sports, hobbies, art, science and other vitally absorbing interests. Take as your major life goal not only the achievement of emotional health but also that of real enjoyment. Try to become involved in a long-term purpose, goal, or interest in which you can remain truly absorbed. For a good, happy life will give you something to live *for*, will distract you from many serious woes; and will encourage you to preserve and to improve your mental health.

10 Try to keep in touch with several other people who know something about RET counselling and who can help go over some of its aspects with you. Tell them about problems that you have difficulty coping with and let them know how you are using rational-emotive principles to overcome these problems. See if they agree with your solutions and can suggest additional and better kinds of disputing methods that you can use to work against your irrational beliefs.

11 Practice using rational-emotive methods with some of your friends, relatives and associates who are willing to let you try to help them with it. The more often you use it with others, and are able to see what their irrational beliefs are and to try to talk them out of these self-defeating ideas, the more you will be able to understand the main principles of RET counselling and to use them with yourself. When you see other people act irrationally and in a disturbed manner, try to figure out – with or without talking to them about it – what their main irrational beliefs probably are and how these could be actively and vigorously disputed.

12 When you are in rational-emotive counselling try to tape record many of your sessions and listen to these carefully when you are in between sessions, so that some of the rational-emotive ideas that you learned in counselling sink in. After counselling has ended, keep these tape

recordings and play them back to yourself from time to time, to remind you how to deal with some of your old problems or new ones that may arise.

13 Keep going back to the rational-emotive reading and audiovisual material from time to time, to keep reminding yourself of some of the main rational-emotive findings and philosophies.

How to Deal with Backsliding

1 Accept your backsliding as normal – as something that happens to almost all people who at first improve emotionally and who then fall back. See it as part of your human fallibility. Don't feel ashamed when some of your old symptoms return, and don't think that you have to handle them entirely by yourself and that it is wrong or weak for you to seek some additional sessions of counselling and to talk to your friends about your renewed problems.

2 When you backslide look at your self-defeating behaviour as bad and unfortunate, but work very hard at refusing to put yourself down for engaging in this behaviour. Use the highly important rational-emotive principle of refraining from rating *you*, your*self*, or your *being*, but of measuring your *acts*, *deeds* and *traits*. You are always a *person who* acts well or badly – and never a *good person* or a *bad person*. No matter how badly you fall back and bring on your old disturbances again, work at fully accepting yourself with this unfortunate or weak behaviour – and then try, and keep trying, to change your behaviour.

3 Go back to the ABCs of rational-emotive counselling and clearly see what you did to fall back to your old symptoms. At A (activating event), you usually experienced some failure or rejection once again. At rB (rational belief) you probably told yourself that you didn't *like* failing and didn't *want* to be rejected. If you only stayed with these rational beliefs, you would merely feel sorry, regretful, disappointed, or frustrated. But when you felt disturbed again, you probably then went on to some irrational beliefs (iBs) such as 'I *must* not fail! It's *horrible* when I do!' 'I *have to* be accepted, because if I'm not that makes me an *unlovable worthless person*!' Then, after convincing yourself of these iBs, you felt, at C (emotional consequence) once again depressed and self-downing.

4 When you find your irrational beliefs by which you are once again disturbing yourself, just as you originally used disputing (D) to challenge and surrender them, do so again – *immediately* and *persistently*. Thus, you can ask yourself: 'Why *must* I not fail? Is it really *horrible* if I do?' And you can answer: 'There is no reason why I *must* not fail, though I can think of several reasons why it would be highly undesirable. It's not *horrible* if I do fail – only distinctly *inconvenient*'. You can also dispute your other irrational beliefs by asking yourself, 'Where is it written that I *have* to be accepted? How do I become an *unlovable*, *worthless person* if I am rejected?' And you can answer: 'I never *have to be* accepted, though

I would very much *prefer* to be. If I am rejected, that makes me, alas, a *person who* is rejected this time by this individual under these conditions, but it hardly makes me an *unlovable*, *worthless person* who will always be rejected by anyone for whom I really care'.

5 Keep looking for, finding and actively and vigorously disputing your irrational beliefs which you have once again revived and that are now making you feel anxious or depressed once more. Keep doing this, over and over, until you build intellectual and emotional muscle (just as you would build physical muscle by learning how to exercise and then by *continuing* to exercise).

6 Don't fool yourself into believing that if you merely change your language you will always change your thinking. If you neurotically tell yourself: 'I *must* succeed and be approved' and you sanely change this self-statement to 'I *prefer* to succeed and be approved', you may still really be convinced: 'But I really *have to* do well and *have got to be* loved'. Before you stop your disputing and before you are satisfied with your answers to it (which in rational-emotive counselling we call E, or an effective philosophy), keep on doing it until you are *really* convinced of your rational answers and until your feelings of disturbance truly disappear. Then do the same thing many, many times – until your new E (effective philosophy) becomes hardened and habitual – which it almost always will if you keep working at arriving at it and re-instituting it.

7 Convincing yourself lightly or 'intellectually' of your new effective philosophy or rational beliefs often won't help very much or persist very long. Do so very *strongly* and *vigorously* and do so many times. Thus, you can *powerfully* convince yourself, until you really *feel* it: 'I do not *need* what I *want*! I never *have* to succeed, no matter how greatly I wish to do so! I *can* stand being rejected by someone I care for. It won't *kill* me – and I *still* can lead a happy life! *No* human is damnable and worthless – including and especially *me*!'

How to Generalise from Working on One Emotional Problem to Working on Other Problems

1 Show yourself that your present emotional problem and the ways in which you bring it on are not unique and that virtually all emotional and behavioural difficulties are created by irrational beliefs. Whatever your irrational beliefs are, moreover, you can overcome them by strongly and persistently disputing and acting against these irrational beliefs.

2 Recognise that you tend to have three major kinds of irrational beliefs that lead you to disturb yourself and that the emotional and behavioural problems that you want to relieve fall into one of these three categories:

   (a) 'I *must* do well and *have to* be approved by people whom I find important.' This irrational belief leads you to feel anxious, depressed, and self-hating; and to avoid doing things at which you may fail and avoiding relationships that may not turn out well.

(b) 'Other people *must* treat me fairly and nicely!' This irrational belief contributes to your feeling angry, furious, violent and over-rebellious.

(c) 'The conditions under which I live *must* be comfortable and free from major hassles!' This irrational belief tends to create your feelings of low frustration tolerance and self-pity, and sometimes those of anger and depression.

3 Recognise that when you employ one of these absolutist *musts* – or any of the innumerable variations on it that you can easily slide into – you naturally and commonly derive from them other irrational conclusions, such as:

(a) 'Because I am not doing as well as I *must*, I am an incompetent worthless individual!' (Self-damnation.)

(b) 'Since I am not being approved by people whom I find important, as I *have to be*, it's *awful* and *terrible*!' (Awfulising.)

(c) 'Because others are not treating me as fairly and as nicely as they *absolutely should* treat me, they are *utterly rotten people* and deserve to be damned!' (Other-damnation.)

(d) 'As the conditions under which I live are not that comfortable and as my life has several major hassles, as it *must* not have, I can't stand it! My existence is a horror!' (Can't-stand-it-itis.)

4 Work at seeing that these irrational beliefs are part of your *general* repertoire of thoughts and feelings and that you bring them to many different kinds of situations that are against your desires. Realise that in just about all cases where you feel seriously upset and act in a distinctly self-defeating manner you are consciously or unconsciously sneaking in one or more of these irrational beliefs. Consequently, if you get rid of them in one area and are still emotionally disturbed about something else, you can always use the same rational-emotive principles to discover your irrational beliefs in the new area and to eliminate them there.

5 Repeatedly show yourself that it is almost impossible to disturb yourself and to remain disturbed in any way if you abandon your absolutist, dogmatic *shoulds*, *oughts* and *musts*, and consistently replace them with flexible and unrigid (though still strong) *desires* and *preferences*.

6 Continue to acknowledge that you can change your irrational beliefs by rigorously (not rigidly!) using the scientific method. With scientific thinking, you can show yourself that your irrational beliefs are only theories or hypotheses – not facts. You can logically and realistically dispute them in many ways, such as these:

(a) you can show yourself that your irrational beliefs are self-defeating – that they interfere with your goals and your happiness. For if you firmly convince yourself: 'I *must* succeed at important tasks and *have to* be approved by all the significant people in my life', you will of course at times fail and be disapproved – and thereby inevitably make yourself anxious and depressed instead of sorry and frustrated;

(b) your irrational beliefs do not conform to reality – and especially do not conform to the facts of human fallibility. If you always *had* to succeed, if the universe commanded that you *must* do so, you obviously *would* always succeed. And of course you often don't! If you invariably *had* to be approved by others, you could never be disapproved. But obviously you frequently are! The universe is clearly not arranged so that you will always get what you demand. So although your desires are often realistic, your god-like commands definitely are not!;

(c) your irrational beliefs are illogical, inconsistent or contradictory. No matter how much you *want* to succeed and to be approved, it never follows that therefore you *must* do well in these (or any other) respects. No matter how desirable justice or politeness is, it never *has* to exist.

Although the scientific method is not infallible or sacred, it efficiently helps you to discover which of your beliefs are irrational and self-defeating, and how to use factual evidence and logical thinking to rid yourself of them. If you keep using scientific analysis, you will avoid dogma and set up your hypotheses about you, other people, and the world around you so that you always keep them open to change.

7 Try to set up some main goals and purposes in life – goals that you would like very much to reach but that you never tell yourself that you absolutely must attain. Keep checking to see how you are coming along with these goals; at times revise them; see how you feel about achieving them; and keep yourself goal-oriented for the rest of your days.

8 If you get bogged down and begin to lead a life that seems too miserable or dull, review the points made here and work at using them.Once again: if you fall back or fail to go forward at the pace you prefer, don't hesitate to return to counselling for some booster sessions.

Encouraging Clients to Become their Own Counsellors

During the beginning stage of counselling, the counsellor is quite active-directive with respect to helping the client to learn the ABCs of RET. In the middle stage of counselling this material needs to be reviewed, but the client should be encouraged to take the lead in applying it to problem areas.

Counsellors are advised to be active and directive when first discussing a particular problem area with a client, but to gradually decrease their activity level as a means to promote the client's own efforts and involvement. Here, the overall goal is to help the client to internalise the rational-emotive method for solving emotional problems. The counsellor thus encourages the client's attempts to identify troublesome emotions and behaviours, relate these to particular activating events, and identify operative irrational beliefs. The client would then be encouraged to dispute these irrational beliefs and to develop alternative, rational beliefs that can replace them. It is also important to prompt clients to look for links between problem areas, with the object of identifying and disputing core irrational beliefs.

Counsellors should increasingly utilise the Socratic questioning technique during the middle stage as a means of encouraging clients to do most of the work of counselling. Didactic teaching should be kept to a minimum. Short, probing questions can be used to promote independent thinking, and to decrease client dependence upon the counsellor's problem-solving skills. Thus, when a client discusses her experiences between sessions in dealing with a particular problem area, the counsellor may ask a sequence of questions such as the following:

'How did you feel when that happened?'
'What were you telling yourself to bring on that feeling?'
'How did you dispute that?'
'How did you block yourself from disputing that?'
'What rational belief could you use to replace that must?'
'How is that rational belief more (logical; realistic; helpful) than that irrational belief?'
'If you really believed that, then how would you tend to act?'
'Could you try that during the coming week?', etc.

Some clients may not respond well to a decrease in the counsellor's level of directiveness. A number of individuals may, for instance, be prone to form dependent relationships with their counsellors because they harbour doubts about their ability to function independently as emotional problem-solvers. Counsellors can attempt to deal with these doubts (e.g., by making reference to prior instances when the client in question successfully coped with a particular upset), and can present a rationale for increased independent effort. When a given client appears genuinely stuck with respect to dealing with a particular problem area, the counsellor can temporarily revert back to a more active-directive stance. As work on this problem area proceeds, the counsellor can then gradually return the responsibility for dealing with it back to the client. When clients respond successfully to decreased counsellor directiveness over several sessions, it can be appropriate to begin taking steps to work towards termination.

THE ENDING STAGE

The ending stage of the counselling process involves working towards the termination of regularly scheduled counselling sessions. Termination may be approached either by collaboratively decreasing the frequency of counselling sessions over time, or by setting a definite termination date. Although it is unrealistic to attempt to establish a perfect point at which termination should occur for a given client, it is possible to identify a number of general criteria that can be applied to termination decisions. These criteria are as follows:

1 The client has internalised RET's approach to emotional problem-solving and has made significant, healthy modifications to her personal philosophy.

2 The client has gone beyond dealing with her initial presenting problems such that other significant problem areas have been tackled as well.
3 Core irrational beliefs have been identified and disputed.
4 The client has developed confidence in her capacity to act as her own therapist.
5 Counsellor and client agree that termination is appropriate.

These criteria can be viewed as constituting an 'ideal outcome' within rational-emotive counselling. In reality, however, ideal outcomes are relatively rare and clients may often want to terminate before these criteria have been reached. It is thus important for counsellors to be aware of various sorts of scenario in which premature termination is a possibility, so that they can respond in an effective manner to these situations.

A number of clients will want to terminate counselling before they have made any real progress in identifying and disputing their irrational beliefs. This scenario can occur when clients' troublesome activating events fortuitously change for the better, so that they are no longer experiencing the upsets that may have contributed to their original decision to seek counselling. When clients leave counselling under such circumstances, they will probably be vulnerable to the same sort of upset in the future. Counsellors can make efforts to explain to them that they have not yet dealt with the philosophical underpinnings of their emotional problems, and can encourage them to remain in counselling as a means for militating against a recurrence of their disturbance. Here, it is noted that much useful work can be accomplished within rational-emotive counselling even when clients are not facing any immediate stressors. If clients are unresponsive to the provision of a rationale for continuing in counselling, counsellors can make it clear to them that they may return if their external circumstances take a turn for the worse and they once again create upsets for themselves.

A certain number of clients will state their desire to terminate counselling after having made some initial progress with respect to their original presenting problems. In this scenario a given client may feel that she has accomplished what she set out to accomplish, and she may regard her counselling as having been very helpful. Her counsellor, however, may see that she probably harbours particular core irrational beliefs which have not yet received formal attention within sessions. As such, it may be unlikely that this client will be able to generalise her rational-emotive counselling gains across problems and situations. Again, it would be appropriate for the counsellor to present a rationale for remaining in counselling, as it could still have much to offer this individual. Ellis's (1984) handout on generalisation and maintenance, reproduced above, could be used to supplement the counsellor's rationale, as it conveys the message that it is possible to make oneself generally less susceptible to emotional and behavioural difficulties. Should the client stand by her preference to discontinue counselling, the counsellor can extend an 'open invitation' to return when she feels that she would like to enhance her treatment gains.

Scenarios also occur in which the client has made some progress in overcoming her emotional problems as per the RET approach, but wishes to terminate formal sessions in order to pursue independent practice of self-counselling. Counsellors will generally want to be supportive of such a preference, although they may wish to engage the client in a discussion concerning the pros and cons of continued counselling contacts. In some instances, such discussion may reveal concerns or issues related to counselling (such as time-scheduling difficulties) that may be easily resolved. If such issues are not a part of the picture and the client maintains her desire to terminate formal contacts, the counsellor may still suggest a limited number of additional sessions that will be focused on facilitating the client's future efforts at self-counselling. The content of these sessions can include recommendations concerning relevant self-help books and audio-tapes, reiteration of rational-emotive strategies for emotional problem-solving, and attempts to help the client anticipate (and hence be better prepared to deal with) activating events that may serve as triggers for future upsets. Whether or not the client agrees to extra sessions, the counsellor can make it clear that it is perfectly appropriate to return for additional contacts when these are viewed as necessary.

In addition to being confronted with situations in which clients may want to terminate prematurely, counsellors will also occasionally encounter individuals who wish to continue counselling sessions beyond an appropriate point. Some clients who have made considerable progress, for instance, may still believe that they need the continued help of their counsellor in order to maintain their counselling gains. Such problems may become manifest when a given client is reluctant either to set a termination date or to decrease the frequency of sessions. When this is the case, the counsellor can work to identify and dispute any irrational beliefs that are in operation (e.g., 'I *must* have the ongoing support of my counsellor; I am incapable of coping on my own'), and can suggest to the client that she attempt an experiment to assess her coping capacity. This could involve helping her to specify the aspects of her life that she thinks she cannot cope with on her own, and then encouraging her to test this out as a homework assignment.

Other clients may be reluctant to terminate counselling because they do not want to lose the special sort of relationship they have developed with their counsellor. Here, it can be appropriate for the counsellor to identify and discuss any feelings of sadness that a client may have about the dissolution of the counselling relationship. It can be emphasised that, while such feelings may be negative in tone, they are an appropriate emotional response to the ending of a significant relationship. If the client believes that she should not have these somewhat painful feelings, the counsellor can encourage her to dispute this irrational belief as a means of helping her to accept this normal part of human experience.

Some counsellors may be unwilling to terminate the counselling relationship with clients who have shown considerable progress. These counsellors may believe that they need to have continued evidence of client progress in order to prove that they are competent practitioners and therefore worthwhile people. Needless to say, it would be highly desirable for such counsellors to identify and challenge their competency needs by using the methods of rational-emotive counselling outlined in this book.

As a final note, counsellors may want to consider building in well spaced out follow-up sessions after regularly scheduled counselling sessions have ended. These follow-up sessions can be used as a means to help clients monitor their future progress. In one respect there is no absolute end to the rational-emotive counselling process, as counsellors would want to encourage their clients to contact them for further assistance when they encounter prolonged difficulties in practising self-counselling.

A Typical Case of Rational-Emotive Counselling

The following account describes a case in which WD [Windy Dryden] was the counsellor.

Mrs Haynes (pseudonym), at the time that I saw her, was a 35-year-old professional married woman who had recently discovered that her husband had been having an affair and had decided to leave her for the other woman. There were no children in this marriage. Mrs Haynes was referred to me for counselling by her general practitioner for depression and anxiety. In the initial session she made it clear to me that she did not want to involve her husband in counselling but rather she wanted an opportunity to focus on her own problems. She further did not think that joining a group would give her sufficient time or privacy to discuss her problems in as much depth as she considered to be most productive for her. We thus decided on a course of individual rational-emotive counselling.

In the initial session, I asked Mrs Haynes to describe her prior experiences with counselling. She reported having had a previous spell of individual counselling with a marriage counsellor who, from her description, appeared to practise a kind of non-directive psychoanalytically oriented counselling. She felt that she did not benefit from this approach, mainly because she was confused and put off by the counsellor's passivity and seeming lack of active involvement. I gave her a thumbnail sketch about what she might realistically expect from rational-emotive counselling, and her initial reaction was favourable. We agreed to meet initially for five sessions. I like to make an initial time-limited contract to enable clients to make a more informed decision about whether or not they think that they will benefit from rational-emotive counselling.

Mrs Haynes saw depression as more of a pressing problem for her than anxiety, and it was the one that she chose to make a start on. Her problem list revealed that she was particularly depressed about her own failure to make her marriage work and blamed herself for her husband's preference for another woman. I helped her to see that it was not his preference for another woman that made her depressed, but her belief about the situation which was, 'I must make my marriage work and I am a failure if I don't!' Before proceeding to help her to dispute this belief in the initial session, I worked patiently with her to enable her to see the connections between A, B and C.

I only started to dispute her irrational belief when she said that she saw clearly that it was this belief that caused her depression rather than her husband leaving her, and that in order to overcome her depression she needed to change her belief. While disputing her belief I helped her to develop a list of self-disputes that she could ask herself in the coming week whenever she felt depressed about her presumed failure in marriage. I gave her a copy of *A New Guide to Rational Living* (Ellis and Harper, 1975) and suggested that in particular she read Chapter 2 ('You feel the way you think') and Chapter 11 ('Eradicating dire fears of failure'). I also offered her an opportunity to take away a tape of our session, which she accepted gratefully. She was thus exposed to the idea of working at homework assignments between sessions.

At the beginning of the following session I asked her for her reactions to both the tape and the reading material. It transpired from this that she had a positive response to both the tape and reading material and she commented that she particularly liked the method of bibliotherapy. Her depression had lifted considerably since our first session, and she was able to use her own self-disputes to come up with plausible answers. In order to reinforce her progress I asked her if she would find it helpful to use one of the written self-help forms that exist for this purpose, and showed her three. She decided to start off with the one which I invented. We first worked on an episode of depression – even though she had progressed on that since our initial session – after we had decided that it was better to get closure on her depression before we tackled her anxiety. We spent the rest of session two filling out this form and at the end I gave her a number of these forms and suggested that she read Chapter 15 of *A New Guide to Rational Living* ('Conquering anxiety') and to use such insights to fill in a form whenever she became anxious.

At the beginning of session three, she reported that she benefited from reading the chapter on anxiety, but had experienced some difficulty in zeroing in on the irrational beliefs which underpinned her own anxiety. Using the inference chaining procedure, I helped her to see that she was anxious about ever finding another man again and ending up an old spinster. As is typical in rational-emotive counselling, I encouraged her to assume the worst and to imagine that she was an old spinster and asked her for her feelings about that. Her reply was instructive: 'Oh God, I couldn't stand the thought of living like that'. I disputed her belief that she needed a man in her life in order to be happy and helped her to see that she could in fact gain a fair measure of happiness in her life being single even though she would prefer to be married and have a family. This led on to a discussion of her immediate anxiety, that is, her feeling that she could not go out on her own because this would be shameful.

Often feelings of shame are related to feelings of anxiety and, assuming this to be the case with Mrs Haynes, I helped her to see that she was saying: 'If I go out on my own then other people will think that I am alone and that would prove that I am worthless'. The rest of the session was spent putting this into ABCDE form using the self-help form. I then suggested that we try rational-emotive imagery as a bridge between changing her attitude in her mind's eye and putting into practice her new belief: 'I have every right to go out on my own and if other people look down on me, then I refuse to look down on myself'. Mrs Haynes had a great deal of difficulty in using rational-emotive imagery (Ellis's version) in the session, and between sessions three and four.

At the beginning of session four I went over the rational-emotive imagery and suggested instead that she say her new rational belief quite vigorously to herself. She was able to do this, first of all out loud and then internally and felt a mood shift which was much more profound than that she was able to achieve by using Ellis's version of rational-emotive imagery. Let me add that her feelings of depression were no longer considered by her to be a problem since session one.

At the end of session four we negotiated an assignment whereby she would go out socially on her own on two occasions, on one occasion to a local evening class and second to a dance hall, while vigorously repeating the rational self-coping statements we developed. This apparently was very helpful to Mrs Haynes, for she reported that she was able to go out on both occasions without undue anxiety. This was our fifth session, the last of our therapeutic contract and I discussed progress with Mrs Haynes and how she wished to proceed in the future. She said that she felt very pleased with her progress and wanted to continue to have sessions every two weeks rather than weekly. Under the circumstances, this appeared to be a reasonable way of approaching termination.

From sessions five to ten Mrs Haynes made great progress. She had a number of dates with men and was able to resist the sexual advances of two of them, which to her was a great stride because in the past she had had great difficulty saying 'No' to men and had for a period prior to her marriage been quite promiscuous, out of desperation rather than out of choice. Between sessions five and ten, I gave her *Why Do I Think I Am Nothing Without A Man* by Penelope Russianoff (1981) and *Living Alone and Liking It* by Lynn Shahan (1981) to read. She also continued to listen to the tapes of her sessions, although I suggested that she review them only once, rather than her accustomed three times, because I wished to encourage her to rely on her own resources rather than to rely on my direction, albeit secondhand, through the tapes. She also continued going out on her own and used vigorous self-disputing to increasingly good effect. It seemed apparent that she was experiencing success in becoming her own counsellor.

As counselling progressed to what I thought would be termination, Mrs Haynes got quite anxious. She said that she felt she had become quite dependent upon my help and was anxious about whether or not she could cope on her own. First of all I disputed her belief that she needed my help, and second, I encouraged her to view a break from counselling as an experiment and suggested a six-week gap between our tenth and eleventh sessions, stressing that she rely more on self-disputing rather than on bibliotherapy. I also suggested that she should not listen to any of the past tapes, so that we could conduct a fair experiment of her inference that she could not cope on her own.

The experiment proved to be a success because she came in and wondered why she even thought that she could not cope on her own, since she had managed the six-week gap very well. I commented that I was pleased with her progress, to which she replied: 'That's nice to know but even if you weren't, I am. I don't need your approval.' Having been firmly put in my place in this regard, we discussed whether she needed any future sessions and finally agreed that we would have a six-month follow-up, although I did suggest that she could contact me if she wanted to in the interim, on the condition that she used her own skills for a two-week period and if she could not cope with any emotional problems which came up in that period then she could contact me.

At the six-month follow-up session Mrs Haynes had attained and enhanced her therapeutic gains. She was productively involved in many social and voluntary activities and had ongoing casual relationships with three men, one of which included sex out of choice and not out of desperation. Her relationship with her husband was reasonably cordial and they were proceeding towards an amicable divorce. In my keenness to encourage her to cope on her own, I made the error of moving towards termination without helping her to anticipate future problems and encourage her to see that she could use her new coping methods to deal with these problems. Although this was an error at the time, Mrs Haynes was able to do this in the intervening period. In addition, I had to do very little work in helping her set goals for increased satisfaction since she was able to do this on her own.

Appendix I: Possible Reasons for not Completing Self-help Assignments

(To be completed by client)

The following is a list of reasons that various clients have given for not doing their self-help assignments during the course of counselling. Because the speed of improvement depends primarily on the amount of self-help assignments that you are willing to do, it is of great importance to pinpoint any reasons that you may have for not doing this work. It is important to look for these reasons at the time that you feel a reluctance to do your assignment or a desire to put off doing it. Hence, it is best to fill out this questionnaire at that time. If you have any difficulty in filling out this form and returning it to the counsellor, it might be best to do it together during a counselling session.

(Rate each statement by ringing 'T' (True) 'F' (False). 'T' indicates that you agree with it; 'F' means the statement does not apply at this time.)

1	It seems that nothing can help me so there is no point in trying.	T/F
2	It wasn't clear, I didn't understand what I had to do.	T/F
3	I thought that the particular method the counsellor had suggested would not be helpful. I didn't really see the value of it.	T/F
4	It seemed too hard.	T/F
5	I am willing to do self-help assignments, but I keep forgetting.	T/F
6	I did not have enough time. I was too busy.	T/F
7	If I do something the counsellor suggests I do it's not as good as if I come up with my own ideas.	T/F
8	I don't really believe I can do anything to help myself.	T/F
9	I have the impression the counsellor is trying to boss me around or control me.	T/F
10	I worry about the counsellor's disapproval. I believe that what I do just won't be good enough for him/her.	T/F
11	I felt too bad, sad, nervous, upset (underline the appropriate word(s)) to do it.	T/F
12	It would have upset me to do the homework.	T/F
13	It was too much to do.	T/F
14	It's too much like going back to school again.	T/F
15	It seemed to be mainly for the counsellor's benefit.	T/F
16	Self-help assignments have no place in counselling.	T/F
17	Because of the progress I've made these assignments are likely to be of no further benefit to me.	T/F
18	Because these assignments have not been helpful in the past, I couldn't see the point of doing this one.	T/F
19	I don't agree with this particular approach to counselling.	T/F
20	OTHER REASONS (please write them).	T/F

References

Beck, A.T., Rush, A.J., Shaw, B.F. and Emery, G. (1979) *Cognitive Therapy of Depression*. New York: Guilford.

Bordin, E.S. (1979) The generalizability of the psychoanalytic concept of the working alliance, *Psychotherapy: Theory, Research and Practice*, 16, 252–60.

Dryden, W. and Yankura, J. (1992) *Daring to be Myself: A Case Study in Rational-Emotive Therapy*. Buckingham: Open University Press.

Ellis, A. (1984) *How to Maintain and Enhance your Rational-Emotive Therapy Gains*. New York: Institute for RET.

Ellis, A. and Harper, R.A. (1975) *A New Guide to Rational Living*. North Hollywood, CA: Wilshire.

Lazarus, A.A. (1981) *The Practice of Multimodal Therapy*. New York: McGraw-Hill.

Maultsby, M.C., Jr (1984) *Rational Behavior Therapy*. Englewood Cliffs, NJ: Prentice-Hall.

Russianoff, P. (1981) *Why Do I Think I Am Nothing Without a Man?* New York: Bantam.

Shahan, L. (1981) *Living Alone and Liking It*. New York: Warner.

16

Compromises in Rational-Emotive Therapy

Windy Dryden

Introduction

In this chapter I will discuss the notion that while RET therapists prefer to encourage their clients to achieve a profound philosophical change by replacing their irrational beliefs with rational beliefs, this is not always possible. In such cases, RET therapists are advised to make various compromises in helping clients deal with their problems in ways which do not involve philosophical change. These alternative strategies are termed 'compromises' in that, while not ideal, they often bear more fruit than the preferred strategies of RET.

I should say at the outset that by RET in this chapter I mean those therapeutic activities which are designed to effect philosophical change – or what Ellis calls 'elegant', 'preferential' or 'specialised' RET. I personally consider that therapeutic activities which are designed to effect other kinds of change (e.g., inferentially based change, behaviourally based change or change in activating events) are best referred to as derived from other approaches to cognitive-behaviour therapy, although Ellis considers such activities to be part of 'inelegant', 'non-preferential' or 'general' RET. Because terms such as 'elegant' vs 'inelegant', 'preferential' vs 'non-preferential' etc. are value-laden and may offend other cognitively oriented practitioners, I prefer to avoid their use and thus distinguish between rational-emotive therapy and other forms of cognitive-behaviour therapy. This distinction is more likely, in my opinion, to promote constructive dialogue among cognitively oriented therapists than the one employed by Ellis (1980b).

Before discussing the various compromises that RET therapists sometimes are called upon to make, it is first important to distinguish between rational-emotive therapy and other approaches to cognitive-behaviour therapy.

Differences between Rational-Emotive Therapy and Other Approaches to Cognitive-Behaviour Therapy

As opposed to other approaches to cognitive-behaviour therapy, rational-emotive therapy:

1. Has a distinct philosophical emphasis which is one of its central features and which other forms of cognitive-behaviour therapy appear to omit. Thus, it stresses that humans appraise themselves, others and the world in terms of (a) rational, preferential, flexible and tolerant philosophies and in terms of (b) irrational, musturbatory, rigid, intolerant and absolutistic philosophies.
2. Has an existential-humanistic outlook which is intrinsic to it and which is omitted by most other approaches to cognitive-behaviour therapy. Thus, it sees people 'as holistic, goal directed individuals who have importance in the world just because they are human and alive; it unconditionally accepts them with their limitations, and it particularly focuses upon their experiences and values, including their self-actualizing potentialities' (Ellis, 1980b: 327). It also shares the views of ethical humanism by encouraging people to emphasise human interest (self and social) over the interests of deities, material objects and lower animals.
3. Favours striving for pervasive and long-lasting (philosophically based) rather than symptomatic change.
4. Attempts to help humans eliminate all self-ratings and views self-esteem as a self-defeating concept which encourages them to make conditional evaluations of self. Instead, it teaches people unconditional self-acceptance (Ellis, 1972).
5. Considers psychological disturbance to reflect an attitude of taking life 'too' seriously and thus advocates the appropriate use of various humorous therapeutic methods (Ellis, 1977, 1981).
6. Stresses the use of antimusturbatory rather than anti-empirical disputing methods. Because it considers that inferential distortions often stem from dogmatic musts, shoulds etc., rational-emotive therapy favours going to the philosophical core of emotional disturbance and disputing the irrational beliefs at this core, rather than merely disputing anti-empirical inferences which are more peripheral. Also rational-emotive therapy favours the use of forceful logico-empirical disputing of irrational beliefs whenever possible, rather than the employment of rationally oriented, coping self-statements. When feasible, rational-emotive therapy teaches clients how to become their own scientists instead of parroting therapist inculcated rational beliefs.
7. Gives a more central explanatory role to the concept of discomfort anxiety in psychological disturbance than do other cognitive-behavioural approaches to psychotherapy. Discomfort anxiety is defined as: 'emotional hypertension that arises when people feel (1)

that their life or comfort is threatened, (2) that they *must* not feel uncomfortable and have to feel at ease and (3) that it is awful or terrible (rather than merely inconvenient or disadvantageous) when they don't get what they supposedly must' (Ellis, 1980b: 331). While other cognitive-behavioural approaches to psychotherapy recognise specific instances of discomfort anxiety (e.g., 'fear of fear' – Mackay, 1984), they tend not to regard discomfort disturbance to be as centrally implicated in psychological problems as does rational-emotive therapy.

8 Emphasises, more than other approaches to cognitive-behaviour therapy, that humans frequently make themselves disturbed about their original disturbances. Thus, rational-emotive therapists actively look for secondary symptoms of disturbances and encourage clients to work on overcoming these before addressing themselves to the primary disturbance.

9 Has clear-cut theories of disturbance and its treatment, but is eclectic or multimodal in its techniques. However, it favours some techniques (e.g., active disputing) over others (e.g., cognitive distraction) and strives for profound philosophical change where feasible.

10 Discriminates between 'healthy' and 'unhealthy' negative emotions. Rational-emotive theory considers such negative emotions as sadness, annoyance, concern, regret and disappointment as 'healthy' affective responses to thwarted desires based on a non-devout philosophy of desires because they do not needlessly interfere with people's goals and purposes. However, it sees depression, anger, anxiety, guilt, shame/ embarrassment, self-pity and feelings of inadequacy usually as 'unhealthy' emotions based on absolutistic demands about thwarted desires. Rational-emotive therapy considers these latter feelings as symptoms of disturbance because they very frequently (but not always) sabotage people from pursuing constructively their goals and purposes. Other approaches to cognitive-behaviour therapy do not make such fine discriminations between 'healthy' and 'unhealthy' negative emotions.

11 Advocates therapists giving unconditional acceptance rather than giving warmth or approval to clients. Other cognitive-behaviour therapies tend not to make this distinction. Rational-emotive therapy holds that counsellor warmth and approval have their distinct dangers in that they may unwittingly encourage clients to strengthen their dire needs for love and approval. When RET therapists unconditionally accept their clients, they also serve as good role-models, in that they also help clients to accept themselves unconditionally.

12 Stresses the importance of the use of vigour and force in counteracting irrational philosophies and behaviours (Ellis, 1979a; Dryden, 1984). Rational-emotive therapy is alone among cognitive-behavioural approaches to psychotherapy in stressing that humans are, for the most part, biologically predisposed to originate and perpetuate their disturbances and often thus experience great difficulty in changing the

ideological roots of these problems. Because it holds this view, it urges both therapists and clients to use considerable force and vigour in interrupting clients' irrationalities.

13 Is more selective than most other cognitive-behaviour therapies in choosing behavioural change methods. Thus, it favours the use of penalisation in encouraging resistant clients to change. Often these clients will not change to obtain positive reinforcement, but may be encouraged to change to avoid stiff penalties. Furthermore, rational-emotive practitioners have reservations concerning the use of social reinforcement in psychotherapy. They consider that humans are too reinforceable and that they often do the right thing for the wrong reason. Thus, they may change to please their socially reinforcing therapists, but in doing so they have not been encouraged to think and act for their own sake. RET therapists aim to help clients become maximally non-conformist, non-dependent and individualistic and would thus use social reinforcement techniques sparingly. Finally, rational-emotive therapy favours the use of in vivo desensitisation and flooding methods rather than the use of gradual desensitisation techniques because it argues that the former procedures best help clients to raise their level of frustration tolerance (Ellis, 1983).

Thus, the major goal of rational-emotive therapy is an ambitious one: to encourage clients to make a profound philosophical change in the two main areas of ego disturbance and discomfort disturbance. This involves helping clients, as far as humanly possible, to give up their irrational beliefs and to replace these with rational beliefs.

In summary, in rational-emotive therapy, the major goals are to help clients pursue their long-range basic goals and purposes and to help them do so as effectively as possible by fully accepting themselves and tolerating unchangeable uncomfortable life conditions. Rational-emotive practitioners further strive to help clients obtain the skills which they can use to prevent the development of future disturbance. In encouraging clients to achieve and maintain this profound philosophical change, rational-emotive therapists implement the following strategies. They help their clients see that:

1 Emotional and behavioural disturbances have cognitive antecedents and that these cognitions normally take the form of absolutistic irrational beliefs. RET therapists train their clients to observe their own psychological disturbances and to trace these back to their ideological roots.
2 People have a distinct measure of self-determination and can thus decide to work at undisturbing themselves. Thus, clients are shown that they are not slaves to their biologically based irrational thinking processes.
3 People can implement their choices and maximise their freedom by actively working at changing their irrational beliefs. This is best achieved

by employing cognitive, emotive and behavioural methods – often in quite a forceful and vigorous manner (Ellis, 1979b).

With the majority of clients, from the first session onwards, RET therapists are likely to use strategies designed to effect profound philosophical change. The therapist begins the process with the hypothesis that this particular client may be able to achieve such change and thus begins to implement rational-emotive methods which he or she will abandon after collecting sufficient data to reject this initial hypothesis. Rational-emotive practitioners regularly implement this viewpoint which is based on the notion that the client's response to therapy is the best indicator of his or her prognosis.

Compromises

When it is clear that the client is not able to achieve philosophical change, whether on a particular issue or in general, the rational-emotive therapist often uses other cognitive-behavioural methods to effect less 'profound' changes. Because in such cases, these methods yield better results for the client than can be achieved by standard rational-emotive methods, they are regarded as compromises yielding an outcome between no change, on the one hand, and profound philosophical change, on the other.

Inferentially Based Change

Inferentially based change occurs when clients do not change irrational beliefs but do succeed in correcting distorted inferences such as negative predictions, overly negative interpretations of events and of the behaviour of others etc.

A good example of such change was reported by a therapist of my acquaintance. He was working with a middle-aged woman who reported feeling furious every time her ageing father would telephone her and enquire 'Noo, what's doing?' She inferred that this was a gross invasion of her privacy and absolutistically insisted that he had no right to act in this way. The therapist initially intervened with the usual rational-emotive strategy by attempting to dispute this client's dogmatic belief and tried to help her see that there was no law in the universe which stated that he must not invade her privacy. Meeting initial resistance, the therapist persisted with different variations of this theme – all to no avail. Changing tack, he began to implement a different strategy designed to help the client question her inference that her father was actually invading her privacy. Given her father's age, the therapist enquired, was it not more likely that his question represented his usual manner of beginning telephone conversations rather than an intense desire to pry into her affairs? This enquiry proved successful in that the client's rage subsided because she began to re-interpret her father's motives.

Another example of inferentially based change occurred with one of my clients, Robert, who was anxious lest people would stare at him for spilling his drink. His hands would shake whenever he attempted to drink in public. I first employed the customary philosophically based RET strategy, encouraging him to assume the worst and imagine that people would actually stare at him when he spilled his drink. This yielded his irrational belief: 'If they stare at me, it would prove that I would be a worthless freak.' However, I could not encourage him to dispute this belief successfully and he still adhered strongly to it after my varied disputing efforts. Changing tack, I took him to several pubs and asked him to observe other people's reaction as I deliberately spilled drinks in public. From this, he came to realise that other people in general did not stare at me when I spilled my drinks and this helped him to change his own inference to: 'It is unlikely that most people will stare at me when I spill my drink.' This inferentially based change enabled him to order and consume drink in public and reduce his social anxiety, although he never did change his aforementioned irrational belief.

Interestingly, in both examples, although my fellow therapist and I returned to disputing our clients' irrational beliefs after helping them to modify their distorted inferences, we never succeeded in helping them to change these beliefs. However, some clients are more willing to re-evaluate their irrational beliefs after they have been helped to correct distorted inferences. Rational-emotive theory holds that irrational beliefs are the breeding ground for the development of negative inferences and thus, when clients succeed in changing their irrational beliefs, spontaneous reduction in the negativity of inferences will follow. However, these two examples show that inferentially based change can occur in the absence of philosophically based change.

Behaviourally Based Change

Behaviourally based change occurs when clients do not change irrational beliefs, but improve by effecting constructive changes in behaviour. Such behaviour change, in my experience, occurs when clients (1) replace dysfunctional behaviour with constructive behaviour and (2) acquire constructive patterns of behaviour which previously have been absent from their skill repertoire. An example of each follows.

Replacing Dysfunctional Behaviour with Constructive Behaviour Sylvia, a first year student, sought therapy for extreme examination anxiety. She predicted that she would fail her first year exams, demanded that she must pass them and concluded that should she fail, this would be the 'end of the world'. No amount of disputing her irrational beliefs yielded any therapeutic gain, so I shifted to her test-taking behaviour. I discovered that Sylvia approached an examination in the following way. She would choose to answer the first question that she knew anything about; she would write everything she knew about that question without first making an answer plan and would often only answer two out of four questions in the entire examination. It thus transpired that her inferences concerning failure were accurate rather than negatively distorted. My subsequent therapeutic approach focused on teaching Sylvia the following examination techniques: allocating sufficient time to answer all questions; analysing the wording of examination questions; making answer plans; answering all parts of a given question; and dealing with 'mind blank' experiences through cognitive distraction. With the help of her department, I arranged for Sylvia to take several 'mock' examinations so that she could practise her newly acquired skills with the result that she performed very well in these examinations. These experiences helped Sylvia to predict success in her 'end-of-year' examinations rather than failure. This led to a significant decrease in her examination anxiety. However, although Sylvia did in fact do very well in her exams, she still held the same irrational beliefs about failure as she did at the outset and did not want to focus on these later as she thought failure to be 'so unlikely that it's not worth considering'.

This example clearly shows that behaviour change often leads to inferentially based change.

Acquiring New Skills Mrs Anderson was referred to me with problems of anger and depression. Her husband and two teenage children expected her to go out to work, do all the housework without help and cater to their every whim. She had done this for several years, but had become increasingly angry and depressed. Her anger was based on the irrational belief that they must not treat her this way and her depression stemmed from the belief that she was no good for failing to please her family. Traditional rational-emotive disputing methods failed to yield any therapeutic gains so I shifted the focus of therapy to a discussion of assertion and the value of politely declining to do the bidding of her family. Through role-play methods it transpired that Mrs Anderson did not have assertive skills in her repertoire because she could only communicate in an aggressive and demanding manner. I thus trained her intensively in polite, negative assertive skills which she was able to put into practice with her family. Surprisingly her family responded quite well to her behaviour, began to share household tasks and made less demands upon her. The result was that Mrs Anderson's depressed mood lifted appreciably and she became far less angry. As in the other examples in this chapter, I returned to disputing her irrational belief as outlined above but again without success.

This example shows that a client's behavioural changes can sometimes elicit constructive behaviour from others leading to healthy changes in the interpersonal system of which the client is a part.

Changing Activating Events

I concluded the above example with the observation that a client's change in behaviour can promote healthy system-based change. However, this does not always occur. In a similar case to that described above, I had to involve the client's husband and children in therapy and encourage them to change their behaviour towards the depressed client, Mrs Curran, because her own assertive efforts did not on this occasion elicit constructive responses from her family members. Once they changed their behaviour towards Mrs Curran for the better, her mood lifted accordingly. Again disputing efforts aimed at helping Mrs Curran to re-evaluate her irrational beliefs, pre- and post-improvement, did not lead to philosophically based change.

In another example of helping clients by promoting changes in activating events, I helped Mr Brown to overcome his depression by encouraging him to change his vocation from accountancy to law. He was depressed because he believed: 'I have to enjoy my job in order to be happy.' No amount of disputing this belief yielded any therapeutic gain so I switched the focus of the sessions to exploring his vocational interests and aptitudes. This led Mr Brown to conclude that he would be happier working as a solicitor than as an accountant. Accordingly, he decided to go to law school. Years later, after he qualified as a solicitor, I met Mr Brown who had effected a successful career change. He still believed he had to be vocationally satisfied in order to be happy but since he was happy working in law he considered that there was no need to re-evaluate his irrational belief.

Challenging but Not Overwhelming: A Compromise in Negotiating Homework Assignments

Ellis (1983) has recently criticised the use of gradual approaches to helping clients overcome their emotional and behavioural problems. His argument is that the use of gradual methods in psychotherapy and behaviour therapy reinforces 'a philosophy that states or implies that (1) emotional change has to be brought about slowly and cannot possibly occur quickly or suddenly; (2) that it must be practically painless as it is occurring; and (3) that it cannot occur with the use of jarring, painful, flooding methods of therapy' (p. 142). Thus, psychotherapeutic gradualism is seen by Ellis as counter-therapeutic in that it basically reinforces clients' discomfort anxiety or philosophy of low frustration tolerance (LFT) which serve to perpetuate rather than ameliorate their problems. He thus prefers wherever possible the use of flooding or 'full-exposure' methods and homework assignments in RET, primarily because they help clients to overcome their discomfort anxiety and to raise their tolerance level for frustration.

However, 'wherever possible' is the important phrase to note here because not all clients will agree to execute flooding or 'full-exposure' homework assignments. That this should be the rational-emotive therapists' initial approach to negotiating homework assignments is not questioned here. In taking this stance, therapists should explain the rationale for this type of homework assignment, emphasise the benefits of such an approach and encourage clients to implement these assignments after thoroughly disputing clients' LFT ideas. What rational-emotive therapists are in fact saying is: 'Such methods are the most efficient means of helping you achieve your therapeutic goals.' It is not surprising that Ellis should recommend such assignments, given his belief in the value of efficiency in psychotherapy (Ellis, 1980c).

However, no matter how therapists try to encourage (or persuade) some clients to execute 'full-exposure' homework assignments, such clients steadfastly refuse to do so. In the face of such opposition, if therapists persist in their persuasive tactics, they will commit two therapeutic errors. First, they will threaten the therapeutic alliance between themselves and their 'resistant' clients. Bordin (1979) has noted that there are three major components of this alliance: goals, bonds and tasks. In such instances, the therapeutic alliance is likely to break down in the *task* domain. Although therapist and client may have a good collaborative relationship (effective bonds) and agree on the client's goals (shared goals), they disagree about the tasks that the client is prepared to do in order to achieve therapeutic goals. Second, such overtly persistent therapists serve as poor role-models because they tend to believe that clients *must* be 'efficient' in their approach to therapy and do 'full-exposure' assignments. Paradoxically, these therapists, by insisting that clients execute certain types of homework assignments, are in fact being inefficient themselves. A breakdown in the therapeutic alliance often leads to therapeutic impasses which in turn often lead to clients dropping out of treatment.

In such cases, what should therapists preferably do? There is no need to return to therapeutic gradualism, for there is another alternative which allows therapists and clients to effect a working compromise. Whenever I encounter clients who steadfastly refuse to execute 'full-exposure' homework tasks and prefer gradual assignments, I explain this therapeutic compromise. I invite them to choose assignments which are sufficiently *challenging* to discourage reinforcement of their philosophy of low frustration tolerance, but which are not *overwhelming* for them. I explain their choices as follows.

There are three ways you can overcome your fears. The first is like jumping in at the deep end. You expose yourself straight away to the situation you are most afraid of. The advantage here is that if you can learn that nothing terrible will happen then you will overcome your problems quite quickly. However, the disadvantage is that some people just can't bring themselves to do this and get quite discouraged as a result. The second way is to go very gradually. On the one hand, you only do something that you feel comfortable doing, while on the other, you don't really get an opportunity to face putting up with discomfort which, in my opinion, is a major feature of your problem. Also treatment will take much longer this way. The third way is what I call 'challenging but not overwhelming'. Here you choose an assignment which is sufficiently challenging for you to make progress but which would not be overwhelming for you at any given stage. Here you are likely to make progress more quickly than with the gradual approach but more slowly than with the 'deep end' approach.

I find that when clients are given an opportunity to choose their own rate of progress, the therapeutic alliance is strengthened. Most clients who refuse to execute 'full-exposure' assignments choose the 'challenging but not overwhelming' approach and only very rarely do they opt for gradual desensitisation therapy. When they do so I try to dissuade them and frequently succeed. In the final analysis, however, I have not found it productive to insist that clients choose a particular way of tackling problems that is against their preferences.

Case Example Mary, a 23-year-old, single woman came to therapy for help in overcoming her anxiety about eating in public. Typically she had both ego and discomfort anxiety-related beliefs (Ellis, 1979c, 1980a), and in the early sessions I helped her to identify and dispute such self-defeating attitudes as: 'I must not be anxious while eating'; 'If other people see me leave my food they will think I'm odd and I need their approval'; 'I am a shameful individual for having this problem'; 'There is something wrong with me because I have a small appetite' and 'I must not make a fuss and draw attention to myself'.

She claimed that her anxiety would be at its peak if she were faced with the prospect of not finishing her food in a crowded, fashionable restaurant. However, although she was successful at verbally disputing both ego and discomfort anxiety-related beliefs about this incident in therapy sessions, she could not initially conceive of putting this into practice in this particular setting even though I presented the rationale for 'full-exposure' homework assignments and emphasised the benefits that she would experience as a result. She literally could not imagine herself doing it (a good sign that such an experience would, in her terms, be too traumatic). She enquired whether there was not a painless method for overcoming her problems. I explained the dangers of such 'painless' methods and introduced her to the idea of 'challenging, but not overwhelming' tasks. She agreed, albeit with some reluctance, to select such an assignment. My hunch was that she would have terminated therapy if I had persisted in persuading her to expose herself fully to her anxieties. Over the following weeks she set herself and successfully executed the following 'challenging, but not overwhelming' tasks while disputing her salient irrational beliefs. These tasks were in temporal order:

1 Eating two squares of chocolate in a public eating place.
2 Eating a meal of fish and chips on her own in a crowded restaurant, full of strangers.
3 Eating out in a snack bar with her boyfriend.
4 Eating out with her parents in a semi-fashionable restaurant.
5 Eating out with her boyfriend in a fashionable restaurant.
6 Deliberately asking for smaller portions in a fashionable restaurant.

7 Eating out with a large group of friends in a very exclusive restaurant, sending back any portions that were too big.

As I have said, each task was seen by the client as 'sufficiently' challenging but not overwhelming and tasks (5), (6) and (7) were initiated by her in a planned break from therapy. This principle allows clients to take responsibility for their therapy quite early on, once they have fully understood it and experienced initial success. On follow-up, she was able to eat out in a variety of settings with a variety of people without anxiety.

Variations on a Theme While I have not used the 'challenging, but not overwhelming' principle in planning a hierarchy of assignments before treatment commences, it can be used in this way. I have not found this necessary because what clients find 'challenging but not overwhelming' changes over time so that the initial hierarchy becomes redundant. Theoretically, therapists could also use SUDS (subjective unit of distress scale) ratings of hierarchy and/or non-hierarchy items, although, again, I have not found this necessary.

While I have used this principle mainly in helping clients set appropriate challenging tasks to overcome their anxiety problems, I have also used it successfully in helping depressed clients set appropriately challenging behavioural tasks. In so doing I stress to clients the importance of defining what is challenging in personal terms in relation to their depressed state rather than in relation to their non-depressed state. The successful execution of small tasks deemed personally challenging by depressed clients when they are depressed, is highly encouraging for such clients and makes them more amenable to the subsequent use of more traditional cognitive changes procedures (Beck et al., 1979).

In conclusion, the negotiation of 'challenging, but not overwhelming' homework assignments is seen as a healthy compromise between therapists and clients when the latter are overly threatened by the prospect of fully exposing themselves to their anxieties. Such tasks enable clients to execute homework assignments without unduly reinforcing their low frustration tolerance ideas and help to preserve the therapeutic alliance between the protagonists. I maintain that in such circumstances it is a highly pragmatic and efficient approach to negotiating homework assignments, in that it provides clients with the best available (acceptable) means to achieve therapeutic ends.

Conclusion

In this chapter I have considered the various compromises that RET therapists may be called upon to make when they cannot help their clients achieve philosophically based change. Rather than persist with traditional rational-emotive methods that do not prove to be effective, RET therapists can still help their clients by encouraging them to change inferences, behaviour or activating events.

There are, of course, problems associated with such compromises:

1 Clients who succeed in changing negative inferences may later encounter events that realise their inferences. As they have not changed their irrational beliefs they make themselves disturbed about such events. Thus, the client of my colleague may later discover that her father in fact had been prying into her affairs and my own client with social anxiety (Robert) may later encounter a group of people who will notice his anxiety and stare at him.
2 Clients who do change their behaviour for the better may still encounter events which serve to activate their latent unchanged irrational beliefs. Thus, Sylvia, my client with examination anxiety, may in the future fail an important examination and Mrs Anderson's family may again make unreasonable demands upon her.
3 Clients who change or remove themselves from problematic activating events may later re-encounter such situations which again may activate their latent unmodified irrational beliefs. Thus, Mrs Curran's family may later mistreat her and Mr Brown's enthusiasm for the law may wane.
4 Clients who overcome their problems by using 'challenging, but not overwhelming' methods are still vulnerable to 'overwhelming' situations.

While I have described cases where productive changes in inferences, behaviour and situations have not led to belief change, other clients do later change their irrational beliefs after effecting such changes. Yet, although RET theory has emphasised the interdependence of ABC factors, I have endeavoured to show here that change, particularly at the level of beliefs ('B'), does not necessarily follow changes achieved at 'A' or 'C'.

The implications of this chapter for empirical study are clear. It would be helpful to research such questions as:

1 'With which clients, and at which stages of the therapeutic process, are belief change (inference change, behaviour change and situation change) methods appropriate?'
2 'Under which conditions do changes in inferences, behaviour and situations lead to belief change and when do they not promote such change?'

Finally, given the way I have chosen to distinguish rational-emotive therapy from other approaches to cognitive-behaviour therapy, and given my arguments about 'compromises' in RET, I conclude with the intriguing notice that RET therapists do not only practise RET! Indeed it would be fascinating to research the question: 'When do RET therapists practise RET and when do they not do so?'

References

Beck, A.T., Rush, A.J., Shaw, B.F. and Emery, G. (1979) *Cognitive Therapy of Depression*. New York: Guilford.

Bordin, E.S. (1979) The generalizability of the psychoanalytic concept of the working alliance, *Psychotherapy: Theory, Research and Practice*, 16, 252–60.

Dryden, W. (1984) *Rational-Emotive Therapy: Fundamentals and Innovations*. Beckenham, Kent: Croom Helm.

Ellis, A. (1972) Helping people get better: rather than merely feel better, *Rational Living*, 7(2), 2–9.

Ellis, A. (1977) Fun as psychotherapy, *Rational Living*, 12(1), 2–6.

Ellis, A. (1979a) The practice of rational-emotive therapy. In A. Ellis and J.M. Whiteley (eds), *Theoretical and Empirical Foundations of Rational-Emotive Therapy*. Monterey, CA: Brooks/Cole.

Ellis, A. (1979b) The issue of force and energy in behavioral change, *Journal of Contemporary Psychotherapy*, 10(2), 83–97.

Ellis, A. (1979c) Discomfort anxiety: a new cognitive behavioral construct. Part 1, *Rational Living*, 14(2), 3–8.

Ellis, A. (1980a) Discomfort anxiety: a new cognitive behavioral construct. Part 2, *Rational Living*, 15(1), 25–30.

Ellis, A. (1980b) Rational-emotive and cognitive behavior therapy: similarities and differences, *Cognitive Therapy and Research*, 4, 325–40.

Ellis, A. (1980c) The value of efficiency in psychotherapy, *Psychotherapy: Theory, Research and Practice*, 17, 414–19.

Ellis, A. (1981) The use of rational humorous songs in psychotherapy, *Voices*, 16(4), 29–36.

Ellis, A. (1983) The philosophic implications and dangers of some popular behavior therapy techniques. In M. Rosenbaum, C.M. Franks and Y. Jaffe (eds), *Perspectives in Behavior Therapy in the Eighties*. New York: Springer.

Mackay, D. (1984) Behavioural psychotherapy. In W. Dryden (ed.), *Individual Therapy in Britain*. London: Harper and Row.

17

Rational-Emotive Therapy and Eclecticism

Windy Dryden

Eclecticism has been defined as 'consisting of that which has been selected from diverse sources, systems or styles' (*American Heritage Dictionary of the English Language*, 1971) and much has been recently written on eclectic approaches in psychotherapy (e.g., Lazarus, 1976; Shostrom, 1976; Dryden, 1980b; Garfield, 1980). However, there have been few attempts to clarify the decisions that clinicians make in broadening their therapeutic repertoire by selecting from diverse therapeutic orientations. The aim of this chapter is to show what guides rational-emotive therapists in such endeavours.

Rational-emotive theory states that much emotional disturbance stems from the faulty inferences and irrational evaluations that patients make in endeavouring to make sense of themselves, other people and the world (Wessler and Wessler, 1980). Examples of faulty inferences have been detailed by Beck et al. (1979) and include arbitrary inferences, overgeneralisations and selective abstractions. Irrational evaluations are based on a philosophy of demandingness which hinders patients from achieving their long-term goals and restricts their opportunities to live effectively and creatively in the world. The major task of rational-emotive therapists is to help patients correct their faulty inferences and to replace their demanding philosophy with a desiring philosophy, that is, one which is characterised by wants, preferences and wishes. To achieve their basic task, rational-emotive therapists focus on cognitive, affective and behavioural factors and consequently RET has been described as a comprehensive system of therapy (Ellis and Abrahms, 1978).

Rational-emotive psychotherapists then are guided by a particular theory of emotional disturbance and personality change (Ellis, 1978) and thus can be contrasted with eclectic therapists who de-emphasise theory. Theory is considered important by rational-emotive therapists for a number of reasons. First, theory provides testable propositions for empirical study. Second, as Frank (1970) has shown theory helps therapists gain emotional support from others with similar views and thus helps sustain the therapist's morale. The third and most important reason is that theory helps guide therapists in their work, helps them correctly select particular therapeutic procedures and gives them a framework for determining the consequences of such procedures. Eysenck (1970) also stresses the need for theory in psychotherapy and warns that without a theoretical framework the practice of eclectic therapists would be characterised by 'a mish-mash of theories, a hugger-mugger of procedures, a charivaria of therapies and a gallimaufry of activities having no proper rationale and incapable of being tested or evaluated' (p. 145).

Therapeutic Practice

In the execution of their major task – effecting cognitive change – rational-emotive therapists attempt to engage patients in a concrete and situationally based exploration of their problems. To encourage concreteness, therapists tend to use explicitly an implicit ABCDE framework in exploring their patients' problems. Point A in the framework represents an event or the patient's perceptions and inferences concerning that event. B represents the patient's beliefs or evaluations about the phenomenal event, while C stands for the emotional and behavioural consequences of the patient's beliefs. At point D the therapist's task is to help the patient challenge his or her faulty inferences and irrational evaluations and replace them with more realistic and rational cognitions which leads to emotional and behavioural change at point E.

In practice rational-emotive therapists tend to start at point C. The major goal here is to help patients acknowledge their feelings (without dwelling on them) and to identify their actions. In doing so the therapist may very well use procedures derived from other therapeutic systems. For example, if a patient experiences difficulty in acknowledging feelings, the rational-emotive therapist might employ a gestalt awareness exercise or psychodramatic technique with the specific purpose at this stage of encouraging the patient to acknowledge feelings.

After helping the patient to identify correctly emotional and behavioural responses, the therapist shifts his or her attention to the context in which such responses arise (point A). Exploration at this point involves the therapist paying attention to the patient's description of the relevant context. The patient is helped to describe his or her perception of the relevant situation fairly briefly. The therapist tends not to dwell upon those events and discourages the patient from presenting too many or problem-irrelevant contexts. The goal of the therapist is to aid the patient in adequately framing the problem so that he or she can assist in the identification and correction of presently held faulty inferences and beliefs. In practice the context tends to be either one that is anticipated or one of recent occurrence and thus RET tends to be a present- and future-oriented approach to therapy. Rational-emotive therapists tend not to focus on events that have occurred in the distant past since it is argued that such exploration does not aid the correction of presently held faulty cognitions

(Ellis, 1962). However, I have found that in certain circumstances such exploration does assist the therapist in his or her dissuasion strategies with some patients (Dryden, 1979). Thus understanding the likely origins of presently held beliefs may motivate such patients to change such beliefs. The point at issue here is that the purpose of exploring such past events is to facilitate the disputing of *presently* held inferences and beliefs.

At point B in the ABCDE framework, the therapist's task is to help the patient identify the irrational evaluations that the latter employs in appraising the relevant context. Here the therapist is not limited to verbal interventions such as: 'What are you saying to yourself?', that are often seen in therapy transcripts. In fact, in the author's experience a common answer to such questions is – 'nothing'. In addition to psychodrama (Nardi, 1979) and gestalt methods, various role-playing and imagery methods may be used as an aid to facilitate the discovery of irrational beliefs. Indeed, person-centred procedures for some patients may be employed. Such patients find the less active-directive style implicit in such procedures helpful in exploring and discovering meanings and beliefs (DiLoreto, 1971). Rather than abandon RET for person-centred therapy, an eclectic rational-emotive therapist would vary his or her therapeutic style but not the theoretical underpinnings of his or her system.

Point D in the framework is also called the dissuasion process (Wessler and Wessler, 1980). On attempting to dissuade the patient, the therapist may use a wide variety of cognitive, imaginal, affective and behavioural methods, and may suggest similar procedures for the patient to use between sessions as the latter strives to put into practice in everyday life what he or she has learned in therapy (point E).

Theory-inspired Guidelines for Choosing Appropriate Therapeutic Procedures

Thus far it has been argued that rational-emotive therapists may choose from a range of cognitive, experiential and behavioural methods to facilitate their task of working within the ABCDE framework. However, rational-emotive therapists are mindful of possible negative effects of employing certain procedures and by no means would employ all available procedures. There are a number of issues that rational-emotive therapists have in mind when deciding whether or not to employ a particular therapeutic procedure.

Helping Patients get Better Rather than Feel Better

One basic aim of rational-emotive therapists is to promote long-term philosophically based change as opposed to helping patients feel better in the short term (Ellis, 1972). Thus rational-emotive therapists may deliberately avoid being unduly warm towards their patients and would be wary of employing cathartic methods. The hazard of undue therapist warmth is that it may lead to increased long-term dependence in patients who may then believe that they are worth while because the therapist is acting very warmly towards them. However, if the therapist or other significant people act coldly towards the patient, he or she may then conclude that he or she is worthless. Thus, undue therapist warmth, although patients feel better when so exposed, tends to distract them from dealing with the more difficult task of accepting themselves unconditionally (Ellis, 1977). For this reason an intense relationship between therapist and patient is generally avoided. The therapist strives to establish and maintain a working relationship with the patient and strives to accept the patient as a fallible human being without being unduly warm towards him or her.

Cathartic methods have the short-term value of encouraging relief of pent-up feelings, but in the long term, if not employed sparingly and briefly, often encourage patients to practise their already well-ingrained irrational philosophies. For example, cathartic procedures which place emphasis on the ventilation of intense angry feelings (e.g., pounding a cushion) run the risk of encouraging processes of blaming which are, according to rational-emotive theory, a feature of the irrational philosophy underlying anger. Rational-emotive therapists might employ such procedures when they wish to help patients to acknowledge their feelings, but the patient would then be quickly encouraged to consider the philosophy underlying such feelings.

Self-esteem versus Self-acceptance

In RET, self-esteem is defined as a form of global self-rating and is to be avoided since according to rational-emotive theory it has problematic long-term implications for patients. Procedures based on self-esteem notions encourage patients to define themselves as worth while or competent so long as they gain approval or succeed at valued tasks. They are thus prone to defining themselves as worthless and incompetent if they receive disapproval or fail at the same task. Furthermore, rational-emotive theory states that it is nonsensical to give humans global ratings since they are on-going, complex, ever-changing organisms who defy such ratings. As an alternative, rational-emotive therapists urge patients to accept themselves as on-going, complex, ever-changing fallible human beings but also encourage them to rate their traits, aspects and behaviour but not their selves. Many procedures do not in fact discourage patients from making such global self-ratings. For example, many therapists give patients homework assignments which are designed to encourage the patient to succeed. Thus a patient who succeeds at approaching a woman at a discotheque may conclude that because he has been able to do this, perhaps he is not worthless after all. The implication would be that if he failed in his assignment then this would be a confirmation of his worthlessness. Rational-emotive therapists, by contrast, may at times encourage patients deliberately to go out and fail since such a failure experience presents them with opportunities to work on accepting themselves as fallible humans rather than subhumans when they fail. In reality, rational-emotive therapists suggest both success and failure-oriented homework assignments to their patients.

Anger versus Annoyance

Rational-emotive theory clearly distinguishes between anger and annoyance. Annoyance results when something occurs that we view as a trespass on our personal domain, which we strongly dislike but which we refrain from demanding should not have happened. There is an absence of blaming of self, other or the world for the deed, that is, the deed is rated but the perpetrator of the deed is accepted. In contrast anger stems from the jehovian demand that the trespass absolutely should not have occurred and the trespasser is damnable. Counsellors from other persuasions often do not make such a clear distinction and thus the therapy procedures which they employ may encourage the full expression and ventilation of anger rather than annoyance. If this occurs then rational-emotive therapists would avoid using these procedures. As mentioned earlier, while the full expression and ventilation of anger helps the person feel better it often encourages adherence to a long-term and damaging anger-creating philosophy. In RET, procedures are used to help patients to acknowledge their anger fully but then they are encouraged to dispute the underlying philosophy.

Desensitisation versus Implosion

Rational-emotive therapists face a choice between two different approaches when the issue of suggesting homework assignments to patients arises (however, see Chapter 16 for a third approach). They can either suggest that patients gradually face their fears and overcome their problems in a slow stepwise fashion while minimising discomfort (desensitisation), or they can suggest that patients take a risk and forcefully confront their fears and their problems while tolerating discomfort (implosion). Rational-emotive therapists very definitely favour implosion-based assignments because they help patients overcome their 'low frustration tolerance' (LFT) or 'discomfort anxiety', constructs which, according to rational-emotive theory, play a central role in preventing change (Wessler, 1978; Ellis, 1979). Consequently such therapists would avoid helping patients to overcome gradually and painlessly their problems because such procedures are viewed as encouraging patients to cling to their philosophy of LFT which actually decreases their chances of maintaining therapeutic improvement and increases the possibility of relapse (Ellis, 1979).

Due to the somewhat unusual stance taken on the above issues rational-emotive therapy has proved rather difficult to combine with other methods derived from different theoretical origins. Garfield and Kurtz (1977) make a similar observation, noting in their study of 154 clinicians' eclectic views that RET was occasionally combined with learning theory-based approaches but was not combined with psychoanalytical, neo-analytical, Rogerian, humanistic or Sullivanian orientations.

Therapeutic Style

Ellis (1976) speaking for rational-emotive theory argues that humans have great difficulty maintaining, in the long term, the changes that they make more easily in the short term because of the strong biological basis to irrational thinking. Because of this difficulty, Ellis urges rational-emotive therapists to adopt an active-directive, forceful and persistent therapeutic style and also encourage their patients to be equally active, forceful and persistent with themselves. However, is such a style beneficial with a wide range of patients? Or should rational-emotive therapists vary their therapeutic style with different patients? If the latter is to be advised, what criteria should be employed to assist rational-emotive therapists in these important decisions?

The first question remains unanswered since there is a lack of research which has systematically studied the effects of active-directive RET across a wide range of patients. There is, however, some research evidence concerning different therapeutic styles with different patients which has relevance for RET practitioners. DiLoreto (1971) in a study using socially anxious patients found that active-directive RET was more effective with introverts than with extroverts in the sample while person-centred therapy was more effective with extroverts. This suggests that RET practitioners might effectively adopt a less directive, more reflective style of RET, when working with socially anxious extroverts. Morley and Watkins (1974) carried out a treatment study with speech anxious patients. They found that active-directive RET benefited external locus of control patients most, while internal locus of control patients profited most from a modified RET approach where rational and irrational beliefs relevant to speech anxiety were merely presented and not challenged in the usual fashion. To what extent these findings can be generalised to other patient populations remains unclear. We must also wait for studies to consider Ellis's point often made in practice that the stronger patients adhere to irrational philosophies the more forceful the therapist had better be.

Carson (1969) advocates an interpersonally based system to help the therapist vary his or her interpersonal style according to the patient's own style. Unproductive interlocking interactional patterns arise when the therapist adopts a manner of relating which confirms the patient in his own self-defeating style. The therapist's task is to adopt an interpersonal style which (1) does not reinforce the patient's dysfunctional style and (2) provides a disconfirming experience for the patient. For example, with a passive patient, it would be important for the rational-emotive therapist to refrain from adopting a very active style which might reinforce the patient's self-defeating passivity.

Thus, rational-emotive therapists had better be mindful of Eschenroeder's question: 'Which therapeutic style is most effective with what kind of patient?' (1979: 5).

Therapeutic Modalities

Rational-emotive theory holds that the important modalities of human experience – cognitive (verbal and imaginal), affective and behavioural – are overlapping rather than separate systems (Ellis, 1962). However, it may be important for RET practitioners to vary the emphasis they place in working within the various modalities with different patients. Which criteria might be important as guides to decision-making in this area bearing in mind that the ultimate goal is a common one (i.e., to effect philosophical changes)? One set of criteria might be the ability of patients to handle verbal concepts. My own experience of working as a counselling psychologist in a working-class region is that with those patients who find it difficult using words it is important for therapists to focus on the behavioural modality both within and between sessions. When teaching rational concepts, important with such patients, then it is essential to use the visual mode of communication as an adjunct to the verbal mode. Thus, I use pen and paper a lot, sketching diagrams to facilitate such patients' understanding of difficult rational concepts. In addition, I have devised a number of visual models to illustrate rational concepts (Dryden, 1980a). When patients employ words to protect themselves from emotional experience, that is, when they employ intellectualisation as a major defensive style, then rational-emotive therapists might more effectively focus on the experiential modality helping such patients to acquaint themselves with that mode of experience from which they have shielded themselves. If therapists spend too much time engaging such patients in traditional rational-emotive Socratic dialogue then they may well reinforce their patients' defensive style. Such speculations of course need to be tested.

Beutler (1979) has suggested a system which combines therapeutic modalities and styles in determining whether certain approaches to therapy are more effective than others with patients on three major patient dimensions. The first dimension is symptom complexity. If symptoms are circumscribed Beutler (1979) hypothesises that a greater behavioural focus would be more effective, whereas if they are more complex a greater cognitive focus is needed. The second dimension is defensive style. According to Beutler, if the patient utilises an external defensive style, the therapist needs to emphasise the behavioural modality in therapy whereas cognitive interventions are required with patients utilising an internal defensive style. The third dimension – reactance – taps the degree to which external events are construed as representing a threat to the person's autonomy. If the patient is high on the reactance dimension, that is, if he or she is predisposed to view external events as autonomy-endangering, then the therapist would be more productive if he or she adopted a less directive, more experiential, therapeutic style. If the patient is low on this dimension then greater therapist direction with a more behavioural focus is needed. Beutler (1979) reviewed empirical studies relevant to his hypotheses but found only meagre to moderate support for these hypotheses. However, these hypotheses were not tested *directly* and Beutler's system remains a promising one in that it provides the rational-emotive therapist with some guidelines as to possible variations in style and modality focus with different patients.

In conclusion, it has been shown how RET practitioners employ rational-emotive theory as a guide in their choice of a wide array of therapeutic interventions. In addition, the argument was advanced that RET practitioners are advised to take into account patient characteristics in making decisions concerning therapeutic style and modality focus. However, the central purpose of the eclectic RET practitioner remains the modification of faulty inferences and irrational beliefs.

References

Beck, A.T., Rush, A.J., Shaw, B.F. and Emery, G. (1979) *Cognitive Therapy of Depression*. New York: Guilford.

Beutler, L.E. (1979) Toward specific psychological therapies for specific conditions, *Journal of Consulting and Clinical Psychology*, 47, 882–97.

Carson, R.C. (1969) *Interaction Concepts of Personality*. London: George Allen and Unwin.

DiLoreto, A.E. (1971) *Comparative Psychotherapy: An Experimental Analysis*. Chicago: Aldine-Atherton.

Dryden, W. (1979) Past messages and disputations: the client and significant others, *Rational Living*, 14(1), 26–8.

Dryden, W. (1980a) Nightmares and fun. Paper presented at the Third National Conference on Rational-Emotive Therapy, New York.

Dryden, W. (1980b) 'Eclectic' approaches in individual counselling: some pertinent issues, *The Counsellor*, 3, 24–30.

Ellis, A. (1962) *Reason and Emotion in Psychotherapy*. Secaucus, NJ: Lyle Stuart.

Ellis, A. (1972) Helping people get better: rather than merely feel better, *Rational Living*, 7(2) 2–9.

Ellis, A. (1976) The biological basis of human irrationality, *Journal of Individual Psychology*, 32, 145–68. (Reprinted by the Institute for Rational-Emotive Therapy, New York.)

Ellis, A. (1977) Intimacy in psychotherapy, *Rational Living*, 12(2), 13–19.

Ellis, A. (1978) Toward a theory of personality. In R.J. Corsini (ed.), *Readings in Current Personality Theories*. Illinois: F.E. Peacock.

Ellis, A. (1979) Discomfort anxiety: a new cognitive behavioral construct. Part I, *Rational Living*, 14(2), 3–8.

Ellis, A. and Abrahms, E. (1978) *Brief Psychotherapy in Medical and Health Practice*. New York: Springer.

Eschenroeder, C. (1979) Different therapeutic styles in rational-emotive therapy, *Rational Living*, 14(1), 3–7.

Eysenck, H.J. (1970) A mish-mash of theories, *International Journal of Psychiatry*, 9, 140–6.

Frank, J.D. (1970) Psychotherapists need theories, *International Journal of Psychiatry*, 9, 146–9.

Garfield, S.L. (1980) *Psychotherapy: An Eclectic Approach*. New York: Wiley.

Garfield, S.L. and Kurtz, R. (1977) A study of eclectic views, *Journal of Consulting and Clinical Psychology*, 45, 78–83.

Lazarus, A.A. (1976) *Multimodal Behavior Therapy*. New York: Springer.

Morley, E.L. and Watkins, J.T. (1974) Locus of control and effectiveness of two rational-emotive therapy styles, *Rational Living*, 9(2), 22–4.

Nardi, T.J. (1979) The use of psychodrama in RET, *Rational Living*, 14(1), 35–8.

Shostrom, E.L. (1976) *Actualizing Therapy: Foundations for a Scientific Ethic*. San Diego: Edits.

Wessler, R.A. (1978) The neurotic paradox: a rational-emotive view, *Rational Living*, 13, 9–12.

Wessler, R.A. and Wessler, R.L. (1980) *The Principles and Practice of Rational-Emotive Therapy*. San Francisco, CA: Jossey-Bass.

AFTERWORD

18

Rational Emotive Behavior Therapy: A Tough-Minded Therapy for a Tender-Minded Profession

Stephen G. Weinrach

Rational Emotive Behavior Therapy (REBT) is a highly popular approach. It is difficult to read a counseling journal without finding articles which incorporate some aspect of REBT. Virtually every graduate program in counseling and related fields includes REBT as part of its required curriculum. Although all approaches have their critics, there is something about REBT that seems especially to rub some people the wrong way (Weinrach, 1990a). The profession has been slow to accept Ellis's many contributions outright. Much of the criticism leveled against REBT is a function of critics' ignorance of developments in REBT since its inception in 1955 (Young, 1979) or Ellis's demonstration with Gloria ten years later (Ellis, 1986; Gandy, 1985; Shostrom, 1965; Weinrach, 1986). In response, the REBT literature has often been devoted to defending itself (Dryden, 1989; Ellis, 1975, 1979, 1981, 1987a, 1987b; Gandy, 1985; Harris, 1977; Saltzberg, 1979; Weinrach, 1980).

Ellis's demonstration with Gloria in *Three Approaches to Psychotherapy* (Shostrom, 1965) remains highly controversial (Ellis, 1986; Gandy, 1985; Weinrach, 1986). Even Ellis recognized its limitations:

> I may have tried to get too much material in a brief length of time, especially considering that Gloria knew she was being filmed and therefore may have been somewhat distracted from my messages. I referred too often to Gloria's *sentences* and *self-statements* and not to her *meanings, evaluations, images*, and other forms of cognition. And I included a few *musts* and *have to's* of my own, which I would not include today. I was at times sexist in my use of language; and I employed the word *patient* instead of, as I now do, *client*. . . . I feel that my RET emotive-evocative methods left much to be desired. (1986: 648; emphasis in original)

Ellis's demonstration with Gloria in 1965 was not a good example of what REBT was then and is certainly not an accurate example of what REBT is currently. In the late 1960s and 1970s, the profession's reluctance to accept REBT may have been in large part a function of how Ellis's demonstration with Gloria was perceived. It is unfortunate that the continued use of this film perpetuates misconceptions about what REBT is today (Weinrach, 1986).

Probably the most common misconception is that REBT does not deal with emotions (Garcia, 1977; Saltzberg, 1979). REBT, as its second initial indicates, deals with emotions, in part by teaching clients how to differentiate between appropriate and inappropriate emotional reactions. REBT holds that emotions are largely, though not exclusively, determined by one's beliefs *about* an event as opposed to there being a direct causal relationship between an event and how one feels about it. It is regrettable that REBT is seen as encouraging counselors to ignore their clients' emotions. In fact, REBT helps clients make cognitive changes solely as a means to an emotionally self-enhancing end. Clients will likely feel better when they think more rationally. Although REBT clearly deals with emotions, it is unlikely that it will ever deal with emotions in the manner of affectively oriented approaches.

Counselors' objections to REBT appear to exceed the mere rational preference for one approach over another. Ziegler (1990) suggests that James's Dichotomy of Types might explain REBT's appeal to some and its failure to attract others. According to James (1907: 11–12), there are two types of people, tender-minded and tough-minded. Ziegler's (1990) hypothesis is explicit, makes sense and warrants empirical validation.

The Study of Types

William James's (1842–1910) typology attributes specific characteristics or behaviors to each type. The two types 'have a low opinion of each other. . . . The tough think of the tender as sentimentalists and soft-heads. The tender feel the tough can be unrefined, callous, or brutal' (James, 1907: 12–13). Although the 'fit' between James's types and REBT is not perfect, and the types are not pure, it is useful for speculating about the characteristics of those who accept as opposed to those who reject REBT.

REBT is tough-minded on the basis of the following Jamesian characteristics: 'Empiricist (going by "facts"), . . . Irreligious, . . . Pluralistic, [and] Sceptical' (James, 1907: 12). Except for REBT's being intellectualistic and free-willist (Ellis and Dryden, 1987), it shares little in common with the tender-minded. REBT does not share the following tender-minded Jamesian characteristics: 'Rationalistic (going by "principles"), Idealistic, Optimistic, Religious, [and] . . . Dogmatical' (James, 1907: 12).

James and Ellis attribute different meanings to the word rational. Ellis and Harper address the distinction this way:

> Rational*ism* [what James is talking about] holds that reason or intellect, rather than the senses, provides the true source of knowledge. This we do not believe.

> Like most modern scientists and empiricists, we see knowledge as significantly influenced by and related to thinking. But we find it basically stemming from and validated by observation: by evidence involving our senses of touch, smell, sight, hearing and taste. (1977: 72–3)

REBT is a predominantly tough-minded therapy, sometimes provided by tender-minded counselors to clients, of whom some are also tender-minded.

Ziegler (1990) believes that the counseling profession attracts primarily tender-minded trainees, people who are warm, sensitive, and caring. Tender-minded counselor trainees are often threatened or alienated by a theory that espouses, 'life is often unfair.' Tender-minded counselors, after several years of experience are probably more likely to realize REBT's value than are neophytes (Ziegler, 1990). Ellis (1990) sees it more cynically: 'The really bright and scientific psychologists often go into experimental psychology. Those with serious problems and who are not very scientific frequently become clinical psychologists. Counselors are often worse than the clinical psychologists because they are less scientific.' In selecting an approach, counselor trainees often seem to ask, 'which approach will make clients *feel* most comfortable?' rather than 'which approach will help clients deal most effectively with their concerns?'

REBT's Tender-minded Critics' Objections

If Ziegler and Ellis are correct, the counseling profession is filled with tender-minded individuals, who by the very definition of the term, are less inclined to be skeptical and empirical than their tough-minded counterparts. Their expectations of the universe, including theories of counseling, are often sentimental as opposed to scientific. Those defending REBT often view its critics as sentimentalists and soft-heads, just as James (1907) predicted the tough-minded would react. Over the past two decades, counselor educators, counselors and counselor trainees have confronted me and others with objections to REBT similar or identical to those that follow (Weinrach, 1990a).

REBT Should be Complex, Deep and Delve into Clients' Past Histories

Ellis's minimizing the importance of past experiences represents one of his major theoretical contributions and digressions from the mainstream of counseling and psychotherapy. In addressing the criticism that REBT is not deep enough, Ellis (1975) argues that there is no evidence that dealing with the origins of one's disturbance in the past (if in fact any given current problem has a historic antecedent) has any direct therapeutic value to helping the client deal with their present disturbance.

There are those who believe that the human condition is so complex that a complex theory is required to explain it. REBT has been criticized for positing a simplistic solution to a complex phenomenon. Although few would disagree that humans are complex, the right question to ask is the extent to which REBT (or any other theory) explains and proposes adequate treatment strategies for the complexities of the human experience. REBT is straightforward and logical, rather than simplistic (Harris, 1977). It is by no means simple as anyone who has tried it knows.

REBT Should be Easier to Master

REBT requires counselors to respond spontaneously to both client affect and content, particularly content within the conceptual framework of the theory. From my experience, counselor trainees find it far more difficult to use REBT correctly than most other approaches. The process involved in accurately reflecting feelings is not as complex as that of analyzing the client's beliefs and helping the client identify the appropriate irrational idea, dispute it, and finally replace it with its rational counterpart. Gandy warns that:

> Unless an individual studies RET very closely, it is easy to misunderstand and misinterpret some of its psychological and philosophical complexities. RET could be described as a system with only a few parts but one in which the interaction of those parts can become very complex. (1985: 31)

Counselor trainees, often struggling with their own perfectionistic tendencies (Weinrach, 1973), find basic REBT hard to master, much less feel comfortable using (Weinrach, 1982). Trainees demonstrating a theory on which they are being graded may be better off selecting a theory where silence is more highly valued than it is in REBT, if for no other reason that one could more easily conceal one's ignorance by remaining quiet during a session. In some respects, students who select REBT (and other directive and active approaches) may be held to a higher standard of performance than their peers who opt for less active approaches. Similarly, counselor educators may find demonstrating REBT and other cognitive behavioral approaches for their students more difficult than less active approaches. Allen Ivey (personal communication, 26 August 1991) suggested that counselor trainees often resist those approaches which are based upon a 'formula', such as REBT and microskills training, precisely because they *are* harder to master.

Ellis (1990) hypothesizes that counselors and counselor trainees often select a theory because it is *easy* for them to do and that they *enjoy* following it rather than because it is effective in helping clients. He proposes that the medical model has something to offer the counseling profession. Physicians, he suggests, follow the facts and use those techniques that work, as opposed to using those they enjoy and which are consonant with their religious or political views.

Because REBT is Largely Efficient, Progress Should be Swift and Easy

According to REBT, all that is required for a client to get better is identify the underlying irrational belief, practice disputing it, learn how to replace the irrational belief with its rational counterpart and do a little homework. Although REBT is efficient when compared to most other approaches, it is clearly not swift and easy.

If One Selects REBT as a Theory of Choice, Everything Albert Ellis Says, Does and Writes Must also be Accepted

Ellis and REBT are distinct entities, one being a human and the other a theory. Admittedly, it is difficult to separate one's images of a theorist from the theory. To wit, Rogers's (Weinrach, 1990b, 1991a), Perls's (Dolliver et al., 1980) and Ellis's (Weinrach, 1986) public personae are intimately wrapped up with viewers' impressions of each one's respective demonstration with Gloria (Shostrom, 1965). Ellis's interpersonal style has been the subject of several articles and parts of books (Dryden, 1989; Sifford, 1988; Weinrach, 1977, 1980; Wiener, 1988). He rightfully enjoys a reputation as an outspoken, humorous and dynamic speaker who peppers his presentations with common everyday curse words. When the *Journal of Counseling and Development* published an interview of Ellis (Dryden, 1989), it replaced those words of Ellis's which some might consider to be offensive with dashes lest any Tender-minded readers become upset (Dryden, 1990). Theories need leaders who attract attention, and Ellis has certainly done this very well.

If there is anything about Ellis that would likely offend the Tender-minded, it is his outspoken attitude toward religion. Ellis is an atheist. Although he is often viewed as anti-religious, he has clarified his position by stating that he opposes religiosity not religion. He defines religiosity as a devout, dogmatic, absolutist and rigid belief in a theological religion (e.g., Christianity or Judaism) or in a secular religion (e.g., Communism or Fascism) (Ellis, 1981, 1987b). Whether Ellis is an atheist or not is irrelevant to the selection of a counseling theory. Rogers's father was a minister. Does it matter to his followers how often Rogers went to church as an adult? Do you suppose that those who are psychoanalytically oriented care if Sigmund Freud kept kosher? It makes no more sense to adopt REBT because one likes Ellis than it makes sense to reject the theory because one finds him outrageous.

Results of REBT Outcome Studies Should be More Convincing than They Are

Some outcome studies have been encouraging. Lyons and Woods conducted a meta-analysis of 70 REBT outcome studies and concluded that:

> The results demonstrated that RET is an effective form of therapy. The efficacy was most clearly demonstrated when RET was compared to baseline and other forms of controls. The differences among comparisons of RET to CBM [Cognitive Behavior Modification] and Behavior Therapy were not significant. . . . Perhaps it is time to stop the needless and inefficient discussion of the efficacy of this

therapy [RET]. Rather, a better focus of investigations and reviews would be to determine which factors, or combinations thereof, contribute most to the effectiveness of RET. (1991: 367–8)

However, Lyons and Woods (1991) identified methodological problems with some of the studies they examined as one of the limitations of their meta-analysis. Haaga et al. have proposed a set of recommendations to address the criticism that much of the research suffers from a 'lack of empirical evidence to confirm that outcome studies have implemented RET as it is theoretically intended and with high quality' (1991: 73). Ellis (1990) criticized REBT outcome studies for having limited their focus primarily to the cognitive restructuring aspects of REBT, as opposed to the combination of cognitive, emotive, and behavioral aspects of REBT.

It is reasonable to invoke the sacred cow of empirical evidence in a chapter about REBT which espouses empiricism probably more than any other approach. However, it is well beyond the scope of this chapter to resolve the issues associated with research in counseling. Suffice it to say, I have seen no evidence that the absence of numerous and convincing outcome studies has ever discouraged supporters of any given approach from practicing it (Belkin, 1984; Brabeck and Welfel, 1985). Nor have I seen evidence that counselor trainees select their theory of choice on the basis of outcome research (Lichtenberg, 1984; Norcross and Prochaska, 1983; Patterson, 1985; Wallace, 1986; Weinrach, 1991b).

In an ideal world, outcome research would influence, if not determine counselor behavior. In the real world, theories appear to be selected for other reasons, not necessarily rational ones. Skovholt and Ronnestad speculate that, 'the need for compatibility with the self seems more powerful in choice of professional role, . . . than does the empirical research base or the professional biases of one's graduate training program' (1992: 510).

Implications for Practice

The application of James's Dichotomy of Types to REBT is more than just an interesting hypothesis; there are explicit implications for counselors and counselor educators. Those who advocate REBT may need to adjust their approach so as to make REBT more palatable to a wider audience. For example, practitioners have always assessed their clients' readiness for counseling. It is often a balancing act between providing a cathartic experience by encouraging clients to tell their story and pressing on to the action phase where clients' discrepancies are confronted (Weinrach, 1991b). It is rather common for clients to enter counseling with the belief that they need their counselor's love and approval. This is especially true for clients who have yet to grant themselves self-acceptance. Wolfe (1976, 1990), who sees REBT as an effective feminist therapy, points out that 'love slobbism' (or an inordinate demand to be loved) is especially rampant among women who are one of REBT's and counseling's major constituencies.

Encouraging clients to deal with painful material prematurely may scare them away. Counselors may wish to pamper tender-minded clients so that they will remain in counseling long enough so that there is an opportunity to lodge a full scale assault on their dire need for love. Tough-minded clients, on the other hand, may find heavy doses of nurturing offensive. According to Beck (Weinrach, 1988: 162) 'Many people, particularly macho men, are either intimidated or nauseated by any display of caring.' Counselors have unfortunately failed to heed Holland's (1973: 5) dictum, 'most people want help not love.'

Because client histories may provide vital information, especially in terms of patterns of behavior, counselors may wish to devote more time to it. Dysfunctional early messages sometimes come from one's family. Clients learn some of their irrational ideas from their parents. In any case, clients tend to enjoy talking about their past and in so doing rapport can be more easily established (Wolfe, 1990).

The disadvantaged and victims of crime or sexual abuse are, according to Wolfe (1990), constituencies which are particularly confronted by a large number of potentially frustrating activating events. Such clients can easily be lost with too rapid an attack on their beliefs or behavior. It would be imprudent to tell them too early that it is not really awful to be a single mother, who is not receiving her welfare payments and whose ex-husband is threatening her with a gun. Minorities and other disadvantaged or victimized clients could benefit tremendously from REBT, and yet they may flee from counseling if their irrational beliefs are too vigorously disputed. It would be wise for REBT counselors to show appropriate empathy to their clients' plight.

Religious faith is prevalent throughout the world. Although Ellis espouses atheism for himself, there is nothing contraindicated about using REBT with clients who hold a deep religious faith (Young, 1989). Nor is there anything about REBT which precludes its use by counselors who possess similar values. Hauck (1972) and Lawrence and Huber (1982) have shown how REBT may be effectively used within the context of pastoral counseling. Young (1989: 78) has described how he used REBT with 'Bible-belt Christians.'

Recognizing how hard counseling is for some clients, Ellis (1990) suggests that tender-minded clients may benefit from having counselors who are easy going and nurturing as a means of 'hooking them' on the counseling process. In the early stages, not contradicting clients may be helpful. According to Wolfe (1990), the more irrationally-inclined the clients, the greater the resistance they are going to have to surrendering their irrational ideas. Therefore, Wolfe asserts, large doses of empathy and relationship-building are crucial. Clients are especially reluctant to accept the fact that the world is unfair. For tough-minded clients and those who have had previous experience with inefficient forms of therapy, jumping right in and challenging their irrational beliefs may be appropriate (Ellis, 1990). Since clients typically seek to get rid of their pain as quickly as possible, a tough-minded approach is clearly more efficient. It would be erroneous to conclude however, that REBT is a predominantly confrontative approach.

What is lacking from most approaches and may serve to overcome some of the resistance to REBT is the advent of concrete strategies for helping clients with specific concerns. Crawford and Ellis developed the 'Dictionary of rational-emotive feelings and behaviors' in an effort to provide specific treatment strategies to correspond with the more common irrational beliefs. Its purpose is:

> To help clients and others to clearly see the differences between their rational Beliefs and their irrational Beliefs, to understand the disordered feelings and behaviors to which the latter lead, and to help them become more rational, less disturbed, and less dysfunctional in their activities. (1989: 3)

The dictionary represents an excellent beginning to a much needed comprehensive treatment manual for REBT counselors and is an example of how REBT is becoming more refined and concrete.

Conclusion

Ellis has worked hard to counteract the counseling profession's own irrational beliefs about the therapeutic process. Freud generated the myth that the key to understanding the present is a preoccupation with the past. Rogers's legacy was a preoccupation with the counseling relationship. Ellis has taught us that a detailed exploration of the past is not a prerequisite to helping a client and that what a counselor *does* in a counseling session is at least as important as how the counselor relates to the client. Good REBT is good counseling and bad REBT is bad counseling. Good counseling requires counselors to establish constructive working alliances with their clients, something REBT counselors routinely do. Except possibly for Ellis's demonstration with Gloria over 25 years ago, what has impeded a wider acceptance of REBT has not been so much a function of anything Ellis has (or has not) done as much as the counseling profession's reticence to change and move forward. The field has had to evolve from Freud through Rogers before it was conceptually ready for Ellis.

REBT is finally receiving much of the attention it rightfully deserves. As a theory of counseling/psychotherapy and personality and a philosophy of life, it has made an enormous contribution to the field since its inception in 1955. There will continue to be tender-minded and tough-minded counselor educators, counselors and clients in the future. The tough-minded will likely continue to gravitate to REBT on rational grounds. The tender-minded will probably continue to resist REBT and occasionally but reluctantly enjoy its benefits. Albert Ellis, the progenitor of REBT will certainly be recorded as among the most important contributors to counseling and psychotherapy during the twentieth century. Since historians often forgive the idiosyncratic behavior of their subjects, after Ellis's death, the centrality of his personality will be appropriately replaced with a greater focus on his theory.

Note

This chapter is based in part upon a presentation entitled, 'Obstacles to a wider acceptance of RET' given at the World Congress on Mental Health Counseling/35th Anniversary Conference on Rational-Emotive Therapy, Keystone, Colorado, June 1990. I am indebted to my co-presenters, Albert Ellis, Janet L. Wolfe and Daniel J. Ziegler, many of whose ideas I have discussed. Michael E. Bernard, Joanne Christopher, Windy Dryden, Gerald L. Gandy, Martin Gerstein and Allen Ivey provided valuable suggestions on a draft version of the chapter. The author assumes complete responsibility for its content.

References

Belkin, G.S. (1984) *Introduction to Counseling* (2nd edn). Dubuque, IA: W.C. Brown.

Brabeck, M.M. and Welfel, E.R. (1985) Truth in counseling theory: a rejoinder to Patterson and Rychalk, *Journal of Counseling and Development*, 63, 354–5.

Crawford, T. and Ellis, A. (1989) A dictionary of rational-emotive feelings and behaviors, *Journal of Rational-Emotive Therapy*, 7, 3–28.

Dolliver, R.H., Williams, E.L. and Gold, D.C. (1980) The art of Gestalt therapy or: What are you doing with your feet now? *Psychotherapy*, 17, 136–42.

Dryden, W. (1989) Albert Ellis: an efficient and passionate life, *Journal of Counseling and Development*, 67, 539–46.

Dryden, W. (1990) Author's response to Ellis article [Letter to the editor], *Journal of Counseling and Development*, 68, 463.

Ellis, A. (1975) Does rational-emotive therapy seem deep enough? *Rational Living*, 10, 11–14.

Ellis, A. (1979) Rejoinder: elegant and inelegant RET. In A. Ellis and J. Whiteley (eds), *Theoretical and Empirical Foundations of Rational-Emotive Therapy* (pp. 240–67). Belmont, CA: Wadsworth.

Ellis, A. (1981) Science, religiosity and rational-emotive psychology, *Psychotherapy: Theory, Research and Practice*, 18, 155–8.

Ellis, A. (1986) Comments on Gloria, *Psychotherapy*, 23, 647–8.

Ellis, A. (1987a) Integrative developments in rational-emotive therapy (RET), *Journal of Integrative and Eclectic Psychotherapy*, 6, 470–9.

Ellis, A. (1987b) Religiosity and emotional disturbance: a reply to Sharkey and Malony, *Psychotherapy*, 24, 826–8.

Ellis, A. (1990) *Obstacles to a Wider Acceptance of RET*. Paper presented at the World Congress on Mental Health Counseling/35th Anniversary Conference on Rational-Emotive Therapy, Keystone, CO.

Ellis, A. and Dryden, W. (1987) *The Practice of Rational-Emotive Therapy*. New York: Springer.

Ellis, A. and Harper, R.A. (1977) *A New Guide to Rational Living*. North Hollywood, CA: Wilshire.

Gandy, G.L. (1985) Frequent misperceptions of rational-emotive therapy: an overview for the rehabilitation counselor, *Journal of Applied Rehabilitation Counseling*, 16, 31–5.

Garcia, E.J. (1977) Working on the E in RET. In J.L. Wolfe and E. Brand (eds), *Twenty Years of Rational Therapy* (pp. 72–87). New York: Institute for Rational Living.

Haaga, D.A.F., Dryden, W. and Dancey, C.P. (1991) Measurement of rational-emotive therapy in outcome studies, *Journal of Rational-Emotive Therapy and Cognitive-Behavior Therapy*, 9, 73–93.

Hauck, P.A. (1972) *Reason in Pastoral Counseling*. Philadelphia: Westminster.

Harris, R. (1977) Rational-emotive therapy: simple but not easy, *Rational Living*, 12, 9–12.

Holland, J.L. (1973) *Some Practical Remedies for Providing Vocational Guidance for Everyone*. Baltimore, MD: Center for Social Organization of Schools, Johns Hopkins University.

James, W. (1907) *Pragmatism – A New Name for Some Old Ways of Thinking: Popular Lectures on Philosophy*. New York: Longmans, Green.

Lawrence, C. and Huber, C.H. (1982) Strange bedfellows? Rational-emotive therapy and pastoral counseling, *Personnel and Guidance Journal*, 61, 210–12.

Lichtenberg, J.W. (1984) Believing when the facts don't fit, *Journal of Counseling and Development*, 63, 10–11.

Lyons, L.C. and Woods, P.J. (1991) The efficacy of rational-emotive therapy: a quantitative review of the outcome research, *Clinical Psychology Review*, 11, 357–69.

Norcross, J.C. and Prochaska, J.O. (1983) Clinicians' theoretical orientations: selection, utilization, and efficacy, *Professional Psychology: Research and Practice*, 14, 197–208.

Patterson, C.H. (1985) New light for counseling theory, *Journal of Counseling and Development*, 63, 349–50.

Saltzberg, L. (1979) The E in RET stands for emotive, *Psychology*, 16, 51–4.

Shostrom, E.L. (Producer) (1965) *Three Approaches to Psychotherapy* (Part 3 – Albert Ellis) [Film]. Orange, CA: Psychological Films.

Sifford, D. (1988) A noted therapist talks about his 'nastiness,' *Philadelphia Inquirer*, 27 November, pp. 1K, 7K.

Skovholt, T.M. and Ronnestad, M.H. (1992) Themes in therapist and counselor development, *Journal of Counseling and Development*, 70, 505–15.

Wallace, W.A. (1986) *Theories of Counseling and Psychotherapy: A Basic Issues Approach*. Newton, MA: Allyn and Bacon.

Weinrach, S.G. (1973) Even counselors have irrational ideas, *Personnel and Guidance Journal*, 52, 245–7.

Weinrach, S.G. (1977) Review of *Five-day intensive practicum in Rational-Emotive psychotherapy* [Workshop led by A. Ellis and Staff], *Personnel and Guidance Journal*, 55, 558–9.

Weinrach, S.G. (1980) Unconventional therapist: Albert Ellis, *Personnel and Guidance Journal*, 59, 152–60.

Weinrach, S.G. (1982) Confessions of a novice rational-emotive therapist, *Rational Living*, 17, 17–22.

Weinrach, S.G. (1986) Ellis and Gloria: positive or negative model? *Psychotherapy*, 23, 642–7.

Weinrach, S.G. (1988) Cognitive therapist: an interview with Aaron Beck, *Journal of Counseling and Development*, 67, 159–64.

Weinrach, S.G. (1990a) *Obstacles to a Wider Acceptance of RET*. Paper presented at the World Congress on Mental Health Counseling/35th Anniversary Conference on Rational-Emotive Therapy, Keystone, CO.

Weinrach, S.G. (1990b) Rogers and Gloria: the controversial film and the enduring relationship, *Psychotherapy*, 27, 282–9.

Weinrach, S.G. (1991a) Rogers' encounter with Gloria: what did Rogers know and when? *Psychotherapy*, 28, 504–6.

Weinrach, S.G. (1991b) Selecting a counseling theory while scratching your head: a rational-emotive therapist's personal journey, *Journal of Mental Health Counseling*, 13, 367–78.

Wiener, D.N. (1988) *Albert Ellis: Passionate Skeptic*. New York: Praeger.

Wolfe, J.L. (1976) Rational-emotive therapy as an effective feminist therapy, *Rational Living*, 11, 2–7.

Wolfe, J.L. (1990) *Obstacles to a Wider Acceptance of RET*. Paper presented at the World Congress on Mental Health Counseling/35th Anniversary Conference on Rational-Emotive Therapy, Keystone, CO.

Young, H.S. (1979) Is it RET? *Rational Living*, 14, 9–17.

Young, H.S. (1989) Practising RET with bible-belt Christians. In W. Dryden (ed.), *Howard Young: Rational therapist: Seminal papers in Rational-Emotive Therapy* (pp. 77–96). Essex, England: Gale Centre Publications.

Ziegler, D. (1990) *Obstacles to a Wider Acceptance of RET*. Paper presented at the World Congress on Mental Health Counseling/35th Anniversary Conference on Rational-Emotive Therapy, Keystone, CO.

Index